Beyond
the Melting Pot

Beyond the Melting Pot

THE NEGROES, PUERTO RICANS, JEWS,
ITALIANS, AND IRISH OF NEW YORK CITY

SECOND EDITION

BY NATHAN GLAZER AND
DANIEL PATRICK MOYNIHAN

The M.I.T. Press

CAMBRIDGE, MASSACHUSETTS, AND LONDON, ENGLAND

Contents

**INTRODUCTION
to the
Second Edition
NEW YORK CITY
IN 1970** vii

vii	The View from 1970
xxiv	The Race Issue in City Politics
xxxi	A Resurgence of Ethnicity?
xliii	Affluent Blacks and Poor Whites
lvii	The Catholics and the Jews
lxxi	The Party of the People
lxxvi	A Note on Ethnic Studies
lxxxiii	For the Present . . .
xci	Notes

**PREFACE
to the
First Edition** xcvii

INTRODUCTION 1

THE NEGROES 24

25	Numbers
29	Jobs
44	Education
50	The Family and Other Problems
53	Housing and Neighborhood
67	Leadership, Politics, Intergroup Relations

CONTENTS

THE PUERTO
    RICANS 86   86 Prologue
                  91 The Migration
                  99 The Island-Centered Community
               110 The Mobile Element
               116 Lower Income
               122 The Next Generation:
                      Family, School, Neighborhood
               129 Culture, Contributions, Color

THE JEWS 137   143 The Economic Base
               155 The Passion for Education
               159 Community, Neighborhood,
                      Integration
               166 Politics
               171 Culture and the Future

THE ITALIANS 181   186 The Community
               194 Family Influences
               202 Religion
               205 Occupations
               208 Politics

THE IRISH 217   219 The Green Wave
               221 The Democratic Party
               230 The Roman Catholic Church
               238 The Wild Irish
               250 "There Are Some of Us Left"
               262 The Party of the People
               274 City of God and Man

BEYOND THE
MELTING POT 288   292 The Jews
               294 The Catholics
               299 Negroes and Puerto Ricans
               301 The Role of Politics
               310 The Future

               317 TABLES
               325 NOTES
               349 INDEX

INTRODUCTION TO THE SECOND EDITION

New York City
in 1970

THE VIEW FROM 1970

THE MAJOR PART OF *Beyond the Melting Pot* DATES FROM
1960–61. It was in those years, at the end of Mayor Wagner's
second term, that we wrote the chapters on the five major
ethnic groups. (Glazer wrote the sections on the Negroes,
Puerto Ricans, Italians, and Jews. Moynihan wrote the
section on the Irish.) Glazer had formulated the major
themes sometime earlier: they were that ethnicity in New
York remains important; that it would continue to be important for politics and culture; that, from the perspective
of New York City, Negroes and Puerto Ricans could be
seen as the latest of the series of major ethnic groups that
had—oddly enough, two by two, beginning with Germans
and Irish, going on to Jews and Italians—come as immigrants to make up the population of the city; that helping
to make each group different, in its own development and
its relation to the rest of the city, were its basic cultural

characteristics, and particularly important among these was family structure.

The conclusion of the book was fashioned and attached in late 1962, and was based, in large measure, on Moynihan's experience in the campaign of Robert Morgenthau for governor of New York State in that year, an experience that seemed to be consistent with and to confirm the basic assumptions of the book. The book was finally published in 1963. An appropriately obscure final paragraph reads: "Religion and race define the next stage in the evolution of the American peoples. But the American nationality is still forming: its processes are mysterious, and its final form, if there is ever to be a final form, is as yet unknown."

It is a combination of obtuseness and perception that more or less sums up how the book reads today. Obviously, in the aftermath of New York's primaries and election campaign of 1969, it hardly seems as though religion defines the present, or the future, major fissures in New York life. Race has exploded to swallow up all other distinctions, or so it would appear at the moment. Yet, ten years ago one of the major splits in New York City was between Catholics and Jews. The rise of the reform Democratic clubs was a means whereby the liberal upper-middle-class Jewish population of the city tried to control the Democratic party, dominated until then by Irish, and latterly some Italian, Catholic politicians. True, the issues on which they divided often seemed less important than the images of the leaders they felt comfortable with. And even in those distant years there was already some narrowing evident between the liberal values of Jews and the conservative values of Irish and Italian Catholics on such a matter, for example, as school integration. But there *were* issues, such as support to parochial schools, and these issues were live enough to help account for the defeat of a new constitution for New York State in 1968.

By now, it hardly seems that the religious split matters. Catholics have become more liberal—in particular, on such matters as the role of traditional authority, censorship, sex, and morals, on which they used to diverge sharply from Jews—and Jews have become far more aware of the virtue of conservative working-class and middle-class values, which they always practiced but refused to celebrate. Even the American Jewish Congress, the most liberal of the major Jewish organizations, seems to spend as much of its energy these days on threats from black militancy as in older concerns such as keeping inviolate the line between church and state. In any case, the administration of President Kennedy seems to have reduced the salience of that latter issue.

And yet, as we shall point out in a later section, "The Catholics and the Jews," the conflict does persist. The religious element in it has been reduced, the ethnic term expanded. But let us not ignore even muted conflicts—they reappear. As a result of the changes among Jews, Mario Procaccino, running against John Lindsay, did better than could ever have been expected a few years ago among the Jewish working and lower-middle classes, just as the Civilian Police Review Board did poorly with the same group in the referendum of 1966. It isn't as if Procaccino were a new type of Italo-American political figure, either. He is one of a long line of similar types, and seems a direct descendant of an earlier comptroller, Lawrence Gerosa, who is described on page 214 as exemplifying the ideological outlook of small homeowners, so typical among New York's Italian Americans, which includes "opposition to high taxes . . . welfare programs . . . 'frills' in schools. . . ." Eight years later, with the welfare population past one million and a higher crime rate, this outlook has a much wider appeal. College-educated and professional Jews may still resist the appeal of conservative issues and candidates.[1] Better-educated and poorer-educated Jews do split drastically on this issue. But lower-middle-class and working-class Jews find conservative candidates more and more attractive.

Thus, religion as a major line of division in the city is for the moment in eclipse. Ethnicity and race dominate the city, more than ever seemed possible in 1963. That was, after all, before the first summer riots. The civil rights revolution had not yet broken out of the South. Nor had it yet raised economic issues, and even less, the issue of potential separatism, that were to prove so much more explosive than issues of political equality, which were, after all, part of the American creed all along. It seemed hardly possible then that the violence one had always associated with Southern race relations could be transferred bodily to New York—its racial violence seemed far in the past (it had not had a mass attack on blacks in either World War I or World War II, as had other Northern cities). One looked at the demands of the civil rights movement in 1963— equality in the vote, equality in the courts, equality in representation in public life, equality in public accommodations—saw that they existed more or less in New York City, and concluded that the political course of the Northern Negro would be quite different from that of the Southern Negro. He would become part of the game of accommodation politics—he already was—in which posts and benefits were distributed to groups on the basis of struggle, of course, but also on the basis of votes, money, and political talent, and one concluded that in this game the Negroes would not do so badly.

A number of considerations led to this outlook, which seemed reasonable enough at the time.

First, other New York groups had started at the bottom economically and politically and had risen. What was to keep the Negro from doing the same, particularly since the crude evidence available suggested there had already been substantial shifts in occupation—from domestics and laborers to clerical workers and semiskilled workers, for example? On the basis of the experience of other ethnic groups, it was hard to see that this economic rise would need any additional direct commitment by local government. It would come through growth in the national economy, change in the structure of job markets, higher levels of education (which were already evident), and movement into specific but rewarding parts of the economy and labor market: certainly the civil service, possibly the great private bureaucracies of New York businesses, hardly through entrepreneurial activity, though there were opportunities there, too.

Second, there seemed to be no major obstacle to this development in the form of a massive, institutionalized racism. There was prejudice, of course, but other groups had met that. And countering the greater scale of prejudice Negroes met, there were now well funded city and state agencies devoted to fighting prejudice and discrimination in jobs, education, housing (though that we admitted to be an enormous problem), and indeed in the actions of both public and private bodies.

Third, *Beyond the Melting Pot* did suggest that a significant check to the economic rise of the Negroes might be found in the values of American Negroes themselves; these played some large but not fully explicated role in economic development. But the suggestion was tentative—no major warning sign was flashed—because the economic and sociological fundamentals seemed so secure.

What was wrong with this optimistic outlook? First, it was based on poor data. The analysis of the distribution of population by income is a late development, and even so we are in bad shape between censuses. When the work on *Beyond the Melting Pot* began, the figures for the decade 1940–1950 were available, and showed remarkable upward change for Negroes, owing to the war. The stagnation of opportunities for Negroes after the Korean War could perhaps be discovered in the statistics available in the early 1960's, but we didn't discover them. There was a serious undercount of Negro males in New York (as in the whole country) which probably led to an overstatement of the economic position of the Negro. The undercount was first pointed out in 1955 in an article by Ansley J. Coale, but it was not until after our book was published, amazingly enough, that this became general knowledge among social scientists, aside from some specialists in demography.[2] Since the analyses of income data were then so scanty, one depended on occupational data, and these, interestingly enough, did show more upward change for Negroes than the income data. After the book was published, Herman P. Miller and others demonstrated that Negro income had moved not at all in relation to white income since the mid-1950's; Michael Harrington helped rediscover poverty; the civil rights movement for the first time took up economic aims (only in 1963, it will be recalled); and the basis for a relatively optimistic view of the Negro's economic future in our book collapsed.[3]

It is not that the black economic position deteriorated either in real or in relative terms. Just the opposite took place. During the second half of the 1960's Negroes made probably the most rapid economic and occupational gains in their history. These were made relative to and often at the expense of whites. However, for a variety of reasons, possibly including the message of deprivation that accompanied the poverty movement, and certainly owing to greater attention being paid to their condition, the *perception* of well-being seems not to have accompanied the reality. To the contrary, the often false optimism of the past was seemingly supplanted by a pervasive sense of deprivation and impending doom among the more vocal and militant elements of the New York City population. This, too, was a reality, and had the effect of reality.

In addition, New York City seems to have fallen behind the rest of the country's cities in the *rate* at which it overcame poverty among blacks. The percentage of nonwhite New York City families in poverty dropped only 2 points, from 26 to 24 per cent, according to census surveys, between 1959 and 1967, while it dropped 11 points, from 37 to 26 per cent, among Negro families in all central cities.[4] The evidence suggests that the sluggishness in overcoming poverty was largely owing to the rise in the number of black female-headed households.

Puerto Ricans are economically and occupationally worse off than Negroes, but one does find a substantial move in the second generation that seems to correspond to what we expected for new groups in the city. Thus, Nathan Kantrowitz, comparing second-generation Puerto Ricans in 1950 and 1960 (small groups in both years, but their numbers are rapidly growing) showed they improved their position, both in terms of numbers graduating from high school and college, more rapidly than other white males in the city. And while the story on occupational mobility is mixed, even there one sees some grounds for optimism in a substantial shift into white-collar work.[5]

We have not seen such an analysis for Negroes (that is, one based on economic and occupational movement of Negroes born in the city), but the basic question remains: If one had it, would it really matter?[6] And one must conclude sadly, it would not. There is one basic reason for this. Perhaps it made sociological sense in 1963 to treat Negroes as an ethnic group in New York, parallel to other ethnic groups, to evaluate their place in the city in contrast to that of immigrant groups, and record how rapidly this position was changing, but it did not make *political* sense. It is even a question, of course, how much sociological sense it made. It made some, we still think. After all, Negroes themselves saw their place in the city in these terms, viewed themselves as fighting to improve their position not in an undifferentiated white society but an ethnically diverse one, and in such a society some groups, for some purposes, were allies. That Negroes were, or were becoming, one group in a society made up of self-conscious groups was the basic assumption of the book—in that sense, it was closer to social reality than some analysts of American society who saw assimilation and integration as already more advanced for most groups in the society than was actually the case.

Where the book failed was in determining what *kind* of group Negroes would form. As an ethnic group, they would be one of many. As a *racial* group, as "blacks," as the new nomenclature has it, they would form a unique group in American society. In a sense, of course, they always have been; they are old settlers whose presence shaped our Constitution, they were the only group held as slaves, they dominate a good part of American culture and literature—no one could forget that or deny that. But New York City, *Beyond the Melting Pot* argued, while it was America, was also different from America. It accentuated and heightened one distinctive goal of American society: its openness to new groups and its even-handed distribution of opportunity. Here, the larger American experience of the Negro, based on slavery and repression in the South, would be overcome, as the Negroes joined the rest of society, in conflict and accommodation, as an ethnic group.

It didn't happen. Groups may preexist in sociological reality, but they shape themselves by choice; they define their own categories (and this, curiously enough, was also a major theme of the book). In 1963, it looked as if the categories could still be defined as ethnic—groups defined by common culture as well as common descent. In 1969, we seem to be moving to a new set of categories, black and white, and that is ominous. On the horizon stand the fantastic categories of the "Third World," in which all the colors, Black, Brown, Yellow, and Red (these are the favored terms for Negro, Mexican-American and Puerto Rican, Chinese and Japanese, and American Indian—a biologically and humanly monstrous naming, it seems to us—among some militants of southern California) are equated as "the oppressed" in opposition to the oppressing whites.

Human groups do not exist in nature, or rather, the part of difference that exists because of nature is unimportant. They are chosen, and whether one chooses to see oneself as Third World, Black, Negro, is not determined by either biology or sociology. It is a free act, even if constrained by social influences. Thus, as Negroes become "black"—and, perhaps beyond that, part of an alliance of the "internally colonized"—one cannot say this was inevitable, that the shaping forces of American society determined it. The experiences of Negroes in New York since the great migration fifty years ago has had a great deal in it, good and bad. If one compared it with the first fifty years of the Irish, the Italians, and the Jews, we are convinced there would be enough in that comparison to justify an ethnic rather than a racial or "internally colonized" self-image.

But the arts of politics, as exercised in the nation and the city, were insufficient to prevent a massive move toward what must be, for the nation and the city, a more damaging identity. The failure is a complex one.

The received wisdom—perhaps the best expression of it is to be found in the report of the National Advisory Commission on Civil Disorders, the Kerner Commission, on which Mayor Lindsay served as vice-chairman and played a major role—was that the failure was primarily in the level of response by government to the needs of Negroes and other deprived groups. It would be a foolish man who would say that more could not have, should not have, been done. And yet what impresses us is the creativity, relatively speaking, of the American political response all through the decade. A large range of civil rights legislation was passed, and some of it was remarkably effective. Toward the end of the decade, the legislation on equality in employment was being enforced with increasing ingenuity, now by a Republican administration that owed little to Negroes. Affirmative action nationally had replaced, by the end of the decade, the requirement at the beginning, in only a few localities, for nondiscrimination. Voting rights legislation had led to the creation for the first time in 70 years of a substantial body of Negro voters in the South, exercising increasing influence in various areas. Discrimination in public accommodation had just about disappeared. The tax cut (and the war) replaced unemployment with labor shortages, and inflation, created in large measure by labor shortages, replaced unemployment as the dominant economic issue at the end of the decade. To deal with inadequate working skills, a variety of manpower training programs of increasing complexity was mounted, all through the decade, and if many were less than successful, no one could say the various levels of government ever stopped trying. Enormous new funds were put into education, largely to support new educational efforts for the poor (and the black) and to increase opportunities in higher education, where discrimination had passed into history and had turned into a positive effort to bring higher education to as many Negroes as possible.

We had seen the sequence of antidelinquency programs, poverty programs, a model cities program, and the rise of the doctrine of government-supported advocacy of radical change and of participation of client groups: the poor, the tenants, the welfare clients, the patients, in the agencies and institutions that affect their lives.[7] In the field of housing, a fantastic new variety of instruments was made available; they were poorly funded, but almost everything was being tried, to some degree. Indeed, in this decade, the United States, instead of being the consumer of European reforms and European mechanisms of social change, became an exporter: the theories of advocacy and participation began to affect English social policy, and poverty was rediscovered in Europe in response to its rediscovery in the United States.

Obviously more could have been done, but we do not feel, on balance, that the primary failure was in the political response of government to recognized need. But by the end of the decade, following the lead of the Kerner Commission, government response was routinely described as a failure and ascribed to an underlying and pervasive "white racism."

We would point to two other areas of failure, at least as important. One was the failure of intellectuals and the mass media to report and analyze what was happening. During this decade intellectuals continued their surprising conquest of the mass media which began after the Second World War, and which by the end of the decade had made such terms as "highbrow," "middlebrow," and "low brow" archaic. The "highbrows," "middlebrows," and "low brows" now merged, under the stewardship of the intelligentsia. And the intelligentsia, as it so often has, lusted after the sensational and the exotic. The hard work of politics and social change bored it. An increasingly dangerous romance with social brinksmanship and violence developed. The main task of intellectuals, keeping the channels of thought and of communication honest, was increasingly abandoned. Thus, until the rise of black militancy a few years ago, it was typical for the intelligentsia to argue that whatever the shape of race relations, whatever the condition of Negroes, it was fully and exclusively to be ascribed to whites. Whites prevented Negroes from rising economically and politically, and whites by their actions consigned Negroes to slums, poor jobs or unemployment, poor schools, and inferior education. This was an exaggerated and distorted view of the situation even five and ten years ago. Whites of course held far more power than blacks; but blacks could (and did) by their own measures shape a good part of their environment, their conditions of life, and their power.

After the rise of Black Power, liberal sentiment, following the new black ideologies, jumped entirely to the other side. Now blacks could exclusively, and without concern for the attitudes, power, and position held by white groups, fully shape their environment, their conditions of life, and their power. This was as extreme a position in ascribing *all* power to the deprived as the previous position was in denying *any* power to the deprived. Both were wrong. The errors of the first position did nothing to encourage blacks to organize, to create social institutions, to dominate their environment with distinctive social and cultural interests and capacities, for just as previous groups of the deprived had shaped their environment, so could blacks. The second position, on the other hand, ignored that other groups did have interests, did have power, and would and could react against militant and arrogant demands, which owed to the black culture of the streets a good deal of their peculiar bite and arrogance. Whatever the effect of this new black style in creating self-satisfaction among those who used it, it did little to reach the other side and create conditions for accommodation. "The dozens" (the ghetto game of verbal abuse, in which each participant tries to see how much his antagonist can take) was not the ideal form for the conduct of public business; it has become, as far as militant blacks are concerned, almost the only form, with the encouragement of a good number of the white intelligentsia.

Instead of introducing clarity and sanity, the intelligentsia devoted itself to encouraging the varied fantasies and the fascination with violence of black militants. Consider two examples: Malcolm X was one of the most impressive black leaders of the sixties. His autobiography has perhaps the strongest claim to be considered a classic of any book by a black writer of the sixties. He broke with the Nation of Islam (Black Muslims) for a number of reasons, but one basis of separation was his growing rejection of black exclusivism, and his conviction blacks could work with like-minded whites. He was assassinated, and at the time most informed observers, black and white, saw little reason to question the widespread assumption that his black killers were associated with the dominant faction of the Black Muslims. Yet by the end of the decade it was nigh universally accepted in the black community, and was also widely believed by young middle- and upper-middle-class whites, that his tragic death was at the hands of whites, and probably at the behest of the United States government.

Another example is immediately at hand. During 1968 and 1969, a number of Black Panthers were killed in shoot-outs with the police in Oakland, Los Angeles, and Chicago, as were a number of police. Conflicting stories resulted concerning who started shooting and for what reason. In December, 1969, after one of the most serious of these shoot-outs in Chicago resulted in the death of two Black Panther leaders, one could read in the most responsible newspapers in the country that "twenty-eight Black Panthers" had been killed by the police. This figure, which one assumes came from Black Panther sources, was immediately accepted, and spread throughout the world. The *New York Times,* in its *News of the Week* section, an authoritative summary of the news, reported flatly, in a headline on December 7, "The Black Panther toll is now 28." A few weeks later, the *New York Times* apparently thought better of its acceptance of this figure, and asked the Black Panther lawyer, Charles Garry, to specify the 28. It turned out he could come up with 19 dead Panthers, except that four were killed by a rival black group; one by a white merchant; one was killed, the New Haven police charged, by other Black Panthers; one was unknown to the police who had supposedly killed him; another in the list, it was asserted, was shot by a "police agent," not further identified. The 28 was down, maximally, to 11. And even in these cases there were guns on both sides, and the question of who started shooting is disputed. The number of dead policemen is not of any interest to the intelligentsia.

The point is that the political failures of the 1960's also include a failure by intellectuals and by the mass media they increasingly influenced to give a true and honest account of the situation. Lies started, and they were not stopped, because those whose task was to monitor words and ideas had less and less interest in doing so. It was no wonder that, even while progress was substantial, fears of genocide rose.

There was another political failure of the sixties, and this was the failure of Negroes (and Puerto Ricans) to develop and seize the political opportunities that were open to them. It was less clear in 1960–61 than in 1969 how massively Negroes (and Puerto Ricans) abstained from politics, in some of the key ways that counted, for example, voting. They abstained *more* in the 1960's than in the mid-

1940's in New York City, and the reasons are unclear. Arthur Klebanoff has studied this for the city, particularly for Brooklyn. Between 1950 and 1965, the proportion of Negroes and Puerto Ricans in Brooklyn rose from 9 per cent to 29 per cent of the population. This should have meant a massive change in political representation, and presumably in rewards. It didn't.

The remnants of the older political machinery, once broad-based, continued to control Brooklyn politics as late as 1966. Jews and Italians ran the stores, owned the apartments, and filled the political clubhouses. This was to be expected. The surprise was the absence of any competing Negro or Puerto Rican organizations. Jews and Italians continued in office long after the districts they represented became predominantly Negro and Puerto Rican. . . . The existing political organizations did not recruit in Negro and Puerto Rican areas because they had no need to. Nonvoters have never been of great interest to politicians in control of a small constituency. And no politician managed to convince Brooklyn's white party machinery that Negroes and Puerto Ricans would ever be anything but nonvoters.[8]

Klebanoff's analysis demonstrated that while Negroes and Puerto Ricans formed approximately 30 per cent of Brooklyn's total population and 25 per cent of its eligible voting population, they were no more than 15 per cent of Brooklyn's registered voters. It is understandable, then, that the Ocean Hill–Brownsville Local Governing Board should have declared, "Men are capable of putting an end to what they find intolerable without recourse to politics." Unfortunately, when they do, only uncertainty, insecurity, and disorder can result.

Beyond the Melting Pot explored some of the reasons why Negroes and Puerto Ricans might not organize as rapidly and effectively as other groups. For the Negroes, it suggested that the mere fact that they did not form a self-consciously foreign group, cut off by barriers of language from English-speaking institutions, meant that the bases for organization were restricted.* For Puerto Ricans,

* One passage in *Beyond the Melting Pot* has given me considerable pain, and the point I make here gives me a chance to correct it. I wrote, in the chapter on the Negroes, that the chances for "massive self-help"

it suggested that the attitudes developed toward the paternalistic government of Puerto Rico were easily transferred to the government of New York City. Thus, in both groups, the push to organization and self-help was somewhat muted. But in the very nature of the ethnic analysis, this could not be expected to last—the groups would become

---

efforts among Negroes, along the lines of some ethnic and religious groups, were not promising, and one reason I suggested was that "it is not possible for Negroes to view themselves as other ethnic groups viewed themselves because—and this is the key to much in the Negro world—the Negro is only an American, and nothing else. He has no values and culture to guard and protect. He insists that the white world deal with his problems, because . . . he is so much the product of America. . . ." (p. 53, first edition).

What I meant, as the context suggests, was *not* that there were no Negro values and culture—something totally at odds with everything in the section and the book—but that, as the text just quoted states, Negro values and culture were so completely *American* in origin that Negroes, as against other groups of foreign origin, had no strong incentives to create schools to preserve a foreign language, hospitals and old-age homes to give comfort to those raised in a foreign culture, or even to develop retail stores to serve a distinctively foreign market.

I based myself on authoritative scholars, among them E. Franklin Frazier, who argued that the Negro had been remade in America, and almost nothing African had survived in American Negro culture. There has been strong challenge to this view in recent years. The rise of Afro-American and Black Studies will undoubtedly turn up a larger measure of African survivals, both specific and general.

Even, however, as I have elaborated it here, this passage I believe was quite wrong. Conceivably the fact that Negroes saw themselves as American had inhibited to some degree the development of a fully elaborated set of strong organizations along the lines of other groups. But after all, as so much in the book argues, a conscious awareness of foreign origin based on the reality of a foreign culture is only one element in the establishment of a strong set of social organizations, and by no means absolutely essential. The creation of the Mormons out of completely American origins—a group that now shows the American ethnic pattern of a group, largely formed through descent, with distinctive values and social organization—demonstrates that foreign language and culture is no requirement for very strong social organization. Out of American origins, one can create a distinctive subculture which generates the need for its own organizations to "guard and protect" it. This has certainly happened as a result of 300 years of Black American history, and could serve as sufficient basis for strong organization, regardless of the contribution of African origins. Even aside from groups formed in America, we have examples of immigrant groups who have become conscious of themselves as distinct entities in America, and on the basis of experience in America.

In this edition, I have edited the original passage, as I quoted it here, to come closer to my original meaning, so that it now at least expresses the error I originally made, rather than one I did not intend.   N.G.

more self-conscious, better organized. What could not be foreseen, of course, was what form this organization would take.

In the Negro communities, we have seen a wholly admirable and impressive rise of self-assertion and pride. The distinctive aspects of the Negro experience in America and Africa are being explored, reported, recorded, analyzed, and increasingly taught, both in private and in public schools. Aspects of Negro experience that were previously considered by Negroes themselves as unimportant, or matter-of-fact, or even shameful are becoming part of the curriculum for this new movement of self-assertion. All this deserves encouragement and support. When it is combined, as it so often is, with an effort to teach an unreal past and an unreal present, one can still understand it—every group has its own similar tendencies. But when it is combined with an effort to separate Negroes from the mechanisms by which varied groups, in this most mixed of nations, participate in a common society and a common state, then we can only be saddened and frightened.

The political costs of separatist rhetoric, and the surprising mobility offered by the ethnic political model, were to be seen at the outset of the 1970's when the issue arose among liberal Democrats of nominating a Negro for Lieutenant Governor in the primary campaigns that were to precede the 1970 general elections. The press reported elaborate calculations as to how this could be done with minimal damage to the party's prospects, especially "upstate." Seemingly ignored in these strategy sessions was the fact that in 1962 the Democrats had nominated a Negro, Edward R. Dudley, for the incomparably more important post of Attorney General and no one had batted an eye. Dudley was nominated by precisely the process, described in our final chapter, "Beyond the Melting Pot," by which Robert M. Morgenthau had been chosen. A Jew, a Catholic, a Negro, et al. His had been almost the classic ethnic political background. A childhood in rural Virginia, Howard University, St. John's Law School, the New Era Democratic Club (a Harlem Tammany group), the legal staff of the National Association for the Advancement of Colored People, followed by a steady rise through appointive positions (Ambassador to Liberia, the Domestic Relations Court), and at length the nomination for Attorney General of New York, a position we noted was held by an Irish patriot as early as 1812. It is important to note that, while Dudley was nominated for Attorney General, a Negro (Ralph Bunche) was also considered in the polling for Governor (p. 306). It was becoming *routine* for Negroes to have "a place on the slate." Only after a decade of intense preoccupation with injustices done black people, with "white racism," "genocide," and the rhetoric of social revolution did it become a chancy thing to nominate a black for the least significant of statewide posts.

We, black and white, continue to grapple with our primal dilemma, the place of blacks in American society, and the range of options that we now see before us is wider than was apparent when we wrote *Beyond the Melting Pot.* At that time, from the perspective of the city, there were seemingly only two options. One was color blindness, with its corollary assumptions that Negroes could be fully assimilated in American society, fully acculturated, that no distinctions of importance would remain in reality, and distinctions based on racist prejudice would finally fall away. We saw this as unrealistic, not so much because racism was so deeply ingrained in American society (though of course it was far more deeply ingrained than the prejudice any other group had met, even the ferocious prejudice that confronted the Chinese and Japanese), but because the model of America was faulty. White groups, we argued, had not yet "assimilated," perhaps they never would. The ethnic pattern was American, more American than the assimilationist. Would not the ethnic pattern prove the model for the incorporation of Negroes into the life of the city, as it had proved for impoverished Irishmen, for Jews and Italians, all of whom, when they had arrived, had been considered by some of the best representatives of the American thought of the time as inferior races?

There was of course a third alternative, which we dismissed completely—separatism, formal minority status—in the pattern that arose briefly between the wars to accommodate the minority groups of Eastern Europe— perhaps a separate nation. This had been proposed, most prominently by the American Communist party in the thirties, who propounded a theory of autonomy to the point, if wished, of separatism for the black majority areas of the South. More recently the Nation of Islam had proposed a separate nation, in a much vaguer form. We did not see this as even a distant possibility. The Communist party was almost totally divorced from American reality. The Black Muslims, to our mind, were more noteworthy for their effort to create a middle-class style for lower-class blacks than for their vague political goals. But this alternative has been raised far more seriously since.[9]

When we wrote *Beyond the Melting Pot,* the alternatives seemed to lie between assimilation and ethnic group status; they now seem to lie somewhere between ethnic group status and separatism. Earlier assimilation seemed to us the unreal alternative, today it is separatism that holds that status. But unreal unfortunately does not mean impossible. Will makes almost all alternatives possible, even those that are disastrous and that seem sure to guarantee a substantial measure of misery and unhappiness.

We now have as alternatives two models of group relations, which we will name the Northern and the Southern. Both reject a total assimilation in which group reality disappears. In the Southern model, society is divided into two segments, white and black. The line between them is rigidly drawn. Other groups must choose to which segment they belong, even if, as many Southern Jews felt, they do not really want to quite belong to either. Violence is the keynote of relations between the groups. And "separate but equal" is an ideology if not a reality.

The Northern model is quite different. There are many groups. They differ in wealth, power, occupation, values, but in effect an open society prevails for individuals and for groups. Over time a substantial and rough equalization of wealth and power can be hoped for even if not attained, and each group participates sufficiently in the goods and values and social life of a common society so that all can accept the common society as good and fair. There is competition between groups, as between individuals, but it is muted, and groups compete not through violence but through effectiveness in organization and achievement. Groups and individuals participate in a common society. Individual choice, not law or rigid custom, determines the degree to which any person participates, if at all, in the life of an ethnic group, and assimilation and acculturation proceed at a rate determined in large measure by individuals. This is at any rate the ideal—prejudice and discrimination often force people into closer association with groups than they wish. The Northern model in group relations is perhaps best realized in New York City.

We have begun to see the Northern model creep into the South. The politics of the city of Atlanta is now one in which various groups compete, bargain, and come to agreements in a style familiar to us from Northern urban politics. But the Southern style is now being brought into the North. Physically, by immigrants, black and white. Ideologically, by sections of the intelligentsia, black and white. Violence is beginning to play a frightening role in politics.[10] The demand for a rigid line between the races is now raised again, more strongly from the black side, this time. We believe the ethnic pattern offers the best chance for a humane and positive adaptation to group diversity, offering the individual the choice to live as he wishes, rather than forcing him into the pattern of a single "Americanized" society or into the compartments of a rigidly separated society. The question is, can we still convince the varied groups of the society that this is still the best solution?

All the work of incorporating Negroes, as a group and as individuals, into a common society—economically, culturally, socially, politically—must be pushed as hard as possible. Negroes who want to be part of a common society—and these are still, from all evidence, the large majority, if a quiet one—must be given every aid and encouragement, and must be associated in every common enterprise. It is hard to believe that the genius for compromise and accommodation which has kept this a single city, despite the fact that it was made of minorities, will now fail. But the possibility, in 1970, is a haunting one.

THE RACE ISSUE IN CITY POLITICS

THE FACT IS, WE ARE ALREADY FAR ADVANCED ON THE ROAD to division, and perhaps the best indication is that the mayoralty election of 1969 was the *first* in New York City's history that was decided principally by the intensity of racial conflict in the city.

The matter, of course, is not one of race alone, particularly not in New York City. Against the stark contrast of black and white that dominates the South, in New York we have, in partial and grudging alliance with blacks, a substantial part of the Puerto Rican group. They are not racially Negro (only a small proportion—in recent censuses, less than 10 per cent—are Negro as well as Puerto Rican), but the two groups share many common elements of social position: both are relatively recent migrants to the city, come from poor areas, and are equipped generally with relatively poor education and poor occupational skills, both suffer from having to take the worst jobs and the worst housing, both feel aggrieved in their relations with the major city services—police, schools, housing, health, fire, sanitation—and both have formed part, on many occasions, of a single political alliance.

The divisions between them however are as important as the similarities. There are conflicts between them over precedence and power in specific functional areas of government and in specific physical areas of the city. Thus, in the new community agencies that handle the programs of the Office of Economic Opportunity and the Model Cities Program, the chief city agencies dominated by blacks and Puerto Ricans, the conflict is often severe. In the Hunts Point area of the East Bronx, it has been particularly fierce. There are cultural and political differences between the two groups. The Puerto Ricans are perhaps more willing to see themselves as one in a sequence of ethnic groups in the city who will eventually through traditional processes of government get their due. Radical elements among blacks, who deny the validity or legitimacy of such a model and such expectations, tend to be stronger, though many young Puerto Ricans are trying to catch up. Puerto Ricans do not express as much resentment and anger, are not as convinced that measures proposed by black activists should be given such high priority (for example, the push to community control of schools and other city functions). Thus, one Puerto Rican daily (of two in the city) endorsed the conservative Democrat Procaccino and the conservative Republican Marchi in the primary, as against Mayor Lindsay or the liberal and radical opponents of Procaccino. And in the final mayoralty vote, the vote for Mayor Lindsay among Puerto Ricans fell far short of the overwhelming support among Negroes.

We also find, in rather firmer alliance with blacks, a good number of whites: "Manhattan," as it is called—and that means whites of high social and economic position, largely Jewish and white Anglo-Saxon in background, with a mixture of better-off Catholics somewhat liberated from their ethnic groups. They were willing to support Mayor Lindsay and liberal Democratic candidates in a primary where the main issue was whether too much was being done for blacks. They took this position presumably because they are better off, better educated, and also because they are somewhat freer of the pressures of ethnic groups that are helping to solidify, elsewhere in the city, a strong resistance to what are seen as pro-black policies.

The opponents of this coalition can once again be described in ethnic and class terms, as well as by race. Whether we say "blue-collar" or "lower middle-class" or "homeowner" in New York City, or whether we say "Italian" or "Irish" is not unimportant, and yet we know we are talking about roughly the same people. So the mass media discourse about the "white ethnic groups" or the "white working- and lower-middle class"—the people are the same, and the issues are the same: their feelings that they have been ignored, have received little from government in recent years, and have borne the brunt of the costs involved in the economic and political rise of the Negroes.

And in the middle in New York is a "swing group," the largest in the city, Jews, and perhaps the single most important development in the current crisis is the shift of middle- and working-class Jews, in large numbers, from one side to another, a move hastened by the referendum on the police Civilian Review Board in 1966, the school strike over decentralization in 1968, and rising black—and occasionally anti-Semitic—militancy. The facts of ethnicity and race, which were for a long time somewhat underground if vital and recognized factors in New York City's life, surfaced everywhere by 1969. Each primary and election was analyzed in ethnic terms, and, where once class and occupational terms obscured the ethnic factors beneath, now ethnic factors were used as the immediate shorthand, covering the economic and social realities they paralleled. Thus, a reporter interviewing Representative Hugh Carey for the magazine *New York* gave the following account of his Brooklyn district (paraphrasing the congressman):

The make-up of the 15th Congressional District is Park Slope—Irish and Italian; Prospect Heights—Black and Spanish-speaking; Borough Park—Hasidic and Sephardic Jews; Sunset Park—Swedish and Norwegian ("8th largest concentration east of Minneapolis," according to Carey); Bay Ridge—Italian, Irish, German, and "maybe the only White Anglo-Saxon Protestants in the district"; and part of Bensonhurst—a racially mixed district.[11]

Herman Badillo, explaining why he would support Mayor Lindsay instead of Mario Procaccino, was quoted in the *New York Times* (July 30, 1969): "When he talks about crime and treating juvenile offenders as adult criminals, he's talking about black and Puerto Rican kids. Everyone knows he's not talking about Jewish and Italian kids. . . ." (Interestingly enough, when you talked about criminals and juvenile delinquents in this city until twenty-five years ago, you *did* mean Jewish and Italian kids.)

The calculations of political leaders, the analyses of journalists, the reporting of the daily papers, all emphasize, perhaps they even overemphasize, the significance of attitudes toward the Negroes, toward policies that are assumed to be designed to help Negroes, and how these attitudes vary depending on whether white voters are Italian or Jewish or Polish, blue-collar or white-collar or professional, high school-educated or college-educated.

But if there is nothing new in the statement of the case, there is something new in that for the first time in New York City's history, as far as we know it, racial conflict, which can also be viewed as ethnic conflict, became determinative for the city's politics.

Ethnic considerations have always been primary in New York City politics, where the three top spots of each party are regularly divided among a Jew, an

Italian, and an Irishman (sometimes a white Protestant noses out one of the others, most recently the Irishman, who now represents the smallest of the three major white ethnic groups); where the Borough Presidency of Manhattan has been reserved to Negroes for some years; where the old Board of Education was regularly divided among three Jews, three Catholics, and three Protestants. What is new?

What is new is that these arrangements, which were adjustments to the reality of race and ethnic difference, have now taken the center of the stage. They did not play an important role as recently as the first Lindsay election in 1965. As between Lindsay and Beame, the issue was still the traditional one of "reform" versus the "machine," and this was true of earlier elections, too. Connected with the fundamental break between reformers and regular politicians were such issues as efficiency, corruption, relations with criminals. These were, it appears in retrospect, the major issues of past New York City elections. Behind them the steady change in position and status of ethnic groups went on, and was marked by nominations by regular parties of members of various groups to new and higher positions, by elections of members of ethnic groups to new positions, by the creation of factions within old parties, and by the establishment of third parties dominated by new ethnic groups. But, once again, these factions and third parties—the Reform Democrats, the American Labor Party, the Liberal Party, the Conservative Party—while they clearly represented disproportionately certain ethnic groups, were not defined primarily in ethnic terms, they were defined by the classic issues of urban government: reform, machines, corruption, efficiency, taxes.

In the past election, however, there was one overwhelming issue: Had Mayor Lindsay done too much for Negroes, and in lesser degree, Puerto Ricans? Could this charge be pinned on him, not directly, but by the fairly unsubtle messages that political candidates in a democratic society will use: Had he favored Manhattan over Brooklyn and the Bronx, what had he done about crime in the streets, what was his role in the teachers' strike and the struggle over expanded black and Puerto Rican enrollment at City

College, and even more directly, had his tenure in office increased racial and ethnic hostility?

In the end, Lindsay won, though with a minority of the popular vote. But it is clear that the big issue of the campaign remains as the main issue of city politics: Do city policies favor poorer blacks as against working-class and lower-middle-class whites, and its corollary, how does one deal with the danger of further polarization between these groups? In New York, as we have pointed out, this issue is inevitably modulated by the complex ethnic mix of the city, and it is this too which gives New York its chief advantages in dealing with it. These advantages should not be ignored. New York was one of the few major Northern cities that avoided an anti-Negro race riot during the period of rapid Negro migration to the Northern cities that opened with World War I. It did not experience anything like a Chicago riot of 1919 or a Detroit riot of 1943. Indeed, its two major race riots, that of 1935 and 1943 in Harlem, reflecting the fact that New York City *was* different, foreshadowed the "commodity" riots of the 1960's: they were not directed by whites against Negroes but by Negroes against the white storekeepers in black areas, expressions of hostility against whites.[12] And even though New York had its share of devastating riots in the 1960's, the great divide in race relations in New York is marked not by a riot but by the teachers' strikes of 1968, in which the violence was almost entirely verbal rather than physical. Physical violence of course there is. But it is still for the most part the random and individual violence of criminals and near criminals. Even if black criminals now add (as many do) racial excuses to the armory of self-justifications that all criminals use, and even if many are encouraged to criminal violence by the inflated and overheated rhetoric of racial anger, what we find for the most part is still the violence of individuals. And as has often been pointed out, other Negroes are overwhelmingly the victims, and whites, despite their reasonable fear, do not suffer as much.

But at any rate one does not sense that whites are arming in New York, or that groups of whites are muttering about beating up or killing Negroes. New

York is still a different city—not Chicago, not Detroit, not Los Angeles. And, undoubtedly, part of what makes New York a different city are traditions arising from its ethnic variety. New York has had more experience than most American cities in living with a large variety of ethnic groups and in seeing their position and power wax and wane. Perhaps most significantly, this ethnic variety is marked by the presence, as still the largest ethnic group, of the traditionally pacific and nonviolent Jews. Despite the example of Israel, New York City Jews are still strangers to arms—or hunting or target practice or the other recreational and cultural pursuits that encourage acquaintance with arms. They have never been workers in heavy industry, which encourages brawn and provides an environment in which violence is more easily accepted. They are in light industry, in commerce, and in the professions, and come out of cultural environments in which violence is limited to language. Even when they are criminals, they tend to make illegal use of brains, not brawn.

Further, no group in New York City is accustomed to domination, though each may have a partial dominance in some area, and no group, therefore, finds challenge unexpected or outrageous. The Irish have withdrawn before the pressure of Italians and Jews; the white Protestants have been a minority for more than a century, and in recent generations a small minority; Italians, despite their huge number as the second largest white group, have always been concentrated in fairly humble occupations; Jews, despite their recent prominence, remember anti-Semitism and the need for prudence and caution. There is a basic reservoir of good feeling in the city that permits accommodation, change, the rise of new groups to new positions of political power and economic well-being. Obviously, saying this, we present a hypothesis but a hypothesis that we must believe in generally, throughout the country, if the nation is to survive without racial warfare. In New York, at any rate, we have more grounds for believing it than elsewhere.

But if this reservoir is to be built on, if New York is to continue to survive as a city with some degree of harmony and accommodation, then there must be wider understanding of the state of race and ethnic relations in the city.

A RESURGENCE OF ETHNICITY?

THE OVER-ALL ETHNIC PATTERN OF THE CITY HAS NOT CHANGED since 1960, though the proportions have. There are still six major, fairly well-defined groups. The most visible is the Negro, which is rapidly increasing its proportion of the city's population, and has risen from 14 per cent in 1960 to an estimated 20 per cent today. The second most visible and sharply defined group is the Puerto Rican, whose proportion within the city population has increased since 1960 from 8 to 11 per cent. Substantial numbers of Latin Americans— Cubans and others—have come into the city since 1960 and tend to be lumped in public identification with Puerto Ricans, though they resist this. The largest single ethnic group in the city is the Jewish. Our data on their numbers are very poor. We guess they are declining from the quarter of the city's population they have long formed, to more like a fifth, but they are still probably more numerous than the Negroes. The next largest white group is the Italian. The Italian-born and their children alone formed 11 per cent of the city's population in 1960, leaving out the entire third generation and beyond. Perhaps they form one-seventh of the city's population. The Irish are a steadily declining part of the city's population, owing to heavy movements to the suburbs (also true, but in lesser degree, of Jews and Italians). They form probably some 7 per cent of the city.[13]

White Anglo-Saxon Protestants form the sixth most important social segment of the city in ethnic terms. If Irish identity becomes questionable in the later generations, WASP identity is even less of a tangible and specific identity. It is a created identity, and largely forged in New York City in order to identify those who are not otherwise ethnically identified and who, while a small minority in the city, represent what is felt to be the "majority" for the rest of the country.

Even in New York they bear the prestige of representing the "majority," whatever that may be, and, more significantly, they dominate the large banks, the large insurance companies, the large corporations that make their headquarters in the city. Young people flock to the city to work in its communications industries, advertising agencies, in the corporate office buildings, and discover they have become WASPs. This odd term includes descendants of early Dutch settlers (there are still a few), of early English and Scottish settlers (there are still some of these, too), immigrants and descendants of immigrants to the city from Great Britain, and migrants to the city from parts of the country which have had substantial proportions of settlers of British, English-speaking background. Merged into this mix may be persons of German background who no longer feel ethnically identified as German-Americans. The Germans, who formed along with the Irish the dominant ethnic group of the late nineteenth and early twentieth century in the city, have not maintained, as a group, a prominence in the city proportionate to their numbers. (And yet in the 1960's the Steuben Day parade became a major event, at which the attendance of city officeholders was obligatory.)

Beyond the six major defined segments that are crucial to politics, to self-awareness, and also to the social description of the city, there are numerous others, but they tend to have a more local significance. In any given area, one must be aware of Poles, Russians, Greeks, Armenians, Chinese, Cubans, Norwegians, Swedes, Hungarians, Czechs, and so on, and so on, but even the largest of these groups forms no more than a few per cent of the city's population.

The Chinese community has grown, owing to the revision of the immigration laws in 1965, which eliminated the last references to race and national origin. The Cuban community is the largest new addition to the city's ethnic array. The over-all pattern, however, remains the familiar one of the early 1960's, with the trends then noted continuing: the growth of the Negro and Puerto Rican populations; the decline of the older ethnic groups, Irish and German; the continued significance of the two major groups of the "new immigration" of 1880 to 1924, the Jews and the Italians. This is the statistical pattern. Politically, economically, and culturally, however, two groups have outdistanced all others in the sixties: Jews and White Anglo-Saxon Protestants. The life of the city in the late sixties reflected nothing so much as an alliance between these groups, or parts of them, and the growing Negro group, against the remaining white, largely Catholic, groups. We shall say more later concerning why this has come about and what it means for the city.

Have ethnic identity and the significance of ethnic identity declined in the city since the early 1960's? The long-expected and predicted decline of ethnicity, the fuller acculturation and the assimilation of the white ethnic groups, seems once again delayed—as it was by World War I, World War II, and the cold war—and by now one suspects, if something expected keeps on failing to happen, that there may be more reasons than accident that explain why ethnicity and ethnic identity continue to persist. In *Beyond the Melting Pot,* we suggested that ethnic groups, owing to their distinctive historical experiences, their cultures and skills, the times of their arrival and the economic situation they met, developed distinctive economic, political, and cultural patterns. As the old culture fell away—and it did rapidly enough—a new one, shaped by the distinctive experiences of life in America, was formed and a new identity was created. Italian-Americans might share precious little with Italians in Italy, but in America they were a distinctive group that maintained itself, was identifiable, and gave something to those who were identified with it, just as it also gave burdens that those in the group had to bear.

Beyond the accidents of history, one suspects, is the reality that human groups endure, that they provide some satisfaction to their members, and that the adoption of a totally new ethnic identity, by dropping whatever one is to become simply American, is inhibited by strong elements in the social structure of the United States. It is inhibited by a subtle system of identifying, which ranges from brutal discrimination and prejudice to merely naming. It is inhibited by the unavailability of a simple "American" identity. One is a New Englander, or a Southerner, or a Midwesterner, and all these things mean something too concrete for the ethnic to adopt completely, while excluding his ethnic identity.

In any case, whatever the underlying fault lines in American society that seem to maintain or permit the maintenance of ethnic identity beyond the point of cultural assimilation, the fact is ethnic identity continued in the sixties.

We have precious few studies of ethnic identity, despite the increasing prominence of its role in the mass media in recent years, and we speak consequently quite hypothetically. Yet we would like to suggest three hypotheses on the changing position of ethnic identity in recent years.

First: ethnic identities have taken over some of the task in self-definition and in definition by others that occupational identities, particularly working-class occupational identities, have generally played. The status of the worker has been downgraded; as a result, apparently, the status of being an ethnic, a member of an ethnic group, has been upgraded.

There is no question that many occupational identities have lost a good deal of their merit and virtue, not to say glamour, in the eyes of those who hold them, and in the eyes of those in positions of significance in communications and the mass media who do so much to dispense ideas of merit, virtue, and glamour. The unions, the organizations of the working class, have certainly lost much of their glamour. What young bright man coming out of college would think that the most attractive, personally satisfying, and useful job he could hold would be to work for a union, as the authors did in 1944? Indeed, the intelligentsia has been quietly departing from unions and moving into government and the universities for ten years and more. But more significant has been the downgrading of working-class occupations. In the depression, in World War II, even after the war, the worker held an honored and important position. Radicals fought over his allegiance, the Democratic party was happy in his support, one could even see workers portrayed in the movies by men such as Humphrey Bogart, John Garfield, Clark Gable, and these heroes portrayed occupations, whether as truck drivers or oilfield workers or even produce marketmen, that had some reputation and value.

Similarly, to be a homeowner after the war, and many workers became homeowners, was meritorious. It indicated rise in status, setting down roots, becoming a part of the community. Today, if one were to test associations to the word "worker" and "homeowner" among television newscasters and young college graduates, one is afraid one of the chief associations would be "racist" and "Wallaceite." It is hard to recall any movie of the late sixties, aside from *Pretty Poison,* in which a factory worker was a leading character, and in *Pretty Poison* the factory spewed chemical filth into the countryside, and the worker himself was half mad.[14]

Lower-middle-class statuses have also suffered, but the clerk or teacher or salesman never did do well in the mass media. The worker did; he formed part of that long-sustained and peculiar alliance that has always seemed to link those of higher status, in particular aristocrats and intellectuals, with lower-class people, leaving the middle classes in the middle to suffer the disdain of both. What has happened in recent years is that the lower pole of the alliance has shifted downward, leaving out the working class, and now hooking up the intellectuals and the upper-middle-class youth with the Negro lower class.

The Wallace movement and the Procaccino campaign were in part efforts to take political advantage of the declining sense of being valued in the working- and lower-middle class, and to ascribe to these groups a greater measure of credit and respect, as against both the more prosperous and better educated, who have supported measures designed to assist Negroes and the poor, and the Negroes and the poor themselves. If these class and occupational statuses have been downgraded, by that token alone ethnic identity seems somewhat more desirable. Today, it may be better to be an Italian than a worker. Twenty years ago, it was the other way around.

Thus, one reason we would suggest for the maintenance of ethnic identities is the fact that working-class identities and perhaps some other occupational identities have lost status and respect.

Let us suggest a second hypothesis as to changes in ethnic identity in this decade: international events have declined as a source of feelings of ethnic identity, except for Jews; domestic events have become more important. The rise of Hitler and World War II led to an enormous rise in feelings of ethnic identification. Nor was there much decline after the war, as the descendants of East European immigrants who had been aroused by Hitler's conquests now saw their homelands become Russian satellites, and as other nations were threatened. But aside from Jews, no group now sees its homeland in danger. (Israel barely qualifies as a "homeland," but the emotional identification is the same.) Even the resurgence of conflict between Catholics and Protestants in Northern Ireland has evoked only a sluggish response among American Irish. By this very token, as involvement with and concern for the homelands decline, the sources of ethnic identification more and more are to be found in American experiences, on American soil. This is not to say that identification with homelands in danger or in conflict cannot rise again. But for the first time a wave of ethnic feeling in this country has been evoked not primarily by foreign affairs but by domestic developments. This is a striking and important development—it attests to the long-lived character of ethnic identification and raises the curtain somewhat on the future history of ethnic identity in this country.

A third hypothesis: along with occupation and homeland, religion has declined as a focus of ethnic identification. Just as ethnicity and occupation overlap, so do ethnicity and religion. For some time, it seemed as if new identities based on religion were taking over from ethnic identities. This was the hypothesis of Will Herberg.[15] The Jews remained Jews, with a subtle shift from an ethnic identification in the first and second generation to more of a religious identification in the third; the Irish became ever more Catholic in their self-image, and so did the Italians. Even the P in WASP stands for Protestant, as part of the identity. Only for Negroes did racial identity seem clearly far more significant than religion. In *Beyond the Melting Pot,* we argued that religion and race seemed to be taking over from ethnicity. Yet in the last few years, the role of religion as a primary identity for Americans has weakened. Particularly in the case of Catholics, confusion and uncertainty have entered what was only a few years ago a very firm and clear identity. Thus, for Irish and Italians alike,

Catholicism once confirmed a basic conservatism; it was not only anti-Communist, obviously, but, more significantly, it took conservative positions on issues of family, sex, culture, education. Catholics formed the core of the Democratic party in New York, which, alongside its pronounced and decisive liberalism in social policy, remained conservative on issues of family and culture. The revolution in the Catholic Church has shaken this monolithic institution, and the identity of Catholic is no longer self-evident, to those holding it or to those outside the Church. The change is symbolized by the radical changes in ritual, in this most conservative of institutions, and in the possibility of changes in such ancient patterns as the celibacy of the clergy.

For the purposes of race relations, the most striking development is the divergence between clergy and laity (some clergy and some laity) on the issue of Negro militancy. When priests marched with Martin Luther King in Chicago, it was reported that Catholic workers who opposed the move of Negroes into their neighborhoods said, "Now even they are with them, and we are alone." Nothing as striking as this has happened in New York, where the laity are not as conservative as in Chicago (with its strong Polish and Lithuanian representation), and where the priests have not come up with a prominent radical leader. But if there is no equivalent of Father Groppi in New York, there are many smaller versions of Father Groppi. Catholicism no longer confirms as fully as it did some years ago the conservative tendencies of Italians and Irish.

We have suggested three aspects of the current prominence of ethnicity: that it is related to the declining merit of certain occupational identifications, that it increasingly finds its sources in domestic rather than foreign crises, and that the revolution in the Catholic Church means that, for the first time, it does not complement the conservative tendencies of Catholic ethnic groups. Now we come to a fourth aspect. In a word, is the resurgence of ethnicity simply a matter of the resurgence of racism, as is now often asserted? Is the reaction of whites, of ethnic groups and the working and middle class, to the increasingly militant demands of Negroes a matter of defense of ethnic and occupational turfs and privileges or is it a matter of racial antipathy, and more of racism, that large and ill-used term, which means, if it means anything, that those afflicted with it see the world primarily in racial categories, in black and white, and insist that black should be down and white up?

In the fifties, Herberg argued that religion was rising, not because of any interest really in its doctrines, but because religion was a more respectable way of maintaining ethnic primary groups than ethnicity itself. To be Italian or Jewish (ethnic rather than religious) was somehow not reputable and raised the issue of conflict with the demands of American citizenship, a potential conflict that became particularly sharp in World War II and that has remained alive for American Jews since the establishment of the State of Israel. Now, it is argued, religion, owing to the liberalism of the clergy, cannot serve to keep the Negroes out—of neighborhoods, schools, jobs. But ethnicity can still serve that function. So, by emphasizing ethnicity and ethnic attachment, the argument goes, one can cover one's racism and yet be racist.

Thus, it may be argued, just as religion in the 1950's covered for ethnicity, ethnicity in the 1960's covers for racism. The issue remains simply one of white against black, and to speak of Jews, Italians, Irish, is merely to obfuscate it. We disagree with this point of view and argue that ethnicity is a real and felt basis of political and social action.

To begin with, we have always been forced to recognize the validity of some degree of discrimination—difficult to call simply racist—if it was for the purpose of defending something positive rather than simply excluding someone because of his race. For example, while city, state, and federal laws prohibit discrimination on account of race, creed, color, or national origin, they do accept the fact that certain institutions will want to discriminate positively, for purposes of the kind of mission in which they are engaged. The headquarters of the Armenian Church will want to hire Armenians, a Polish cultural foundation will hire Poles, and so on. Similarly, when Jewish organizations fought discrimination in vacation resorts in New York State in the 1940's and 1950's, they had the difficult issue of deciding whether the note in resort advertisements, "churches nearby," indicated discrimination. The argument was made that Jewish resorts could freely advertise, "dietary laws observed." In both cases, one could argue, something *positive* was being accented, rather than something defined as negative excluded. To emphasize the virtues of maintaining an ethnic neighborhood is different from emphasizing the exclusion of Negroes, in sense and logic, though the acts that serve one aim are hard to distinguish from the acts that serve the other.

Legally, the problem of permitting this kind of positive discrimination is enormously difficult. Morally and socially, it appears to have some value. Just as blacks now want to gather together in distinctive institutions where they can strengthen specifically black social, cultural, and political tendencies, so do other groups; in both cases, the pervasiveness of antidiscrimination statutes and regulations introduces difficulties.

It may be granted that there is some legitimacy to what we call positive discrimination, which can be defined simply as the effort to bring together people of distinctive backgrounds or interests or potential interests for some socially valued end. "Religion" is such an end. "Ethnicity" can be considered such an end. But what about "race"? "Race," we all agree, has been rejected as such an end. Thus, we do not want to see "white" institutions maintained or established in this country. For the purpose of "white," as most of us see it, is not to defend or maintain a "white" culture or religion but to exclude blacks. By the same token, is not the maintenance and creation of black institutions illegitimate? We do not think so, because whatever some black militants may think, "black" defines not a race but a cultural group, in our terms, an ethnicity. Thus, it is hardly likely that Moslem, Swahili-speaking blacks of Zanzibar would find much in common with the black institutions and culture that are now being built up in this country. They would not have any predilection for soul music or soul food, would find the styles of dress, hair, walk, and talk that are now popular as defining blackness distinctly foreign. "Blackness" in this country is not really and simply *blackness*, it is an American Negro cultural style. Blackness would be as unacceptable in this country as whiteness, if it were really only blackness. We can accept it because we recognize in blackness not simply the negative exclusion of white but the positive discrimination designed to strengthen and develop a distinctive group, with a distinctive history, defined interests, and identifiable styles in social life, culture, and politics.

But the matter is not so simple. This is one way of seeing blackness, of course, and a way that makes it conformable to the main trends in American society, where ethnic distinctiveness is to some degree accepted and accommodated. But it is not necessarily the way blacks see it today or will see it. Certainly, many blacks *do* insist on the racial formulation. They base it on the common oppression of all "colored" races by all "whites," and even more by "capitalistic" and "imperialistic" whites, something that is a rough summary of history, but very rough indeed, when one considers that Japan built up a great empire over other yellow and brown people, that Arabs for centuries dominated and enslaved black Africans, that Russia maintains dominion over white groups, and so on. To our minds, whether blacks in the end see themselves as ethnic within the American context, or as only black—a distinct race defined only by color, bearing a unique burden through American history—will determine whether race relations in this country is an unending tragedy or in some measure—to the limited measure that anything human can be—moderately successful.

Indeed, much of the answer to the question we have posed—ethnicity or racism?—is a matter of definition and self-definition, and much of the future of race relations in the city and the country depends on what designations and definitions we use. For just as a "nigger" can be made by treating him like a "nigger" and calling him a "nigger," just as a black can be made by educating him to a new, proud, black image—and this education is carried on in words and images, as well as in deeds—so can racists be made, by calling them racists and treating them like racists. And we have to ask ourselves, as we react to the myriad cases of group conflict in the city, what words shall we use, what images shall we present, with what effect? If a group of housewives insists that it does not want its children bussed to black schools because it fears for the safety of its children, or it does not want blacks bussed in because it fears for the academic quality of the schools, do we denounce this as "racism" or do we recognize that these fears have a base in reality and deal seriously with the issues? When a union insists that it has nothing against blacks but it must protect its jobs for its members and their children, do we deal with those fears directly, or do we denounce them as racists? When a neighborhood insists that it wants to maintain its character and its institutions, do we take this seriously or do we cry racism again?

We believe the conflicts we deal with in the city involve a mixture of *interests:* the defense of specific occupations, jobs, income, property; of *ethnicity:* the attachment to a specific group and its patterns; and of *racism:* the American (though not only American) dislike and fear of the racial other, in America's case in particular compounded by the heritage of slavery and the forcible placing of Negroes into a less than human position. We believe we must deal with all these sources of conflict, but to ignore the ethnic source, or the interest source, in an exclusive fixation on the racist source, will undoubtedly encourage the final tearing apart of the community and the country between groups that see each other as different species rather than as valued variants of a common humanity.

Politically, we think it is wise to recognize these varied sources of conflict. Empirically, we think that to insist that ethnic concerns are only a cover for racism is wrong. Recent research throws some light on the persistence of ethnic cohesion, and it lasts longer than many people believe. The sociologist Nathan Kantrowitz, studying the patterns of residence of racial and ethnic groups in the New York City metropolitan area, points out that the degree of separation between white groups that we often consider similar is quite high. No group, except the Puerto Rican, is as segregated from others as the Negro. When we contrast the residence of Negroes as compared with the residence of foreign-born whites and their children, we find a "segregation index" averaging 80; that is, 80 per cent of Negroes would have to move to be distributed throughout the metropolitan area the way specific groups of foreign-born whites and their children are. We find the same figure when we compare the residences of Puerto Ricans and foreign-born whites and their children; by this measure, then, Puerto Ricans are as segregated as Negroes. But when we compare different *white* groups, we also find a high degree of separation. Thus, for example,

The segregation index between Norwegians and Swedes, 45.4, indicates a separation between two Protestant Scandinavian populations which have partially intermarried and even have at least one community in common (the Bay Ridge neighborhood in Brooklyn). But the high [segregation index] does represent ethnic separation, for each national group still maintains its own newspaper, and each lives in neighborhoods separate from those of the other. If Swedes and Norwegians are not highly integrated with each other, . . . they are even less integrated with other ethnic populations.[16]

And if this is the case for these groups, we would expect Italians and their children, immigrants from Russia and their children to have even *higher* segregation indices—and indeed they do.

　　　　Thus, the data show, on at least this point of residential segregation, that the pattern of distinctive residence characterizes almost all ethnic groups. This is not to say that they all face discrimination: they do not. Negroes do face discrimination in housing, and as we know, severe discrimination. But if groups that do *not* face discrimination *also* show a high degree of segregation, we must resort to two additional explanations of the Negro pattern of residence: one is the economic—they can't afford to move into many houses and many areas (as is true of Puerto Ricans, and, in lesser degree, of other groups); and the second is simply that there is also a positive element in the association of Negroes in given areas, something which is very often totally ignored. Formal and informal social life, churches and other institutions, distinctive businesses, all serve to make neighborhoods that are desirable and attractive for a given group, and to think that this pattern, which operates for all groups, is suspended for Negroes, is to be racist indeed.

AFFLUENT BLACKS AND POOR WHITES

THE SAME KIND OF DIVERSITY WE FIND AMONG WHITES PREVAILS among the newer and poorer groups that are now considered in opposition to whites, that is, Negroes and Puerto Ricans (who are also mostly white, which demonstrates one weakness in phrasing the struggle in racial terms). Indeed, much of our thinking about racial and ethnic conflict in the society has been badly flawed by our tendency to see two "sides," and to ascribe uniformity of one kind or another to both. All the whites are affluent, all the blacks and Puerto Ricans are poor. Or all the whites are racists, all the blacks are militant. (Once again, people think less about Puerto Ricans.) These black and white visions have limited the range of possible tactics and policies by political leaders and administrators, and indeed, have helped encourage the creation of a situation in which all the blacks would, in fact, become militant and all the whites racists, even if they did less to create a situation in which all the whites became rich and all the blacks poor. The emphasis on black poverty was designed to increase sympathy. But in the white working class it very often created a mystified response: Why such poverty and misery? Jobs are available (every issue of the newspaper reported job shortages). Why were there so many children in the television reports and so few men? What was going on and wasn't it their fault? And if it was their fault, why the militancy, the insults, and the denunciation? The prevalent style of reporting and of political response only increased the fear and antagonism.

The fact is, of course, that there are many, many working-class and middle-class Negro and Puerto Rican men, working hard and supporting families—indeed, far more than those who are not—but they are rarely considered. These elements of the community were ignored by almost all those engaged in the problem. They were ignored by the black militants, unless they were denounced as Uncle Toms, or more recently "Negroes" (this term, for which various Negro organizations had fought, now became to many militants a sign of unworthy and unmanly accommodation to "the man"). They were ignored by the white mass media. They were very often ignored by the political leaders. As a result, the self-confidence of these elements disintegrated. The Invisible Man once meant the black man without a job, without a home, truly invisible, not even counted in the census. In the 1960's, the black Invisible Man became the working class and the middle class, people who had been leaders in their communities. They were now pushed aside by young militants, who were supported by white mass media and some white political leaders.

Thus, a good deal of the practical, effective work in raising the income and power of individual blacks and of the black communities was totally ignored by whites and blacks. Perhaps the best criticism of this whole style in race relations was made by Matthew Holden, Jr., a political scientist now at the University of Wisconsin, at a conference, typical of the times, held in 1967 by the City of New York Commission on Human Rights on "Community Values and Conflict." The nature of the conference can be well imagined by anyone who has participated in other similar exercises. What was completely not to be expected was Professor Holden's remarkable critique at the end. He began with a criticism of the character of the conference, asserting it had

resolutely refused to face the most critical issues which have to be understood if there is to be a forward movement in American race relations. It has not dealt in realities, but in rituals. . . .

If . . . the conference has ducked, rather than faced, the hard issues . . . , is not one reason that the very structure of the conference is decisively unrepresentative of the urban Negro communities? Every important segment in the urban Negro communities ought to be represented. . . . However, there are at least two vital segments which are absent, which ought to be present, and their presence would have changed the tone of the discussion.

First, this conference distinctly under-represents, and systematically under-represents, the urban Negro middle class. The 1960's have seen a novel phenomenon in American history. For the first time, there is an urban Negro middle class which is substantially similar to the urban white middle class, in its educational levels, its income levels, and its occupational tendencies. That Negro middle class, embodied in such people who can raise more than $100,000 in Detroit (via a $100 per couple dinner) for the Legal Defense Fund, is playing an increasingly crucial role in public affairs generally, and is increasingly ready to assume a full responsibility within the Negro community. To come here and pretend that it does not exist is sheer fantasy. To come here and denounce it for "deserting" is sheer dishonesty.

Secondly: this conference also neglects and ignores the Negro "working class." Every city in the country has a fully stable and responsible Negro population, which is just above the poverty line (and sometimes below it), the interests of which have not been articulated here in the past two days. These people do not go to national conferences. . . . They are the mainstay of the religious, fraternal, and other private institutions within the Negro communities. They are the prime support of Negro politicians and Negro business establishments. They are the people whose children, deep in the worst slum schools, provide the stabilizing element which makes it possible for teachers to teach at all. . . . Their aspirations are as "middle-class" as you can get, and they . . . need little except to have institutional barriers knocked down. They are the people who *actually* provide "grass-roots" leadership. (Who else were the elected candidates in poverty agencies in Cleveland and Philadelphia?)

Any public policy which ignores both these groups will be based upon unreal expectations.[17]

And yet in large measure, public policy in New York City in recent years has ignored both these groups. In doing so, it even fosters the illusion in the black community itself that they do not exist. When militant groups—representing whom, no one knows, and at best only a handful of the population—took over the site of the proposed state office building on 125th Street in Manhattan, a spokesman was quoted in the *New York Times* as saying of the people who came to camp on the site, "They were the people who truly represent the community—the welfare mothers, the students, a lot of the young bloods." What a fantastic view of the community! What a degrading one! And what an amazing transvaluation of values! (Presumably, even in referring to "students," the spokesman did not have in mind those who were studying but those who were demonstrating.) Thus, excluded from the community were the professional men, the businessmen, the civil servants, the workers, all of whom might well have given overwhelming approval to the building of a state office building in Harlem.

The 1960's have seen an enormous increase in the number of Negroes in stable jobs, with some degree of security; it has simultaneously seen an enormous increase in militancy. It is quite common for spokesmen for Negroes, in the multifarious public bodies that now exist, to insist that nothing has changed, indeed that blacks are worse off than before, and to act as if they are totally ignorant of the real changes. We think one policy in improving the tone of race relations in New York City would be to give a fair and honest picture of the Negro and Puerto Rican communities. The image projected by political leaders and mass media should not fudge the reality of poverty and degradation: poor housing for very large sections of these communities, high rates of unemployment, the grim fact that one-third of the black and more of the Puerto Rican population are dependent on welfare. But it should not limit the story to this.

While our statistics are poor, and we do not know the full range of change in New York's deprived groups during the past decade (even after the 1970 census, we will still wonder whether we have managed to count the black males of whom probably 60,000 in the city alone were missed in 1960), we still know enough to know there has been substantial progress in the creation of a stable working and middle class among Negroes in New York City. The following are only a few of the evidences:

One-half of the Transport Workers Union of 36,000 are now estimated to be Negro. These now have the security of well-paid jobs with many fringe benefits, including retirement after twenty years of service if the employee is fifty years or over.

About one-third of the members of the American Federation of State, County and Municipal Employees union, which represents 115,000 city workers in varied agencies and occupations, are Negro and Puerto Rican, and they are covered by strong contracts that will give a minimum of $7,000 a year to every city employee by June, 1970.

There has been a transformation in the position of voluntary hospital employees, largely Negro and Puerto Rican. The union that represents them, local 1199 of the Drug and Hospital Workers Union, has 40,000 members, in large measure Negro and Puerto Rican, and has changed their position in ten years from wages below the minimum wage, to wage levels considerably above the minimum wage.

We have seen a transformation in the position of Negro and Puerto Rican workers who formerly had no or weak unions and worked at low wages, and we have seen the movement of Negroes into existing strong unions. We are now seeing Negroes moving into many skilled trades where formerly their representation was infinitesimal. In the Cutters local of the International Ladies' Garment Workers' Union—the highest-paid occupation in the industry—there were, in 1962, about 250 Negro and Spanish-speaking cutters, mostly the latter. In 1968, of 6,843 dress cutters, 283 were Negro and 513 Spanish-speaking; and in that year, of 392 new members of the union, 178 were Negro and Spanish-speaking.

Among the Cloak Pressers, another high-paid local of the I.L.G.W.U., of 1,396 members, 659 are now Negro, Spanish-speaking, or Oriental.*

* These estimates and figures are from union officials and from stories in the *New York Times* (and once again these are probably from union officials). A letter to the *New York Times* on December 3, 1969, from the chairman of the Rank and File Committee of the Transport Workers Union, Mr. Joseph S. Carnegie, asserts 70 per cent of operating personnel of the transit system are black. The letter is moderate and persuasive and suggests that the voice of many unionized black employees is quite different from that of black militants who get more publicity. Mr. Carnegie writes:

The Rank and File Committee of the Transport Workers Union . . . was formed nine years ago to promote democratic reforms within that union. It has never been 100 per cent black, although its leadership has been predominantly black. As a matter of fact, in 1965 the Rank and File Committee ran a slate in opposition to the leadership of the T.W.U. for top offices, and four of our six candidates were white. . . . The leadership of the T.W.U. has always reflected the group which once made up the majority of its workers: The Irish. Why are we now labeled "black separatist" when we only seek to organize a democratic union which will fight in the interests of all workers and reflect in its leadership the ethnic composition of the industry?

Mr. Carnegie's letter has certainly not hurt his cause.

NEW YORK CITY IN 1970

As is well known, the construction industry (except for laborers) has remained for many years almost Negro-free, and its complex modes of recruitment—through apprenticeship, and through the adoption of journeymen who have achieved membership in other cities—have been peculiarly resistant to efforts to bring Negroes into these high-paying trades. Bald or subtle discrimination has played an important role in severely limiting jobs for Negroes in the building trades. Finally, after many years of frustration, Negroes are coming into these unions. One of the most impressive roles in bringing this about has been the Joint Apprenticeship Program of the Workers Defense League and the A. Philip Randolph Educational Fund. The story of how they decided to train young Negroes to the point where they could pass the difficult examinations required for entry into apprenticeship is a remarkable one, for it involved the devising of new teaching techniques to do in a few weeks what the schools had not done in years. In the last three years, 700 to 800 have been placed in building and apprenticeship programs in New York City. Minorities are now beginning to enter these most difficult-to-enter trades in proportions closer to their proportion in the city's population as a whole. About 20 to 30 per cent of new apprenticeship classes are black or Puerto Rican. Since apprenticeship training is not open to workers over 26, there is a serious need for *lateral* entry into the building trades of black and Puerto Rican journeymen and journeymen-trainees. Lateral entry is common in the building trades, but Negroes have rarely entered that way. The idea of journeymen-trainees is important because there are many partially skilled Negroes over twenty-six who could become journeymen with some intensive on-the-job training. If this is done in tandem with apprenticeship programs, blacks and Puerto Ricans will soon control a fair share of the high-prestige, high-wage building trades jobs.*

* See "Testing Human Potential: Report of Conference for Testing New Techniques for Selecting Employees from Minority Groups, April 25, 26, 1968" (mimeographed), The City of New York Commission on Human Rights, pp. 68–71, for an impressive account of the work of this project by Dennis A. Derryck. An earlier publication of The City of New York Commission on Human Rights gives a picture of the slow progress and the complex barriers in this field, "Bias in the Build-

There have been similar changes in the area of white-collar work. Negroes have shown a much greater increase in the percentage holding white-collar jobs than whites. The percentage of Puerto Ricans holding white-collar jobs has, according to the same surveys, declined. But as we pointed out earlier, those of Puerto Rican parentage, born on the mainland, do show a substantial increase in percentage holding white-collar jobs.[18]

In March, 1968, the Commission on Human Rights held hearings on minority employment in the

---

ing Industry, an updated report, 1963–67." It reports that in 1963 and 1964 changes in federal and state legislation provided for the selection of apprentices on the basis of merit. As New York State law and implementing regulations put it, "Apprentices shall be selected on the basis of qualifications alone, as determined by objective criteria which permit review." "As a result," the report continues,

the previous "father-son" clauses and the "sponsorship" requirements were eliminated. . . . The new procedures based on objective criteria showed the first encouraging results at year-end 1966 and in early 1967. The statistics and the testimony indicate that non-white apprentices have been admitted into certain crafts for the first time. In some cases, they represent a substantial percentage of the new admissions. The most dramatic results took place in the Ironworkers. Of 55 applicants admitted, 15 were Negroes, 2 were Indians, and 1 was a Filipino. In the Sheetmetal Workers, 14 out of 60 were non-whites in one test, and 24 out of 60 passed the last test . . . in the Stone Derrickman's Union, 3 of the 8 successful candidates were non-whites; . . . in the Electricians union . . . 40 of the 161 successful candidates were non-whites.

The commission notes with interest that all except one of the successful candidates were recruited and tutored for the tests by a private civil rights agency, the Workers' Defense League in association with the A. Philip Randolph Educational Fund. (Pp. 31–32)

There are three observations to be made on this story: (1) One area of control in the hands of skilled workers has been reduced—the "father-son" clauses and the "sponsorship" clauses permitted fathers and uncles to make it easier for sons and nephews to get into high-paid occupations. Admittedly this reduction of power was necessary to increase opportunities for blacks. Yet middle-class professionals who secure their children's futures by means of expensive private school and college education should appreciate the feelings of workers who secure their children's futures, insofar as they can, through control of jobs. And if blacks are resentful because they lack sufficient power, understandably workers become resentful at the loss of some part of theirs. (2) The shift to merit standards, combined with the creative tutoring and training programs of the Joint Apprenticeship Program, was able to secure substantial percentages of places for blacks and other minority group members. (3) In 1969 quite new tactics to increase these proportions of blacks in the building trades made their appearance: blocking construction on various sites (Chicago, Pittsburgh, and Tufts and Harvard Universities) and the demand for fixed quotas.

advertising and broadcasting industry. It had surveyed the degree of such employment in September, 1967. A program of affirmative action was devised after the hearings, and a new survey of minority employment was conducted in September, 1968. One year after the first survey, and only seven months after the hearings, the following changes were recorded:[19]

	September, 1967		September, 1968	
	Number	Per Cent	Number	Per Cent
Thirty-five Advertising Agencies				
Total employees	17,008		16,062	
Negro	609	3.5	829	5.1
Puerto Rican	265	1.5	287	1.8
Three Broadcasting Networks (ABC, CBS, NBC)				
Total employees	10,888		10,703	
Negro	572	5.3	721	6.7
Puerto Rican	141	1.3	216	2.0

Obviously, there are various ways of looking at these figures. As Daniel Bell says about a glass with water halfway up to the brim, we can consider it half-full or half-empty. Regardless of how we consider it, the change in one year, in industries with declining or stable numbers of employees, is remarkable. It is quite clear that new employees are being drawn disproportionately from minority groups, a situation which is as it should be if they are to improve their economic position.

Of course, these percentages are averages between tiny proportions of Negroes and Puerto Ricans, if any, in high-paying and policy-making jobs, and larger proportions in jobs of inferior income and status. Yet the numbers in the higher levels increased at a faster rate than the over-all increase in Negro personnel. And this was the work of one year. How much we may ascribe to the action of the Commission on Human Rights and how much to the simple reality of increasing numbers of qualified Negro and Puerto Rican individuals getting jobs through the regular operations of the labor market is unclear, but we suspect as much is owing to the latter as to the former.

We may point to other areas where Negroes are taking up not only white-collar jobs with security but jobs with some authority. Substantial numbers of Negroes hold important jobs in city government. The number of Negro professional employees in the unions with large Negro membership has in the last few years increased rapidly. For example, 40 of the 100 professionals on the staff of the State, County and Municipal Employees union are now Negro and Puerto Rican. In other unions, Negroes are now pushing to take over top leadership. (Top leadership in unions, as is generally known, is peculiarly long-lived.) But Negroes are still underrepresented in the top offices of unions in which they form a large part of the membership. We expect this will change rapidly in the next few years.

Another area of professional jobs and policy-making in which Negroes now dominate is the neighborhood-oriented programs spawned by the poverty program and the related programs of manpower development, model cities, neighborhood school districts, and the like. These programs, whatever changes occur at the top, are here to stay. Some form of community organization and community-related social programming is inevitable. How many Negroes and Puerto Ricans work in this field it is hard to say, but 14,300 persons are employed in the anti-poverty programs of the Human Resources Administration, and the great majority of these are Negro and Puerto Rican.[20]

There are scattered figures that we suggest mark a trend: the incorporation of greater and greater numbers of Negroes and Puerto Ricans into stable working-class and white-collar occupations, with some degree of security and of the fringe benefits—vacations, medical benefits, sickness pay, retirement benefits—which the ordinary American worker has achieved. Yet the official orientation to race relations in the city has ignored this large, stable working-class and middle-class group. If policy-makers had been more consistently aware of this group, the perverseness of believing, as some seemed to, that the Negro community is made up only of welfare mothers, demonstrating students, and "young bloods" would have been avoided.

The more conservative tendencies in the Negro community have gone underground, for a variety of reasons. One is that the mass media and public figures did not recognize them, and certainly we are given a sense of

our identity and numbers by an outer, symbolic acknowl-
edgment. The mass media and public figures did recognize,
seek out, and direct the full thrust of their policy to the
excluded groups, a laudable aim but one which also had
the political disadvantage of losing white sympathies, as
they, too, fell in with the illusion that this was all that the
Negro community consisted of. In addition, the militant
elements gained support from the youth of the better-off
working-class and middle-class Negroes. These were influenced by the great change that overtook American political
thinking in the 1960's, a change which reawakened and
strengthened many old radical interpretations and under-
standings of American society. The force and strength of
these new tendencies, in the black communities as well as
the white, silenced older and more moderate elements,
which (and again these tendencies were supported by the
mass media) were confused by self-doubts.

In the case of the Puerto Ricans, militant
elements were weaker, and conservative, traditional, and
reformist elements were stronger.[21] Puerto Ricans received
only a fraction of the attention that policy-makers and mass
media lavished on black militants. Traditional approaches
to social mobility, such as the work of "Aspira" in getting
Puerto Rican youngsters into college, played a larger role
in the over-all pattern than in the black community.

And yet a policy that assumed that all Ne-
groes were militant, just as a policy that assumed all were
poor, was seriously mistaken.

First, the facts themselves indicated that
militants could elect almost nobody in black communities;
the elected officials tended to be from the major moderate
groups, even though their rhetoric began to reflect the
change in the Negro communities.

Second, certain policies were adopted which
ignored the feelings and desires of the stable working-class
and middle-class groups. One example of such policies was
the effort to build public housing on land adjacent to the
apartment houses and homes of the stable working class
and middle class. One of the chief misfortunes facing Negroes in this city, as we pointed out in *Beyond the Melting
Pot,* is that, owing to discrimination in housing and a lim-

ited housing choice, they cannot choose their neighbors. The respectable are forced to live next to those they dislike and despise. A policy that insists that housing for the lower classes should be built in carefully protected stable neighborhoods hurts working-class and middle-class blacks more than it hurts whites. For the whites *did* have larger choices, the blacks were more limited. To a liberal mind, it seems reasonable that all people should live together. To a man painfully working himself up, the opportunity to escape from his problem-ridden neighbors is far more important than this abstract ideal. This was true for the immigrants of the early twentieth century. It was only ironically when the Negroes were ready to make this change that ideology insisted they should not escape.*

Third, policies directed to the militants strengthened the militants. Very often what they wanted was so poorly thought out or presented that no policy could accommodate them, but they personally could be accommodated. They could be listened to by boards and commissions, placed on them, given television time, taken seri-

* For a criticism of this policy, see Irving Kristol and Paul Weaver, "Who Knows New York? Notes on a Mixed-up City," *The Public Interest*, No. 16, Summer, 1969, pp. 41–63. Mark Zussman, "Superblock in Bed-Stuy," in *The Village Voice*, December 11, 1969, describes the effects, in one case, of ignoring the reality that there are middle-class and working-class stable homeowning black families as well as lower-class unstable ones, and that the first do not think their children or their immediate neighborhoods will be improved by close contact with the second. The story records the effort of the Bedford-Stuyvesant Restoration Corporation to build a "superblock," linking two blocks more closely together through elegant contemporary urban design. The better-off families on one of the blocks resisted the link.

A story in the *New York Times* of December 28, 1969, gives another example of the conflict between poorer and better-off blacks. It reports the dismay of homeowning Negroes in two school districts on Long Island at the increase in the number of welfare families (black) among them. The issue is not racial at all: white homeowners would resist the increase in welfare families (white or black), and black homeowners resist the increase in welfare families (white or black).

Many black middle class residents in both communities have come to resent the fact that their schools have had to absorb such a large number of welfare students. Many feel that the quality of education in their district has gone down because of the high proportion of students on welfare: 50 per cent in Wyandanch and 30 per cent in Roosevelt. The children of the welfare clients are often behind in reading and other subjects. As a result, some middle-class blacks have become part of a second migration out of the communities. . . .

ously. Their nonsense was very often accepted as simple decent common sense that everyone must accept.

One of the most striking examples of the disasters that ensued from considering militants the sole voice of the Negroes and Puerto Ricans could be seen at the City College of New York in the spring of 1969. Here Negro and Puerto Rican militant students demanded 50 per cent of the entering places at the college for Negroes and Puerto Ricans. Apparently no one argued with them, to say, for example, that this was far more than their proportion among high school graduates in the city; that to abandon standards for admission was to reduce the value of the City College diploma for those who did get in; that it was unfair to hundreds of Negroes and Puerto Ricans (leaving aside others) who had worked to attain the high standards for admission; that it would destroy a major resource by which poor groups in the past had improved themselves. That resource, the City College of New York, was created not by a distinguished faculty, or lavish resources, or prestige based on class and connections but by only one thing—a student body selected on the basis of academic qualifications alone. Destroy that, and City College would mean no more for those who attended it than a hundred community colleges around the country.

All these, and there were probably other good arguments, seem to have played no role in the negotiations that followed (which were, in any case, conducted in private). From whatever leaked out, the only point of the negotiations was to determine how the initial demand could be accommodated without it appearing as if a simple racial and ethnic quota had been established. It was no wonder that when candidate Mario Procaccino, a City College graduate, went to court to force the reopening of the College, he created what turned out to be one of the most potent issues in the Democratic primary.[22]

We do not know how hard-working middle-class and working-class Negroes and Puerto Ricans responded to this sad story. One suspects they were at least torn, for their efforts to instill in their children the desirability of hard work and discipline were undermined by such a demand.

Just as one illusion of racial politics in the 1960's in New York was that all blacks were poor and militant, another illusion was that all whites were affluent. Most of the Irish had taken three generations to work themselves out of poverty, the Italians two, the Jews had moved somewhat faster. But all these groups knew they had worked their way out of poverty at a time when government aid to the poor was nonexistent or more moderate, when mass public education was more restricted, when manpower development programs did not exist, and they found it difficult to understand the demand of "high income and high position now." That was in effect the demand: not jobs now, because jobs existed; not poverty-level maintenance income for those who could not work, for that, too, existed; but high income and high position now.[23] These groups had been trained in working and waiting a long time to achieve high income and high position. We have pointed out in *Beyond the Melting Pot* how endless was the process whereby, in the Irish Catholic controlled Democratic party, a man achieved high position. He began work at the bottom, in the precinct, and might in decades work himself nearer to the top. The same was true in the government jobs that many Irish, Italians, and Jews took.

The white ethnic groups were familiar with the processes of bureaucratic advancement—how long a time was necessary at one level to reach the next. Many Negroes, excluded from this kind of experience, were not, and were unaware when they made demands for Negroes in high position in various bureaucratic organizations, government and nongovernment, how shocking and immoral these demands appeared to those who had served their time.

At one of those conferences in which businessmen meet with Negroes (generally, alas, black militants who move from conference to conference providing denunciation for whites), a company president described the program of his company in bringing Negroes into various jobs. A Negro demanded: "How many Negroes run your plants?" The businessman, taken aback: "None." "Why not?" "Well, it takes a long time to learn how to run a plant, maybe twenty-five or thirty years. It's a very responsible job, most of our Negro employees have only been with the company a short time." "Do you expect Negroes to wait *that long* for a good job?"

There is an answer to this, "Everyone else has." Unfortunately, many Negroes, and in particular militant leaders, are not aware of this. And if everyone else has waited, they don't see why Negroes shouldn't wait, too. Obviously, there are rights on both sides here. Negroes must be advanced rapidly to high and authoritative positions as symbols of the fact that they form a full part of the society, as encouragement to others, to utilize their real talents, and primarily to create a unified and integrated society. But if one does not recognize that there are rights on *both* sides, one's policies will be clumsy, obtuse, and ineffective.

One key fact that is often ignored is that most members of the white ethnic groups are *not* successful. And just as race relations policy should take into account working-class and middle-class Negroes, so should it take into account not-so-affluent whites. We do not know just how ethnic groups are distributed by income and occupation, since the census gives us little assistance and is, in any case, badly out of date. But a sample survey of New York adults taken in 1963 offers some ground for thought on this issue. Thus, if we consider professional employment alone, 9.5 per cent of Negroes were so engaged, compared to 3 per cent of Puerto Ricans, 5 per cent of Italians (first and second generation), 9 per cent of Irish (first and second generation), 11 per cent of other Catholics (including third and higher generations of Italian and Irish), 10.5 per cent of foreign-born Jews, 21.5 per cent of native-born Jews, and 22 per cent of white Protestants. From the point of view of the Puerto Rican, using this measure alone, the Negro is doing quite well; from the point of view of the Italians, Negroes include a large number of professionals. More of the Negro professionals are women. But even when we consider men alone, 8.5 per cent of Negroes are professionals, compared to 4.7 of Puerto Ricans, 7.7 of Irish first and second generation, 8.1 of Italian first and second generation, and higher proportions of the other groups. The proportion of Negroes who are in professional statuses one would guess has increased more rapidly than for other groups since 1963.[24] But the point of these statistics is simply to argue that it is not true that every white sees every Negro in an inferior and deprived position. In consequence, it is not true that every white opposing policies and demands that are aimed at raising the number of Negroes in good jobs and high-paying jobs is simply acting out of racism. He may be acting as much out of a sense of fair shares, the proper reward for merit, the right relation between effort and income. In this case, to attack his resistance on the ground that he is being racist and selfish is politically totally ineffective and self-defeating; to understand that his resistance is based on a sense of what is right and proper, a sense that we would not want to destroy, is to come closer to finding approaches to moderating white resistance to policies that will improve the economic position of Negroes.

THE CATHOLICS AND THE JEWS

CONTRIBUTING TO THE MALAISE OF THE WHITE WORKING AND lower middle classes in the city has been the startling decline in the power of the Irish and Italian groups, and by the same token, of Catholics, for in New York, as we have pointed out many times, to name an occupational group or a class is very much the same thing as naming an ethnic group, and to name an ethnic group is very much the same thing as naming a religious group.

Among the most notable events in New York City during the 1960's was the decline, almost the collapse, of Catholic power. This is not a misnomer. "New York," we wrote in the opening sentence of the chapter on "The Irish," "used to be an Irish city." That meant a Catholic city as well: one in which the Church had temporal as well as spiritual power. This culminated, even as it declined, in the long reign of Francis Cardinal Spellman as Archbishop of New York, ruling from his episcopal throne in St. Patrick's Cathedral. Spellman was feared, disliked, and heeded. It went on too long by half. His successor, whom he had chosen (having first, some said, laid it down to Rome that either he would be permitted personally to pick the next man or he would refuse to die), seemed almost to sense this and promptly assumed a posture much more in keeping with reality. New York's Catholics might still be, probably were, a majority of the population, but

in all other senses—of political power, of wealth, of intellect, of energy—they were a minority and had best get used
to behaving as such.

A series of events brought all this about. As
with all ethnic history in New York, the most important
event was the arrival of new groups. The era of Catholic
ascendancy in New York came to an end in the aftermath
of the arrival, for the first time in large numbers, of the Jews
and then the Negroes. The process was slow at first but then
accelerated and became almost vengeful. By the end of the
decade, in the entire hierarchy of government officials
elected in statewide or citywide elections, there was but one
lonely Catholic, Malcolm Wilson, the lieutenant governor.
In New York City, following the 1969 election, the powerful
Board of Estimate, consisting of the mayor, the comptroller,
the president of the council, and the five borough presidents,
consisted of five Jews, one white Protestant, one black Protestant, and, again, one lonely Catholic, Robert T. Conner.
(Significantly, both he and the lieutenant governor were
Republicans. Catholic Democrats had disappeared altogether.) In the weighted voting of the Board of Estimate,
Jews had fourteen votes, Protestants six, Catholics two. In
1963 when *Beyond the Melting Pot* was first published, the
Catholic representation was quite the reverse. The Board
of Estimate had five Catholics, two Jews, and one black
Protestant. The voting strength was Catholics fourteen, Jews
six, and Protestants two.

This process had been predictable enough
with respect to the decline of Irish power, and we had so
predicted. But the decline of Catholic power was not, at
least by us, foreseen. Nor, in retrospect, is it easily explained.

One element not to be overlooked is the
almost mechanical process whereby a dominant group fractionates and creates the conditions for its own decline. Once
securely in power, Catholics began to fall out with one another, in the seemingly fixed pattern of these things. (Al
Smith remarked that the only time the Irish stood together
was for the Last Gospel at Sunday Mass.) Interestingly, it
is the Jews, who have replaced the Irish in power and influence, who are now the most politically divided group in

the city. But this is not the whole of the story. The Jews did not merely fill a vacuum; their success involved something more than "just being around," the phrase with which Smith was wont to describe the source of his rise in the scheme of things. The Jews also *ousted* the Catholics. They did this in direct toe-to-toe encounter in a hundred areas of the city's life, and, also, they carried out a brilliant outflanking maneuver involving the black masses of the city, which combined in inextricable detail elements of pure charity, enlightened self-interest, and plain ethnic combativeness.

A full analysis of this complex process has to consider some matter-of-fact political realities. Before the fifties, Jews in New York City were divided among the Democratic party, Republican party and fusion, and left and liberal third parties—Socialists, American Labor, Liberals. In the fifties and sixties, they increasingly concentrated in the Democratic party. Meanwhile, Catholics, concentrated in the Democratic party in earlier decades, divided by moving into the Republican and new Conservative parties. But simultaneously Jews maintained their attachment to liberals of any party and religion. The result was to eclipse Catholic power within the Democratic party, and limit any rise outside it. But this is only one element in Catholic decline.

At the beginning of the century, the Catholic population had its share, at very least, of the most vibrant people of the city in politics, in business, and in the arts, and were quite dominant in areas of immigrant achievement such as sports (where, indeed, they had created a pattern of upward mobility via the prize rings, and the like, that others were to follow precisely). A third of a century later, this was no longer so clearly the case. The Jews were beginning to make their impact. They dominated radical politics, were well established in business, and already intellectually ascendant (withal the nation did not yet realize it). The La Guardia administration for the first time brought Jews in large numbers into positions of political influence.

In the middle third of the century that followed, the Jewish position was expanded and consolidated. This process was hastened, and even in ways made possible, by the rise of Hitler in the 1930's and the extraordinary economic expansion in the United States that commenced in the 1940's. The first led to an intense sense of group identity and group interests among New York Jews—a tradition common enough with them in any event—and also added to their numbers through immigration a small but amazingly gifted group, the German and Central European refugees.[25] The founding of Israel further intensified this development. Economic expansion brought wealth to the businessmen, influence to the professionals, and something very like power to the Jewish scientists and intellectuals. It may be the cold war should be listed here as well. Jews were the dominant group in the American Communist party during the thirties and forties.[26] But they were also the dominant group among the Socialist groups, of the left and right, that opposed the Communists, and dominant in the increasingly important intellectual opposition to the Communists that grew in this country in the thirties and the forties. When the cold war broke out, they inevitably supplied a good number of the experts—who else had spent their college (and even high school) years fighting the Stalinists? And, in addition, Jews had entered the new social sciences in enormous numbers: sociology, economics, political science. Thus, Jews were prominent among the intellectuals who developed the military and diplomatic strategies of the 1940's and 1950's—and also among those who opposed them.

In the new scientific elite, which also played its role in the developing cold war, Jews were again everywhere and often on both sides of each issue. Oppenheimer confronted Teller, and Lewis Strauss turned the issue into one of the great dramas of postwar American history.

The point is that the Jews were everywhere, doing everything. In New York, with the largest Jewish population in the world, they simply outclassed their competition, which was Protestant in business, professional, and intellectual circles, and Catholic in the political ones.

Of all the triumphs of the Jewish style in America of the 1960's, none, surely, was as bizarre or unlikely as the radicalizing of the elite youth of the Eastern seaboard patriciate. By the end of the 1960's, the best preparatory schools of the area were torn with doctrinal disputes between leftist factions anathematizing one another over alleged deviations from doctrines setting forth the true role of the working class in a prerevolutionary phase. Pure C.C.N.Y., circa 1937. And if the prep school boys did not do it especially well, it must surely be marveled, as Dr. Johnson said of the lady preacher, that they did it at all.

All this happened to Jews at a time when rather the opposite was happening to Catholics. The intellectual and cultural sterility described in *Beyond the Melting Pot* gave way before the combined influence of Pope John and the *embourgeoisement* of large sectors of the Catholic population, and was followed by a period of considerable vitality, in comparison at least with the past, but also considerable fractionating.* The embattled solidarity of the anti-Communist period also broke up as that issue gradually became, or seemed to become, less central to the nation's life. Catholics started popping up on every side of the political and moral issues of the day. Thus, in 1969, Monsignor, now Bishop, Fulton J. Sheen declared himself in favor of the United States getting out of Vietnam, and doing so quickly. The nation, he declared, was suffering a nervous breakdown over the whole affair. Doubtless, good sense. But, also, in a curious way, a confession of failure. All those speeches to the Friendly Sons of St. Patrick had been pretty poor stuff, had they not? Poor *intellectually*. The New York Catholics had been so very right about a limited number of things—Joseph Stalin was *not* a nice man—only in the end to be judged to have been wrong about most. Their cultural history, like the history of their politicians, would be written by their enemies or their betters. After fifty years and more of maintaining the loyalty of the American working class to democratic institutions, they would be judged to have done little more than to have

* The 1960's were not at all a barren period for Catholic scholarship. To the contrary, in a period when Jewish and Protestant radical intellectuals became political actors of some consequence, with an accompanying decline in the quality of their work, theologians at institutions such as Fordham began to do quite serious work. It was just that— serious work—and had no popular impact save indirectly through the peace movement, but the foundations of some future influence were perhaps being laid. It is at least worth noting that Eugene McCarthy was by far the most intellectual political figure the Democrats had produced since Wilson.

contributed the term "McCarthyism" to the language. And now, they couldn't even get elected to the Board of Estimate any more.

In largest measure, the passing of the Catholic ascendancy, as a normal, predictable, understood fact about the city, arose from a failure of intellect. There just weren't enough smart Catholics around: smart as district leaders, as playwrights, as professors of molecular biology. The century and a half of unprecedented support of a private educational system had come to little, certainly nothing distinctive. But there was a further factor involved. The 1960's brought the issue of race to the city as it had not existed before. In New York, as elsewhere in the North, this created a range of conflict situations in which Negroes confronted *Catholics.* Not just Irish and Italian Catholics, but also a great range of middle Europeans with very little political or public presence (so little that they could all be lumped under the common term of "Ethnics") but with a sizable interest in the maintenance of patterns of residency, employment, and education that Negroes now threatened by the simple fact of their presence and consequent need for a place to live, a job to provide income, a school to provide education. There followed a classic encounter between working-class and middle-class styles in politics, which, in New York, had come to be Catholic and Jewish styles, respectively. A clue can be found in Selig Perlman's analysis of trade unionism, which arose, he concluded, from a pervasive sense among workers of the scarcity of economic opportunity. (Middle-class intellectuals typically get this wrong, ascribing all manner of universalist and egalitarian intention to what is in fact an effort to keep other people from invading what is seen as a limited and threatened means of making a living.) The newcomers inevitably aroused anxieties. Theirs was a very real threat, and it soon enough acquired substance as black neighborhoods grew, job markets were transformed, schools changed, and so through the various forms by which a new group makes its presence felt.

In New York a game followed in which there were in essence the five players constituting the groups described in *Beyond the Melting Pot* and, in addition, an elite Protestant group. The play went something as follows. The Protestants and better-off Jews determined that the Negroes and Puerto Ricans were deserving and in need and, on those grounds, further determined that these needs would be met by concessions of various kinds from the Italians and the Irish (or, generally speaking, from the Catholic players) and the worse-off Jews. The Catholics resisted, and were promptly further judged to be opposed to helping the deserving and needy. On these grounds their traditional rights to govern in New York City *because they were so representative of just such groups* were taken from them and conferred on the two other players, who had commenced the game and had in the course of it demonstrated that those at the top of the social hierarchy are better able to empathize with those at the bottom. Whereupon ended a century of experiment with governance by men of the people. Liberalism triumphed and the *haute bourgeoisie* was back in power.

The ethnic politics of New York in the 1960's can be understood only if this not especially pleasant process is seen for what it is. Or was. The Catholic ascendancy in New York had been based first on numbers, but second on a reasonably well grounded assumption that they, normally as Democrats, would best look after the interests of ordinary people, and would be especially concerned for the least well off, being themselves only recently emerged from that condition. The Protestant elite of the city had always challenged that assumption, asserting instead that the Tammany bosses were boodlers, pure and simple, or in a slightly different formulation, such as that of Lincoln Steffens, were merely paid lackeys of the really Big Boodlers. Either way the charge was that they did not truly represent the people as they claimed to do. In three elections out of four, the masses would choose to believe Charlie Murphy's version rather than that of the *New York Times.* But the effort persisted and in the 1950's acquired a new and devastating tactic. The educated middle class, mostly in the form of young Jewish liberals, began competing for control of the Democratic party machinery itself. In the 1960's they succeeded in breaking Carmine DeSapio, who will probably be regarded as the last of the powerful Democratic party chieftains. (As remarked in *Beyond the Melting Pot,* they could destroy DeSapio, but they could not replace him. In the process, they had destroyed a style of politics.) And almost at that moment, the central issue of politics in the city turned from "Bossism" to "Racism," and here, the Catholics were wholly outclassed. And also, in a way, outmaneuvered. For when the city turned to the issue of race in the mid-1960's, it did not thereby turn away from the issue of who would control the political system. To the contrary, the struggle over racial issues became in many ways a surrogate struggle for control of the city government and the Democratic party. In the end, the Catholics, who had dominated both, lost out.

Many things happened, of which the most important is that from the outset, Jews, in a great variety of roles, defined the new problem. (Not all of them public roles by any means. During this period, if a famous civil rights leader made a speech, the chances were at least even that it had been written by a Jewish speech writer.) And the first thing they did was to define the difficulties facing the Negroes as being in most respects identical to those earlier faced by Jews. In essence, this was the situation of the approach of a highly competitive group so threatening to the established position of others that artificial barriers are raised to restrict and limit the success experienced by the new group (for example, quotas in medical schools).

Reality was almost completely the opposite. The black immigrants in New York City in the 1950's and 1960's were a displaced peasantry, not at all unlike their Irish and Italian predecessors, most, in truth, like the Irish, who arrived with all the stigmata acquired from living under rulers of a different race. (The gulf between ruler and ruled in, say, eighteenth-century Ireland was just as great as that between black and white in the American South.) The Negroes were not highly competitive; they were undercompetitive. They had been raised that way in the South, and were not instantly transformed by Bedford-Stuyvesant, which became not a ghetto but a slum. Taking all references to racial or ethnic identity out of university admission applications, and forbidding photographs, would not automatically double or triple the proportion of Negroes admitted to the Columbia Medical School. It might have quite the opposite effect. But, nonetheless, in one form or another, the situation of the black masses was likened to that of an earlier group that had been artificially and systematically denied successes that would otherwise have accrued to them by a process of discrimination. The response of society would have to be to forbid such discrimination and to punish the discriminators by opening up their restricted preserves to equal opportunity.

Stated in these terms, which are simplified but not exaggerated, it will be seen that this interpretation of the situation of the blacks served a very considerable agenda. It was, first of all, responsive to the genuine concern of New York Jews for the desperate conditions in which so many blacks lived in New York, and the hideous past from which they had escaped. (How could they fail to interpret such things in light of their own experience?) It was responsive to the enlightened self-interest of the Jews, and any other group in the city, to see the black newcomers grow prosperous and successful, as had their predecessors in one degree or another. *But it also served to ascribe, or impute, a good deal of wrongdoing to working-class Catholics who weren't especially conscious of wrongdoing at all.* Moreover, it set up situations of conflict between black and white working-class interests which, no matter who won the battle, ended with the white workers losing the war. No matter what happened, *they* ended up as "racists" and "bigots." And at no cost to upper-middle-class players. It was demanded that trade unions be opened up to the newcomers, with all the primitive fears that would arouse. But it was rarely argued that blacks must be admitted to brokerage firms or law offices. (More to the point, when it was so argued, concessions were easy to make. The upper-middle-class persons involved were not gripped by concern over the scarcity of opportunity. They were more likely to be concerned by the scarcity of Harvard Law School graduates to help with the burgeoning practice. Significantly, when the generalized threat of black competition made its way into the school system, where lower-middle-class Jewish teachers —persons not unlike building trade unionists, trained to one job, and not likely to get another one as good—were exposed, New York experienced the most dangerous racial crisis in its history.) In any event, as this process continued, the fitness of the Catholic majority of the city to govern was increasingly and effectively challenged. On the day after Mayor Lindsay, in 1969, was defeated by an Italian Catholic for renomination by his own party, he ascribed his defeat to "bigots." And although he was later thought to be paying not a little attention to the bigot vote, the fact is that, on this issue, he won reelection against quite extraordinary odds. It was in this election that the Catholic ascendancy in New York City finally dissolved. Without doubt, there will be periods of Catholic rule in the future. But the era is over.

One aspect of the decline of Catholic power has been the failure of the Italians to make a larger impact on the city scene. Everything we have said of the Catholics holds even more strongly for the Italians. The working-class style as against the middle-class style marks them, even as they move in larger and larger numbers into the middle class. Their ability to take over leadership, in the mass media, in education, in the newer sectors of economic development, in politics, even in the Church, has been limited. In *Beyond the Melting Pot* we explored some of the aspects of the Italian-American cultural and social style that seem to have contributed to these limitations. The ties of family, neighborhood, friends, the choice of these over against the claims of higher education and lonely ambition, have produced many of the most attractive families, neighborhoods, and friendships in New York. (Italians have a genius for making cities livable.) But somehow the ethos has not gone beyond that to create a presumption of leadership in city affairs.

The reasons are complex. But high among them would have to be listed the curse of the Mafia. In the 1960's the curse compounded. Not only did the Italian population continue to suffer from the exactions of its criminal element—a basic ecological rule being that criminals prey first of all on those nearest them—but also the charge, or fear, or presumption of "Mafia connections" affected nearly the entire Italian community. Injustice leading to yet more injustice: that is about what happened. During the 1960's the mass media, *and the non-Italian politicians,* combined to make the Mafia a household symbol of evil and wrongdoing. Television ran endless crime series, such as *The Untouchables,* in which the criminals were, for all purposes, exclusively Italian. Attorneys General, of whom Robert F. Kennedy was the archetype, made the "war against organized crime" a staple of national politics. As Attorney General, Kennedy produced Joseph Valachi, who informed the nation that the correct designation of the syndicate was not Mafia but "Cosa Nostra"—"Our thing." True or not, the designation was solemnly accepted by the media, with an air almost of gratitude for the significance of the information thus divulged. On the occasions that a reputed "family head" would pass away (often as not peaceably, amidst modest comfort in Nassau County), the *New York Times* would discourse learnedly on what the probable succession would be.

This is rather an incredible set of facts. Ethnic sensitivities in New York, in the nation, have never been higher than during the 1960's. To accuse a major portion of the population of persistent criminality would seem a certain course of political or commercial disaster. But it was not. The contrast with the general "elite" response to Negro crime is instructive. Typically, the latter was blamed on white society. Black problems were muted, while Italian problems were emphasized, even exaggerated. Why?

We do not know. There may have been some displacement of antiblack feeling to Italians, possibly as a consequence of the association of the Mafia with the drug traffic, and the latter's association with high rates of black crime.* It may be that society needs an unpopular group around, and the Italians were for many reasons available. Democratic reformers, in largest number Jews but also including among them political figures who had come from the Irish Catholic and white Protestant groups, were

* Blacks were increasingly sensitive to this issue. In 1969 a pamphlet distributed by the Blackman's Development Center in Washington, D.C., raised the matter directly. There are relatively few Italians in the capital, but the appearance of the drug traffic there was generally attributed to the New York Mafia. The leaflet called for action. "The only people that can break white-face dog Mafia, Mafiosi and Costra-Nostra [sic] selling illegal heroin and other dope to our school children, our families is *ourselves.*"

able to use the Italian association with crime to topple any number of Italian political leaders and, perhaps more important, to prevent others from acquiring any ascendancy.* Many political figures thus gained advantage. But in the end it was the weakness of the group itself that was decisive.

This might be symbolized by the near to total failure of the Italian-American "Anti-Defamation League" established during the 1960's to combat anti-Italian prejudice. It was not only modeled, it was apparently named after the Anti-Defamation League of B'nai B'rith, but the results were in no way similar. The ADL has access to an extraordinary range of Jewish intellectuals, writers, professors, publishers, publicists, moving picture and, more recently, television executives, who happen to be Jewish. These in turn connect with almost the entire network of public opinion making in America. In New York this is known as clout. It is something which in this field Italians simply do not have. Whether they shall ever, as a group, remains to be seen. There are uncertain signs. Mario Puzo's *The Godfather,* a benign, even romanticized account of the long life and happy death of a particularly repelling brute of a Mafia chieftain, was 40 weeks on the *Times* Best Seller list for 1969, equaling *Portnoy's Complaint.* This is the mark of an emergent self-consciousness but not necessarily of emerging competence in the encounters that count. It is likely that Portnoy will continue to be "Assistant Commissioner for the City of New York Commission on Human Opportunity" under the Lindsay Administration and its successors (there is money to be made in poverty), while the sons and daughters of Puzo's saga will continue to find themselves exploiting themselves and exploited by others. For the rest of the city it has at least been an example of reasonably good grace under pressure.

Of the Catholic groups of the city, none ended the 1960's in less-promising circumstances than did the Puerto Ricans. The expectation voiced in *Beyond the*

---

* The reformers' luck held in one respect. At the end of the decade DeSapio was convicted on a corruption charge of the kind repeatedly insinuated when he was in power.

Melting Pot that they would leapfrog their black neighbors does not seem to have occurred. To the contrary, Puerto Ricans emerged from the decade as the group with the highest incidence of poverty and the lowest number of men of public position who bargain and broker the arrangements of the city. They had no elected officials, no prominent religious leaders, no writers, no powerful organizations. In the 1969 municipal elections, all 5 of the Puerto Rican candidates (among 246 running for office) lost. Their relations with blacks were not good, especially as the latter took advantage of the opportunities for middle-class persons created by the antipoverty program. But neither could they make much common cause with the coreligionists who had preceded them to the city. In a way, this left the Catholic Church with one of the most serious problems it had yet faced. The religious observance of Puerto Ricans was mixed, but so was that of Italians when they first arrived. Prosperity makes persons more, not less, concerned with such matters. But Puerto Ricans also showed great interest in Pentecostal Protestantism. (An interesting continuity. The first Irish and then Italians to rise to prominence in public affairs in the city were Protestant. So with the first Puerto Rican, Herman Badillo.) If the Puerto Rican mass should abandon Catholicism, or split on the issue, Catholics would shortly become a numerical as well as a political and cultural minority in the city.

And yet, even though Puerto Ricans have done badly, economically and politically, the seventies may be the decade in which the optimism of *Beyond the Melting Pot* is fulfilled. It may still be argued that their poverty and powerlessness is accompanied by little despair and a good deal of hope. Certainly, even though the Negroes are (statistically) better off economically and have much larger representation politically, they show much more despair and much less hope. The explanation for this paradox, we suggest, is that Puerto Ricans still see themselves in the immigrant-ethnic model; that is, they see their poor economic and political position as reflecting recency of arrival and evil circumstances that can still be overcome. Thus, they have an explanation for their poor circumstances that does not demand revolutionary change. This immigrant-ethnic model is strengthened by the fact that so many new Spanish-speaking immigrants to the city during the 1960's are refugee Cubans and voluntary migrants from various Central and South American countries, who, even more than the Puerto Ricans, see themselves as classic immigrants, fleeing political persecution and economic deprivation to find opportunity in a new country. These non-Puerto Rican Spanish-speaking migrants are, willy-nilly, identified by the rest of the city as "Puerto Rican." Perhaps a new ethnic group, the "Spanish-speaking," is emerging to replace the Puerto Rican. Certainly, the term is coming into widespread use in the city. The Puerto Ricans have to struggle between a conception of themselves as "colonized" and, therefore, "exploited," and a conception of themselves as "immigrants." The first leads to bitterness, the second to hope. The other Spanish-speaking migrants have much less occasion to think of themselves as colonized (though there is an ideology to justify that, too!).

Not that the "colonized" pattern does not have attractions for Puerto Rican youth and intellectuals. There are some stirrings of alliance with blacks who think in this way. A stronger drive in Puerto Rico for independence will affect Puerto Ricans on the mainland. The radical white college youth, who are now so influential in the mass media, will try to convince them they are "colonized." And yet, one detects a strong resistance to this interpretation of the Puerto Rican position becoming popular.

What are the signs that the Puerto Ricans might be following the ethnic-immigrant pattern rather than the colonial pattern? Some are the moderate tone of their politics; their resistance to full identification with militant blacks; the emphasis of their social institutions, few as they are, on personal mobility; their continued emphasis on business, and creating new business, with little outside support (the colonized pattern would be to call for "expropriation"). The 1960's may go down as the worst decade for the Puerto Ricans in New York. Or, we may be wrong, and the long-range economic and political changes in city and country may record the continued agony of the Puerto Ricans in the city.

THE PARTY OF THE PEOPLE

AT THE CLOSE OF THE 1960'S, THE DEMOCRATS WERE MORE
completely out of power in New York state and city government than almost at any time in their history. The oldest
organized political party in the world was reduced by way of
officeholders to the comptroller in Albany, Arthur Levitt,
who had long since become a politically neutral figure,
and the comptroller in New York City, Abraham D. Beame,
whose career would have to be judged to have passed its
apogee.

The decline of the Democrats accompanied,
and to some degree merely reflected, the collapse of Catholic
power. On the other hand, it is not likely to be a permanent
or even a prolonged condition. In party politics prolonged
failure typically creates the conditions of eventual success.
Thus, by 1970, as Governor Rockfeller completed his third
term in office, Republicans had controlled the state government for all but four of the preceding twenty-eight years.
By definition, Democratic chances became better. Similarly,
the prospect of Mayor Lindsay succeeding to a third term,
or of his being followed by another Republican, would not,
on form, be good. The Democrats will rise again.

They will not, however, ever be the same.
The process of disestablishing the party machinery, which
was described in *Beyond the Melting Pot*, has continued almost to the point where there is no machinery. In any number of Eastern cities the decline or destruction of the Democratic working-class parties was followed by the rise of
organized crime as the single most effective system for organizing power and influence. (It was, and remains, the
theme of many middle-class commentators that organized
crime was somehow brought into existence by the "corrupt"
party machines. This would seem not at all the case. The
relationship was more often that of competing power systems, with an Irish-Italian overlay.) When the Democratic
party declined in New York, a quite different group took
over, one which had helped engineer that decline, and
which benefited from it. It is a group impossible to locate
and difficult to describe save perhaps to say that its nucleus,
or one of its nuclei, could be said to be those persons who,
at a succession of breakfast meetings in Manhattan in 1968–

69, raised fortunes for the campaigns of first Eugene Mc-Carthy, then Hubert H. Humphrey, then John V. Lindsay, and then began gathering to consider who they would raise money for in the coming gubernatorial and senatorial campaigns. Although of distinctly liberal cast of mind, the general sociological point could be made that, in terms of occupation and income and social background, the group was not greatly to be distinguished from the patriciate-plutocracy that in most American cities does try to have a say in things, and usually manages to do so.

To identify this group as "limousine liberals," as Mario Procaccino did in the 1969 mayoralty campaign, or to refer to it as "the Manhattan arrangement," is not far from the facts. It is also a fact that this group beat Procaccino. And herein lies the problem that will continue to plague the Democrats and the city for years to come, whatever the ups and downs of party politics. The Democratic coalition in New York City was shattered in the 1960's. It will never be put back together as a normal condition of politics. In rough terms, this was a coalition of Irish, Italians, Jews, and blacks against the field. They added up to a majority, and they usually won, but those days are now past.

The sources of Irish and Italian-Catholic distaste for and fear of the commercial success and high culture of the Jews (a success increasingly taking the form of familiar WASP power) were described in *Beyond the Melting Pot.* A word may be in order about reciprocal distaste and not so much fear as disdain by the ascendant group.

In an important article that appeared in 1969, Michael Lerner laid out the essentials of this relationship.

When white . . . students denounce the racist university or racist American society, one has little doubt about what they refer to. One also has little doubt about the political leanings of the speaker. He is a good left-liberal or radical, upper-class or schooled in the assumptions of upper-class liberalism.

Liberal-to-radical students use these phrases and feel purged of the bigotry and racism of people such as Chicago's Mayor Daley. No one could be further from bigotry, they seem to believe, than they.

But it isn't so. An extraordinary amount of bigotry on the part of elite, liberal students goes unexamined. . . . Directed at the lower middle class, it feeds on the unexamined biases of class perspective, the personality predilections of elite radicals and academic disciplines that support their views.

There are certainly exceptions in the liberal-radical university society—people intellectually or actively aware of and opposed to the unexamined prejudice. But their anomalousness and lack of success in making an ostensibly introspective community face its own disease is striking.

In general, the bigotry of a lower-middle-class policeman toward a ghetto black or of a lower-middle-class mayor toward a rioter is not viewed in the same perspective as the bigotry of an upper-middle-class peace matron toward a lower-middle-class mayor; or of an upper-class university student toward an Italian, a Pole or a National Guardsman from Cicero, Illinois—that is, if the latter two cases are called bigotry at all. The violence of the ghetto is patronized as it is "understood" and forgiven; the violence of a Cicero racist convinced that Martin Luther King threatens his lawn and house and powerboat is detested without being understood. Yet the two bigotries are very similar. For one thing, each is directed toward the class directly below the resident bigot, the class that reflects the dark side of the bigot's life. Just as the upper class recognizes in lower-class lace-curtain morality the veiled uptightness of upper-middle-class life, so the lower-middle-class bigot sees reflected in the lower class the violence, sexuality and poverty that threaten him. The radical may object that he dislikes the lower middle class purely because of its racism and its politics. But that is not sufficient explanation: Polish jokes are devoid of political content.[27]

Significantly, by way of illustration, he cited a world-famous Yale professor of government who, at dinner, "on the day an Italian American announced his candidacy for Mayor of New York," remarked that "If Italians aren't actually an inferior race, they do the best imitation of one I've seen." (It was later also said of Mario Procaccino that he was so sure of being elected that he had ordered new linoleum for

Gracie Mansion. No one said much of anything about John J. Marchi, the Republican and Conservative candidate, whose Tuscan aristocratic style was surely the equal of Lindsay's WASP patrician manner, and who conducted perhaps the most thoughtful campaign of the three.) Procaccino was made out a clod, and was beaten.

These are not unfamiliar sentiments in the world. But they do destroy coalitions, and that has happened in New York. Moreover, in New York City, ethnic tensions were greatly exacerbated by the rise during the 1960's of a peculiarly virulent form of black antiwhite rhetoric that the white elites tolerated and even in ways encouraged because it was, in effect, directed to the same lower-middle-class and working-class groups which they themselves held in such disdain. Lerner* noted an essential fact concerning the Yale professor's comment about Procaccino. "He could not have said that about black people if the subject had been Rap Brown."

Even more essential is the reverse fact that Rap Brown was, at this time, in a metaphoric sense, pretty much free to say anything he wished about the professor, or rather, about "whitey." Indeed, the more provocative the remark, the more likely it was to be taken seriously. This constituted a grievous departure from the rules of ethnic coalition and clearly made an enormous impact on the Democratic party.

In the course of the 1960's, the etiquette of race relations changed. It became possible, even, from the point of view of the attackers desirable for blacks to attack and vilify whites in a manner no ethnic group had ever really done since the period of anti-Irish feeling of the 1840's and 1850's. This was yet another feature of the Southern pattern of race relations, as against the Northern pattern of ethnic group relations, making its impress on the life of the city. There was, of course, an inversion. The "nigger" speech of the Georgia legislature became the "honky" speech of the Harlem street corner, or the national television studio, complete with threats of violence. In this case, it was the whites who were required to remain silent and im-

---

* Note, there was seemingly no Italian about in 1969 to make Lerner's analysis.

potent in the face of the attack. But the pattern was identical. The calamity of this development will be obvious. The whites in the North responded much as did the blacks in the South. In New York City it was especially difficult for the white working class to understand. What had *they* done? What were the blacks complaining about? The point here is that the white worker in New York in the 1960's readily enough came to see that *a portion* of the black population of the city had achieved what was, in effect, a privileged status. Thus, Whitney M. Young, Jr., in a public address, could dismiss whites as "affluent peasants," [28] in the certainty that such abrasiveness would in no way jeopardize his well-paid job as director of the National Urban League, his office as president of the National Association of Social Workers, and so through the very considerable perquisites of a race man in New York in the 1960's. Young would reply, and with justice, that such rhetoric was necessary to maintain his "credibility" with black militants. (He was speaking to the separatist, or separated, Association of Black Social Workers, whose numbers in New York alone came to 3,000.) But this hardly improved his credibility with white workers, who almost certainly at this time could sense that social workers are not an especially exploited people.

Doors were opened to blacks everywhere in the city, which would never have been opened to a Pole or a Slovak with similar credentials. And the blacks took it as their due.* Which, in any large perspective of American history, it most certainly was, but this was not necessarily self-evident to white workers two or three generations away from the life of peasants on the feudal estates of Europe. Their reaction to the black rhetoric, increasingly accompanied by threats of violence (again the Southern model), was predictable, and it was not always attractive. The anguish of the black slums was something they knew too little (or too much) of to keep steadily in mind. The ag-

* Early in 1969, the black director of an urban studies program at one of the major universities of the city, a fine man with a fine career behind him, including an ambassadorship bestowed by President Kennedy, noted in an address that he was a lawyer, one of his brothers a doctor, and the other a dentist. These, he explained, had been the only occupations open to blacks when he was a boy.

gression of the black leaders against whites in general was, in any event, too threatening, too disorienting to maintain a focus on these other matters. On every hand, persons in positions of ostensible authority seemed to be denying reality. (In his address, Young, a fair man, had noted that "being black can be an asset" to a fortunate minority of the black population. This became a self-evident fact in New York in the 1960's. But all the white elite leaders talked about was discrimination. A similar phenomenon arose as the white elites persistently denied the growing problem of crime, imputing racist motives to anyone who made an issue of it, when for the great mass of the city population it had become a very real issue indeed.) The result was a further delegitimation of authority, a general rise in fear of aggression from other groups (many Negroes at this time became obsessed with the prospect of genocide), and a spreading conviction that the city was "sick" and "ungovernable."

In New York, the 1960's ended much worse than they began. It will now be much more difficult to bring about the gradual incorporation of blacks into the ethnic pattern of the city. If it should turn out to be impossible, the 1960's will be the period in which the direction of things turned.

A NOTE ON ETHNIC STUDIES

IN THE OPENING SENTENCE OF *Beyond the Melting Pot,* WE describe it as "a beginning book." It was, we said, "an effort to trace the role of ethnicity in the tumultuous, varied, endlessly complex life of New York City." By "beginning," we meant it was partial and incomplete, and we hoped there would be more. There is a magnificent tradition of course of immigrant and ethnic group history and sociology. After the work of Marcus Hansen, Oscar Handlin, W. I. Thomas, Robert E. Park, Louis Wirth, Everett C. Hughes, to mention only some leading scholars, we could scarcely make any claim to originality in directing attention to ethnic issues. But at the time we wrote, most of the major work in ethnic history and sociology was already old, not much new was being done, and many seemed to think there was not much more to say. We disagreed.

We had hoped, writing at the outset of the 1960's, that some higher level of intellectual effort and scholarly attention might be paid to the persistence of ethnic ties in American society, a phenomenon that had not been forecast and had to be explained. This was, moreover, not an isolated phenomenon but, rather, one central to the American experience. Andrew Greeley (a Catholic priest and a sociologist), speculating as to what the social historians of, say, the twenty-third or twenty-fourth century will find notable about our era, lists three things: the demographic revolution, the Westernization and industrialization of the non-Western world, and "The formation of a new nation on the North American continent made up of wildly different nationality groups." [29]

We would agree, and we would suppose that, by now, the subject would be considerably developed as an aspect of American studies. But, in this, we would be wrong. Writing now, at the beginning of the 1970's, we find the literature of ethnicity hardly more advanced than when we sent forth our "beginning book."

One would have thought that the crisis of race relations would have led to a better and fuller knowledge by now of the life of blacks and Puerto Ricans in New York and other Northern cities, even if white European immigrant ethnic studies were ignored. On the contrary, those peaks of black scholarship of the forties, E. Franklin Frazier's *The Negro Family in the United States* (Chicago: University of Chicago Press, 1939) and St. Clair Drake and Horace Cayton's *Black Metropolis* (New York: Harcourt, Brace, 1945) stand alone, even more alone than ten years ago. The sixties, whatever they have done for black self-consciousness and pride, have not seen any flowering of black scholarship. One looks back on the sixties and finds only two books that serve as a somewhat adequate general introduction to the situation of blacks in the urban North: Charles Silberman's *Crisis in Black and White* (New York: Random House, 1964) and Kenneth B. Clark's *Dark Ghetto* (New York: Harper & Row, 1965). There are valuable and insightful works of urban ethnography: Elliot Liebow's *Tally's Corner* (Boston: Little, Brown, 1967) and Charles Keil's *Urban Blues* (Chicago: University of Chicago Press,

1966). The work directed by Lee Rainwater in St. Louis has provided important additions to our knowledge of the urban black situation, but as yet only one book, David A. Schulz's *Coming Up Black* (Englewood Cliffs, N.J.: Prentice-Hall, 1969), gives a hint of the further insights locked in doctoral dissertations and unpublished research.

Gerald D. Suttles's *The Social Order of the Slum: Ethnicity and Territory in the Inner City* (Chicago: University of Chicago Press, 1968) deals with more than Negroes. His analysis of ethnic groups in contact in Jane Addams's old Near West Side Chicago neighborhood—Italians, Negroes, Mexican Americans, Puerto Ricans—contains some of the most insightful and perceptive sociology of the 1960's.

The situation of Puerto Rican studies is hardly better. One must record with a sense of shock that the only broad general survey of New York Puerto Ricans is based on research of the mid-forties, C. Wright Mills, Clarence Senior, and Rose Goldsen's *The Puerto Rican Journey* (New York: Harper, 1950). The major addition to the literature on Puerto Ricans in New York since the publication of *Beyond the Melting Pot* is Oscar Lewis's *La Vida* (New York: Random House, 1965), a powerful but limited book. Black academic intellectuals seem to have been largely silent during the sixties, except on political issues. Puerto Rican academic intellectuals have only barely begun to appear.

The fertile Jewish group continues to provide analyses of its own group as well as others, but even though the literature on American Jews has been enriched by Marshall Sklare and Joseph Greenblum's *Jewish Identity on the Suburban Frontier* (New York: Basic Books, 1968), the first analysis of some length of the upper-middle-class style of Jewish life that is becoming the norm for the group, any serious analyst of American Jewish affairs is aware of enormous gaps in knowledge. Even the size of the Jewish population in New York City is unknown. It was once possible to estimate it, badly, by school absences on Yom Kippur. Yom Kippur is now a school holiday. We are, consequently, left in the dark on even the size of the Jewish population of New York.

We are left even more in the dark when it

comes to other groups of the second migration: Italians, Poles, South Slavs, and others, who make up so large a part of the white population of New York and other cities. Leonard Covello's valuable thesis, *The Social Background of the Italo-American School Child* (Leiden: E. J. Brill, 1967), is now available in more than the one copy in the New York University Library that was once the only means of reading it. Ironically, it has been published in the Netherlands. Another Netherlands publisher has printed the report of the major research undertaking of Joshua Fishman, *Language Loyalty in the United States* (The Hague: Mouton, 1966), which throws further light on some of these groups.

Our theoretical understanding of ethnicity in American life is scarcely better advanced. One must mention here Milton Gordon's useful *Assimilation in American Life* (New York: Oxford, 1964). There, the complex issue of what "assimilation" of ethnic groups in the United States actually has been, its forms and distinctions, and what it might be, is considered and illuminated. And one must mention, too, Milton Gordon's valuable Prentice-Hall series on American ethnic groups: Sidney Goldstein and Calvin Goldscheider's *Jewish Americans* (1968), Alphonso Pinkney's *Black Americans* (1969), and Harry Kitano's *Japanese Americans* (1969) have already appeared; Murray Wax's *Indian Americans* and Joseph Fitzpatrick's *Puerto Rican Americans* are on the way.

There is one area in which new statistical techniques have given us a better understanding of one important aspect of ethnicity, residential segregation and integration. Two works in particular should be mentioned: *Ethnic Patterns in American Cities,* by Stanley Lieberson (New York: The Free Press, 1963), and *Negroes in Cities,* by Karl E. and Alma F. Taeuber (Chicago: Aldine, 1965). We have already referred to the work of Kantrowitz on the same theme (see pp. xli–xlii).

There is another area in which our understanding of ethnicity has been advanced by new techniques of research. The monumental study of *Equality of Educational Opportunity* (James Coleman and others, U.S. Department of Health, Education and Welfare, Office of Education, 1966) provided a mass of material on the educational achievement of whites, blacks, American Indians, and Oriental Americans. It has been subjected to intensive reanalysis, which has perhaps raised more questions than it has answered, but still our understanding of the complex relationships between group social characteristics, family characteristics, and school characteristics has been considerably advanced. (This analysis has been presented in a special issue of *Harvard Educational Review,* Vol. 38, No. 1, Winter, 1968, and is developed at much greater length in the forthcoming collection of studies on the Coleman report edited by F. Mosteller and D. P. Moynihan.)

One must record the work of Susan S. Stodolsky and Gerald Lesser on the distinctive patterns of achievement of different ethnic groups. Their paper, "Learning Patterns in the Disadvantaged" (*Harvard Educational Review,* Vol. 37, No. 4, Fall, 1967, pp. 546–593), presents research of extraordinary elegance and insight. Four groups of school children—Chinese, Jews, Negroes, and Puerto Ricans—were selected for study. Two samples of each were selected—a lower-class and a middle-class sample. Four tests (of verbal ability, reasoning, number facility, and space conceptualization) were given. The striking results were that, for each group, a distinctive profile of achievement emerged, which remained the same for the middle-class and the lower-class children. Though the middle-class children scored, in each case, better than the lower-class children, the profile remained intact. Chinese scored highest on space conceptualization, Jewish children highest on verbal facility.

The study is of particular virtue in marking the beginning of quantified and replicable observation of ethnic distinctness. It also raises, only by implication, the sober question of how a society dedicated to achieving a larger measure of equality responds to such striking and enduring differences.[30] There would appear to be reasons beyond any conscious policy, for example, that might explain the Chinese bulge in schools of architecture.

The work of historians, on whom we have leaned so heavily in *Beyond the Melting Pot,* and on whom we must all depend for an understanding of ethnic groups and their relations, has proceeded during the 1960's, but no more—and probably less—has been added than in the previous decades. Once again, it seems not to have been a decade for ethnic studies. One historian remarks to us that this was the decade of urban history rather than ethnic history. The history of racism, slavery, and the American Negro has however been illuminated by a number of valuable works, among them Leon F. Litwack, *North of Slavery* (Chicago: University of Chicago Press, 1961); Gilbert Osofsky, *Harlem: The Making of a Ghetto* (New York: Harper & Row, 1965); Winthrop D. Jordan, *White Over Black* (Chapel Hill: University of North Carolina Press, 1968); Allan H. Spear, *Black Chicago: The Making of a Negro Ghetto, 1890–1920* (Chicago: University of Chicago Press, 1967); August Meier, *Negro Thought in America, 1880–1915: Racial Ideologies in the Age of Booker T. Washington* (Ann Arbor: University of Michigan Press, 1963); Henry A. Bullock, *A History of Negro Education in the South: From 1619 to the Present* (Cambridge: Harvard University Press, 1967).

Thomas N. Brown's *Irish-American Nationalism, 1870–1890* (Philadelphia and New York: Lippincott, 1966) is a model of ethnic history, pointing out *inter alia* the role of nationalist sentiment ostensibly directed to the politics of the old country in giving cultural validity and political cohesion to the immigrant group in the new one.

As usual, the newer white ethnic groups, aside from Jews, have received little attention, though that hopefully is changing. One should mention the work of Timothy L. Smith, who has conducted and directed a good deal of research into these less-studied white ethnic groups; there are already interesting findings, and one looks forward to more (see "Immigrant Social Aspirations and American Education, 1880–1930," *American Quarterly*, Fall, 1969, pp. 523–543.)*

In the near future, we believe the need

* It cannot be without interest to the student of ethnic matters that, to our knowledge, half of the approximately thirty authors and scholars mentioned are Jews, three Negroes, three or four Catholics. This brief survey of some of the work relevant to ethnic studies in the sixties is, we know, partial, reflecting limitations of knowledge, and we present it without any implied judgment on other work and writers.

for ethnic studies will become ever more urgent, simply because ethnic issues have been raised as policy issues so sharply in the sixties. Initially, of course, they have been raised by Negroes. But there has been a response by Mexican Americans, American Indians, and other groups that find themselves in similar depressed circumstances. All of them have become more self-conscious. Now white ethnic groups seem to be developing a perhaps protective greater measure of self-consciousness.

We think the gap in ethnic studies is a misfortune, because such research potentially can be of considerable value to the larger society, primarily by sensitizing it to the opportunities and the difficulties involved in certain types of social change. A society more sensitive to these matters would, for example, have seen with Greeley that "The term 'white ethnic racist' is as pejorative and deceptive as the term 'nigger' or 'damn Yankee' (and perhaps every bit as much a therapeutic ink blot, too)." Such a society would have been much more sensitive to the tradeoffs between one group and another when large social undertakings are launched. It would, if we are correct in our analysis, have perceived and responded to the black experience in the North in quite different terms from those that actually shaped the legislation and domestic programs of the decade, a decade which ended in an ominous mood of more trouble to come.[31]

The rise of the black studies movement would appear to be the first systematic effort to teach ethnic history in elementary and secondary schools and in colleges and universities. We welcome this altogether. However, we would argue that if it is to be *only* black studies, the result will be very much less than satisfactory, for here we are again with the Southern model of race relations: blackey and whitey, two characters in a Beckett play. Doomed together. Polish history and Italian history and Southern white history, all those histories need to be studied and taught. Not least important, if blacks are to learn the history of slavery and not know anything of the histories of how other peoples treated one another in other countries and continents, they can become only yet more persuaded of the fundamental evil of American society. Similarly, if all whites know about the ethnic past is that blacks were slaves, never learning a thing really about the life of the Polish peasant, a not dissimilar distortion of reality is encouraged. Either way, separatism grows.

A point we also tried to make in our opening paragraph was that ethnic studies can be very painful. Carried at the level of the speech to the American Irish Historical Society (p. 253), "While we know that an Irishman was in Columbus' crew on his first voyage to the New World . . . ," they do no great harm, but neither is it clear how much good they do. That is to say, ethnic studies as a form of self-celebration and group reassurance have a place in the scheme of things. But there is also a place for a true historical, sociological effort. *And this will not be pleasant. The results will not be welcomed.* But the effort is necessary if we are going to acquire a deeper understanding of ourselves and a better capacity to determine our future.

FOR THE PRESENT . . .

POLICY, OF COURSE, IN MOST AREAS, CANNOT WAIT ON RESEARCH, however enlightening research might be. What proposals for an ethnic policy—a policy conscious of the reality of the distinctive ethnic and racial groups, with distinct interests, with specific and general conflicts, some reaching to the foundations of the society—can one give? We orient our suggestions to New York City, though they are applicable in major degree to every large city in the country. They are offered in humility, but actions will be taken, and these considerations, we suggest, should guide action.

First, we must be aware that all policies in the city *are* inevitably policies for ethnic and race relations. This is inevitable, because the ethnic and racial groups of the city are *also* interest groups, based on jobs and occupations and possessions. Nor are they interest groups alone; they are also attached to symbols of their past, they are concerned with the fate of their homelands, they want to see members of their group raised to high position and respect. But, aside from all this, owing to the concrete nature of their jobs (or lack of jobs), their businesses, and their professions, they are also defined by *interest*. And since they are interest groups, and since all policies affect interests differently, they also affect group relations. This is the first thing one must be aware of. If one does something that affects the position of organized teachers, one does something that affects the attitudes of the Jewish community, for half the teachers are Jews, and they have relatives. If one does something that affects policemen, one affects by that token the attitudes of the Irish, for a substantial part of the police force is Irish, and they have relatives. (How many is impressive: the study of Brooklyn voting on the police civilian review board shows that 54 per cent of Catholics in Brooklyn have relatives or close friends on the police force. Even 21 per cent of Jews have relatives or close friends on the police force!)[32] If one affects the position of people on welfare, one immediately touches one-third of the Puerto Ricans and Negroes in the city. If one affects the interests of small homeowners, one touches the Italian community. If one affects the interest of small shopkeepers, one has touched the Jews and Italians. And so it goes. Thus, a policy that affects race relations for the city must be a policy that affects all policies in the city. Each of them must be judged from the point of view of its impact on race relations. This impact must be a criterion, not the sole criterion, in every policy one undertakes. It should not be possible for a political leadership ever again to find itself in the position of pressing for a major policy, such as school decentralization, without at least considering in advance its impact on race relations, and how it might be moderated.

Second, policies must be based on the reality that the great majority of the people of the city are workers, white-collar workers, businessmen, and professionals, white and black, who are not aware that their position in life is based on massive governmental assistance. The great majority do not believe that they subsist on the basis of the exploitation of the black and the poor. And their interests and morality must serve as major limits to policy. Many people believe if the interests and morality of these groups are determinant, then nothing can be done for the poor and the black, and, therefore, the interests and morality of the workers and the middle class must be attacked in head-on and destructive conflict. Thus, one often hears the argument that one reason that the people on welfare have such a hard time is that whites and middle-class people refuse to see that work is not superior to nonwork, a point which is presented as an essential insight for the better society of the future. If, indeed, the progress of the poor and the black depends on such a change of values, then we will have to wait a long time for progress. Or we will have to devise means, in a democracy, by which policies can be carried out in the face of the opposition of the great majority. But to say that policies must take into account the interests and morality of the workers and the middle class is not to say that no decent policies are possible. The people of the city do support strongly policies to root out discrimination and prejudice. They do support policies to increase the number of jobs, income from jobs, security from jobs. Policies along these lines, which, of course, must involve state and federal as well as city government, would do much to make jobs more attractive and, by the same token, welfare less attractive.

Third, policies must accept the reality, at least for some time to come, of ethnic communities with some distinctive social concerns, and of people who prefer living with other members of their group. The positive aspects of ethnic attachment should be recognized; the general approval of efforts to build up black pride and self-confidence and self-assertiveness will encourage this. This is perhaps the most difficult point to make, for we believe it would be a disaster for the city if ethnic divisiveness is fostered. But we can *accept* the reality of group existence and group attachment, yet not allow it to become the sole basis of public decisions. The city should not be a federation of nations, with protected turfs and excluded turfs. The organization of the groups should be, as it has been in the past, voluntary. Public action should operate not on the basis of group membership but on the basis of individual human qualities. It has been the curse of this country for so long that this did not happen in fact, and that Negroes—and other groups, in lesser degree—were excluded from even-handed public action. We must not now move to another extreme, in which the sense of injustice is implanted in other groups.

A subtle mix of policies has emerged in the city, in which group existence is recognized and tolerated, in which groups move upward, economically, politically, socially, in which individuals are free to associate with ethnic groups or not as they will, in which groups are given recognition informally but not in formal and fixed procedures. In other words, New York City is neither Lebanon, where Moslems and Christians have formal and fixed constitutional roles, nor Malaysia, where, again, the groups are recognized in public policy and their place and privileges fixed. Nor should it be. How to maintain respect for group feeling and identity while maintaining the primacy of individual rights and responsibilities is perhaps the most difficult task of government, yet the history of New York City gives us some insight into this difficult task, and should not be ignored.

Fourth, one of the chief problems of race relations in this city is the disproportionate presence of Negroes and Puerto Ricans on welfare. As long as one-third or more of the members of these groups are on welfare, as long as welfare remains, as it has become, the largest single item of expenditure in the city, it is hard to see how race relations in the city will not be basically and deeply affected. (One could say the same of the disproportionate Negro role in street crime and crimes of violence.) We know this is a national problem, but it is in even larger measure a New York City problem, for no other city, even those with higher proportions of Negroes and equally generous welfare provisions, shows such huge numbers on welfare. Obviously, this is a problem in its own right, and it is not easy to know what one might do about it. The solution to this problem, if there is one, lies more at the federal than the city level. The Nixon administration has moved strongly to propose a radical revision of the welfare system, one which would tie it in more closely to work, encouraging those requiring government aid to work on the one hand and giving government aid to those who work at low wages on the other, while providing assistance to city and state governments suffering under the strains of increasing welfare needs. This is not the place for an analysis of the problem of welfare in its own right. But there is a role for city government in this respect. As long as the great majority of the population is a working population and a tax-paying population, and as long as welfare aid goes disproportionately to certain ethnic and racial groups, the city government must not place itself in the position of appearing to encourage welfare or of actually encouraging it. Aid to the deprived is a right and an obligation of government. But, as Tocqueville pointed out long ago, rights vary in dignity and virtue. The right to welfare should not be endowed with the same dignity and virtue as the right to work. This can only exacerbate racial and ethnic tensions in the city. Meanwhile, the amelioration of the problems of welfare, which must be sought at many levels both of government and policy, should be pursued.

Fifth, a higher level of civic amenity must be attained to reduce the frustrations and miseries of the poor and the indignation of Negroes and Puerto Ricans. It is easy to say this, impossible to prescribe within present budgetary limits. The mayors are already a powerful lobby demanding more help from the federal government for this purpose. The streets should be cleaner, the subways less of a misery, the parks and playgrounds more numerous, policing—including local constabularies—more effective, and so on. If more money can regularly flow to such urban needs, one hopes that, in some measurable degree, anger will decline.

Sixth, one must beware of encouraging and supporting purely divisive groups and philosophies. The difficult question that we face today is whether black groups that insist—rhetorically or not, who is to tell?—on armed revolution, on the killing of whites, on violence toward every moderate black element, should be tolerated. Even if they are, however, they should not receive public support and encouragement. Intellectuals in New York have done a good deal to encourage and publicize this kind of madness.* The strong corporate feeling today in black commu-

* Not just in New York. The president of a middle western university, prominent in civil rights activities, learned of this phenomenon in a most direct way. He recruited to his campus a young Negro law professor and gave him special responsibilities to deal with minority students. Before many months had passed, the professor submitted his resignation. His life had been threatened. The president was indignant: he asked for the name of the student and vowed he would be off the campus in twenty-four hours. The professor was not moved. Not just his life had been threatened, but that of his wife and child. He had no

nities makes actions against even the least representative and most dangerous groups difficult. Persecution will probably make these groups stronger and will gain them sympathy from moderate blacks, not to mention white liberals. Perhaps the most that can be said at this point is that they should not be encouraged. More positively, this means that every element in the Negro community that *does* believe an integrated, democratic society is possible should be encouraged. There are many such people, and many of them are now cowed by the verbal (and not only verbal) violence of black militants and the unthinking and dilettantish support they now receive from such wide strata of white intellectuals and liberals. Those elements that do believe there is hope for American society should be given recognition and support. They have organizations: these should be given important roles to play in the economic and political improvement of the Negro communities. They have leaders: they should be recognized. They have ideas: they must have the opportunity and power to carry them out.

Seventh, all institutions that wield great power—we think primarily of government, business, labor unions, universities and colleges, hospitals—must be constantly aware of the need to place significant numbers of blacks and Puerto Ricans in posts of responsibility and power. To prescribe how this is done in each area is beyond the confines of this article. Government has been perhaps most active in this respect. Labor unions have been among the more backward, yet owing to the large numbers of Negroes and Puerto Ricans who now make up the working population of New York, and who will make up ever larger proportions in the near future, they have a particular responsibility to develop Negro and Puerto Rican leadership more rapidly. They should have more black and Spanish-speaking business agents, organizers, representatives, union presidents. One can envisage the New York City labor council conducting a serious leadership training for young blacks

---

choice but to leave. The incident is worth reporting because the university president in question had earlier been thoroughly resistant to the idea that such things were taking place. In truth, white liberals have come close to sacrificing the interests of black moderates in order to sustain their own threatened ideology of race relations.

and Puerto Ricans, both in and outside the labor movement, with a guarantee of jobs to successful graduates. This might provide one kind of constructive channel for the driving energy of so many young blacks today, and it might help to provide new vigor to an institution in American life that has done more than any other to raise the position of the poor and the worker. Obviously, similar programs would be a good idea in other major institutions, too.

Eighth, a good deal still devolves upon the complex public and private machinery that has been built up in the city to promote good race relations. We think in particular of the Jewish defense organizations, which have substantial resources and staffs, and which represent the largest single group in the city, the traditional Negro organizations (NAACP, Urban League), the City Commission on Human Rights, and the state agency with parallel responsibilities to fight discrimination and promote good race relations. Obviously, as we argued in our first point, race and ethnic relations are no longer specialized functions for specialized groups. They are issues that must be in the consciousness of public and civil leaders, no matter what area of policy they deal with. Yet there is one major area of tension and conflict in which these specialized agencies can play an important role, and that is the area of Negro-Jewish relations. We discussed the reasons for this tension in *Beyond the Melting Pot* in 1963, and they remain the same. The ironies of history have placed Jews disproportionately in positions of landlord, merchant, doctor, teacher, and social worker; and Negroes, disproportionately, in the positions of tenants of these landlords, customers of these merchants, patients of these doctors, pupils of these teachers, and clients of these social workers. These primary reasons for conflict have existed for a long time, and they have by now, in large measure, effaced the strong alliance that, in the forties and fifties, made New York State and New York City a leader in the passage of civil rights legislation and the development of programs for integration. New sources of tension have been added, in particular, the alliance between American black militants and the revolutionists of the third world. This turns many black leaders into stated enemies of Israel, even if this is not a particularly salient part of their political outlook.

There is no easy way to get at the sources of the conflict. Changes are occurring. Tenement landlords are, owing to varied developments, rapidly abandoning many of their properties, and small businessmen are abandoning theirs. The American Jewish Congress has been instrumental in launching a program to transfer Jewish business properties in black areas to blacks. There are programs to increase the number of Negro doctors. There has been a huge increase of Negroes and Puerto Ricans in the City Colleges, which will increase the number of teachers and social workers. One can think of many other programs that will perhaps more rapidly increase the number of Negro and Puerto Rican landlords, merchants, doctors, teachers, and social workers. All these will have a potential for increasing conflicts between groups, but in the long run we believe they must reduce them.

The voluntary organizations and the city and state agencies can play important roles in all these areas. The voluntary agencies in particular can and should continue the efforts they have carried on throughout the years to promote more direct discussion and meeting between people of different groups. In the end, a good deal must depend on the political intelligence of Jews and Negroes, the two chief groups in conflict. Leaders on both sides can inflame passions. The voluntary organizations that have worked together in the past should be in the best position to educate members of both groups to the enormous dangers in such a path, to spread sound information, to promote tolerant and understanding attitudes.

This is a small budget of suggestions, indeed, for a big problem. Certainly, we are now living through the severest test that New York as a multiethnic society has ever experienced. As we see how other multiethnic and multiracial societies solve or, rather, do not solve their problems, we cannot be too encouraged. And yet, in some respects, the United States, and in particular the great cities, have developed unique approaches to a multiethnic and multiracial society. They may be sufficient for the test.

.   .   .   .

For the second edition of *Beyond the Melting Pot,* we have not attempted any extensive revision or updating of the text of the book. In the seven years since the book was published, errors have been pointed out to us, interpretations have been attacked and challenged, and, most important, enormous changes have occurred in the relationships of racial and ethnic groups, in the country as a whole and in the city. This introduction to the second edition tries to take account of some of these changes. But we have not tampered with the text of the book, aside from the correction of a few errors, the straightening out of some clumsy language, and the correction of a few formulations. The distance between 1963 and 1970 is simply too great to permit extensive revision and updating of a book conceived in the late fifties. The body of the book must stand uncorrected as a record of whatever understanding we had of these issues when we composed it. We wish to express our gratitude to David Riesman, Seymour Martin Lipset, and Joe Glazer, who read drafts of this introduction and provided insightful comments and helpful data.

Parts of this introduction, in somewhat different form, appeared as articles by Nathan Glazer in *The Public Interest* ("A New Look at the Melting Pot," No. 16, Summer, 1969, pp. 180–187) and in *Agenda for a City: Issues Confronting New York,* edited by Lyle C. Fitch and Annmarie Hauck Walsh, Sage Publications, 1970.

Cambridge, Massachusetts　　　Nathan Glazer
January, 1970　　　Daniel P. Moynihan

NOTES

1. *See Police, Politics, and Race: The New York City Referendum on Civilian Review,* by David W. Abbott, Louis H. Gold, and Edward T. Rogowsky, with an Introduction by Daniel P. Moynihan, Cambridge, Mass.: Harvard University Press, 1969; and Arthur Klebanoff, "Is There a Jewish Vote?" *Commentary,* Vol. 49, No. 1, January, 1970, pp. 43–47. These two studies trace the history of the split in Jewish political orientations in New York, along the lines indicated in the text.

2. For the history and analysis of the undercount of Negroes in the census, see "Social Statistics and the City," David M. Heer, Ed., *Report of a Conference Held in Washington, D.C., June 22–23, 1967,* Joint Center for Urban Studies of the Massachusetts Institute of Technology and Harvard University, 1968.

3. For one attempt to determine the distribution of in-

come in New York City by income classes and ethnic groups, see David
M. Gordon, "Income and Welfare in New York City," *The Public Interest*, No. 16, Summer, 1969, pp. 64–88. This argues the case that there
has been real stagnation in the economic position of Negroes and Puerto
Ricans in New York City during the sixties. But the matter is still not
beyond dispute. Among the challenges to David Gordon's estimates is
an analysis of census data by the Center for New York City Affairs of
the New School for Social Research (*New York Times*, February 23,
1970).

4. See "Trends in Social and Economic Conditions in
Metropolitan Areas," U.S. Bureau of the Census, *Current Population
Reports*, Series P-23, February 7, 1969, pp. 55, 61.

5. Nathan Kantrowitz, "Social Mobility of Puerto Ri-
cans: Education, Occupation, and Income Changes Among Children of
Migrants, New York, 1950–60," *International Migration Review*, Vol. 2,
No. 2, Spring, 1968, pp. 53–71.

6. After the writing of the passage in the text, the following data came to hand: In 1968, Negro husband-wife families outside
the South, with heads of family aged 14 to 24 years, had median incomes that were 99 per cent of the median incomes of comparable white
families. For Negro husband-wife families with family heads aged 25 to
34, outside the South, median income was 87 per cent of the comparable
white families. (U.S. Department of Commerce, Bureau of the Census,
Special Tabulation.) It remains the fact that convergence in material
circumstances has been accompanied by increasing strength for militant
political attitudes based on the denial that anything of the sort is
happening.

7. See Daniel P. Moynihan, *Maximum Feasible Misunderstanding*, New York: The Free Press, 1969, for an analysis of the
rise of this doctrine.

8. Arthur Klebanoff, "The Demographics of Politics:
Legislative Constituencies and the Borough of Brooklyn, 1950–1965,"
unpublished senior honors thesis, Yale University, 1969.

9. See Theodore Draper, "The Fantasy of Black Na-
tionalism," *Commentary*, Vol. 48, No. 3, September, 1969, pp. 27–54, for
a scholarly and insightful history and analysis of black separatism.

10. For a description of the Southern model, nothing
will serve better than this letter, published in the *New York Times* on
December 29, 1969. The writer, Mr. Vincent S. Baker, is second vice-
president, New York City Branch, NAACP.

The Convention held in Harlem on the proposed state
office building has implications far more important than the building,
and the truth about what happened there should be known and re-
membered.

Though the convention chairman, Judge James Watson,
tried to be fair, free discussion could not take place in that atmosphere
of violence and intimidation. The fact that an effort was made to drag
me from the hall, and that my life was twice threatened by speakers on
the convention floor without a word of reprimand from convention officials leaves no doubt that anyone wishing to disagree with the hooligan
element could do so only at the risk of personal injury or even
death. . . .

The truth is that the Dec. 13–14 Convention, whatever
the intention of its planners, was the opening phase of a drive by

latter-day fascists to impose upon Harlem a despotic rule for their own power and profit. . . ."

New York, Dec. 17, 1969

11. Fred Ferretti, "Carey into the Breach," *New York Magazine,* March 24, 1969, p. 44.

12. For the remarkable similarity between the Harlem riots of 1935 and 1943 and the Northern urban riots that began in New York City in 1964 (and went on to strike every major Northern city), see Harold Orlans's contemporary account of the 1943 riot, "The Harlem Riot: A Study in Mass Frustration," Social Analysis Report No. 1, 1943. The pamphlet is not easily accessible, but it is quoted in Nathan Glazer, "The Ghetto Crisis," *Encounter,* Vol. 29, No. 5, November, 1967, pp. 15–22.

13. The estimates of Negroes and Puerto Ricans in the city have some official standing; they are from the City Planning Commission. The others are based on sample surveys conducted for the 1969 election. These are rather contradictory, and we have simply made some educated guesses.

14. See William Simon, John H. Gagnon, and Donald Carns, "Working-Class Youth: Alienation Without An Image," *New Generation,* Vol. 51, No. 2, Spring, 1969, pp. 15–21.

15. Will Herberg, *Protestant, Catholic, Jew,* New York: Doubleday, 1955.

16. Nathan Kantrowitz, "Ethnic and Racial Segregation in the New York Metropolis, 1960," *American Journal of Sociology,* Vol. 74, No. 6, May, 1969, 685–695.

17. From *Community Values and Conflict, 1967: A Conference Report,* sponsored by the City of New York Commission on Human Rights; the Lemberg Center for the Study of Violence, Brandeis University; and Brotherhood-in-Action, in cooperation with the Community Relations Service of the Department of Justice, 1967, pp. 116–119.

18. Data of the Health Population survey of New York City, compared with Census data of 1950 and 1960, show the following changes in the percentage of nonwhites and Puerto Ricans in white-collar occupations between 1950 and 1965:

Percentage Employed in White-Collar Occupations

	Employed Men		Employed Women	
	1950	*1965*	*1950*	*1965*
Total	45.9	47.2	56.7	61.3
Nonwhite	21.4	28.5	16.1	31.0
Puerto Ricans	17.3	12.1	12.5	24.9

The increase in the number of nonwhite professional and technical workers was from 3.3 per cent in 1950 to 8.3 per cent in 1965. (M. J. Wantman, "Population Health Survey Research Memorandum," RM 1–67, Health Services Administration and the Center for Social Research of the Graduate Center, The City University of New York.)

For the more substantial progress of second-generation Puerto Ricans, see Note 5.

19. These tables are compiled from two reports of the City of New York Commission on Human Rights, "Report of the Public Hearing on the Employment Practices of the Broadcasting and Advertising Industries . . . held by the City of New York Commission on Human Rights, March 11–12, 1968," and "Report, Affirmative Follow-up to Advertising and Broadcasting Hearing, November, 1968."

20. The figure is from Daniel Bell and Virginia Held, "The Community Revolution," *The Public Interest,* No. 16, Summer, 1969, pp. 142–179. This article also gives the best current account of the developing pattern of community government in New York which is providing the jobs for Negroes and in much lesser degree Puerto Ricans that the old political machine system once provided for earlier groups. This pattern was radically restricted by the rise of civil service, which, whatever its other virtues, has made it very difficult for some branches of city government (for example, the public school system) to reflect in its better jobs the changing ethnic composition of the city. There are still only 35 Negroes among the 900 principals of New York City's public and high schools, and of these only 4 are regularly licensed. (*New York Times,* November 5 and 13, 1969.)

21. For a picture of Puerto Rican leadership in New York which supports this characterization, see John Warren Gotsch, *Puerto Rican Leadership in New York,* Master's thesis, Department of Sociology, New York University, 1966.

22. The best account of the City College story is by Lloyd P. Gartner, "The Five Demands at New York City College," *Midstream,* Vol. 15, No. 8, 1969, pp. 15–35.

23. For the argument that welfare in New York City provides poverty-level maintenance, see Nathan Glazer, "Beyond Income Maintenance—A Note on Welfare in New York City," *The Public Interest,* No. 16, Summer, 1969, pp. 102–122. Two signs of the times on the argument as to what kinds of jobs are available: a headline in the *Boston Globe,* December 18, 1969, reads, "Puerto Ricans face $2.00 an hr. or relief." The point of the article is that the only alternative to welfare is work at $2.00 an hour. A placard in the New York City subways in November, 1969, reports the availability of $143 a week jobs for helpers in many categories in the transit system; the jobs give vacations with pay, social security, sick leave, retirement at half-pay after twenty years, and require either a trade-school diploma or some experience.

24. Jack Elinson, Paul W. Haberman, and Cyrille Gell, "Ethnic and Educational Data on Adults in New York City, 1963–64," School of Public Health and Administrative Medicine, Columbia University, 1967; and Note 18.

25. See Donald Fleming and Bernard Bailyn, Eds. *The Intellectual Migration: Europe and America, 1930–1960,* Cambridge: The Belknap Press of Harvard University Press, 1969.

26. Nathan Glazer, *The Social Basis of American Communism,* New York: Harcourt, Brace, 1961, Chapter IV.

27. Michael Lerner, "Respectable Bigotry," *The American Scholar,* Vol. 38, No. 4, Autumn, 1969, pp. 606–607.

28. *New York Daily News,* October 27, 1969.

29. Andrew Greeley, "The Alienation of White Ethnic Groups," Paper delivered at a Conference on National Unity, Sterling Forest Gardens, October 21–22, 1969, Mimeographed, p. 4.

30. Some of these implications are considered in Nathan Glazer, "Ethnic Groups and Education: Toward the Tolerance of Difference," *Journal of Negro Education*, Vol. 38, No. 3, Summer, 1969, pp. 187–195.

31. This, of course, has taken the form, *inter alia*, of considerable trouble for the Democratic party. In his study, *The Emerging Republican Majority* (New Rochelle: Arlington House, 1969), Kevin P. Phillips contends that, as the Democrats shifted from the economic populist stand of the New Deal to what he terms "social engineering," their coalition collapsed. As a result, he writes, "In practically every state and region, ethnic and cultural animosities and divisions exceed all other factors in explaining party choice and identification."

32. See p. 27 of Abbott, Gold, and Rogowsky, Note 1.

Preface

This is a beginning book. It is an effort to trace the role of ethnicity in the tumultuous, varied, endlessly complex life of New York City. It is time, we believe, that such an effort be made, albeit doomed inevitably to approximation and to inaccuracy, and although it cannot but on occasion give offense to those very persons for whom we have the strongest feeling of fellowship and common purpose. The notion that the intense and unprecedented mixture of ethnic and religious groups in American life was soon to blend into a homogeneous end product has outlived its usefulness, and also its credibility. In the meanwhile the persisting facts of ethnicity demand attention, understanding, and accommodation.

The point about the melting pot, as we say later, is that it did not happen. At least not in New York and, *mutatis mutandis,* in those parts of America which resemble New York.

This is nothing remarkable. On the contrary, the American ethos is nowhere better perceived than in the disinclination of the third and fourth generation of newcomers to blend into a standard, uniform national type. From the beginning, our society and our politics have been at least as much concerned with values as with interests. The principal ethnic groups of New York City will be seen maintaining a distinct identity, albeit a changing one, from one generation to the next. One group is not as another and, notably where religious and cultural values are involved, these differences are matters of choice as well as of heritage; of new creation in a new country, as well as of the maintenance of old values and forms. Our discussion of these differences necessarily touches, even dwells, on the consequent, widely varying patterns of achievement in areas such as education, business, and politics. Understandably enough, the unevenness of achievement in such matters is the source of resentment and even bitterness by many individual members of the different groups. It may be that our discussion will also be resented by such persons, for much the same reason. We would therefore, in advance, ask a measure of forgiveness for taking up a subject which needs to be discussed, but which cannot be aired without giving pain to some.

The Joint Center for Urban Studies of the Massachusetts Institute of Technology and Harvard University sponsored this study, and its indefatigable director Martin Meyerson sustained it in adversity. A grant from the New York Post Foundation made possible much of the research and writing. We are singularly indebted to a great many scholars and fellow New Yorkers who have given us information, ideas, and encouragement. We would like particularly to acknowledge the counsel of Daniel Bell, Leonard Covello, Father Joseph P. Fitzpatrick, S.J., Herbert J. Gans, Frederick L. Holborn, Will Maslow, Michael Parenti, and Lloyd Rodwin. Nancy Edelman and Victor Gioscia helped with research on the Puerto Rican and Italian sections. Professor James S. Coleman generously provided an analysis of the results of the 1962 New York gubernatorial election.

This work was conceived and organized by Nathan Glazer. He wrote "the Negroes," "the Puerto Ricans," "the Jews," "the Italians," and most of the "Introduction." Daniel Patrick Moynihan wrote "the Irish" and most of the last chapter, "Beyond the Melting Pot." We have discussed and criticized each other's writing, and worked together to formulate the thesis that the book presents.

Washington
April, 1963
Nathan Glazer
Daniel P. Moynihan

Introduction

In 1660 William Kieft, the Dutch governor of New Netherland, remarked to the French Jesuit Isaac Jogues that there were eighteen languages spoken at or near Fort Amsterdam at the tip of Manhattan Island. There still are: not necessarily the same languages, but at least as many; nor has the number ever declined in the intervening three centuries. This is an essential fact of New York: a merchant metropolis with an extraordinarily heterogeneous population. The first shipload of settlers sent out by the Dutch was made up largely of French-speaking Protestants. British, Germans, Finns, Jews, Swedes, Africans, Italians, Irish followed, beginning a stream that has never yet stopped.

The consequences of this confusion, soon to be compounded by the enormous size of the city itself, have been many. Not least has been the virtual impossibility ever of describing New York City or even the state in simple terms. By preference, but also in some degree by necessity, America has turned elsewhere for its images and traditions. Colonial America is preserved for us in terms of the Doric simplicity of New England, or the pastoral symmetry of the Virginia countryside. Even Philadelphia is manageable. But who can summon an image of eighteenth-century New York that will hold still in the mind? A third of the battles of the Revolution were fought on New York soil, but Bunker Hill and Yorktown come easiest to memory, as do Paul Revere and Patrick Henry.

History, or perhaps historians, keep passing New York by. During the Civil War "New York [State] provided the greatest number of soldiers, the greatest quantity of supplies, and the largest amount of money. In addition, New York's citizens paid the most taxes, bought the greatest number of war bonds, and gave the most to relief organizations." [1] Yet it is recalled as a war between Yankees and Southerners. The Union preserved, the American mind roams westward with the cowboys, returning, if at all, to the Main Streets of the Midwest. The only New York image that has permanently impressed itself on the national mind is that of Wall Street—a street on which nobody lives. Paris may be France, London may be England, but New York, we continue to reassure ourselves, is *not* America.

But, of course, it *is* America: not all of America, or even most, but surely the most important single part. As time passes, the nation comes more under the influence of the city—consider the effect of television in the past fifteen years. As time passes, the nation comes more to resemble the city: urban, heterogeneous, materialist, tough; also, perhaps, ungovernable, except that somehow it is governed, and not so badly, and with a considerable measure of democracy.

With all this, our feeling for the city is at best remote. Even New Yorkers seem to avoid too direct an involvement. The taverns of the West Side of New York boast tunes as old and as good as many gleaned in Appalachian hollows, but when the latter-day folk singers of Morrisania and Greenpoint take to the night clubs, they give forth with "Barbree Allen" and the "Ballad of the Boll Weevil." Even the sociologists, wedded to complexity and eager for fresh subjects, have tended to shy away from the city. Chicago has been far more thoroughly studied, in part because of the accident of the existence of a great department of sociology at the University of Chicago. But it is no accident that a department of equal distinction at Columbia University during the 1940's and 1950's had almost nothing to do with New York. Big as it was, Chicago still offered a structure and scale that could be more easily comprehended.

When magazines on occasion devote issues to San Francisco or Chicago or Houston, and publish pictures of well-dressed and distinguished people in elegant settings, and tell us that these are the important people in this city, it is easy to believe them. When the same magazines get to New York and do the same, the informed reader cannot help but think they are indulging in a game. True, there *must* be important people in New York, but are they this banker, this publisher, this playwright, this society leader? The head of a huge corporation or financial complex in Chicago or Pittsburgh or Boston does play an important role in his city. He will be a central figure in a great movement to reform city government or rebuild the city center. In New York, the man who heads an institution or corporation of equal size is only one of many. The men who can sit around a table and settle things in smaller cities would here fill an auditorium. Indeed, in New York one can fill an auditorium with people of many kinds, who in other cities can sit around a room—high school principals, or educational reformers and thinkers and leaders, police captains and experts on crime and law enforcement, housing project managers and experts on housing and urban renewal, hospital directors and specialists in any field of medicine, directors of societies that help the poor and organizations that raise money from the rich, professors of sociology and owners of art galleries.

Of course there are important people in New York. But they have been men like Robert Moses, who has no equivalent in any other city in the United States, and whose major virtue was that he was well enough connected with enough of the centers of power to get something done, to get things moving. Everyone was so astonished at this fact that for a long time it hardly mattered that what he was getting done on a scale appropriate to the city's size was brutal and ugly, and only exacerbated its problems. The Rockefellers are also important in New York City. Perhaps only their combination of wealth and energy and political skill makes it possible for them to approximate the role that the Mellons play in Pittsburgh. But really there is no comparison. The Mellons can be a moving force in remaking the center of Pittsburgh, and in reshaping the image of that city. But all the wealth and skill of the Rockefellers, wedded to the power of Robert Moses, produce a smaller impact on New York. Robert Wagner, the mayor of New York, is an important man. He probably has never met, and never consults, men who in cities of a million or two million people would be movers of city affairs.

We must begin with this image of the city. New York is more than ten times as large as San Francisco, and twice as large as Chicago, but this does not suggest how much more complicated it is. For in the affairs of men, twice as large means four or eight times as complicated. Twice as large means that the man on top is perhaps four or eight times away from what happens on the bottom. But attempts at calculation understate the complexity. When you have 24,000 policemen in a city, it not only means that you need a few additional levels of authorities to deal with them— those over hundreds, and five hundreds, and thousands, and five thousands—but it also means (for example) that there are enough Jewish or Negro policemen to form an organization. And they too can fill a hall.

The interweaving of complexity that necessarily follows from its size with the complexity added by the origins of its population, drawn from a staggering number of countries and from every race, makes New York one of the most difficult cities in the world to understand, and helps us understand why so few books try in any serious way to understand it.

Ideally, if we are to describe one aspect of a city, in this case its ethnic groups, we should begin by spreading out as a background something about the city as a whole. We should speak about its politics, its economic life, its culture, its social life, its history. But none of these aspects of the city can be adequately described or explained except by reference to its ethnic groups.

Consider the politics of New York. Major changes are now taking place in the city. The power of the regular Democratic party—the "machine"—to name its candidates has been broken. In 1961 Mayor Robert F. Wagner, having been denied the nomination, ran in opposition to the regular party, and won. To explain what happened, we have to say that he won with the support of lower-class Negro and Puerto Rican voters, and middle-class Jewish voters who together were enough to overcome the opposition of Italian, Irish, and white Protestant middle-class and upper-working-class voters. One could describe his victory and the political transition now underway in the city without using ethnic labels, but one could barely explain it. For in New York City ethnicity and class and religion are inevitably tied to each other. The votes of the poor and the well-to-do cannot be understood without looking into the question of who the poor and the well-to-do are, without examining their ethnic background.

Similarly, to describe the economy of New York fully, one would have to point out that it is dominated at its peak (the banks, insurance companies, utilities, big corporation offices) by white Protestants, with Irish Catholics and Jews playing somewhat smaller roles. In wholesale and retail commerce, Jews predominate. White-collar workers are largely Irish and Italian if they work for big organizations, and Jewish if they work for smaller ones. The city's working class is, on its upper levels, Irish, Italian, and Jewish; on its lower levels, Negro and Puerto Rican. Other ethnic groups are found scattered everywhere, but concentrated generally in a few economic specialties.

Despite all this, it remains something of a question just what role the ethnic groups play in the development of New York economy. New York is affected by the growth of suburbia, where it is easier to locate plants and shopping centers, and where the middle class prefers to live —and presumably this would be happening no matter what ethnic groups made up the city. New York is affected by the growth of the Far West and Southwest, for more and more productive and commercial facilities are located in those areas. New York is affected by the power of unions in old centers, just as Detroit and New England are, and this encourages some plants to move away. Its original growth was touched off presumably by the fact that it was the terminus of the best level route to the Midwest, both in the canal era and the railroad era, and that it has the best natural port on the Northeastern Seaboard. These factors are quite independent of the nature of its population.

But there are other elements in the relationship between the population of New York and the economic development of New York. New York is now plagued by low wages in manufacturing. In the years since the end of the Second World War, the city has declined, relative to other cities, in the wages paid in manufacturing industries. This is a very complicated matter. Yet it must be of some significance that its manufacturing wages have fallen at a time when it has had a vast influx of relatively unskilled and untrained manufacturing labor. If through some historical accident the immigrants of the period 1946–1960 had been of the same level of education and training as the refugee German and Austrian Jews of 1933–1940, might not the economic history of the city have been different? Clearly, the main lines of the economic history of New York have been fixed by great factors that are quite independent of the nature of the population. Yet obvious as this is, there are important connections between what a people are, or what they have been made by history and experience, and their economic fate, and as economists now become more and more involved in considering the development of people of widely different cultures, they may learn things that will throw more light on the economic development of New York.

New York's culture is what it is presumably because it is the cultural capital of the richest and most important nation in the world. If America's culture is important, New York's culture must be important, and this would be true even if New York were all Anglo-Saxon and Protestant. And yet, the fact that the city is one-quarter Jewish, and one-sixth Italian, and one-seventh Negro—this also plays some part in the cultural history of New York. Ethnic identity is an element in all equations.

The census of 1960 showed that 19 per cent of the population of the city were still foreign-born whites, 28 per cent were children of foreign-born whites, another 14 per cent were Negro, 8 per cent were of Puerto Rican birth or parentage. Unquestionably, a great majority of the rest (31 per cent) were the grandchildren and great-grandchildren of immigrants, and still thought of themselves, on some occasions and for some purposes, as German, Irish, Italian, Jewish, or whatnot, as well as of course Americans. Of the foreign-stock population (immigrants and their children), 859,000 were born in Italy or were the children of Italian immigrants; 564,000 were from the U. S. S. R. (these are mostly Jews); 389,000 from Poland (these too are mostly Jews); 324,000 from Germany; 312,000 from Ireland; 220,000 from Austria; 175,000 from Great Britain; almost 100,000 from Hungary; more than 50,000 from Greece, Czechoslovakia, Rumania, and Canada; more than 25,000 from Yugoslavia, around 10,000 from the Netherlands, Denmark, Finland, and Switzerland; more than 5,000 from Portugal and Mexico. There were more than a million Negroes, and more than 50,000 of other races, mostly Chinese and Japanese. From almost every country in the world there are enough people in the city to make up communities of thousands and tens of thousands with organizations, churches, a language, some distinctive culture (see Table 1).

Let us introduce some order into this huge buzzing confusion. The best way to do so is historically. English stock has apparently never been in a clear majority in New York City. In 1775 one-half of the white population of the state was of English origin, but this proportion was probably lower in New York City, with its Dutch and other non-English groups, and with its large Negro population.[2] After the Revolution and the resumption of immigration, English and Scottish immigrants as well as migrants from New England and upstate New York probably maintained the British-descent group as the largest in the city through the first half of the nineteenth century.

In the 1840's Irish and Germans, who had of course been present in the city in some numbers before this time, began to enter in much larger numbers, and soon

7

became dominant. By 1855 the Irish-born made up 28 per cent of the city, the German-born 16 per cent of the city;[3] with their children they certainly formed a majority of the city, and they maintained this dominance until the end of the century. In 1890 Irish-born and German-born and their children made up 52 per cent of the population of New York and Brooklyn (then separate cities).[4]

In the 1880's Jews and Italians began to come in large numbers (there were of course sizable communities of both groups in the city before this time), and this heavy immigration continued until 1924, and on a reduced scale after that.

The Negroes began to enter the city in great numbers after World War I, the Puerto Ricans after World War II.

Thus six great groups have entered the city two by two, in subsequent epochs; and to these we must add as a seventh group the "old stock," or the "white Anglo-Saxon Protestants." The two terms are of course not identical, but the overlap among those they comprise is great. The "old stock" includes those New Yorkers who descend from families that were here before the Revolution. They were largely of English, Scottish, and Welsh origin, but also included Dutch, French, and other settlers from Northwestern Europe. It has been relatively easy for later immigrants of the same ethnic and religious background—from Canada and from Europe—to assimilate to this "old stock" group if they were in occupations of high status and of at least moderate affluence.[5]

What is the relative size of these seven groups in the city today? For all except the Negroes and the Puerto Ricans, who are listed separately in the census, it is difficult to give more than a very general guess. The accepted religious breakdown of the city population, based on sample surveys and estimates by various religious groups, indicates that less than a quarter of the population is Protestant, and more than half of that is Negro.[6] The white Protestants of course include many of German, Scandinavian, Czech, and Hungarian origins. It is thus not likely that more than about one-twentieth of the population of the city is "old stock," or "WASP." Public opinion polls which ask for "national origin" suggest that about a tenth of the population is Irish, another tenth German. The same sources suggest that about a sixth is Italian. Jewish organizations estimate that one-quarter of the population is Jewish. The census reports that Negroes form 14 per cent of the population, Puerto Ricans 8 per cent. We have accounted for about 90 per cent of the population of the city. (In Table 2 we have arranged from the various censuses since 1900, when New York assumed its present physical extent, figures indicating the changing size of these various elements in the population of the city.) These figures, aside from being inexact (less so for Puerto Rican and Negro), also assume that everyone in the city can be neatly assigned to an ethnic category. Of course this is in large measure myth; many of the people in the city, as in the nation, have parents and grandparents of two or three or four groups.

Despite the immigration laws, old groups grow and new groups form in the city. Thus, Batista and Castro, as well as the growing size of the Spanish-speaking population, have encouraged the growth of a large Cuban community of 50,000. For despite the stringent immigration laws, the United States is still the chief country of immigration in the world, and 2,500,000 were able to enter this country as immigrants between 1950–1959. Very large numbers of these immigrants settle in New York and its region, where large communities of their compatriots make life easier and pleasanter. Buried in this vast population of the city are new groups (such as 18,000 Israelis) that in any other city would be marked and receive attention. In New York their coffee shops and bars and meeting places and political disputes and amusements and problems are of interest only to themselves. Only when an immigrant group reaches the enormous size of the Puerto Ricans does it become a subject of interest, attention, and concern.

New York cannot be read out of America because of its heterogeneity; but it is true its heterogeneity is to some extent extreme, even among the heterogeneous cities of the Northeast. The cities of the South, except for the presence of Negroes, are far more homogeneous. They are largely inhabited by white Protestants whose ancestors came from the British Isles. The cities of the Great Plain—

from Indianapolis to Kansas City—are also somewhat less mixed. Their largest ethnic element is generally German; and Germans have also found it easiest to assimilate to the white Anglo-Saxon Protestant culture that is still the norm in American life. The cities of the Far West, too, are in their ethnic aspect somewhat different from the cities of the Northeast. Their populations, if we trace them back far enough, are as diverse as the populations of Northeastern cities. But these immigrants have come from the East, Midwest, and South of the United States, rather than from Europe. This second immigration to the Far West has made them more alike. If you ask people there, "Where did you come from?," the answer is Illinois or Iowa, Oklahoma or New York. In the Northeast, the answer is more likely to be Germany or Sweden, Russia or Italy. In terms of immediate origins, the populations of Far Western cities consist of Iowans and Illinoisans and New Yorkers, rather than Germans, Jews, and Italians.

But now what does it mean for New York that most of its population is composed of people who think of themselves—at least at some times, for some purposes—as Jews, Italians, Negroes, Germans, Irishmen, Puerto Ricans? Is New York different, because of this fact, from London, Paris, Moscow, Tokyo?

Do we not, in every great city, meet people from all over the world? We do; but we should not confuse the heterogeneity of most of the great cities of the world with that of New York. The classic heterogeneity of great cities has been limited to the elite part of the population. It is the small numbers of the wealthy and exceptional who represent in those other cities the variety of the countries of the world, not, as in the United States, the masses. This for the most part is still true of the great cities of Europe, even though large numbers of Irishmen and colored people now form part of the working class of London, large numbers of Algerians part of the working class of Paris. Those with very special skills and talents have always been drawn from all over the world into its great cities. Thus, the specialized trading peoples—Phoenicians, Syrians, Greeks, Jews—have formed, for thousands of years, part of the specialized commercial and trading classes of the Mediterranean cities. And even today, trade with foreign countries is still in large measure carried on by nationals of the countries involved, who have special knowledge of language and conditions and local laws and regulations. There is also to be found in all great cities the diplomatic corps, now enormously swollen by international agencies of all sorts. There are the people involved in cultural and artistic activities, who may be of any part of the world. These elites, commercial, political, cultural, today give such cities as London, Paris, and Tokyo an international flavor. It is these people we think of when we say that people from all over the world flock to its great cities; they do, but they are relatively few in numbers.

The heterogeneity of New York is of the masses—numbers so great that Negroes are not exotic, as they are in Paris, Puerto Ricans not glamorous representatives of Latin American culture, as they might be in London, Italians not rare representatives of a great nation, as they are in Tokyo. Here the numbers of each group are so great, so steady and heavy a presence, that it takes an effort of mind to see that all these group names describe a double aspect: those one sees around one, and those in some other country, on some other continent, with a different culture.

Admittedly, even this heterogeneity of the masses is not unique to the cities of the United States. The cities of Canada and Latin America have also drawn their populations from varied groups (though none equals New York in its variety). Even in the great cities of the past one could find sizable differences among the masses. In Athens one might presumably find countrymen from every deme, in Paris workers from every province. There was probably a tendency for them to cluster together. Even though all spoke the same language, they spoke different dialects. Even though they were all of the same religion, they may have preferred to worship among friends and relatives. Even though they all participated in some forms of a growing national culture, they must have preferred their own provincial specialties in food, folk music, and dancing.

But in New York the masses that make up the city have come not from different provinces but different countries. Their languages have been mutually unintelligible, their religion radically different, their family structures, values, ideals, cultural patterns have been as distinct as those of the Irish and the Southern Negro, of urban Jews and peasant Italians.

This is the way it was, but will it be relevant for New York City much longer? The foreign-language press declines rapidly in circulation; the old immigrant quarters now hold only some of the old-timers. The immigrant societies play little role in the city's politics. The American descendants of immigrants diverge markedly from the people of the old country. American descendants of Germans seem no more committed to the unity of Germany and the defense of Berlin than other Americans, the foreign policy of the American Irish seems to have nothing in common any more with the foreign policy of a neutral Eire, and the political outlook and culture of Americans of Italian descent seem to have little in common with what one can see in Italy. (New Italian movies exploring the limits of modern sensibility are as incomprehensible to Italian immigrants as to other immigrants.) And perhaps the Jewish commitment to Israel is best explained by the recency of the establishment of the state and the permanent danger surrounding it. American culture seems to be as attractive to the children of immigrants as the descendants of pioneers (and indeed, as attractive to Indonesians or Russians as to Americans). The powerful assimilatory influences of American society operate on all who come into it, making the children of immigrants and even immigrants themselves a very different people from those they left behind. In what sense, then, can we put immigrants, their children, their grandchildren, and even further descendants into one group and speak of, for example, "the" Irish? Must we not speak of the middle-class Irish and the working-class Irish, the big-city Irish and the small-town Irish, the recent immigrants and the second and third and fourth generation, the Democrats and the Republicans; and when we do, is there any content left to the group name?

Perhaps the meaning of ethnic labels will yet be erased in America. But it has not yet worked out this way in New York. It is true that immigrants to this country were rapidly transformed, in comparison with immigrants to other countries, that they lost their language and altered their culture. It was reasonable to believe that a new American type would emerge, a new nationality in which it would be a matter of indifference whether a man was of Anglo-Saxon or German or Italian or Jewish origin, and in which indeed, because of the diffusion of populations through all parts of the country and all levels of the social order, and because of the consequent close contact and intermarriage, it would be impossible to make such distinctions. This may still be the most likely result in the long run. After all, in 1960 almost half of New York City's population was still foreign-born or the children of foreign-born. Yet it is also true that it is forty years since the end of mass immigration, and new processes, scarcely visible when our chief concern was with the great masses of immigrants and the problems of their "Americanization," now emerge to surprise us. The initial notion of an American melting pot did not, it seems, quite grasp what would happen in America. At least it did not grasp what would happen in the short run, and since this short run encompasses at least the length of a normal lifetime, it is not something we can ignore.

It is true that language and culture are very largely lost in the first and second generations, and this makes the dream of "cultural pluralism"—of a new Italy or Germany or Ireland in America, a League of Nations established in the New World—as unlikely as the hope of a "melting pot." But as the groups were transformed by influences in American society, stripped of their original attributes, they were recreated as something new, but still as identifiable groups. Concretely, persons think of themselves as members of that group, with that name; they are thought of by others as members of that group, with that name; and most significantly, they are linked to other members of the group by new attributes that the original immigrants would never have recognized as identifying their group, but which nevertheless serve to mark them off, by more than simply name and association, in the third generation and even beyond.

The assimilating power of American society and culture operated on immigrant groups in different ways, to make them, it is true, something they had not been, but still something distinct and identifiable. The impact of assimilating trends on the groups is different in part because the groups are different—Catholic peasants from Southern Italy were affected differently, in the same city and the same time, from urbanized Jewish workers and merchants from Eastern Europe. We cannot even begin to indicate how various were the characteristics of family structure, religion, economic experience and attitudes, educational experience and attitudes, political outlook that differentiated groups from such different backgrounds. Obviously, some American influences worked on them in common and with the same effects. But their differences meant they were open to different parts of American experience, interpreted it in different ways, used it for different ends. In the third generation, the descendants of the immigrants confronted each other, and knew they were both Americans, in the same dress, with the same language, using the same artifacts, troubled by the same things, but they voted differently, had different ideas about education and sex, and were still, in many essential ways, as different from one another as their grandfathers had been.

The initial attributes of the groups provided only one reason why their transformations did not make them all into the same thing. There was another reason—and that was the nature of American society itself, which could not, or did not, assimilate the immigrant groups fully or in equal degree. Or perhaps the nature of human society in general. It is only the experience of the strange and foreign that teaches us how provincial we are. A hundred thousand Negroes have been enough to change the traditional British policy of free immigration from the colonies and dominions. Japan finds it impossible to incorporate into the body of its society anyone who does not look Japanese, or even the Koreans, indistinguishable very often in appearance and language from Japanese. And we shall test the racial attitudes of the Russians only when there are more than a few Negroes passing through as curiosities; certainly the inability of Russians to get over anti-Semitism does not suggest they are any different from the rest of mankind. In any case, the word "American" was an unambiguous reference to nationality only when it was applied to a relatively homogeneous social body consisting of immigrants from the British Isles, with relatively small numbers from nearby European countries. When the numbers of those not of British origin began to rise, the word "American" became a far more complicated thing. Legally, it meant a citizen. Socially, it lost its identifying power, and when you asked a man what he was (in the United States), "American" was not the answer you were looking for. In the United States it became a slogan, a political gesture, sometimes an evasion, but not a matter-of-course, concrete social description of a person. Just as in certain languages a word cannot stand alone but needs some particle to indicate its function, so in the United States the word "American" does not stand by itself. If it does, it bears the additional meaning of patriot, "authentic" American, critic and opponent of "foreign" ideologies.

The original Americans became "old" Americans, or "old stock," or "white Anglo-Saxon Protestants," or some other identification which indicated they were not immigrants or descendants of recent immigrants. These original Americans already had a frame in their minds, which became a frame in reality, that placed and ordered those who came after them. Those who were like them could easily join them. It was important to be white, of British origin, and Protestant. If one was all three, then even if one was an immigrant, one was really not an immigrant, or not for long.

Thus, even before it knew what an Italian or Jew or an Irishman was like, the American mind had a place for the category, high or low, depending on color, on religion, on how close the group was felt to be the Anglo-Saxon center. There were peculiarities in this placing. Why, for example, were the Germans placed higher than the Irish? There was of course an interplay to some extent between what the group actually was and where it was placed, and, since the German immigrants were less impoverished than the Irish and somewhat more competent craftsmen and farmers, this undoubtedly affected the old American's image of them. Then ideology came in to emphasize the common links between Englishmen and Germans, who, even though they spoke different languages, were said to be really closer to each other than the old Americans were to the English-speaking, but Catholic and Celtic, Irish. If a group's first representatives were cultured and educated, those who came after might benefit, unless they were so numerous as to destroy the first image. Thus, German Jews who arrived in the 1840's and 1850's benefited from their own characteristics and their link with Germans, until they were overwhelmed by the large number of East European Jewish immigrants after 1880. A new wave of German Jewish immigrants, in the 1930's, could not, regardless of culture and education, escape the low position of being "Jewish."

The ethnic group in American society became not a survival from the age of mass immigration but a new social form. One could not predict from its first arrival what it might become or, indeed, whom it might contain. The group is not a purely biological phenomenon. The Irish of today do not consist of those who are descended from Irish immigrants. Were we to follow the history of the germ plasm alone—if we could—we should find that many in the group really came from other groups, and that many who should be in the group are in other groups. The Protestants among them, and those who do not bear distinctively Irish names, may now consider themselves, and be generally considered, as much "old American" as anyone else. The Irish-named offspring of German or Jewish or Italian mothers often find that willy-nilly they have become Irish. It is even harder for the Jewish-named offspring of mixed marriages to escape from the Jewish group; neither Jews nor non-Jews will let them rest in ambiguity.

Parts of the group are cut off, other elements join the group as allies. Under certain circumstances, strange as it may appear, it is desirable to be able to take on a group name, even of a low order, if it can be made to fit, and if it gives one certain advantages. It is better in Oakland, California, to be a Mexican than an Indian, and so some of the few Indians call themselves, at certain times, for certain occasions, "Mexicans." In the forming of ethnic groups subtle distinctions are overridden; there is an advantage to belonging to a big group, even if it is looked down upon. West Indian Negroes achieve important political positions, as representatives of Negroes; Spaniards and Latin Americans become the representatives of Puerto Ricans; German Jews rose to Congress from districts dominated by East European Jews.

Ethnic groups then, even after distinctive language, customs, and culture are lost, as they largely were in the second generation, and even more fully in the third generation, are continually recreated by new experiences in America. The mere existence of a name itself is perhaps sufficient to form group character in new situations, for the name associates an individual, who actually can be anything, with a certain past, country, race. But as a matter of fact, someone who is Irish or Jewish or Italian generally has other traits than the mere existence of the name that associates him with other people attached to the group. A man is connected to his group by ties of family and friendship. But he is also connected by ties of *interest*. The ethnic groups in New York are also *interest groups.*

This is perhaps the single most important fact about ethnic groups in New York City. When one speaks of the Negroes and Puerto Ricans, one also means unorganized and unskilled workers, who hold poorly paying jobs in the laundries, hotels, restaurants, small factories or who are on relief. When one says Jews, one also means small shopkeepers, professionals, better-paid skilled workers in the garment industries. When one says Italians, one also means homeowners in Staten Island, the North Bronx, Brooklyn, and Queens.

If state legislation threatens to make it more difficult to get relief, this is headline news in the Puerto Rican press—for the group is affected—and news of much less importance to the rest of the press. The interplay between rational economic interests and the other interests or attitudes that stem out of group history makes for an incredibly complex political and social situation. Consider the local laws against discrimination in housing. Certain groups that face discrimination want such laws—Negroes, Puerto Ricans, and Jews. Jews meet little discrimination in housing in New York but have an established ideological commitment to all antidiscrimination laws. Apartment-house owners are against any restriction of their freedom or anything that might affect their profits. In New York, this group is also largely Jewish, but it is inhibited in pushing strongly against such laws by its connections with the Jewish community. Private home-owners see this as a threat to their homogenous neighbor-hoods. These are largely German, Irish, and Italian. The ethnic background of the homeowners links them to com-munities with a history of anti-Negro feelings. The Irish and Italian immigrants have both at different times com-peted directly with Negro labor.

In the analysis then of the conflict over anti-discrimination laws, "rational" economic interests and the "irrational" or at any rate noneconomic interests and atti-tudes tied up with one's own group are inextricably mixed together. If the rational interests did not operate, some of the older groups would by now be much weaker than they are. The informal and formal social groupings that make up these communities are strengthened by the fact that Jews can talk about the garment business, Irish about politics and the civil service, Italians about the state of the trucking or contracting or vegetable business.

In addition to the links of interest, family and fellowfeeling bind the ethnic group. There is satisfac-tion in being with those who are like oneself. The ethnic group is something of an extended family or tribe. And aside from ties of feeling and interest, there are concrete ties of organization. Certain types of immigrant social organiza-tion have declined, but others have been as ingenious in remolding and recreating themselves as the group itself. The city is often spoken of as the place of anonymity, of the breakdown of some kind of preexisting social order. The ethnic group, as Oscar Handlin has pointed out, served to create a new form of order. Those who came in with some kind of disadvantage, created by a different language, a different religion, a different race, found both comfort and material support in creating various kinds of organizations. American social services grew up in large part to aid in-coming immigrant groups. Many of these were limited to a single religious or ethnic group. Ethnic groups set up hos-pitals, old people's homes, loan funds, charitable organiza-tions, as well as churches and cultural organizations. The initial need for a separate set of welfare and health institutions became weaker as the group became more prosperous and as the government took over these functions, but the organizations nevertheless continued. New York organizational life today is in large measure lived within ethnic bounds. These organizations generally have religious names, for it is more acceptable that welfare and health institutions should cater to religious than to ethnic communities. But of course religious institutions are generally closely linked to a distinct ethnic group. The Jewish (religious) organizations are Jewish (ethnic), Catholic are generally Irish or Italian, now with the Puerto Ricans as important clients; the Protestant organizations are white Protestant—which means generally old American, with a smaller German wing —in leadership, with Negroes as their chief clients.

Thus many elements—history, family and feeling, interest, formal organizational life—operate to keep much of New York life channeled within the bounds of the ethnic group. Obviously, the rigidity of this channeling of social life varies from group to group. For the Puerto Ricans, a recent immigrant group with a small middle class and speaking a foreign language, the ethnic group serves as the setting for almost all social life. For Negroes too, because of discrimination and poverty, most social life is limited to the group itself. Jews and Italians are still to some extent recent immigrants, and despite the growing middle-class character of the Jewish group, social life for both is generally limited to other members of the group. But what about the Irish and the Germans?

Probably, many individuals who by descent "belong" to one of these older groups go through a good part of their lives with no special consciousness of the fact. It may be only under very special circumstances that one becomes aware of the matter at all—such as if one wants to run for public office. The political realm, indeed, is least willing to consider such matters a purely private affair. Consciousness of one's ethnic background may be intermittent. It is only on occasion that someone may think of or be reminded of his background, and perhaps become self-conscious about the pattern formed by his family, his friends, his job, his interests. Obviously, this ethnic aspect of a man's life is more important if he is part of one group than if he is part of another; if he is Negro, he can scarcely escape it, and if he is of German origin, little will remind him of it.

Conceivably the fact that one's origins can become only a memory suggests the general direction for ethnic groups in the United States—toward assimilation and absorption into a homogeneous American mass. And yet, as we suggested earlier, it is hard to see in the New York of the 1960's just how this comes about. Time alone does not dissolve the groups if they are not close to the Anglo-Saxon center. Color marks off a group, regardless of time; and perhaps most significantly, the "majority" group, to which assimilation should occur, has taken on the color of an ethnic group, too. To what does one assimilate in modern America? The "American" in abstract does not exist, though some sections of the country, such as the Far West, come closer to realizing him than does New York City. There are test cases of such assimilation in the past. The old Scotch-Irish group, an important ethnic group of the early nineteenth century, is now for the most part simply old American, "old stock." Old Dutch families have become part of the upper class of New York. But these test cases merely reveal to us how partial was the power of the old American type to assimilate—it assimilated its ethnic cousins.

There is also, in New York, a nonethnic city. There are the fields that draw talent from all over the country and all over the world. There are the areas, such as Greenwich Village, where those so collected congregate. On Broadway, in the radio and television industry, in the art world, in all the spheres of culture, mass or high, one finds the same mixture that one finds in every country. Those involved in these intense and absorbing pursuits would find the city described in these pages strange. Another area of mixture is politics. It is true that political life itself emphasizes the ethnic character of the city, with its balanced tickets and its special appeals. But this is in large part an objective part of the business, just as the Jewish plays on Broadway are part of the business. For those in the field itself, there is more contact across the ethnic lines, and the ethnic lines themselves mean less, than in other areas of the city's life.

How does one write about such groups? If one believes, as the authors of this book do, that the distinctions are important, and that they consist of more than the amusing differences of accent and taste in food and drink, then it is no simple matter to decide how to describe and analyze this aspect of American reality. For it has been common to speak about the ethnic groups in terms of either blame or praise.

It is understandable that as foreigners flooded American cities all the ills of the cities were laid on their shoulders. It is also understandable that the children of the immigrants (and they had the help of many other Americans) should have defended themselves. They had become part of America; they spoke the language, fought in the wars, paid the taxes, were as patriotic as those who could count more generations in the country—and just as they had become Americanized and good citizens, others would. There is no way of discounting the polemical impact of anything written on this question. How many and of what kind to let into this country is a permanent and important question of American public life. It is a permanent question in American life what attitudes to take on matters of public welfare, public education, housing, toward increasing numbers of new groups in American cities. These are matters that involve the chances for decent lives for many Americans, and mobilize the deep and irrational passions of many others. On such issues, most people will simply have to use arguments and facts and ideas as weapons, and will not be able to use them for enlightenment. Even scholarship is generally enlisted in the cause, on one side or another. And yet beyond personal interest and personal commitment, it is possible to view this entire fascinating spectacle of the ethnic variety of the American city and to consider what it means.

At least, this is the point of view we have tried to adopt in this book. It is inevitably filled with judgments, yet the central judgment—an over-all evaluation of the meaning of American heterogeneity—we have tried to avoid, because we would not know how to make it. One author is the son of a working-class immigrant, the other, the grandson; there is no question where their personal interest leads them. On the other hand, we would not know how to argue with someone who maintained that something was lost when an original American population was overwhelmed in the central cities by vast numbers of immigrants of different culture, religion, language, and race.

But the original Americans did choose this course; the nation stuck with it for a hundred years; and despite the policy of 1924, which was supposed to fix the ethnic proportions of the population then attained, these proportions change continually because the immigration policy of the United States is still the freest of any great nation. And enormous internal migrations continue to change the populations of the cities as rapidly and on as great a scale as in the era of free immigration.

A nation is formed by critical decisions, and the American decision was to permit the entire world to enter almost without restriction. The consequences of this key decision, despite the work of such major figures as Marcus Hansen and Oscar Handlin, have received surprisingly little attention. Popular writing, scholarly writing, novels, and plays, all seem to find the beginning of the process of assimilation most interesting. It is when the immigrants first arrive that everyone is aware of them. By the time the problems are less severe, or have become largely personal, local color has been dissipated in the flush of Americanization, and the writers find less to write about. Because of the paucity of the literature and the size of the subject, it has proved beyond our capacities to present our theses wholly in terms of objective and verifiable statements. It would be quite impossible to write a book such as this exclusively on the basis of concrete data which are either now available or which could, with reasonable effort, be obtained. We have nonetheless gone ahead out of the strongest possible feeling of the continuing reality and significance of the ethnic group in New York, and by extension, in American life. This is what we think we know about the subject: this is all we can say except that if we are subsequently proved wrong, we hope we shall have at least contributed to a continuing discussion.

Some of the judgments—we will not call them facts—which follow will appear to be harsh. We ask the understanding of those who will be offended. The racial and religious distinctions of the city create more than a little ugliness and complacency. But they are also the source of a good deal of vigor, and a kind of rough justice that is not without attraction. Melbourne is said to have expressed a particular fondness for the Order of the Garter, which was awarded, as it were, on the basis of blood lines "with no damned nonsense about merit." This, precisely, is the principle of the balanced ticket and a thousand other arrangements, formal and informal, that the people of New York have contrived to bring a measure of social peace and equity to a setting that promises little of either.

The body of the book describes five major groups of the city. There is no great significance to the order in which they are arranged. We begin, as the visitor might, with what immediately strikes the eye, and proceed from there.

the Negroes

To most New Yorkers today
to whom the word means anything, "Fort Greene" means
the Fort Greene Houses, the largest public housing project
in the city, which stands between downtown Brooklyn and
the Brooklyn Navy Yard. To the eye, it is mostly Negro,
though the official figures show that a fifth of the 3,500
apartments are occupied by whites, and another fifth are
occupied by Puerto Ricans. It would probably surprise
New Yorkers who recall stories of gang fighting in the Fort
Greene area to discover that above the housing project, in a
little park, stands one of the major monuments in the city.
It commemorates the prison ship martyrs of the Revolution
and was designed by the great architects of New York's age
of elegance, McKim, Mead & White, who also built the
University Club, the Columbia University campus, the
N.Y.U. Hall of Fame, the Pennsylvania Station, and the
Brooklyn Museum. This monument contains a great central

column standing amidst urns and eagles, a magnificent staircase down which one may approach the project, a comfort station designed like a Greek temple which puts the utilitarian structures of Mr. Moses to shame. From the site one may view the entire housing project and a good deal besides. All this provides a rather grander setting for gang rumbles than they usually find.

It does not pay to extract too much symbolism from the accidental coming together of a mostly Negro housing project and a great monument erected by an earlier city. And yet, one does not have to force the symbolism, because between the New York represented by the monument and the New York of the housing project there is a close and intimate link. Historical irony makes the elite of that older New York and the poor Negroes of the project both, for the most part, Protestant. Indeed, more than half the Protestants of New York, who are only a quarter of the population, are colored. And since the work of the city is so often divided along religious lines, it means that the old elite and its institutions—churches, charitable societies, hospitals—often find they have inherited a special responsibility for the Negro.

Fort Greene is rich in symbols. Bordering the park to the south stands the huge bulk of the Brooklyn Technical High School, one of the specialized high schools of the city system which have often served as the first step in the economic and social advance of many boys from earlier immigrant groups. It is the potential bridge between the project and the monument.

NUMBERS

IN 1960 THE CITY HAD 1,088,000 NEGROES. THERE HAD BEEN an increase of 340,000 in ten years, coming after an increase of 290,000 during the 1940's. During the 1950's the white population of the city dropped by almost a half-million. The New York of 1960 was one-seventh Negro (see Table 3).

New York of course is not alone in this great shift in population. Indeed, it has a smaller proportion of Negroes than other great Northern cities. In 1960 Chicago was 24 per cent Negro, Philadelphia was more than one-quarter Negro, and Cleveland and Detroit had even higher proportions—both 29 per cent. New York is so enormous that even large population changes affect the proportions slowly. In Newark, for example, which is a city of 400,000, the Negro population increased by 63,000 between 1950 and 1960, and Newark became one-third Negro. But the kind of change that transforms a city the size of Newark is for New York only a neighborhood shift.

The Negro population is younger than the white, though not as young as the Puerto Ricans. Thus, it forms a higher proportion of both the school population and the juvenile delinquent population for demographic reasons alone. (There are of course other reasons why there are more Negro juvenile delinquents.) In the next decade, owing to the fact that about three-tenths of New York's schoolchildren (almost all white) attend parochial and private schools, the Negroes and Puerto Ricans will together exceed the rest of the public school population.[1]

The Negro population is still in large part new to the city. In 1960 half of the entire nonwhite population of the city above the age of 20 had come from the South.[2] These Americans of two centuries are as much immigrant as any European immigrant group, for the shift from the South to New York is as radical a change for the Negro as that faced by earlier immigrants.

The Negro immigrant has not had the good fortune of arriving with useful skills and strong institutions, nor has he found a prosperous, well-organized Negro community to help him.[3] The Negro community in the city is indeed an old one, but age has done nothing to prepare it to meet the problems of mass migration. In 1910, before the first decade which saw a sizable migration from the South, New York had 90,000 Negroes, less than 2 per cent of the population. Negro writers who remember that antebellum New York community often write about it with something like nostalgia, but in those days, aside from a tiny Negro "upper class" of minor government employees and professionals, the community consisted almost entirely of domestics, laborers, waiters, unskilled workers. Negroes accepted an inferior place in society; and in this inferior place, despite the existence of distinctions of class and status, poverty was matter-of-course and segregation was universal. This group could do little for Negroes coming up from the South and from the West Indies.

During the First World War the Negro population increased rapidly. In 1920 it was 150,000, about 3 per cent of the population. In the 1920's mass immigration from Europe came to an end, and the Negro population of the city more than doubled. The migrants poured into a New York in which they could not eat in a first-class restaurant, go to a first-class hotel, or get a job in the white world (aside from some specially reserved government jobs) above menial labor. And yet the city did offer a large variety of jobs, at pay much higher than Negroes could get in the South, and, as important, it offered Harlem, a more exciting and stimulating environment for Negroes then than any other place in the country.

Segregation helped make Harlem alive. It is hard to envisage, as one walks the streets today, with the buildings forty years older, and the population greatly changed, what Harlem was like in the 1920's. In those days, Negro entertainers and musicians were a rarity on Broadway, and one had to go above 125th Street to find them. Because of the unbroken pattern of segregation, Harlem included everyone in the Negro community—the old tiny "upper class," the new professionals and white-collar workers, the political leaders just beginning to take over the old political clubs, the artists and entertainers and writers, as well of course as the domestic workers, the laborers, and shady characters.*

Writing in 1930, James Weldon Johnson described a Harlem few of us would now recognize, but he helps explain the enormous attractions of New York, even though the city did not offer the advantages of jobs in heavy industry available to Negroes in Chicago and Detroit: "In nearly every other city in the country," Johnson wrote,

* We are today very conscious of the role of public services, in particular relief, among Negroes, and the charge is often made that it is really relief that is bringing in large numbers of poor newcomers. This is part of the story; but it is interesting to recall that in the twenties, when there was no such thing as relief and the poor were dependent on private charity, the Negro population of New York leaped from 150,000 to 327,000. And that in the next decade, when public relief did become a reality, the increase was much smaller.

"the Negro section is a nest or several nests situated somewhere on the borders; it is a section we must 'go out to.'
In New York it is entirely different. Negro Harlem covers
one of the most beautiful and healthful sites in the whole
city. It is not a fringe, it is not a slum, nor is it a quarter
consisting of dilapidated tenements. It is a section of new-
law apartment houses and handsome dwellings, with streets
as well paved, as well-lighted, and as well-kept as any in the
city. . . . The question inevitably arises: will the Negroes
of Harlem be able to hold it? Will they not be driven further northward? Residents of Manhattan, regardless of race,
have been driven out when they lay in the path of business
and greatly increased land values. Harlem lies in the direction that path must take; so there is little probability that
Negroes will always hold it as a residential section." [4]

This makes strange reading today; it made
strange reading only ten years later, when another major
Negro writer, Claude MacKay, wrote a book on Harlem.
Ten years of depression had been for the Negroes a disaster
that almost rivaled slavery. MacKay quoted estimates that
60 per cent of the population was on relief, 20 per cent held
WPA jobs.[5] Dependent on casual labor and household service, without salaried jobs, without businesses, Harlem's residents suffered far more from the depression than any other
part of the city. White workers knew what it was to go two
or three years without steady work, but a case of special
distress in the white world was the norm in the Negro
world. Harlem became more frightfully crowded than ever
—even though there were high vacancy rates in adjacent
East Harlem—because the population was so impoverished.
The Negro population continued to rise through natural
increase and migration, but much more slowly than in the
1920's. In 1940, on the eve of World War II, it stood at
450,000.

With the war, a new period in the history
of the Negro in New York City began. The age of Harlem,
as the seat of the Negro renaissance and of depression
misery, drew to a close as new areas of Negro settlement,
in Brooklyn, the Bronx, Queens, and the suburban counties, were opened up and rapidly increased. The war created
a new New York for the Negroes—new in the kinds of

neighborhoods where they lived, the kinds of jobs they held, the role they played in politics and social life, and in their image of themselves and their relation to other groups. Central in this transformation of the Negro position was a revolution in the level of income that was typical, and in the kinds of jobs that became accessible.

JOBS

DURING THE DEPRESSION, THE NEGRO WORKER, WHEN HE worked, made a little better than three-fifths what the white worker made in New York City, and the wages of the white workers were barely above what was needed to survive. As a result of the war, and the entry into new types of employment, a great change occurred; unemployment fell sharply (though it was still higher than among whites), wages increased, and the gap between Negro and white income narrowed. In 1949 the Negro in New York State made about seven-tenths as much as the white worker. During the fifties the gap has remained at about this figure. The 1960 census reported that the median income of Negro workers in the New York metropolitan area was about 70 per cent of the white median. For nonwhite families, it was 73 per cent of the median of all families, reflecting the fact that more members of a Negro family work.[6]

In other Northern cities during the fifties, this gap was smaller. New York was behind Detroit and Chicago in wages because it did not have the same concentration of auto plants, steel mills, stockyards, and other heavy industry, in which powerful and progressive unions had achieved high wages and a strict equality in pay between Negroes and whites. Incomes in New York, with its great variety of low-wage and service industries, lag behind those for white as well as Negro workers in the big, heavy-industry cities. However, as the economy slowed down in the late fifties and the early sixties, New York was spared the high Negro unemployment of the heavy-industry cities. In 1961 the National Urban League estimated that about 10 per cent of Negro workers in the New York metropolitan region were unemployed. This was less than the national figure of 14 per cent and much less than the figure of 17 per cent in Chicago, 20 per cent in Cleveland, or 39 per cent in Detroit.[7] (The 1960 census reported 6.8 per cent of male nonwhite workers unemployed, as compared with a New York City rate of 4.9 per cent.)[8]

Before the onslaught of the industrial unemployment of the late 1950's and early 1960's, Negro men whether unskilled or semiskilled generally could find better jobs in the Midwest than in New York. But the situation for Negro women was better. New York is not a workingman's town. Its big individual employers are nonunionized banks, insurance companies, corporation front offices, "communications" industries, retail stores. At the lower levels of skill, there are better jobs for women than for men. In 1960 the median income for Negro women was 93 per cent of the median for white women; for Negro men it was only 68 per cent of the white median.[9]

But it is not only today that we see a peculiar and characteristic difference between the economic power and capacity of Negro men and women. In 1940 in New York City, almost as many Negro women as men were employed—81,000 to 88,000. By contrast, among whites, two and a half times as many men as women worked. More than three-fifths of Negro women then worked as private household workers. The enormous Negro community of 450,000 was in large part supported by the domestic labor of women, which was the single most important source of income. About a third of the men were engaged in various service jobs—as superintendents, bootblacks, watchmen, and the like. A quarter worked in skilled and semiskilled crafts, a seventh as laborers (see Table 4).

There were in 1940 only small groups of professionals and clerical and sales workers. But perhaps most striking was the almost complete absence of a business class, and this is still true today. The small shopkeeper, small manufacturer, or small entrepreneur of any kind has played such an important role in the rise of immigrant groups in America that its absence from the Negro community warrants some discussion. The small shopkeepers and manufacturers are important to a group for more than the greater income they bring in. Very often, as a matter of fact, the Italian or Jewish shopkeeper made less than the skilled worker. But as against the worker, each businessman had the possibility, slim though it was, of achieving influence and perhaps wealth. The small businessman generally has access to that special world of credit which may give him for a while greater resources than a job. He learns about credit and finance and develops skills that are of value in a complex economy. He learns too about the world of local politics, and although he is generally its victim, he may also learn how to influence it, for mean and unimportant ends, perhaps, but this knowledge may be valuable to an entire community.

The small businessman creates jobs. In the depression, the network of Jewish businesses meant jobs for Jewish young men and women—poor paying, but still jobs. The impoverished businessman still needed a delivery boy, the small furniture manufacturer needed someone to help with the upholstery, the linoleum retailer someone to help him lay it. These were not only jobs, they also taught skills. In addition, the small businessman had patronage—for salesmen, truck drivers, other businessmen. In most cases the patronage stayed within the ethnic group. The Chinese restaurant uses Chinese laundries, gets its provisions from Chinese food suppliers, provides orders for Chinese noodle makers. The Jewish store owner gives a break to his relative who is trying to work up a living as a salesman. The Jewish liquor-store owner has a natural link to the Jewish liquor salesman. These jobs as salesmen are often the best the society offers to people without special skills and special education. As such, they can be important to Negroes, as the picket lines before liquor stores in Harlem in 1960, demanding the use of Negro liquor salesmen, attested. A Negro action committee threatened that the pickets would soon be in front of the grocery stores. But how different matters would be if Negroes owned the grocery stores they patronized to begin with, as most groups in the past have, and as Puerto Ricans today do.[10]

One may scoff at the small businessman as pursuing an illusion—who can fight the A & P? For a community, however, regardless of what the balance sheet showed, the small businessman was important.

Much has been written about the failure of the Negro to develop an entrepreneurial class.[11] In the early 1900's, Booker T. Washington and W. E. B. Du Bois, one an accommodationist and the other a militant, both exhorted the Negro to go into business, to develop wealth and power. Today Negro business is if anything less important than fifty years ago. The catering business, in which Negroes played a role of some significance in the late nineteenth century, has declined and fallen into other hands. The only important forms of Negro business are beauty parlors, barber shops, the preparation of special cosmetics, and undertaking parlors. Negro insurance companies (which once developed because Negroes found it hard to get insurance from established companies), banks, the Negro press, Negro real estate, whatever their importance symbolically, are of small importance economically in supplying jobs, economic contacts, skills. Perhaps one may make an exception to some extent for real estate, for a sizable amount of savings has been invested in houses and business property, and there are now a good number of real estate brokers and operators. And yet, this is for the most part all on a remarkably small scale. When anything even as extensive as a building of an apartment house is planned by a group of Negroes, this is news in the community newspapers.[12]

There are some obvious explanations for lack of Negro businesses. Negroes emerging from slavery had no experience with money, and had no occasion to develop the skill in planning and foresight that even the smallest businessman must have. In this respect, the European peasant, whose standard of living may have been as low as a slave's, was better off, for he had to market his produce and manage a small stock of money and goods. The upper class of slaves, the house servants who might have been given some small education, had as models the lavish expenditure of a plantation society, and it was easier for them to observe the processes of consumption than those of production and marketing.[13] The freed slaves and later the migrants to the North were absolutely without financial resources, even the scanty sums needed for tiny businesses. They met unbending prejudice and discrimination in their efforts to get stock, capital, or space for rent.

Yet surely there were in the great Negro city that grew up in Harlem in the 1920's opportunities for the business-minded to get a foothold by serving their own, as so many ethnic groups had done before them. But other factors came into play to inhibit the rise of Negro businessmen. One of them was that the Negro, while a migrant, was not like the immigrants bearing a foreign culture, with special needs that might give rise to a market. There was no local demand for a Buitoni and a La Rosa to make pasta, for a Goodman and a Manischevitz and a Schapiro to supply matzos and kosher wine. The only demand was for undertakers, hairdressers, and cosmetics. As we know, in time these small beginnings in supplying members of one's own ethnic community might grow into sizable enterprises which laid fee on a world of customers that extended beyond the initial ethnic base.

Perhaps another way in which Negroes differed from European immigrant groups was that they did not develop the same kind of clannishness, they did not have the same close family ties, that in other groups created little pools for ethnic businessmen and professionals to tap. There was little clubbing together of the South Carolinians versus the North Carolinians versus the Virginians—life in these places was either not different enough, or the basis of the differences was not attractive enough, to create strong local groups with strong local attachments. The Negro family was not strong enough to create those extended clans that elsewhere were most helpful for businessmen and professionals. Negroes often say, "Everyone else sticks together, but we knock each other down. There is no trust among us." This is a stereotype and probably has the same degree of truth that most stereotypes have, that is, a good deal. Without a special language and culture, and without the historical experiences that create an elan and a morale, what is there to lead them to build their own life, to patronize their own? The one great exception to this is the Negro church, and it is perhaps no accident that tight churchlike groupings among the Negroes have often branched out into business enterprise, as was true of Father Divine and Daddy Grace and is now true of the Nation of Islam.[14]

In the end, the most important factor is probably the failure of Negroes to develop a pattern of saving. The poor may have had nothing to save; but even those better off tend to turn earnings immediately into consumption. The reasons are clear enough to anyone sensitive to the frustrations under which almost all Negroes in America live. They are sufficient to explain the search for pleasure in consumption which makes the pattern of saving and self-denial so rare. To quote Elijah Muhammed addressing a great throng in Harlem (and more authoritative voices, such as that of the sociologist Franklin Frazier, could be added): "You're a sporty people! . . . You look fine and well-dressed. . . . But you haven't got anything. You spend more than your rich white master and your children! You spend your paycheck back for sport! And your masters wait for the money they just gave you to come back home." [15]

But if problems of incapacity for business prevailed among Negroes coming up from the South, it did not among that large part of the Negro population of New York that comes from the West Indies. We cannot help, when we talk about any group, obscuring differences that are important within it. When we say "Negroes," we speak of those born in the city as well as those coming from the South, the middle class as well as the lower class, the native-born as well as the foreign-born, the light-skinned as well as the dark, the speakers of French and Spanish as well as those who speak English. To the external white eye all these distinctions seem of no importance. This tendency to create a group by perceiving people as being all one occurs not only in the case of Negroes: very different groups of Jews were merged by the perception of the outer world, more than by their own self-perception of similarity. But this process affects Negroes more harshly because the outer world makes so few distinctions among them.

Alongside the stream of migrants from the South was a stream from the West Indies, primarily the British West Indies, and mostly from the single most populous island, Jamaica. After 1925 this immigrant stream became much smaller; most of the New York West Indian element was established in the city by the mid-twenties. In 1930, no less than 17 per cent of the New York City Negroes were foreign-born, and with their native-born children they certainly formed between a fifth and a quarter of the Negro population.[16] They were viewed from the beginning by native American Negroes as highly distinctive—in accent, dress, custom, religion (they were Anglican), and allegiances (they celebrated the King's birthday). Distinctive as they were, they were forced to live in the same quarters as other Negroes. Furious at a prejudice far greater than that among whites in their home islands, they were helpless to do much about it. Many, as a consequence, turned radical. Negro Communists and labor leaders, it has been said, were disproportionately West Indian.[17]

But the West Indians' most striking difference from the Southern Negroes was their greater application to business, education, buying homes, and in general advancing themselves. James Weldon Johnson (whose parents stemmed from British West Indies) described them in 1930: they "average high in intelligence and efficiency, there is practically no illiteracy among them, and many have a sound English common school education. They are characteristically sober-minded and have something of a genius for business, differing almost totally, in these from the average rural Negro of the South." [18] They contributed disproportionately, all observers have agreed, to the number of Negro leaders and accomplished men. Claude MacKay, himself a Jamaican, pointed out that the first Negro presidential elector in New York State, the first elected Negro Democratic leader (Herbert R. Bruce, in 1935), one of the first two Negro municipal judges, were West Indians. Marcus Garvey, who in the 1920's, led one of the greatest Negro political mass movements in American history, was a Jamaican.[19] A sociologist wrote (in the only book-length study ever made of the foreign Negro in America) in the late 1930's, "It is estimated that as high as one-third of the Negro professional population—particularly physicians, dentists, and lawyers—is foreign-born." [20]

The ethos of the West Indians, in contrast to that of the Southern Negro, emphasized saving, hard work, investment, education. Paule Marshall has described this ethos in a remarkably revealing novel about Barbadians in Brooklyn. Here is a wife denouncing a husband who has not measured up to Barbadian ("Bajan") ideals:

No . . . he ain no Bajan. Look Percy Challenor who was working the said-same job as him is a real estate broker and

just open a big office on Fulton Street. More Bajan than
you can shake a stick at opening stores or starting up some
little business. They got this Business Association going
good now and 'nough people joining. . . . Every West
Indian out here taking a lesson from the Jew lanlord and
convertin these old houses into rooming houses—making
the closets-self into rooms some them!—and pulling down
plenty-plenty money by the week. And now that the place is
near overrun with roomers the Bajans getting out. They
going. Every man-jack buying a swell house in dichty Crown
Heights. . . .[21]

The West Indians have by now pretty much
merged into the American Negro group, and their children
do not feel themselves to be particularly different. They
never found it possible to create a separate residential area.
They are citizens, have given up the Queen, and lost their
accents. The group might have been maintained by renewed
immigration which reached a thousand a year from Jamaica
alone after World War II; but the new McCarran-Walter
immigration law of 1952 radically cut the numbers eligible
to come in from the British West Indies, and the stream was
deflected to England, thus becoming indirectly responsible
for the development of a new, large Negro community there.
One can still detect the West Indian stream in New York
from first names such as Percy, Cecil, Chauncey, Keith.

No one has studied why the West Indians
were superior in business enterprise and educational achievement to the native Negro. Very likely the fact that they came
from islands which were almost completely Negro, and in
which, therefore, Negroes held all positions in society except
the very highest, inhibited the rise of a feeling of inadequacy and inferiority, and gave them the experiences and
self-confidence that Southern Negroes on the whole lacked.
And the Barbadians in particular were rather better educated than Southern Negroes.

In any case, notwithstanding the West In-
dian difference, Negro business did not develop, despite the
fact that business is in America the most effective form of
social mobility for those who meet prejudice. The young
man of ethnic background who encounters discrimination
may find a place in a business of his own or that of a rela-

tive. Thus the Chinese in America, a small group who never dreamed until World War II of getting jobs in the general American community, had an economic base in laundries and restaurants—a peculiar base, but one that gave economic security and the wherewithal to send children to college. It has been estimated that the income of Chinese from Chinese-owned business is, in proportion to their numbers, *forty-five times* as great as the income of Negroes from Negro-owned business.[22] Jews, Greeks, and Armenians, while not as specialized as Chinese, show a similar history.

Professional men, despite their much higher status than shopkeepers among Negroes, have not been common either among Negroes, but their history is quite different. For while businessmen have always been infrequent, a professional class did develop in the Negro community in the fifty years after slavery, but its growth has been slow. Thus there were in the nation 3,400 Negro physicians and surgeons in 1910, and only 4,000 in 1950. There were only 1,450 Negro lawyers in 1950, and the increase since 1900 had kept pace only with the increase in Negro population. There were only 1,500 dentists—a sevenfold increase from 1900, but still very small in relation to the Negro population.[23]

But even though the numbers of businessmen and professionals did not grow importantly, great changes did take place in the Negro community in the 1940's and 1950's. The dependence on menial labor has been broken. In 1960 a relatively large proportion of women still work—49 per cent of nonwhite women work, compared to 36 per cent of white women. But now only one-quarter of the women work in domestic households, as against the almost two-thirds of 1940; and these are the older women. More than a quarter work as professionals and white-collar employees.

Among the men, the changes in occupation have not been as striking, but in their case as well there has been a sizable reduction of service workers and laborers and an increase in skilled and unskilled workers. A fifth of Negro men are employed in professional, technical, managerial, clerical, and sales work[24] (see Table 4).

In a peculiar way, as we shall see again and again, the problem of the Negro in America is the problem of the Negro men more than the Negro women. It was the woman who could get whatever work was available even in the worst times. It was the man who was seen as a threat and subject to physical violence. It was the woman who came in touch with the white world, and for whom favors, if any were forthcoming, were more common. Perhaps it was easier for whites to be gracious to the women, who, because they were women, could be seen as accepting subordination with more grace and with less resentment and sullenness. Already a member of one underprivileged group (that of women), membership in another (that of Negroes) did not perhaps weigh so heavily upon her, or so it might appear to the white world.

In New York, the problem of the Negro man is if anything exaggerated. What kind of job is he to get? Here, as we have said, there is little heavy industry, where skilled or unskilled labor, if unionized, can get a good wage. He has mostly depended in New York on unskilled labor and services. We are dispensing with unskilled labor by new machines, better organization, poorer maintenance, and simply learning to do without.[25] Just as the Negro Southern agricultural laborer has been displaced by machinery, so too the Negro urban unskilled laborer is being displaced. In the long run, this may be a blessing. In the short run (which is likely to be quite long) and for the individual, it means strain and suffering and a high rate of unemployment. It means strong and increasing pressure on the Negro male to qualify himself for jobs that demand special skills. It means a particularly desperate problem for the Negro boy coming out of high school, with or without a diploma, and looking for a job in a market where there are few jobs for the unskilled, and in a neighborhood and a community in which there are few businessmen or professionals or skilled workers to give him a break or tell him about the breaks (this is the way the unqualified of other groups get started). This is the "social dynamite" that so shocked James Bryant Conant in the Negro slums of the great Northern cities in the late fifties,[26] and that reduces social workers to despair in Bedford-Stuyvesant in Brooklyn and Harlem in Manhattan. The problem is *not* those with the capacity to go on to college or even get a good commercial high school education—there is always, at least, a government job for them. The problem is those who will have to work with their hands, in a society that has less and less work for people with only hands.

The array of jobs potentially available for Negro men and boys in New York raises special problems. There is a great clothing industry, but although the Jewish male found work at sewing machines no threat to his manliness, other males have not been so adaptable. Neither the Negro nor the Puerto Rican man seems to find the garment industry attractive. In any case the best jobs demand skills and training that tend to be kept within the ingroup. The same pattern, in even more extreme form, is found in a wide variety of skilled trades. Who can become an electrician, a plasterer, a bricklayer, a machinist, unless he has connections? The problem is not just discrimination against the Negro but discrimination against any outsider. Here again we see the problem created by the lack of a Negro business class. There are Irish and Italian skilled workers, in part because Irish and Italians were prominent in contracting and construction.

For women there is a great variety of clerical and sales jobs, technical and semiprofessional jobs, and there are no restrictive and monopolistic unions in these fields. The educational attainments required are often moderate, and in any case Negro girls seem to do better in school than boys. (In a lower-class group, school is a threat to masculinity, but not to femininity.) And a woman too will be satisfied with a clerical and sales job and income that will not satisfy a man.

Both the NAACP and the State Committee Against Discrimination are concerned with the skilled crafts, hoping to effect a breakthrough in Negro employment. Less than 2 per cent of 15,000 registered apprentices in the state are Negroes.[27] The difficulties in increasing the number are great. Negro youths have little contact through family and friends with the skilled trades. They have little experience with apprenticeship, and do not always see any point in long training at low wages. Skilled labor of any kind does not have great prestige among Negroes. Many managements are indifferent to the measures necessary to reach Negro youth, or positively antagonistic, for they see no reason to believe they will be good workmen. A shift into the skilled trades thus involves changes in the unions, in management, in the Negro community.

There are jobs that involve relatively little training but are likewise restricted by a union-employer network. The State Commission Against Discrimination (SCAD)* and the National Urban League have made intensive efforts to get Negroes jobs in breweries, as truck drivers, and as bakery driver-salesmen.[28] These efforts have brought small results. The employers blame the unions, the unions point to their rules on getting membership (which are generally very complicated), and both point to the Negroes— they do not come looking for the jobs. But why should they, when there are so many problems in getting them, and in any case the man on the inside, with the contacts, will get it?

As one examines the employment picture among Negroes, a number of major conclusions become obvious. One is that it is easier to change employment patterns in huge, bureaucratically organized, strongly led organizations than in small ones, which are the characteristic employers of skilled labor.

It is the small organization that hires friends and relatives, or people of the same ethnic background, and where the personal prejudices of the boss can come into play. According to the law in New York State, discrimination in small organizations (as long as they have six employees) is as illegal as discrimination in large ones. But one feels that SCAD is perhaps being more diligent than it has to be—or than is rewarding—when it turns its eagle eye on a small Italian restaurant where it turns out only Italians are employed.

In large organizations, everyone has to learn to play according to the bureaucratic rules, to mute his personal feelings, and keep them from affecting his actions. The small business in New York finds it easier to be tricky and evasive than the big one. For the big organization has

* The name was changed in 1962 to the State Commission for Human Rights.

personnel directors, formal application forms, formal tests, formal rating arrangements, formal rules, all of which SCAD is empowered to observe or study.

A second major conclusion is that the strictly legal approach to discrimination will have to be supplemented with new approaches. The major advances possible through legal measures alone have, in New York City, been made. The major success of both the law and the voluntary organizations has been with the big organizations; and there are not many big divisions left to be captured. The law can handle pretty well the problems of discrimination in *initial* employment, and these have been greatly reduced. This is not to say that every job is available on equal terms—when is this ever the case? and what law can ever overcome the prejudice in favor of pretty girls?— but that enough are, as many as there are qualified personnel to fill them. But now problems develop that are much harder for SCAD to deal with—the problems of advancement in bureaucratic organizations. In a big organization this must be based theoretically on capacity and accomplishment. But how is one to be fair about that? There are many ways of getting ahead, and many ways of finding oneself stuck at the lowest rungs of the ladder. Within the organization there are a thousand subtle factors affecting advancement that no outside agency can police.

A third major point: in the follow-up of opportunities—following up the first few Negroes into an organization, and moving up the bureaucratic ladder— one needs people with training and motivation, with the ability and skills and education required to hold jobs and to advance in them. For one reason or another (and they are not, at least on the surface, hard to understand) there are today problems in finding enough colored Americans with the motivation, training, and ability to fill the opportunities that are available.

The NAACP report on the apprenticeship problem supplies much food for thought in this connection. It speaks of "pre-training," and says:

Indenturing units [that is, firms that have apprenticeship programs] almost universally demand that apprentices register a good scholastic record, as is evidenced by completion of either academic or vocational high school. . . .

Available evidence indicates that Negro youth are deleteriously placed with respect to the pre-training factor. Nationally, fewer Negroes attend secondary school than whites. They also evidence a lower rate of completion. Because of a lack of motivation, derived in part from acknowledged parental frustrations in the field of employment, portions of Negro youth completing high school are not apt to have treated their educations with the attention commensurate with its importance in later years. . . . Negro youths do not emerge from high schools in desirable numbers, nor, if they do, is their training on a par with that of white youth. . . .[29]

Again and again, one finds that a breakthrough in Negro employment has not been followed up. For example, SCAD has issued a report on employment in banks. Each of a number of huge banks, with thousands of employees, has a few hundred Negro employees, generally about 2 per cent of the total employment.[30] There are certainly attitudes and practices in these elite institutions which restrict Negro employment at higher levels. A few hundred is, however, more than token employment, and yet Negro employment shows little tendency to grow since these jobs were opened.

The only areas of white-collar employment in which there are really large numbers of Negroes are in government agencies, city, state, and federal. This perhaps suggests one clue to the Negroes' slowness to seek private employment. Negroes still *expect* discrimination and rebuffs. Only in government is this feeling overcome, for there the civil service laws ensure impartiality, and Negro political strength backs it up. Elsewhere, cases are won, changes are made, but the follow-up is slow.

And yet this is not the whole story. One finds other cases of relatively sluggish follow-up in which discrimination or fear of it could not play a major role. It is interesting to note some contrasts between Negro and Puerto Rican employment patterns. Negroes and Puerto Ricans both work in sizable numbers in hotels. Puerto Ricans entered after Negroes, and it is not likely that they face less discrimination. Yet many more Puerto Ricans than Negroes are employed in the hotel industry.³¹ The same thing holds in branches of the garment industry. Perhaps the difference can be ascribed in part to the relative weakness of clan and extended family feeling among the Negroes. One Puerto Rican may be quicker to bring in another, and there seems more of a tendency for family and related groups to work together.

Finally, it is the general economic situation that will do most to break down discriminatory employment patterns, regardless of people's attitudes or the law. The big change in Negro employment was a result of wartime shortages of labor. Negro unemployment is always higher than white, but the gap becomes greatest in times when the general unemployment rate rises. Newest in jobs, with least protection from seniority, they are the first to go. Disproportionately represented among those with poor training and undeveloped skills, they are also less capable of holding on to jobs in times of difficulty.³² The critical problem of Negro employment today has been created by a general economic change—the rapid elimination of unskilled and semiskilled jobs. This social change has nothing to do with discrimination, and yet it has dealt Negroes (and the whole community, picking up the tab in the form of increased costs of relief, youth projects, police, and so on) as severe a blow as discrimination.

Aside from all the problems we have discussed, the facts still show that Negroes, at the same levels of education as whites, do not get as good jobs, as high incomes. These are still the crude, brute facts of discrimination. And yet the same facts can be responded to in different ways. The Japanese in California before the war found it impossible to get good jobs outside the Japanese community; Jews until the Second World War took it for granted that they would find few jobs in engineering or with large corporations. But at the same time, Japanese attended college in phenomenal numbers; they became the best educated racial group in California. Jews did the same. This meant frustration for Japanese and Jews who could not find jobs for which they had trained and were qualified. Graduate Jewish chemists peddled cosmetics that they had concocted and bottled, graduate Japanese technicians worked as busboys.

But this overtraining also meant that when the barriers came down these groups were ready and waiting. The Negro today is not. It is true his experience has been more frustrating, prejudice more severe, personality damage more extensive. And yet in some ways the situation is better; never has there been more opportunity for education and training at government expense, never has there been a more favorable environment for minority students in colleges, never have there been so many opportunities making the struggle of education light in contrast to the rewards held out. Important leadership elements in the Negro community are aware of this situation; but can they successfully communicate a sense of urgency to great numbers?

EDUCATION

THERE ARE SOME CRUCIAL FACTS ABOUT NEGRO EDUCATION IN New York City. One-quarter of the city's elementary school population was Negro in 1960; a fifth of the junior high school population; only a tenth of the academic high school population.[33] There are no figures by race on the graduating classes of the city academic high schools, but they are certainly less than 10 per cent Negro. When we come to the free colleges that are the peak of the city's educational system, we do not have figures by race, but it is clear that they in no way represent the very large numbers of Negroes in the low-income population. New York Negroes do go to college in fairly large numbers. In 1960 nonwhites formed more than 6 per cent of the college graduates of the city, more than 10 per cent of those with some college education. But these figures conceal a much greater gap in quality.[34]

The vocational high schools are more than one-fifth Negro. The New York City vocational high schools teach trades, but it is also well known that they serve to keep poor students off the street until they reach the legal age for dropping out of school. They serve this function for many Negro youths.

At first glance, the picture may remind us of some European immigrant groups of peasant background who have little contact with education, little knowledge of what value or use it might be, and in which the parents are interested in getting the children out of school and at work or married as soon as possible. In these groups, very often a close-knit family positively discourages further education. The failure of children to pursue their education is not a product of social disorganization but of the fact that the values of the parents were not the standard American values, and they gave no support to education.

The Negro situation is different. Negroes do place a high value on education.[35] The educational attainments of young men and women are emphasized in news stories and announcements. Negro professionals stand at the top of the social ladder, and make the highest incomes. Parents continually emphasize to children the theme of the importance of education as a means of getting ahead; and this is true among the uneducated as well as the educated, the failures as well as the successful. And yet the outcome is a poor one.

There are not as many good Negro students coming out of the high schools as there are places in colleges to put them. Indeed, the major task of the National Scholarship Service and Fund for Negro Students, which has for years been working on the problem of getting places and scholarships for Negro students in colleges, is to find enough qualified students, or to get colleges to accept those who formally fall below the admission requirements but who NSSFNS feels can make the grade. Richard Plaut, President of NSSFNS, has written that "places [in Northern colleges] for five times as many [Negro students as were actually placed] might have been found had that number been qualified and available." [36] The former principal of a New York City high school reports that one of the best colleges in the Northeast was willing to accept Negro students on his say-so, regardless of formal record.[37]

Even money is in some cases no longer a problem. A meeting of Medical Fellowships, Inc., revealed "that the chief bottleneck in efforts to increase the number of Negro physicians is not . . . finding available openings in medical schools or even the monies required for a medical education but . . . finding college graduates interested in medicine who have the requisite high academic standing." [38] We have pointed out that the number of Negro physicians has been almost static for fifty years—there is certainly no question of the rewards that await Negro doctors.

Studies of Negro students in schools reveal too that aspirations are high. One also sees many Negro students who remind one of the students of other minorities that have met discrimination, students whose motivation and drive are great. The emphasis on the values of education does have a real effect on many children, though there are still many who are unaffected.

We can think of many reasons why this should be so, after the fact. There is of course the poor education Negroes have received in the South; and so many students in the New York schools are transfers from the South. There is the long heritage of prejudice and discrimination that convinces so many of them that it is not worth trying.

In the minds of most Negroes in New York City, the problem of education is essentially the problem of segregation. In the South their children are forced to attend all-Negro schools with inferior teachers, buildings, standards; in New York City their children may attend all-Negro schools, with the same deficiencies. Since the Supreme Court decision on segregated schools in the South, segregation in New York schools has been a major political issue in the city. In 1954 Professor Kenneth Clark of City College, who had testified for the Supreme Court as an expert on the psychological effects of segregation, argued that the decision should be applied in the schools of the North that were segregated by the effects of the combination of neighborhood concentration of Negroes and neighborhood school zoning. The Board of Education requested the Public Education Association to investigate the problem. A year later it reported that in schools of high Negro and Puerto Rican concentration the children scored much below children of other schools in various tests. The city spent more on the education of children in these high-concentration schools, supplied more staff. The buildings however were older, and there was a higher proportion of substitute teachers. And the results were worse.

The Board of Education then started its ponderous machinery in motion to come up with ways of "integrating" the schools. To Negro parents the issue was simple—the children go to school with other Negro children, their education must be worse. The Board of Education, confronted with enormous Negro areas supplying tens of thousands of schoolchildren, and resisting the notion of doing away with the neighborhood school, tried to reinterpret the problem as one of education alone, and most of its measures adopted in the course of the integration controversy were designed to improve the education of Negro and Puerto Rican children in schools that it saw no way of desegregating. Thus, it supplied larger and larger numbers of specialized personnel to the so-called "special service" schools (those with high proportions of Negroes and Puerto Ricans); it supported the Demonstration Guidance and Higher Horizon projects, which experimented with substituting trips to the opera and more intensive reading instruction for the presumed lack of an appropriate home background; it insisted that new regular teachers be assigned to the difficult schools—as a result, many preferred to hold on to their substitute status, or teach in the suburbs. It rezoned schools, tried to place new schools in border areas. By the time they were built, the areas were generally all Negro or Puerto Rican. It replaced the old schools in the slum areas.

From the point of view of the militant elements in the Negro community, all this was irrelevant—the issue was simply the fact that their children had to go to schools that were almost entirely Negro and Puerto Rican. (The Puerto Rican community actually played little role in the controversy.) Meanwhile, this situation became worse. In 1957 the Board of Education began to keep meticulous records of the numbers of Negro, Puerto Rican, and "other" children in each class and in each school, so as to determine the effect of measures to integrate the schools. In despair, they saw the proportion of Negro and Puerto Rican children rise from 36 to 43 per cent of the elementary school population of the schools by 1960. In Manhattan 75 per cent of the elementary school population was Negro or Puerto Rican! What was an "integrated" school under these circumstances? In 1960, 95 of 589 elementary schools contained more than 90 per cent Negro and Puerto Rican children, 22 of 125 junior high schools held more than 85 per cent Negro and Puerto Rican children (these figures serve to separate "segregated" from "integrated" schools in the peculiar language used in New York City to discuss this problem; yet it is doubtful that many parents in a school with an 80 per cent Negro and Puerto Rican enrollment would consider the school "integrated").[39] The situation is aggravated by the large number of children attending parochial and other private schools. The executive director of the United Parents Association pointed out that while only seven in the city in the 5-to-14-year age-group was Negro, one out of three-and-a-half in the public schools was Negro. From 1950–1951 to 1960–1961, enrollments in private and parochial schools rose from 307,000 to 415,000, an increase of 35 per cent, while public school enrollment rose only 11.5 per cent.[40]

Meanwhile, in September 1960 the Board of Education succumbed to the pressure of Negro parents demanding the right to send their children out of the districts in which they lived to schools with small proportions of Negroes and Puerto Ricans. Negro parents, led by Paul Zuber, a Manhattan lawyer, and the Reverend Milton Galamison, minister of the Siloam Presbyterian Church in the Bedford-Stuyvesant section of Brooklyn, had forced the change by school strikes and threats of further school strikes. The Board announced a program of permissive zoning, whereby the children attending the "segregated" schools would be allowed to transfer to "integrated" schools with space available. The first major test of the program came in February, 1961, when the parents of 15,000 children headed for junior high schools were allowed to request transfers. Almost 4,000 requested the transfer to "unsegregated" schools, indicating how strongly Negro parents felt about the issue. Of those requesting transfers some, however, were the parents of "other" children who sought the privilege of transferring even more eagerly than did the parents of Negro and Puerto Rican children. P.S. 197, a new school surrounded by middle-class housing projects in Harlem—Riverton and Lenox Terrace—showed the highest percentage of requests.[41]

And yet it is not likely that "permissive zoning" will have much impact on the education of Negro children in the city, despite the passion with which it has been espoused by middle-class parents. Even in 1960, before the impact of permissive zoning had made itself felt, more than half the Negro and Puerto Rican children in the city attended "integrated" schools. No one has examined these schools to see whether a school that is 50 per cent Negro and Puerto Rican is by that fact alone better than one that is 90 per cent Negro and Puerto Rican. In the South, where segregation is the formal and legal embodiment of society's effort to keep the Negro in a less than human position, there is no question its effects are damaging. In New York, where it is simply the expression of the existence of the Negro ghetto, it is doubtful whether a purely formal effort to change the proportions of black and white in a school will have much effect, even though it will reduce the political pressure of parents desperately eager to get their children off to the best possible start.

In the end, the Board of Education accepted the principle that the concentration of Negro and Puerto Rican children was *itself,* and independently of the factors of poverty and background, educationally disadvantageous. And yet one cannot help asking: why were schools that were indifferent to the problems of the children of other groups, forty and fifty years ago, adequate enough for them, but seem nevertheless inadequate for the present wave of children? Why is the strong and passionate concern of the Negro community and Negro parents for education so poorly rewarded by the children?

There is little question where the major part of the answer must be found: in the home and family and community—not in its overt values, which as we have seen are positive in relation to education, but in its conditions and circumstances. It is there that the heritage of two hundred years of slavery and a hundred years of discrimination is concentrated; and it is there that we find the serious obstacles to the ability to make use of a free educational system to advance into higher occupations and to eliminate the massive social problems that afflict colored Americans and the city.

THE FAMILY AND OTHER PROBLEMS

THERE WERE IN 1960 IN THE NEW YORK METROPOLITAN AREA 353,000 Negro families; a quarter were headed by women. In contrast, less than one-tenth of the white households were headed by women.[42] The rate of illegitimacy among Negroes is about fourteen or fifteen times that among whites.[43] When we find such an impossible situation as that discussed in the New York press in 1960, in which babies are abandoned in hospitals by their mothers, and live there for months on end, for there is no room for them anywhere else, most of them are Negro children.[44]

There are not enough foster homes for the Negro children who need care; there is a desperate shortage of adoptive parents for Negro children, for there are so many of them who need adoption.

More Negro children live apart from parents and relatives; more live in institutions; more live in crowded homes; more have lodgers and other related and unrelated persons living with them.[45]

Broken homes and illegitimacy do not necessarily mean poor upbringing and emotional problems. But they mean it more often when the mother is forced to work (as the Negro mother so often is), when the father is incapable of contributing to support (as the Negro father so often is), when fathers and mothers refuse to accept responsibility for and resent their children, as Negro parents, overwhelmed by difficulties, so often do, and when the family situation, instead of being clear-cut and with defined roles and responsibilities, is left vague and ambiguous (as it so often is in Negro families).

We focus of course on one side of the problem—there are more unbroken than broken homes among Negroes, more responsible than irresponsible parents, more nonworking than working mothers, more good homes for children than poor ones. There is a whole world in which these problems do not exist. But the incidence of these problems among Negroes is enormous, and even those who escape them feel them as a close threat. They escape, but family, relatives, friends, do not.[46]

All this cannot be irrelevant to the academic performance of Negro children, and indeed it is relevant to a much wider range of problems than educational ones alone. In particular, it is probably the Negro boy who suffers in this situation. With an adult male so often lacking, there is a much greater chance of psychological difficulties. Certainly, even without the problems of a figure with whom to identify and on whom to model himself, the Negro boy, as was pointed out in talking about jobs, would have problems enough. But it is understandable that his knowledge of the adult male world should be weak and uncertain, that his aspirations should be unrealistic, that his own self-image should be unsure and impaired. And this indeed is what studies show. One psychologist reports on a comparative study of Negro boys and girls in a New York elementary school: the girls "generally have better academic performance, a greater span of attention, report more positive family atmosphere, have more positive and realistic self-concepts." [47]

We do not propose a single explanation of the problems that afflict so many Negroes; obviously, if the schools were better, the students' performances would also be better. If housing and job conditions were better, there would be less illegitimacy. If the police were fairer, there would be less arrests of Negroes. If Negroes had better jobs and higher incomes, fewer of them would be sentenced, fewer criminals would be made in prisons and reformatories.* All these things are true. And since it is easier to do something about education, housing, jobs, and police administration than many other things, there is where we should put our emphasis, and there is where we begin. But I think it is pointless to ignore the fact that the concentration of problems in the Negro community *is* exceptional,

* The New York City Police Department does not keep records by race. The Department of Correction, however, does. In 1958 more than two-fifths of all male first admissions and more than three-fifths of all female first admissions to institutions of detention or sentence were Negro.[48]

and that prejudice, low income, poor education explain only so much.

Migration, uprooting, urbanization always create problems. Even the best organized and best integrated groups suffer under such circumstances. But when the fundamental core of organization, the family, is already weak, the magnitude of these problems may be staggering. The experience of slavery left as its most serious heritage a steady weakness in the Negro family. There was no marriage in the slave family—husbands could be sold away from wives, children from parents. There was no possibility of taking responsibility for one's children, for one had in the end no power over them. One could not educate them, nor even, in many cases, discipline them. The sociologist Franklin Frazier, in one of the most important books written on the American Negro, has traced the history of the family, from slavery, to the Southern postslavery situation, to the Northern city. What slavery began, prejudice and discrimination, affecting jobs, housing, self-respect, have continued to keep alive among many, many colored Americans.

This is the situation in the Negro community; it will be the situation for a long time to come. The magnitude of the problems in the lower-class and disorganized sector of the population is so great that the middle-class element is inadequate to deal with them, as other middle-class elements, of other ethnic groups, dealt in the past (and deal today) with their problems. Consequently, while the problems of other groups are in large measure their own, the problems of the Negro community become the problems of all of us. It is true (as is often pointed out by sociologists) that we do not hear of Jewish illegitimacy or juvenile delinquency because the community is so blanketed with institutions that it gets them before the public agencies do. But this works only because the proportion of problem-solvers to problem-producers in this community is so large.

The Negro middle class suffers deeply from the burden of Negro social problems. For as against other groups—even the Mexicans in the Southwest, and certainly most European ethnic groups—the middle-class Negro cannot hide his membership in a community that includes so many who make problems. The image of the Negro is still predominantly that created by the problem element. But it is also true that the Negro middle class contributes very little, in money, organization, or involvement, to the solution of Negro social problems. Conceivably, institutions organized, supported, and staffed by Negroes might be much more effective than the government and private agencies that now deal with these problems.

But it is not likely that we will see a massive self-help effort. For one thing, the middle-class Negro, separated by a thin line from the lower-class Negro, is often too busy maintaining his own precarious adaptation to offer sympathy or assistance. But more important, it is not possible for Negroes to view themselves as other ethnic groups did because the Negro is so much an American, the distinctive product of America. He bears no foreign values and culture that he feels the need to guard from the surrounding environment. He insists that the white world deal with his problems because, since he is so much the product of America, they are not *his* problems, but everyone's. Once they become everyone's, perhaps he will see that they are his own, too. For even if he has not *chosen* his group (and who has?), even if he finds nothing positive in it, the group does exist. Groups are formed in strange ways. The word Slav comes from the word for Slave. The Hebrews were created by a group of wandering outcasts. However formed, eventually those who are part of groups must make peace with them and accept them.

For the Negro, this acceptance must mean, in the end, a higher degree of responsibility by the middle-class and well-to-do and educated Negroes for the others.

HOUSING AND NEIGHBORHOOD

THE GREATEST GAP BY FAR BETWEEN THE CONDITIONS OF LIFE of New York's population in general and the specific part of it that is Negro is to be found in housing. Here is the greatest and most important remaining area of discrimination—important in its extent, its real consequences, and its social and psychological impact.

The Negro ghetto in New York City has not dissolved, neither in Manhattan nor in the other boroughs, for the poor or the well-to-do.[49] The ghetto is not surrounded by a sharp line, and there is less sense of boundaries in New York than there is in many other cities. But in each of the four main boroughs there is a single concentrated area of Negro settlement, shading off at the edges to mixed areas, which tend with the increase in Negro population to become as concentratedly Negro as the centers. If one looks at a map of New York City on which the places of residence of the Negro population have been spotted, one will find many areas with small percentages of Negroes, and it may look as if the Negro population is spreading evenly through the city, is being "integrated." But a closer examination will reveal that these small outlying areas of Negro population are generally areas with public housing projects, and the Negro population is there because the housing projects are there. The projects in the outlying boroughs are partly Negro islands in a white sea.

There are laws forbidding discrimination in renting and selling housing, just as there is a law forbidding discrimination in employment. The city and state laws have steadily increased their coverage to the point where all housing but rooms or apartments in one's own home, and units in two-family homes in which one is occupied by the owner, must be made available without discrimination on account of race, religion, or national origin. Ninety-five per cent of city housing is now covered by the law. But the law forbidding discrimination in housing is much less effective than the law forbidding discrimination in employment. It is weaker, and provides no specific penalties, though if a landlord remains adamant, the city can bring him into court.

But the main reason the law against discrimination in housing can do less to change this situation than the law against discrimination in employment is that apartments are not controlled by big bureaucratic organizations. The big projects can be prevented from discriminating by law. But most apartments are in existing houses owned by small landlords. Long before the complaint can possibly be acted on, the apartment is gone. There is also little danger in a landlord practicing evasive action. It is fair to say that this is a law to which the run-of-the-mill landlords have responded with massive evasion. It takes really elaborate measures to get an apartment the way the law is now written. One needs a respectable-looking white friend to find out first that the apartment is available; a Negro who really wants it and is ready to take it then asks for it and is told it is not available; a second white is then required in order that he may be told that the apartment is still available, so as to get a sure-fire case; then direct confrontation plus rapid action in reporting all the details to the City Commission on Human Rights* is required. At this point, the landlord will often succumb. The Committee on Racial Equality (CORE) as well as Reform Democratic clubs and other organizations have supplied the whites for this sandwiching technique, and the elaborate advance planning and chance for immediate gratification have supplied perhaps a more satisfying activity to CORE than picketing local branches of Woolworth's. (The white pickets were generally in the majority, and were unhappy at the Negroes going past them.)

Perhaps even more significant in reducing the effectiveness of the law than landlord resistance is the perpetual housing shortage in New York City. This "temporary" situation is now as permanent as anything in life ever is. Someone beginning school in New York City during the Second World War may now be married and having children in a housing market that has the same "temporary" shortage that it had at the end of the war. Even in the absence of discrimination, the low-income tenant would find it very hard to find cheap housing when it is being demolished faster than it is being built. The housing shortage means that we deal with a situation of "discrimination for" as well as "discrimination against." Just as good jobs are reserved for friends, relatives, and insiders, so are good apartments. Indeed, the better apartments in New York descend through a chain of relatives and friends, year after year, decade after decade. The most valuable of these valuable commodities are of course the rent-controlled apart-

* Formerly the Commission on Intergroup Relations. The name was changed in 1962.

ments. Rent-controlled apartments mean, as a matter of course, discrimination against everyone who has come into the city since 1943. Even *without* any discrimination on the ground of color, Negroes (and in larger measure Puerto Ricans) would be getting a poor share of the housing market, and paying more for it, because they are in larger measure latecomers.

But the law is not only interested in improving the housing available to Negroes, it is also interested in breaking down the pattern of segregation in housing. And here it is hard for the law to be very effective, whether in conditions of housing shortage or housing plenty. It is again instructive to compare housing with jobs. The breakthrough into an area of employment *does* mean a racially mixed working force; the breakthrough into an area of white housing has up to now generally meant a period of transition ending with the extension of the all-Negro and mostly Negro neighborhood. It has not meant, the objective that so many feel is desirable and that seems so unattainable, a stable, racially mixed area.

This pattern of white withdrawal or flight before incoming Negroes is found everywhere in the nation. It is perhaps mildest in New York City, for in Manhattan, if not in the other boroughs, people act as they do nowhere in the nation. Manhattan is unique because the struggle for space is so intense, and so many people want to live there, that the flight of some white elements means their immediate replacement by other white elements. In Manhattan, therefore, one does find mixed areas of whites, Puerto Ricans, and Negroes, and it is likely the island will become even more mixed in the future. But one of the reasons that people live so closely together there is because they can have so little to do with each other. Manhattan has few communities to protect, for here a variety of "communities" as well as many people who are connected to none share the very same ground. One element goes to a church, a second to a synagogue, a third to neither. One patronizes one kind of store, another a store with a somewhat different line of similar goods, or a different price range, located right next door to the first. One group sends its children to public school, another to parochial school, another to private school, and a fourth, surprisingly large, has no children at all—which, again, is one of the reasons they are willing to live so close to Negroes and Puerto Ricans. If the groups do not share the same apartment houses, they do share the same blocks, parks, shopping streets. But they are willing to share as much as this, and be as close as this, because they really share so little. These are important considerations, and the reason why it is unrealistic to compare Manhattan with the other boroughs, or the rest of the metropolitan area. These areas outside Manhattan are, to a much larger extent than Manhattan, communities, and when a community feels threatened by what it feels is an alien element, there is a strong tendency for those in it to move away and reconstitute something like it, or to find something like it.

In other cities, less tolerant than New York, the community, instead of fading away, may put up a hard shell and fight. Here, sentiment, the governmental authorities, and the law give little support to any violent effort to prevent Negroes from moving into white areas. The resistance comes mostly from landlords, operating out of prejudice or calculations of rational advantage, less from tenants or homeowners. There are two other reasons New York has had little violent resistance to the expansion of Negro neighborhoods: many are renters who will not fight for their houses; many are Jews who would not resist a Negro move with violence.

Around the edges of Harlem, of Bedford-Stuyvesant, and of the other major centers of population, then, there is "integration," if one thinks in terms of people living near one another. In the middle-class suburban areas around New York, there are a few integrated communities, but they tend, more or less rapidly, to become more and more Negro, or less and less white, unless the houses are quite expensive—a fact that automatically limits the Negro market. The Negro population of the city and the metropolitan area is rising, and the Negro population of high and steady income is also rising; it is understandable that the Negro proportion in a desirable and pleasant area, where Negroes can buy homes, will also rise. This would be so in any case; it is also true that the transition is often speeded up by real estate men, Negro and white, encouraging people to move out. In southern Queens, in the Springfield Gardens, Laurelton, Rosedale area, a Tri-Community Council exists, and the real estate men are countered by a community organization that encourages white homeowners to stay. The same kind of effort to freeze the changeover from white to Negro occupancy is to be found in Teaneck, New Jersey, in Lakeview, Long Island, and other suburban areas. Such organizations, which tend to bring together the new and old elements in a changing community, and to teach people the great truth that people are very much alike, are desirable. They slow down the transition. Certainly they make life pleasanter while the transition goes on, and have important educational effects. But if we look at the over-all picture, we cannot but conclude that in most cases the tendencies for an area to become mostly Negro is irreversible.

Often prejudice has nothing to do with it at all, or hardly anything, and indeed the movement into the area may have begun because it showed the *least* prejudice, the *least* resistance. But the older group may still desire to live in a community of "their kind." Rising incomes and rising land prices and house prices make mobility easy. Often there are differences aside from color between the old community and the newcomers. And often the older settlers, living in older homes, and now without young children, needed only a little push to do what they were already thinking of, to move out into a smaller and more convenient house, or into a suburban apartment. Prejudice is extensive but is rarely unmixed or pure. Economic advantage in selling out, higher income permitting better housing, changing needs and wants, social interests, and other factors may play a role in the moving out of the whites.

The effect of these patterns of growth and movement has been to spread the Negro population through the city and metropolitan area, but its spread has been around a single main concentration in each borough. Harlem in Manhattan (the term has grown with the Negro community, and it is now almost synonymous with the main area of Negro occupancy) has already reached its peak as a center of Negro population. Manhattan had still in 1960 more Negroes than any other borough (397,000), but its rate of increase in 1950–1960 was by far the smallest. Meanwhile, the centers of Negro population in the other boroughs have grown rapidly. The Bronx, which had only 25,000 in 1940, had 164,000 in 1960. Queens, which also had about 25,000 in 1940 had 146,000 in 1960. Brooklyn has grown from 110,000 in 1940 to 371,000. Manhattan, which had two-thirds of the city's Negro population in 1940, has only a little more than a third today.[50]

Beyond the borders of the city, in other cities such as Newark and in suburban areas, there has been a great increase in the Negro population. Westchester has risen from 32,000 Negroes in 1940 to 56,000 in 1960. Nassau and Suffolk in this time more than doubled their Negro population. In these counties, older Negro settlements that very often consisted of servants and handymen have expanded and been joined by very different, prosperous, middle-class communities.[51]

While discrimination is the main channelizer of this population movement, we tend perhaps to minimize other factors at work in this process of Negro community formation. Even with much less prejudice directed against them, Jews have formed dense and concentrated suburban settlements. Great Neck did not become Jewish because Jews could not move anywhere else, but because it was an attractive community, and once there were enough Jews to organize synagogues and temples, to support social circles and associations, bakeries and delicatessens, it became even more attractive. There may be less in the way of specialized tastes in food and certainly less in the way of specific cultural attachments to differentiate the Negro middle class from the great American average. But there is a distinctive and important religious and organizational life, and in time, and indeed perhaps the time is now, we shall have to recognize that a community that is Negro is not necessarily the outcome of discrimination, just as a Jewish community is not necessarily the product of discrimination. In the absence of discrimination these clusters would continue to exist. But there is no question that today, in a Negro community, compulsion and limitation are felt more strongly than the free decision to come together.

No one has thought very seriously about what truly integrated communities would be like. What

would be the basis for common action, for social activities
bringing together people of different groups? The communities of New York have always been in large measure
ethnically and religiously delimited, and the social and organizational life of suburbia is lived within the distinctions
created by religious affiliation. If Jews set up clubs and
recreational activities and social activities largely on the
basis of affiliation to synagogues and Jewish community centers and other Jewish organizations—as, outside of Manhattan, they increasingly do—then what areas are left for the
mingling of Negroes and Jews? They only rarely meet at
work, and that does not generally affect the communities
to which the workers return to live. If Catholics do the
same, there is again little room for social intercourse with
Negroes. There remains local politics, and one of its chief
virtues is that it does remind people of the variety of our
communities, and does require them all to come together.

It is the white Protestants on whom the
moral injunction to form a community together with Negroes falls most heavily, at least from a theoretical point of
view. For in America religion is a legitimate basis on which
to erect partially distinct communities, and neither Jews
nor Catholics need feel that they act in discriminatory fashion when they base their social life on a religious affiliation
which does not include Negroes.* But the basis for the
separation of white and Negro Protestants is much less
clear. The white Protestants were generally the first settlers
in the older suburban communities into which Negroes are
moving. But by now, white Protestant dominance in many
of these has ended in the face of a heavy Catholic and
Jewish movement. Many of the white Protestants of these
communities left long before the Negroes got there, two
migrations back, so often there are not many white Protestants left to wonder about the basis of the division of Negro
from white Methodists, Negro from white Episcopalians

* Negro Jews are actually only one of the many city sects that have
grown up among Negroes in imitation of exotic religions. They are for
the most part not really Jews, just as most Negro Muslims are not really
Muslims, for they have not gone through the prescribed process of conversion. There is a sizable body of Negro Catholics, but the issue of the
"integration" of Negro and white Catholics in the North does not as
yet seem to have greatly concerned whites or Negroes.[52]

and Congregationalists, Negro from white Baptists. Many Protestant ministers are aware of their responsibility and their failure, and there is a good deal of discussion and soul-searching as to what can be done. Community with the Negro will become more and more a Protestant problem as religion comes more and more to serve as the major legitimate basis for separate communities within the larger community.[53]

In the center of the city, among the poor, the problem of integration is a very different one. Indeed, the search for a decent place to live is so intense that for most the additional social goal of a mixed community seems a utopian and irrelevant consideration. But ironically enough, it is here, in the center and among the poor, that the goal of integration is most earnestly sought and most widely found, for a great public agency plays an important role today in the housing of the poor in New York. The New York City Housing Authority now controls a major part of the shelter of the poor in the city of New York, and its decisions affect the way they live. In mid-1962, more than 450,000 people lived in the 116,000 apartments of the New York City Housing Authority. Nineteen thousand more apartments were under construction and being occupied, with an estimated population of 72,000, and 17,000 more apartments were being planned. Within a few years, the public housing pool will contain more than 150,000 apartments, and 600,000 people! About 40 per cent of public housing is occupied by Negroes, which means that about one out of every five or six Negroes in the city is living in a project. The project is now beginning to rival the slum as the environment for poor Negroes, and it consequently becomes more and more important to consider what kind of life is lived there, and what kind of communities are created in them.

The projects are of course integrated. There are none without some Negroes and only a few that are entirely Negro. The Housing Authority is concerned over the fact that in many projects there is a strong tendency for the white population to decline. A few years ago, it attempted to keep many projects integrated by favoring the applications of white prospective tenants in some, and of

Negro and Puerto Rican tenants in others.[54] Challenged by complaints to SCAD, and by articles in the Negro press, the Authority has limited its integration efforts in recent years to the attempt to recruit a balanced tenant population for new projects. But since the over-all tendency is for the white population to fall, it is largely white tenants that are favored, within of course the over-all maximum income limitations, and the complex system of priorities that the Authority must observe. This is part of the Authority's over-all policy, within recent years, of attempting to make each project a community. Thus the Authority has also tried in many projects to reduce the numbers on relief (for some projects once contained a very large proportion of families on relief), just as it tried to get a mixture of different ethnic groups.

But the creation of a good community is a difficult thing, and the existence of a housing project that is divided between Negroes, Puerto Ricans, and whites may mean (and often does mean) only the physical proximity of groups that have very little to do with each other. In a middle-class community as we have seen, the two races separate, among other reasons, because there are too few elements of community to bind them, and their active social life goes on within racial and religious groups. In the housing project, the situation is generally worse, for the absence of ties across group lines is generally accompanied by the absence of ties even *within* the group. A powerful bureaucracy manages the project, and, whatever its intentions, its mere existence and its large functions inhibit the development of a community. There are few churches or any other kind of organization within the projects. Social isolation of tenant from tenant is common, because after all people have been bureaucratically assigned to projects and apartments, within a limited choice, rather than having located to be near friends, family, or institutions. Suspicion is also common, in part because there is fear of having transgressed one of the many rules of the Authority, and many tenants take the point of view that the less the neighbors know of them the better. The weakness of the bonds of community within the projects is true whether they are all Negro or partly Negro.

The problem of creating a community is an enormous task, and it may seem unfair to demand of a landlord that he undertake this task. But the landlord of 100,000 families is more than a landlord, and the Authority accepts, as the integration policy shows, its responsibility for helping to create community within the projects. And yet one wonders whether the mixing of the races in proper proportions will play much role in creating good communities. The improvement of the projects as communities probably depends on a host of measures that are even more difficult than affecting their racial composition: involving the people of the projects in their management and maintenance, encouraging and strengthening forms of organization among them (even when the main purpose of these organizations seems to be to attack the management), encouraging forms of self-help in them, varying their population occupationally as well as racially by greater tolerance in admissions, reducing the stark difference of the projects from their surroundings by changing their appearance, considering more seriously the impact of their design on the social life that they enfold, all this and more have been suggested. Some of the projects are integrated without any efforts by the Authority. These are the projects that for various reasons do overcome the many drawbacks and become so attractive that whites as well as Negroes want to live in them.

Integration in the projects is probably best achieved not by policies to directly affect the mixture but by policies to create good communities, making them attractive to more families. But in any case, there is not much the Authority can do to affect proportions, for the number of Negroes in public housing will depend on their future economic fate in New York. If most of the poor in New York are Negro, then most of the housing project population will have to be Negro, and the Authority will be helpless to affect the situation, short of radical changes in the entire idea of public housing.

The projects are important not only for themselves; they are also important for their impact on the rest of the city. And perhaps their most important effect has been in upsetting the balance of the slums. Large numbers of normal families living in slums (the chief candidates for the projects) have been withdrawn from them, leaving the remaining slums to become the homes of the old, the criminal, the mentally unbalanced, the most depressed and miserable and deprived. The slums now contain the very large families that are not eligible for public housing because they would overcrowd it; the families that have been ejected from the projects (or were never admitted) for being antisocial; those who have either recently arrived in the city and hardly adapted to urban life, or those who may have been here a long time but never adapted; as well as the dope peddlers and users, the sex perverts and criminals, the pimps and prostitutes whom the managers reject or eject to protect the project population. All these are now concentrated in the slums that ring the projects, and areas that were perhaps barely tolerable before the impact of the projects are now quite intolerable. As we tear down the slums, those that remain inevitably become worse. And what after all are we to do with the large numbers of people emerging in modern society who are irresponsible and depraved? The worthy poor create no serious problem—nothing that money cannot solve. But the unworthy poor? No one has come up with the answers.

The structure of the Negro neighborhood and the Negro community means that the Negro middle class, in the city at any rate, rarely escapes from the near presence of the Negro poor, as well as of the depraved and the criminal. The middle-class neighborhoods border on the lower-class neighborhoods, and suffer from robberies and attacks, and the psychic assaults of a hundred awful sights. There are the additional frustrations of the difficulty of getting a taxi to take one home, the saturation of the area by police (whose numbers make it harder to escape a summons for a minor traffic violation). Within the city, it is not easy to escape, for few neighborhoods are pure. In the small suburban towns, with their high-cost houses, strict zoning regulations, informal controls for identification and ejection of the unwanted and the troublesome, the situation is different. There, if the colored middle-class family is successful in entering, it, like the white middle class, is protected from the pressure of the social problems thrown up by modern society, and most heavily concentrated among the colored. There it can enter into the community activities that encompass both races without being burdened by the problems, social and psychological, of the Negro poor. Its success in integration is there aided by the fact that it is successfully segregated from the Negro poor.

But in the city, no one can protect himself, for the city is free and open, and cannot fence itself off. There is thus scarcely a middle-class Negro area that does not know that close to it, on its borders and in measure in its midst, are all the problems that are so heavily concentrated in the Negro community.

This is the over-all picture, and yet, despite the housing shortage, the segregated new housing, the community problems, New York will very likely in the end be an integrated city—or rather something even better, a city where people find homes and neighborhoods according to income and taste, and where an area predominantly of one group represents its positive wishes rather than restricting prejudice.

We see the signs everywhere. In Manhattan, the western edges of the Harlem ghetto show not only the hardly integrated pattern of Negroes, mainland whites, and Puerto Ricans of different economic levels and different family patterns, close together but not mixing. There is also a large Negro element that is on the same level, economically and socially, as most of the old and new non-Puerto Rican white population. This group has older established people (as in the Morningside Gardens co-ops) and young couples and single young people, scattered through the brownstones and apartment houses. Here Negroes and whites do begin to form an interracial community that is rapidly being taken for granted, and one in which a mixed couple (the West Side is the area where they are most numerous) no longer leads to the turning of heads.

In the higher-income public projects of the City Housing Authority, the so-called middle-income housing, in co-ops like Morningside Gardens, in Title I projects like Park West Village, we find families living together, not in the indifference of forced association but in what are in large measure real communities, and where common tastes and backgrounds create interracial groups that are more than a self-conscious demonstration.

Up to now, there has been little Negro interest in co-ops, except for Morningside Gardens. But this is changing. Co-op housing is increasingly becoming the most popular answer to the problems of middle-income housing in the city. It will also draw less and less on the special type of person who is interested in the cooperative idea from an ideological point of view (that pool is becoming exhausted) and become attractive to large numbers. There is also now the model of Morningside Gardens as a successful co-op community. For all these reasons, the new co-ops have somewhat larger Negro contingents. The Negro often buys a house because he cannot get a good apartment. In the discrimination-free co-op housing, Negroes who prefer the city can find a way to stay that is not more expensive than suburban housing.

Even in Brooklyn, the Bronx, and Queens, we find, in addition to the dense all-Negro stretches, lower-income and middle-income, many individual families scattered through the most middle-class neighborhoods. Teachers, social workers, and other white-collar and professional workers may be found living on pleasant tree-lined streets with friendly neighbors.

In Greenwich Village, where few of the young bohemians who crowd the streets and coffee houses can afford to live, established Negro writers and artists live, again without meeting discrimination; and the younger and less successful find relatively easy access to the cold-water flats of the Lower East Side.

Even in suburbia, the stronghold of middle-class values, exclusiveness, and discriminatory behavior, we find the matter-of-course mixing of colored and white in many towns. In 1961 on Long Island and in Westchester and New Jersey, groups sprang up in a number of suburban communities—Great Neck was perhaps the leader—which attempted to break down their all-white character, to get sellers and real estate agents to show houses to Negroes, and to get Negroes to move in. Frances Levinson, of the New

York State Committee Against Discrimination in Housing, was active in trying to coordinate the work of these varied groups. In places like Great Neck and Scarsdale, though this is only the beginning, it was apparently easier to get houses that the owners were willing to sell to Negroes than to find Negroes who could afford such houses and who wanted to move to such communities. It is perfectly understandable that if one can afford a big house in suburbia, Mount Vernon and New Rochelle and some other towns that already have large middle-class Negro communities have more to offer. For some people and in some places, we are approaching the point where we may discover that discrimination is only the first crude barrier to integration, and that people are more complicated than either racists or those who deny the reality of race believe.

It is still an effort for a Negro individual or family to live in a non-Negro neighborhood, but it is an effort that it is no longer exceptional; we can scarcely guess at the numbers who live in all the situations we have described. These situations in which white and colored live together without tension and without problems, and perhaps even comfortably enough with each other to begin finally to appreciate their real differences, mark the course of the future in New York. The only question is, how fast, and against how much resistance.

LEADERSHIP, POLITICS, INTERGROUP RELATIONS

WHATEVER THE SITUATION IN OTHER COMMUNITIES, THE Negroes of Harlem and other New York communities are deeply involved in politics. They register and vote in substantial proportions, their newspapers keep up a continual flow of political news, they are active in club membership and in the support of political leaders. Clearly politics is seen as an area in which to advance the interests of the individual and the group.[55]

What do Negroes want out of politics? What everyone else wants: jobs, on all levels from the most humble to the highest; recognition and prestige; and the advancement of group interests.

It is perfectly clear on the national level
what policies are necessary to advance group interests. But
New York is not Washington and not the South. There is
no insuperable problem in getting almost any law or policy
against discrimination, in almost any area, adopted, and in
getting it enforced. The issue is, will it really be helpful?

If it is a matter of getting the right to regis-
ter and vote, or integrating the restaurants, political activity
can be clear, direct, and effective. But there are no such
simple political objectives left for Negroes in New York.
There are already laws against discrimination in employment and housing, and while their administration can undoubtedly be improved, the agencies that enforce them (the
City Commission on Human Rights and the State Commission for Human Rights) have Negro heads or high
officials and Negro staff members—there is not much more
to be done along this line. The Board of Education actively
tries to integrate the schools. There is no discrimination in
higher education. There is probably no discrimination in
restaurants and hotels. It is hard to see how it could be
maintained in the face of the influx of African emissaries
and officials. The Committe on Civil Rights in Manhattan
found in a sampling of East Side restaurants in 1950 that
more than two-fifths were discriminating. It rechecked in
1952, and discrimination had dropped to 16 per cent. Since
1953 it has had only five reports of discrimination, and it
now considers this problem settled, and the main problem
to be housing.[56]

In New York City, it seems, there are no
easy problems any more, or easy solutions. The improvement of the Negro economic position requires such complex
and far-flung operations that it is hard to see how it can be
made a simple political issue. It involves such matters as
retraining the unskilled, better education all along the line,
stronger motivation so that people will take advantage of
retraining and education opportunities, changing the structure of New York's economy, changing the role of the
unions. Even if New York were to adopt a minimum wage
of $1.50 an hour, the effect might well be to increase the
level of unemployment among Negroes to a Midwest level
rather than to improve their general economic situation.

In housing, as in wages and employment, the need is for radical policies that make improvement in the situation in general, and these are not particularly attractive to Negro political leaders in the city (or any others, for that matter). They do not urge that low-cost and other government-supported housing be restricted to vacant land sites, which is the one sure way of increasing the over-all supply of low-cost housing in the city. Such a policy would mean that they preside over areas of decaying slums while their supporters escape to greener fields. Instead one finds the popular program of attacking landlords for inadequacy of maintenance, proposing ever harsher measures to enforce good maintenance, demanding more frequent and more severe inspections by city agencies. These are worthwhile policies, but to concentrate on inspecting a declining and aging stock of low-cost housing does little to increase it, or to deal with the conditions that make it possible for landlords to get high rents for crumbling apartments. The kind of political courage that would be involved in tracing out the real impact of rent control on different groups in the city is simply not heard of in American politics.

In effect, there is little public discussion among those active in city politics of *policies,* except in response to the most blatant scandals. There is certainly no more than this low average of discussion among Negro political leaders; there is probably less.

In recent years the emphasis has been on political jobs. All good things are scarce and involve conflicts, and on the question of the proportion of jobs in city elective and appointive posts held by Negroes we find rancor and bitterness, and strains on old political alliances and allegiances. There is nothing really new here—every new group tries to get the nominations and jobs it feels it is entitled to, and these are always more than the older groups, which fought their way up to a certain proportion of jobs and nominations in the past, feel the new group has a right to.

But who is to determine what is the "right" proportion? Congressman Powell in 1960 demanded that Negroes should get 21 per cent of the jobs in a Democratic city administration, since 21 per cent of the enrolled Democrats in Manhattan are Negro.[57] He said they held only 6 per cent of high political posts—Commissionerships, board memberships, judgeships. Even so, Negroes are doing better at getting political jobs in New York than anywhere else in the country.

James Q. Wilson writes:

> Chicago, having about 750,000 to 850,000 Negroes, has only three Negro judges. . . . New York, having about 1,000,000 Negroes, has seventeen judges, two Supreme Court Justices, one General Sessions Judge, four City Magistrates, three Domestic Relations Court Judges, six Municipal Court Judges, and one City Court Judge. [This comes to just about 6 per cent of the judicial offices in the city.] In addition, in New York City (unlike Chicago) many Negroes hold administrative positions at the Cabinet and sub-Cabinet level.[58]

Whatever the strains in politics, the clubs and committees form one of the most important arenas in which the people of different groups meet and test each other's feelings and capacities and powers. New York's politics serves much more as such a meeting ground than its business, certainly more than its formal social life, and probably as much as its cultural life. New York has good race relations, and it has been helped in this by a number of factors. The city does not have politically powerful neighborhood homeowning groups, electing their representatives to the city councils to fight the spread of the Negro community and the tax-supported expansion of social services. In any case, the City Council in New York is weak. It is the Board of Estimate, dominated by officials elected by the entire city electorate, and the mayor, who wield effective power—and these are far more susceptible to the citywide Negro vote. The important role of culture in the city means that talent and genius have a status which transcends group membership and which is not found as commonly in other American cities. And then the remarkably varied group life all through the city's history means that all the groups have been somewhat mellowed in their attitudes toward other groups, and that New York's Irish and Italians are probably somewhat more tolerant in their outlook than Irish and Italian groups in other cities. This mellowness is aided by the large proportion of Jews, who traditionally (and probably because of their traditional lack of power) have learned to eschew violence and favor negotiation and conciliation and live-and-let-live policies.[59]

And yet, within this context of over-all good relations, it is just in relations with the Jews, despite their generally liberal outlook, nonviolent temperament, and their similar experience as a minority facing problems of discrimination, that an observable level of tension has recently developed.[60] It would be easy to exaggerate this tension. Sensitive, just as the Negroes are, and also timid and vulnerable, Jews inflate small incidents. Then, contributing to our awareness of this tension, there is the fact that the Jewish community supports (as Italians and Irish do not) professional organizations devoted to good intergroup relations. This means that any sign of tension immediately becomes the focus of specialized professional concern (sometimes from several different Jewish groups) and is rapidly brought to the attention of leaders in the Jewish and Negro groups, and appropriate governmental agencies—SCAD, COIR, the police, the mayor's office, the governor perhaps. So it is easy to exaggerate the degree of tension that exists between Negroes and Jews. And yet it exists; its existence at all is paradoxical; and since it also involves to some extent the somewhat frayed relationship of the Negroes to political liberalism in general, it is worth examining.

To begin with, anti-Jewish feeling is endemic among Negroes (as Professor Kenneth Clark and novelist James Baldwin have at different times observed in the Jewish magazine *Commentary*[61]) because the Negroes keep bumping into the Jews in front and ahead of them. Expanding into Jewish neighborhoods in Manhattan, the Bronx, and Brooklyn (less so in Queens), Negroes become the customers of the many Jewish shopkeepers that have remained behind. They become the tenants of the Jewish owners of property. Whatever the personal qualities of shopkeepers and landlords, Negroes are thus often in contact with Jews who are making a living from them. The tension between landlord and tenant in New York, and particularly landlord and low-income tenant, is in any case extreme, and it is understandable that it takes very little for it to become tinged with anti-Semitic feeling.

But in addition to this large range of unfortunate contacts, the Negro also meets the Jew as an employer. This is likely in a city that is one-quarter Jewish; the likelihood is increased because of the heavy Jewish concentration in the city's small manufacturing. In garment factories, in small plants assembling electrical products, toys and novelties, plastic products, and the like, the Negro operative in low-wage jobs is likely to find he has a Jewish employer. Once again, here is a situation in which a natural conflict of interests can be interpreted in group terms, and is likely to contribute to the strengthening of traditional stereotypes of Jews to boot. The Negro is even likely to find, in many of the New York industries in which he is employed, that the union has a Jewish leadership and Jewish staff, and he resents this. Thus, in the low-wage laundry industry a Negro and Puerto Rican working force is represented by a union whose top leadership is Jewish. The worker does not know, nor perhaps is it relevant, that these men may have built this union at great sacrifice twenty and thirty years before. All he knows is where his dues are going, and who is on the payroll.

There is one particular form of Negro-Jewish conflict which is too important not to mention, trivial as it may appear, and that is the large number of Negro women engaged in domestic labor for Jewish housewives. Many of these contacts have produced good relationships, but they have also led to the feelings of exploitation and resentment that are almost inevitable in the master-servant relationship in a democratic society. One can hazard the guess, too, that the democratic ethos of Jewish life—which explains why Jewish waiters are the worst in New York— probably also helps to make many Jewish women poor employers of domestic help. The democratic camaraderie of the Jewish housewife with her Negro servant, alternating with the uncomfortable haughtiness of someone not used to a servant, might both tend to create more resentment than the steady formal relationship maintained by housewives with a longer tradition in the use of domestic help.

Perhaps, too, the liberal Jewish housewife feels guilty in relationship to her Negro servant, and this, too, might lead to the complementary feeling that the guilt is justified. In any case, it is interesting that one study which has gone into this matter shows a stronger feeling of anti-Semitism among Negro women than Negro men, and the authors suggest that this master-servant relationship may be the cause.[62]

Even the middle-class Negro often meets the Jew in a situation in which one is formally an inferior, the other formally a superior. As Negroes move into the governmental agencies, which are one of the most important areas of employment for the upwardly mobile, they come into contact with all the groups that have preceded them. But in particular they come into contact with the group that got there before them—Jews, who in the 1930's entered government service in large numbers. This means that the Negro schoolteacher now often works under a Jewish principal, that the Negro social worker very often has a Jewish supervisor. (The top social worker, James Dumpson, Commissioner of Social Welfare, is a Negro.) On the whole, these relationships between teachers and social workers, whose training and work tend to develop a high degree of tolerance and insight, have been productive of some of the healthiest and most satisfying interracial relationships that one may find anywhere. Nevertheless, the relationship between inferior and superior in a hierarchy is inevitably tension-producing, and the conflict between different people is always subject to interpretation in group terms.

Thus, the dissatisfaction over social services for Negroes, and in particular the fact that they are run by whites and do not give sufficient jobs to Negroes, often takes the form of complaints against Jews and Jewish agencies, an inevitable by-product of the distribution of wealth, teachers, doctors, and social workers in the city.

For example: Under a banner headline, "They Let Them Die," the *Amsterdam News* reported on February 4, 1961: "Dr. Raphael Gamso, the new superintendent of Harlem Hospital, admitted to the *Amsterdam News* that he ignored Dr. Aubrey Maynard, director of surgery, when he permitted resident doctors from Mt. Sinai to enter Harlem Hospital and pick out a number of Negro patients whom they carried off to Mt. Sinai for experimentation." (What actually happened was that service at the city Harlem Hospital almost collapsed as a result of a shortage of physicians, and Mt. Sinai, a Jewish voluntary hospital, agreed to take a number of cases. It seems to have selected, over Dr. Maynard's protest, some of the more interesting ones.)

A month later the *Amsterdam News* attacked the Higher Horizons program, and in particular, its director, Daniel Schreiber, and its reporter wrote: "While the program experiments with Negro children there is a dearth of Negro teachers connected with the program, particularly at the administrative or policy making level" (*Amsterdam News*, March 4, 1961).

Disproportion in wealth and power introduces a hazardous element into the best relationships. Our Latin American neighbors, who know us so well and in so many ways, seem capable of turning in the twinkling of an eye from friends to enemies. So, too, in the case of Negro-Jewish relationships. The good relationships cannot help but be affected by the disproportion in power, whatever the good will on both sides. Just as in underdeveloped countries governments insist that the foreign investor take on a certain proportion of native employees, so have the political organizations of Harlem insisted that the Jewish storekeeper have Negro employees, and so, too, they now demand that he use Negro salesmen. They lack only the ultimate power of expropriation, but if they did, Jewish and other white business might fare as badly in Harlem as the American investments in Mexican oil, or in Cuba.

We can press our colonial analogy a bit further. For, if the Jews, in an earlier parallel to colonialism, may be seen as exploiters, they are also, paralleling the later development of colonialism, those who help and assist the deprived group. This role is if anything more exasperating than the former one. Negroes know that in New York Jews play a disproportionate role in pushing for the kind of policies that help Negroes. It is true that these policies—fair employment practices, fair educational practices, fair renting practices—had their origin on the agenda of Jewish organizations at a time when they were as important for

Jews as they were for Negroes; but the fact is that as times changed, as they became more definitely policies in which Jewish self-interest was less clearly involved, Jewish organizations, with their rich resources in money, staff, and contacts, continued to press for them. Very often Negroes were drawn into these activities. And while they played an important role, the (largely Jewish) liberal organizations pushing for these policies soon became aware of the very different levels of participation, organization, and money-raising capacity in the two communities. James Wilson tells the story of the most effective of these organizations which had their origin in the activities of Jewish liberal civil rights agencies:

> The fight for an open occupancy ordinance in New York City [the bill banning discrimination in housing] was led by the New York State Committee Against Discrimination in Housing (NYSCDH). . . . It was created largely at the instigation of the leading Jewish organizations in New York in 1949 after the failure of a court attack on the Stuyvesant Town anti-Negro policies. . . . Four major state laws and two New York City ordinances were passed in large part due to the efforts of this and related organizations. White (primarily Jewish) groups have been the most important single factor in the Committee. From the first, an effort was made to involve Negroes in its work, and a sizeable number of prominent Negroes have played important roles and occupied top positions. Most of this Negro support has come from the ranks of Negro professionals who are officers or executives of other organizations (public and private) with an interest in . . . housing. . . .
> Some important white leaders of the Committee, however, . . . wish in addition for Negro grass-roots support.[63]

Those who work together in such organizations represent part of that alliance of liberal and minority forces which has played such an important role in the city for thirty years. But on the other side there are the grass-roots elements who are relatively distant from such activities, and the press and political leaders who talk to them, and it is as easy to arouse resentment and prejudice against a more advantaged group that is being helpful, particularly if there are other contributing factors, as against another that is more distant, more powerful, and more hostile.

Finally, there is, and again the colonial analogy is helpful, the central problem of political representation. Jewish (and of course non-Jewish, too) political leaders who have for years represented neighborhoods that have changed to Negro and Puerto Rican occupancy have discovered that regardless of their votes in civil rights and other issues, the Negroes want the job for themselves.

It is against this background that the exposure in 1960 of Borough President Hulan Jack's connection with a (Jewish) real estate developer, and his trial for accepting a financial favor from him, was particularly exasperating. For it so happened that it was the crusading *New York Post* that uncovered this relationship in the course of a long-extended investigation into public policies affecting housing. The *New York Post* had a Jewish publisher, a Jewish editor, and a large Jewish readership. It is also true it has the most distinguished Negro reporter in the city, it had the only Negro columnist (on a non-Negro newspaper), and a large Negro readership. But all this did not matter.[64] The *Post* became the villain of the case, of what was referred to darkly as the "plot" to drive Negroes from public life and it was implied, too, that it was a liberal and Jewish plot—in view of the prevailing political outlooks in New York, a Jewish plot would have to be a liberal plot, and vice versa. Meanwhile, about the same time the long-delayed trial of Adam Clayton Powell for income tax evasion came up. Even though Jews had little to do with this, and even liberals had little to do with it, the threat to the top elective jobs which Negroes held touched such sensitive spots that this was irrationally also considered part of the Jewish and liberal betrayal of the Negro.

And indeed, there is a strong element of rationality in the irrational amalgam. For whatever the attitudes of liberals on civil rights, in New York City they are tied up with good government forces (represented best by the Jewish-owned *New York Times*), and a large part of the Negro community will not feel very sympathetic toward those who search out every example of financial gain from public office. While no leader in the group will openly favor illegal gain, it may seem unfair to Negroes that their representatives in public office do not get the gains from it that members of other groups have in the past. Alas, times have changed, and it is harder and harder to make anything from public office. In any case, whatever some Negroes thought privately about Hulan Jack's dealings with Unger, hardly a voice was raised against him. Everyone supported him—even the ministers.[65]

Now admittedly everything we have to say to explain Negro-Jewish relations is also true (to some extent) of Italian-Negro and Irish-Negro relations. And yet there is less feeling expressed against the Irish and Italians. Perhaps for many Negroes, subconsciously, a bit of anti-Jewish feeling helps make them feel more completely American, a part of the majority group.[66] There are probably other irrational bases for this anti-Jewish feeling—anti-Semitism is a complicated thing—and yet the special tie-up of Jews with liberalism is certainly important.

But political issues, as well as personalities, symbols, and the fate of private attempts at gain, do play a role in the developing tension between Negroes and liberals. Despite the fact that the battle over civil rights is a regular occasion for Northern liberals to match themselves against Southern Democrats at national political conventions, Negroes cannot help feeling that liberals do not quite do enough. The liberals are part of the same party that includes the South (as well as most of the New York Negro voters) and are always open to the charge of holding back in the fight for civil-rights bills. How much of one's time and influence should one devote to this issue? How much else should one let go? From the Negro point of view, whatever time and effort one devotes are hardly enough. What this means then is a steady strain between the liberal and the Negro which can often become quite bitter.

The bill of complaint then is that the liberals frame the Negroes, they don't put up enough of them or give them enough recognition, they don't fight hard enough for civil rights—in fact, they hypocritically fight just hard enough to get Negro votes. And the reaction has been a new rise of Negro exclusivism and nationalism: the feeling that Negroes have to go it alone and should trust no one but themselves, and the idea that any disinterested common action with democratic-minded whites for public policies to improve the condition of Negroes is an illusion.

An extremist element has been a permanent part of Northern Negro life since the 1920's; it has recently rapidly increased in strength, stimulated by frustration over the South and the rise of independent African states. The Nation of Islam (Black Muslims) and similar groups are not likely, in view of the much higher level of education and sophistication among Negroes today, to be anywhere nearly as successful as Marcus Garvey was in the 1920's. More important, however, is the adoption of this exclusivist feeling by a wide range of Negro leaders, publicists, and intellectuals. This development has been as rapid and sudden as the leap in the number of independent states in Africa—and the two phenomena are not unrelated. The impact of twenty independent Negro states, all with representatives at the U.N. in New York, is already striking, and while some of the Africans are patronizing the beauty parlors of Harlem, many American Negroes, going the other way, are discovering that *they* can leave their hair unstraightened. There is quite a difference between the subtle and complicated early essays of James Baldwin on the relationship of Negroes to America, and his writing in 1961— scarcely less subtle, but envisaging the possibility of a much more radical divorce of the Negroes from white America than he had earlier contemplated. There is an even sharper difference between the subtle and somewhat amused treatment of African nationalism in Lorraine Hansberry's play, *Raisin in the Sun,* and the passion of her advocacy of African (and American Negro) nationalism in 1961.[67]

There are obviously many types of exclusivism, and even so, this is only one part of the spectrum of opinion to be found among Negro leaders. A. Philip Randolph's American Negro Labor Council, organized in 1960, was established primarily to exert pressure on a labor movement from which he does not wish, if possible, to isolate himself. The leaders of the National Urban League and the NAACP and CORE resist the exclusivist trend and still include many whites, though the proportion of whites in leadership and on the staffs declines as men of ability and training in the Negro community grow more abundant. These organizations still represent the old Negro–liberal alliance. The local NAACP branches in New York, and elsewhere, include few whites and are far more exclusivist in their outlook. And the gap between them and the new nationalist groups is not great.

It is to this grass-roots nationalism and exclusivism that Adam Clayton Powell and the *Amsterdam News* appeal. Here, when an attack is made on liberal allies, the assumption is that they are not allies at all but enemies. What the future of this exclusivist outlook and feeling will be, it is hard to say. But it does not seem that it can be more than a temporary tendency. No group or interest gets very far alone in American politics. Particularly in New York City, there are too many groups, too many interests, for anyone to adopt the attitude that its strength, its numbers, require little cooperation with and accommodation to others. Whatever the psychological satisfactions of the present mood, it is doubtful that it is the way to get gains for the Negro community, in jobs, in influence, in prestige, or in practical policies. One can reject white standards of beauty, one can devote oneself to the study of African history and culture, one may support the policies of African states. There will be more and more of this, and this is all to the good. But Africa and nationalism and exclusivism will have as little to do with changing the conditions of American Negro life as Israel and Zionism have to do with the conditions of American Jewish life. Emigration is only for the few. The problems are here, and they must be solved here, and the main impact of the nationalist mood (sincere and passionately felt as it is) will be to serve more flexible politicians and leaders in getting gains and concessions.

We have indicated often enough our feeling that Negro communal organization is weak, and insufficient to make much impact on the great needs of the poorer and disorganized part of the community. As Oscar Handlin wrote in his study of Negroes and Puerto Ricans in New York:

. . . the ability [of new groups] to develop an adjustment that would assure the individuals involved a healthy creative life depended both on the nature of the hurdles to be surmounted and on the resources available for doing so. The hardships of the Negroes and Puerto Ricans arise from the fact that the hurdles are unusually high and the resources unusually meager.[68]

One must read the Negro New York newspaper, with its regular appeals to the community to raise pitifully small sums for the local Y or other institutions, to discover how fantastically difficult it is to raise money in the Negro community. Handlin points out that when Sydenham Hospital was integrated, it also shifted from a voluntary to a municipal hospital.[69] Two sets of institutions manage to raise money: those fighting segregation and for equal rights (NAACP, NUL, CORE), though they raise less than they need, and much of that comes from whites; and the Negro churches.

In the Negro communities of New York, as elsewhere in the country, it is difficult to underestimate the importance of the Negro churches. When one says "Negro church," it is possible the image of the storefront sect, stomping and hollering, taking outlandish names, and twisting the common heritage into strange forms, still comes to the mind of many whites. It is not these churches that we speak of, though they of course exist, are important in the lives of the people involved, and are also of some weight in politics. We have in mind the large institutional churches, in well-equipped buildings, with various group activities, with associated social services, with a large membership and a prominent minister. These churches, which elsewhere in America, for most groups, and for most vital areas of concern, are fifth wheels, are in colored America, and in colored New York, in the center of things. And they play a role in politics that the churches of no other group can aspire to, or would dare to.

It is not unimportant that Adam Clayton Powell, New York's first Negro Congressman, is a minister; that Gardner Taylor, the only Negro member of the New York Board of Education in 1960, was also a minister—and that both men lead particularly large churches (Baptist), claiming 10,000 members. It is also not without significance that Milton Galamison, former head of the NAACP of

Brooklyn and one of the most prominent figures in the fight to "desegregate" schools, is also a minister of a large church (Presbyterian). James H. Robinson of the Presbyterian Church of the Master ran for borough president on the Liberal Party ticket and was spoken of as a successor to Hulan Jack. There are other ministers who play some role in politics, and the New York Negro minister is in general far less cautious in indicating his preferences from the pulpit than the white minister.

The Negro newspapers regularly devote a great deal of space to church activities and report on the politics of the national denominations in the greatest detail. In 1960 and 1961 there was a bitter struggle going on in the National Baptist Convention for leadership between Gardner Taylor of New York and J. H. Jackson of Chicago. It was headline news in the Negro press. (It is not untypical of Negro church politics that after a wild convention in 1960 the matter ended up in court—but the court refused to take jurisdiction.) This battle involved the fundamental question of the attitude of the church to the new militancy of Negroes in South and North. But the main point to notice is that it is not often that an issue that is as central as this to a group becomes the basis of struggle in white denominations. (When J. H. Jackson was victorious in 1961, one of his first steps was to remove Martin Luther King from a position in the Baptist organization.)

We have magnificent descriptions of the old fundamentalist storefront church in literature (for example, James Baldwin's *Go Tell It on the Mountain*), and we have good sociological descriptions of these churches. No one has yet described the Negro middle-class churches which seem often to make up for the loss of fundamentalist fervor by becoming as heatedly involved in the secular political struggles that affect Negroes. It is this kind of church that is rapidly becoming the dominant type of church. We find, as part of the middle-class development among Negroes, that the same social changes that have made the city church a problem for white Protestants may begin to make it a problem for Negroes. Members are beginning to move away from the areas in which the big churches are located to the suburbs; the church becomes to some degree the institution of an absentee membership; and new ethnic elements move into the neighborhood around the church, with no relationship to it. And just as the white churches long ago had to consider what to do as their neighborhoods changed—and the majority sold out and followed the membership, with a few remaining to serve a peculiar function as city churches —so we find some Negro churches considering the problem of a new Puerto Rican group around its doors. Here and there, in Brooklyn and the Bronx, Negro ministers are beginning to think in terms of a mission to the Puerto Ricans, just as some white churches are finally beginning to think in terms of a mission to the surrounding Negroes. And just as conservative members of the white Protestant churches find it hard to think in terms of a universal church, open to all, so do some Negroes, used to the comfortable community church, the only institution that is entirely theirs, find it hard to envisage bringing in Puerto Ricans.

But the mere fact that Negro churches must begin to think in these terms shows to what an extent they have become part of American Protestantism, participating in its intellectual and theological development and its problems. (Gardner Taylor has served as head of the Protestant Council of New York; J. Archie Hargraves, minister of Brooklyn's Nazarene Congregational Church, became secretary of the Board of Home Missions of the Congregational Christian Church in 1961.) Since the same factors affect them that long ago made their impact on white Protestants, one may see the signs of the time when secularization and specialization will affect the Negro churches, as they affect the older Protestant denominations, and when these churches will be less flamboyant, but also very likely less influential. The day will come in the Negro church when the minister is not wealthier than his parishioners, and at that time, the minister will not wield the influence that he does today.

Interestingly enough, even the development of Elijah Muhammed's Temples of Islam suggests the change in Negro religion and politics. It does not have the flamboyance of either Marcus Garvey or Father Divine. It emphasizes traditional virtues, as do all storefront churches (no smoking, drinking, women), but less because these are sinful than because by saving his money and devoting himself to his business the Negro may make himself wealthy and successful. This is indeed a nationalist and racist movement. But it is surprising how much of Horatio Alger there is in it, too—and that reflects a great change in the Negro community. Elijah Muhammed's young men remind some people of fascists, and yet they wear dark business suits and are proud of their self-restraint and their discipline. The Temple of Islam service, an admirer of the movement tells us, is sober and restrained—only hand-clapping greets a point well made. Thus, even the most extreme of present-day Negro movements suggests the extent of the shift to middle-class patterns, and the power they now possess.

In a community of a million people, one can see pretty much what one wants, and this is as true for Negroes as for any other group. One can see the large mass of problems that are high up on the agenda of city government and civic groups—crime, delinquency, the breakdown of family responsibility. And one can see the increasing numbers who achieve middle-class status, and for whom the only problems are those created by the prejudiced and discriminatory behavior of others. One can see demagogic self-serving leaders in politics and church and civic activity, incapable of seeing any problems except those created by the white man; and one can see an increasing body of competent leaders, very often professionals on the staffs of private and public agencies, quite up to facing directly and squarely the problems of the group and who yet give no ground in their insistence on equality. One can see the huge ghetto concentrations, and one can see the ever larger areas of integration in work, civic activity, politics, housing. One can dole out an even-handed justice, saying, on the one hand there is this, on the other, that, and it is true among a million people there will be enough examples for any argument. And yet, how do we cast the final balance, how do we envisage the future? Here there are no agreed-on scales, there is only the judgment of those who try to see the whole picture, in the light of past history, and to discern future trends. Our own judgment is that, in the North, a new phase in Negro leadership must begin. The era of the leaders who sought "accommodation" to an exploitative white world has come to an end everywhere, even in the South. The era of the leaders of "protest" has been in full swing in New York for a good twenty-five years, though it has only recently arrived in the South. Its achievements in the city have been great, but it is now entering an era of diminishing returns. And because there are as a matter of fact few additional gains to be made in New York City by protest, the protest leadership shows a tendency to become irrational, shrill, and ineffective. (The situation in other cities—for example, Chicago—and in the South is entirely different.)

But the worst of it is that important tasks, necessary ones on the agenda of American Negroes, are shirked and ignored. These are tasks that conceivably no one but Negroes can do. It is probable that no investment of public and private agencies on delinquency and crime-prevention programs will equal the return from an investment by Negro-led and Negro-financed agencies. It is probable that no offensive on the public school system to improve the educational results among Negroes will equal what may be gained from an equivalent investment by Negro-led and Negro-financed groups, and an increase in the numbers of Negro teachers and principals. It is possible that no effort to change the patterns of the Negro lower-class family will be effective at a time when the white family is in disorder, when strong families of whatever kind, native and ethnic, show signs of disintegration; but if anything can be done, it is likely that Negro agencies will be far more effective than public agencies and those of white Protestants.

Succeeding the period of accommodation, then, and the period of protest, one can detect the need for a period of self-examination and self-help, in which the increasing income and resources of leadership of the group are turned inwards. And already a few voices are raised to make just this point. This is the argument that John H. Johnson, publisher of *Ebony* and *Jet,* suggested at the 1960 Convention of the National Urban League.[70] (*Ebony*, it should be pointed out, is itself rather more self-help oriented than the protest-rooted Negro newspapers, and its circulation in New York is probably greater than that of the local New York weekly Negro community newspaper, the *Amsterdam News*.) This is the argument of Carl T. Rowan, the distinguished Negro reporter, in an article in the *Saturday Evening Post*.[71]

Everywhere in America the argument can be met by the counterargument—let the white world reform itself first. Even in New York one can say this, and most Negro leadership does; but the question is: whatever the origins of the burden, on whose shoulders does it fall, and how can it best be overcome?

the Puerto Ricans

IF SOMEONE TWENTY-FIVE YEARS AGO HAD LOOKED AROUND AT the potential sources of new immigration to New York City, his eye might well have fallen on Puerto Rico: he would also have concluded that the Puerto Ricans, if they were potential migrants, would have a very hard time adapting to New York City and indeed might well be considered the migrants least likely to succeed.

Puerto Rico in the middle 1930's, after thirty-five years of American administration, was a scene of almost unrelieved misery. Rexford Tugwell, the American governor of the island during the early forties, titled his big book on Puerto Rico *The Stricken Land.* Its 3,435 square miles—a tiny area—held a population of one and three-quarter millions. Its death rate had been reduced from the very high figure of about 30 per thousand at the time of the American occupation at the end of the nineteenth century to about 20 per thousand; but its birth rate remained among

86

the highest in the world, and the population grew rapidly. The island lived off a cash crop—sugar—that had collapsed with the depression; it had almost no industry; in any case even in the best of times the agricultural workers who made up the majority of the population lived under incredibly primitive conditions that some observers have described as no better than were to be seen in the villages of India or China. Sanitary facilities were primitive; shoes were rarely worn in the country districts; the ground was infested with sewage and parasites and so, too, was the population; and a prevalent malnutrition produced a stunting of growth and susceptibility to a wide range of diseases. The details of the infant mortality rate, death rates from various causes, all showed the effects of a grinding poverty that is scarcely imaginable in contemporary industrial countries. Most of the population was unemployed and underemployed and suffered from hunger.

It is true there was something of a Puerto Rican upper class, which lived at the same level as the rich in all countries. This tiny upper class had never given much signs of energetic leadership or substantial ability. Puerto Rico had been a neglected part of the Spanish colonial system. It had been somewhat less neglected by the Americans, but here inconsistency in policies effectively prevented occasional good intentions from making their full impact felt. Illiteracy had been reduced from 83 per cent in 1898 to 31 per cent in 1940; the proportion of children attending school had been greatly increased; but shifting policies as to whether to teach in English or Spanish, and at what levels to introduce which language, led to a relatively ineffective education. If Puerto Ricans were not illiterate in both languages, it is certainly true that on the whole they learned English poorly, and at the same time the Spanish cultural heritage was transmitted inadequately.

The kind of economic situation that prevailed in Puerto Rico was of course the situation of most of the world, and indeed it was often pointed out that the economic situation of Puerto Rico was better than that of Latin America in general, even in the middle 1930's. But rural poverty of the kind that prevailed on the island is often relieved by two considerations: first, the existence of a

network of culture, religion, art, custom that gives strength
and grace and meaning to a life of hardship; and second,
the existence of a strong family system that again enhances
life. And both a rich culture and a strong family system, in
addition to their immediate rewards, are often the basis
for an improvement in life. The net of culture keeps up
pride and encourages effort; the strong family serves to
organize and channel resources in new situations.

In both these aspects Puerto Rico was sadly
defective. It was weak in folk arts, unsure in its cultural
traditions, without a powerful faith. Folk arts existed to a
limited extent: there was a tradition of folk and dance
music, and a great love of dancing and singing. Indian
culture was still meaningful in Mexico and Peru, Afro-
American culture in Brazil and Haiti. But Puerto Rican
Indians had long before been absorbed into the population,
and its large African population of former slaves, almost
one-half of the total population in the middle 1860's, had
not retained the rich array of African cultural survivals
that enlivened other parts of the Caribbean. Even Puerto
Rican Spiritualism, while it owed something to traits bor-
rowed from Haiti and Cuba (and thus indirectly from
Africa), seemed to be based more directly on the works of a
nineteenth-century French writer on occult matters.[1] The
great Spanish cultural tradition to which Puerto Rico was
linked also led a pale existence there. The Catholic Church,
the formal religion of most of the population, reflected the
weaknesses of the Church throughout much of Latin America: there was a tiny clergy (Puerto Rico has one priest for
7,000 Catholics, New York has one for 750),[2] in large measure foreign, and not closely attached to the national ambitions of the people or their daily life. The Church was seen
as something for the rich—one could not expect that if the
people migrated, their priests would follow them, as did the
spiritual leaders of the many streams of European immigrants to this country. And indeed, they did not. There was
a strong Protestant group, which was quite different in
character, but it affected only 15 per cent of the population.

Nor was there much strength in the Puerto
Rican family. In some ways, it was similar to the family
type of peasant Europe, patriarchal and authoritarian, the

man reigning as absolute despot, demanding obedience and respect from wife and children. And yet, this was not the family of the Polish or South Italian peasant. The major difference was the wide extent of consensual or common-law marriage; more than one-quarter of the marriages were of this type, and as a result about one-third of the births were formally illegitimate. The evaluation of the consensual marriage form is a difficult thing—was it only the consequence of the distance between the Church and the people, the absence of priests, the expense of church ceremonies and formal weddings? This is the explanation that is often given. Yet consensual marriage also reflected an instability in the marriage form. The breakup of consensual marriage was common. More serious for the strength of the family were the widespread existence and acceptance, in legal and consensual marriage, of concubinage and sexual adventurism on the part of the men, which meant that children often grew up in confused family settings, and which introduced a strain between husbands and wives. Children were loved in Puerto Rico—this was fortunate since there were so many. And yet many observers believed that their mothers often loved them to the point of overprotection to make up for neglect by their husbands.[3]

Both the European peasant and the Puerto Rican jealously guarded the virginity of the female children, and superstitiously kept them apart from men. But while the European peasant could often then arrange the marriage of his virginal daughter or of his son so as to enhance his property situation, marriage in Puerto Rico was more typically a matter of an early escape of the young daughter with a man whom her parents had not chosen and whom she herself scarcely knew. Marriage at the age of 13 and 14 was not uncommon. Indeed, a random sample of the island's population in 1947–1948 showed that 6 per cent of the married women had been married at 14 or earlier, a fifth had been married at the ages of 15 or 16, a quarter at the ages of 17 and 18, another fifth at the age of 19 or 20— seven out of ten were married before 21![4] This, combined with the feeling that a man and woman married or living together should have children as soon as possible, meant a very early induction into childbearing on the part of women, an early induction into responsibility for many children on the part of men. Adolescence did not exist for most Puerto Ricans, who moved directly from childhood to adult responsibility.

And yet, the family, despite these weaknesses, was perhaps one of the stronger elements in the Puerto Rican situation. Men might have children with a number of women, but they took responsibility for all of them. There was a relatively high degree of breakup of marriage (for a peasant culture), and yet there were always places in families for the children. The institution of the godparents, the *compadre* and *comadre* who were "co-parents" for each child, meant that a second set of parents stood ready to take over if the first was overburdened with too many children, too many woes, or was broken up by death or desertion. Children were overprotected, it seems true, but they were not resented and neglected; and perhaps the second is worse than the first.

But in competition with the more tightly knit and better integrated family systems of, say, Chinese and Japanese peasants, the Puerto Ricans did badly. In Hawaii, where at different times Chinese, Japanese, and Puerto Ricans had been imported to work on the plantations, the Chinese and Japanese rapidly moved out of the plantations, into the cities and into better-paying occupations, achieving positions of such high prestige that their descendants now sit in Congress. There were few Puerto Ricans, but they often left the plantation only to fall into dependency in the cities. In 1930, they showed the highest rate of juvenile delinquency of any of Hawaii's many ethnic groups; the highest proportion on relief. "The Puerto Ricans," an authority reported, "have constituted an exceptionally heavy charge on the community, while the Japanese and Chinese have required the least." [5]

There was no reason to think the Puerto Rican would make a better adjustment than this in the more demanding and less tolerant atmosphere of the New York City of the thirties. And indeed, he did not. When Lawrence R. Chenault made the first book-length study of New York Puerto Ricans in the mid-1930's, there were 45,-000 migrants from Puerto Rico in the city, and he found that they were heavily overrepresented on the relief rolls. As early as 1930 a social worker at a meeting of the National Conference of Catholic Charities stated that the Puerto Rican family was the biggest social work problem in New York at the time.[6] Nothing—in education, in work experience, work training, or work discipline, in family attitudes, in physical health—gave the Puerto Rican migrant an advantage in New York City.

Against this background, one might have expected massive Puerto Rican migration to New York to be a disaster. It is not, and part of the reason why not is the transformation of the island itself, a transformation so startling, and so little heralded by anything in Puerto Rico's earlier history that it is reasonable for two books on Puerto Rico published in 1960 to bear the titles *Puerto Rico: Land of Wonders* and *Puerto Rico: Success Story*.[7] New York must be as grateful to the leader of this transformation, Luis Muñoz Marin, as the people of Puerto Rico itself: for the great advances in education, health, self-respect, work capacity, and training that have taken place under Muñoz Marin's regime have meant a steadily rising level of New York's Puerto Rican population.

THE MIGRATION

NEW YORK CITY HAD 500 PERSONS OF PUERTO RICAN BIRTH IN 1910; 7,000 in 1920; 45,000 in 1930.

This group already included some professional people and businessmen in small stores, but the overwhelming majority of the employed men and women were engaged in unskilled work, as laborers, porters, factory operatives, and domestic workers. The center of the community was East Harlem, from 97th Street to as far as 125th Street, from Fifth Avenue to Third Avenue. There was also a small group around the Brooklyn Navy Yard and in South Brooklyn. In Manhattan, where three-quarters of the Puerto Ricans lived, they met the old East Harlem Italian community on the east, and the growing community of Negroes to the north and west.[8] There was also a large Jewish group in East Harlem, withdrawing to other parts of the city, principally to the Bronx. The paths of migration through the city are fixed by such matters as lines of transportation and availability of housing at the next highest level one can afford to pay. Just as the Jews moved out of East Harlem along the IRT subway to the East Bronx, so, too, did the Puerto Ricans, when in 1945 the East Harlem community began to fill up and overflow.

But until the 1940's there was plenty of room in the old-law tenements of East Harlem—vacancy rates in the middle thirties there were 15 per cent.[9] There is no history of any conflict with the Jewish group. With the local Italians, relations were cool. The tight Italian community did not find it easy to open up to strangers; the youth, of course, simply followed in the pattern of adolescent ethnic hostility, and the mild Puerto Ricans, whose history had had plenty of misery but remarkably little violence, were taken aback. Even the Italian adults have at times been violent in their sentiments, for during the depression it was easy to blame anyone for one's troubles.[10]

Even in these early days a characteristic pattern of response to the American Negro could be seen in the Puerto Rican community. For the Puerto Ricans are a mixed people. And while in their own minds a man's color meant something very different from what it meant to white Americans, they knew very well its meaning for Americans. About one-fifth of the Puerto Rican group in New York in the thirties was listed in census returns as Negro (a slightly smaller proportion than were then listed as colored in the Puerto Rican census). Chenault believed "The American Negro is inclined to resent all of the people from the West Indies [he includes the Puerto Ricans in this group] because of their competition in the labor market. . . ." While on his part "The Puerto Rican, if white or slightly colored deeply resents any classification which places him with the Negro. . . . Finding the American-born Negro confronted with serious disadvantages in this country, the Puerto Ricans want to maintain their own group and to distinguish themselves from him. . . . People who have studied the relations of the West Indian groups in Harlem report that . . . the darker the person from the West Indies is, the more intense his desire to speak only Spanish, and to do so in a louder voice." [11]

But whatever the complications introduced in attitudes toward Negroes by this factor of color in the Puerto Ricans themselves, relations actually seem to have been pleasanter than with the Italians. In later years, the young people coming into this first section of Puerto Rican settlement, "El Barrio," would find their adjustment complicated by the hostility of Italian youth, while Negro youth was more willing to accept them.[12]

In 1940, the group was still small—70,000— still predominantly concentrated in East Harlem, with a sizable subconcentration in Brooklyn along the waterfront, and a small group in the Bronx. The census showed a sharp reduction in the number of Negroes, to about 11 per cent. Whether this was the result of a change in the composition of the group that took place in the depression years is hard to say; it would seem unlikely that so great a change should have taken place, and perhaps the uncertain census takers were for some reason listing more mixed Puerto Ricans as white. (By 1960 the proportion of colored among the New York Puerto Ricans was only 4 per cent.)

During the war, Puerto Rico, four days from New York by boat, was cut off to normal passenger movements. There was almost no addition to the Puerto Rican population until 1944. Then there was a heavy inmigration of 11,000. The next year, with the end of the war, air service between San Juan and New York was introduced. The situation of the potential migrant was transformed. In 1945, 13,500 entered the city; in 1946, almost 40,000. And New York was in the middle of a mass migration rivaling the great population movements of the first two decades of the century.

The movement ebbed and flowed with economic conditions in the city. During the early years the movement to the mainland was almost exclusively to New York City, and very few Puerto Ricans went beyond the city to settle elsewhere. By 1950 the census showed 187,000 Puerto Ricans in the city, and 58,000 children of Puerto Rican parents, making a community of more than a quarter of a million. The peak year of the migration was 1952–1953, when 58,500 settled in the city. Toward the end of the fifties, with worsening economic conditions, the migration tapered off—to 31,500 in 1956–1957, 16,200 in 1957–1958, 22,700 in 1958–1959, 14,200 in 1959–1960, and only 8,000 in 1960–1961. (By this time, only three-fifths of the migrants to the mainland were settling in New York.) However, these figures are of net migration. The actual numbers moving back and forth for permanent or temporary settlement are much greater, and two or three times these numbers of "new" Puerto Rican migrants are probably added to the city each year.

In 1961, before the release of census figures, it was estimated there were 720,000 of Puerto Rican birth or parentage in the city.[13] The census, however, revealed only 613,000 of Puerto Rican birth or parentage in the city. The great movement of migration seemed to have come to an end, but the high birth rate of the Puerto Rican population guaranteed that those of Puerto Rican origin would make up an increasing proportion of the city. In 1961, more than one-seventh of the births in the city were of Puerto Rican parents (24,746 out of 168,383).[14] The crude birth rate of the Puerto Rican population of New York was 40 per thousand. (For nonwhites, it was 30; for others, 20.)

By 1960 El Barrio in East Harlem was only one of the important Puerto Rican areas of the city. A heavy concentration of the Puerto Rican population in East Harlem was prevented first by the desperate housing shortage, which made it impossible for El Barrio to expand into the areas to the north, east, and west, and second, by the vast program of slum clearance and public housing, which broke up the Puerto Rican concentrations (in the oldest and most decrepit housing, of course) as soon as they were formed, and prevented new concentrations from forming. And so Puerto Ricans spread rapidly throughout the city in the late 1940's and 1950's—to the West Side, to Washington Heights, to Chelsea, the Lower East Side; and outside of Manhattan, in the downtown Brooklyn and the near Bedford-Stuyvesant areas; in the Bronx, through the Morrisania, Melrose, and other districts; into sections of Queens; and outside the city into Newark and other communities in New Jersey. There was scarcely an area in the older boroughs in which Puerto Ricans were not to be found.

Thus because of the housing shortage and slum clearance they rubbed shoulders with everybody in the city.[15]

All through the forties and fifties Puerto Rico itself was undergoing great changes. The chief impact of the New Deal on Puerto Rico had been somewhat larger sums for relief—there seemed no solution to the chronic problems of unemployment and underemployment, poor living conditions, and poor health conditions. A succession of American governors found it impossible to do much, perhaps because it is always hard for a colonial country, whatever its good intentions, to do something *for* a colony. In 1940, however, Luis Muñoz Marin's new Popular Democratic Party won an election. The American government obliged him with a governor of his own choosing, Rexford Tugwell, who had already spent some time on the island in the middle thirties trying to develop a plan to pull it out of its chronic misery. The Second World War provided the new government a nest egg with which to work, for the excise tax on Puerto Rican rum, which came to replace in part scarce wartime whisky, was held by the federal government for Puerto Rico.

Muñoz first thought primarily in terms of solving the agrarian problem by the distribution of the large estates, and while something was done along these lines, it was not the main engine of Puerto Rican transformation. Puerto Rico was too crowded to think in terms of prosperous family-type farms; it needed its main cash crop, sugar, and other cash crops; and at the same time, to compete, it needed efficient organization, higher mechanization, and thus even *less* labor than was then employed in agriculture. The emphasis of the Muñoz–Tugwell regime was put on developing industry, at first through direct government building and operation, and later, and far more successfully, through the stimulation of outside mainland investment. Puerto Rico finally found a major virtue in its connection with America—the American market, and access to American investment capital and economic skills. Six hundred new factories were tempted to open in the island by tax exemption, government-supported economic and market analysis, and by a variety of other means. Forty-one thousand jobs were created by the new factories, paying average wages far, far greater than those in agriculture. One-quarter of U.S. brassieres and electric shavers now come from the island.[16]

What this meant was a steadily rising income on the island, increase in numbers of workers with experience in manufacturing, an increase in urban population. It meant money for improved health services and schools, and better living quarters for the poor. All this was done by a freely elected Puerto Rican government. In 1948 Puerto Rico elected its first native governor, and in 1952, under a constitution it had itself drawn up, it was granted as much of independence as it wanted, and remained part of the United States as a Commonwealth.

The bearing of all this on New York is that the Puerto Rican migrants in the 1950's were not the same as those of the 1920's and 1930's. On the whole the migrants were better educated than the average Puerto Rican; they had a somewhat higher level of skill; they tended to come from the urban areas.[17] Whatever their drawbacks in relation to the older established New Yorkers, they were a better-than-average representation of the people of Puerto Rico, and the average itself rose rapidly from 1940 on. The early fears of an importation of tropical diseases were unfounded; health conditions on the island itself rapidly improved, and in New York certain diseases could not be transmitted because of the prevalence of aqueducts, sewers, concrete sidewalks, and shoes.

The economic and political transformation of the island did not, however, mean that all the Puerto Ricans were happy to stay at home. The reconstruction of the island destroyed almost as many jobs—poor ones, it is true, but jobs—as it made. The fine needlework that had occupied women at home, in line with Puerto Rican mores, was reduced by foreign competition, which paid even less than the miserable wages this provided in Puerto Rico. The increasingly mechanized sugar industry needed less labor all the time. And while the new jobs in the new factories paid good wages for Puerto Rico, wage rates in contrast to those in the United States remained low. Whatever the situation in other tropical islands, in Puerto Rico, where almost everything, including most food, has to be imported, prices are high, and low incomes mean only a low standard of living. Eighteen per cent of the working force was unemployed in 1939–1940, 13 per cent was unemployed in 1957–1958—twice as many as were then unemployed on the mainland.[18] But the two unemployment rates have been converging. In 1962 the unemployment figure on the island was 11 per cent.

Unquestionably, economic factors were and are decisive in explaining the great migration out of the island. And yet there were other matters, too. There was first the growing impact of contact with the mainland—its products arousing dreams of material comfort, its mass media publicizing them, its merchandising techniques spreading the desire for change to every hamlet on the island. There was the additional experience of the Puerto Rican GI's. Over 65,000 had served in the Second World War, 43,000 in the Korean War. Their experience of the normal level of material comfort taken for granted in the U.S. Army was impressive. (Indeed, 40,000 of those who served in the Korean War were *volunteers,* despite the Puerto Rican experience with a segregated army in the Second World War.)[19] The American standard of living, experienced indirectly and directly through mass media and personal contacts, was a powerful agitating force. And as the Puerto Rican population of New York itself grew, and migrants and their children went back and forth by cheap airplane, everyone had direct personal knowledge of what life was like in New York. Once the stream is started and the road open, once the path is made easy, any minor cause may be sufficient to decide to try one's luck in New York: a poor marriage, overbearing parents, a sense of adventure, a desire to see New York itself. One must not underestimate another set of material advantages: the schools, hospitals, and welfare services. These are good on the island, comparatively speaking—they are of course much better in the richest city in the world. These, too, played a role.

Finally, there was the complex impact of the population problem. The economic pinch on the individual grew tighter because, just as his demands and desires were rising, his family was growing, too, and to sizes that were exceptional even for Puerto Rico. For while the death rate, and in particular the infant mortality rate, dropped, the birth rate did not.

The island government needed emigration as well as economic development to cope with these problems; if it did not encourage emigration directly (an unnecessary provision), it planned for and assisted it.

A characteristic of countries with both high birth rates and the benefits of modern medicine is that the death rates drop earlier, and faster, than the birth rates. This was the case in Puerto Rico. But in 1950 the birth rate began to decline. The decline has continued throughout the decade.[20] Some demographers believe the decline is in large part caused by the removal of so many people in the most fertile age-groups from the island to New York—in effect, the population problem has been transferred rather than transformed.[21] But there is no question that the situation is changing, and that long-range decline, even if delayed a few years, will finally set in.

During the forties, Puerto Rico's population problems were studied with the same intensity and skill that were devoted to its economic and social problems. Despite the fact that 85 per cent of the population were nominally Catholic, the Church, the study showed, played little role in molding attitudes toward family size. It had had an impact in preventing during the thirties the free operation of birth-control clinics. But its political power on the island was less than on the mainland, and certainly less than in New York City. Muñoz Marin's government was, if not anticlerical, humanist, and certainly did not take the opposition of the Church to a rational approach to population problems seriously. Contraceptive advice and devices were made available, and an operation for sterilization of women was made cheap and easy, and widely publicized (in part by the Church's denunciation). The studies showed that while the upper-class and middle-class groups used contraceptive devices to a large extent, this was not popular among the great majority. The sterilization of women who had had a number of children was more popular. Indeed, many New York Puerto Rican women will go back to the island to have children so they can take advantage of this operation. In one group of Puerto Rican families in an East Harlem slum area, for example, no less than 20 of the 75 mothers had had the sterilization operation performed—a startling proportion.[22] In 1949, on the island, 18 per cent of the mothers giving birth in hospitals took the opportunity to be sterilized.[23] There seems to have been no decline in the popularity of the operation since.

The reasons why contraception did not work are interesting. There was first of all the problem of using it under the incredibly crowded sleeping conditions in Puerto Rico, and in the absence of modern sanitary facilities. There was second the attitude of the Puerto Rican male to his sexual rights. He dominated the sexual relationship, expected the woman to be passive and submissive, and would not take kindly to the notion of giving her some control of sexual relations by cooperating in contraception. Then, too, man and wife simply did not discuss sex—both might be wrong about what the other thought, but they did not know it. So, for example, investigators discovered that husbands and wives both wanted less children than they had, but each thought the other did not care or preferred more children than they actually did! There was, too, the traditional suspicion and jealousy involved in these marriages, which not only prevented frank discussion but also meant that men suspected that women who fitted themselves with diaphragms were planning to be unfaithful. In this complex situation, contraception would have a hard time of it, and when tried, would fail. Under the circumstances, sterilization, which required one action, little discussion before and none afterwards, no male complaints of deprivation, and was certain, was the most favored course.[24]

In New York, of course, things are different. The relations between men and women change, children are raised differently, the attitudes toward having children change. But old attitudes exist alongside new ones, old-style families alongside new ones, and meanwhile there is a very heavy Puerto Rican birth rate in the city.

THE ISLAND-CENTERED COMMUNITY

THE LINKS BETWEEN THE NEW YORK PUERTO RICANS AND THE island Puerto Ricans are close and complex, and quite different from the relationship of earlier migrant groups to their homelands. Puerto Rico is a part of the United States, and there is no control over movement between the island and the mainland. Puerto Rico is brought relatively close by air, and air passage is not too expensive. The island government takes a strong interest in its people. Indeed, many would be hard put to say whether they belonged to the city or the island. A great part of the movement between New York and San Juan consists of people going back and forth for visits, to take care of sick relatives or to be taken care of, of children being sent to stay with one family or another. One index of the movement is entries into and withdrawals from New York public schools. In 1958–1959, 10,600 children were transferred from Puerto Rican schools, and 6,500 were released to go to school in Puerto Rico.[25] Going back is not, as it was in earlier migrations, either the return of someone who is defeated and incapable of adjustment, or of someone who has made a small competence that will look big in the homeland, although there is more and more of this movement. Going back is too easy for it to have such great significance.

Something new perhaps has been added to the New York scene—an ethnic group that will not assimilate to the same degree as others do but will resemble the strangers who lived in ancient Greek cities, or the ancient Greeks who set up colonies in cities around the Mediterranean.

So, for example, Luis Ferré, a candidate for governor of Puerto Rico in 1960, arrived for a spell of campaigning in the city—after all, as it was pointed out, 30,000 Puerto Ricans from the city return to the island every year. This is consequently as important a bailiwick in which to get votes as many on the island. Nor is there for Puerto Ricans any problem of dual loyalty—on the island they vote in its elections, in New York in its elections —just as one votes in California one year, and if one moves to New York, there the next.

But there are interesting consequences for the community. To continue on the problem of politics, relatively few Puerto Ricans, compared with Negroes in the city, or with the non-Puerto Rican white groups, register and vote. A huge campaign was mounted in 1960 to register

100,000 Puerto Ricans in the city. It was estimated at the beginning of the drive that only 100,000 of a potential 300,000 voters had been registered in 1958. This drive claimed it had registered 230,000 Spanish-speaking citizens; a year later, however, after the primary that renominated Mayor Wagner, his campaign manager said that only 120,-000 Puerto Ricans were registered to vote (New York has permanent registration; perhaps the extra 110,000 of the earlier claim reflected non-Puerto Rican Spanish-speaking). One of the difficulties in registering Puerto Ricans is that the state constitution requires that one demonstrate literacy in English. After Mayor Wagner's election to his third term in 1961, it was estimated that no less than 200,000 Puerto Ricans were in effect disfranchised by this provision of the state constitution, and in December, 1961, the city filed a proposal for a constitutional amendment that would permit residents to take literacy tests in any language in which a daily or weekly newspaper was published in the state.[26] Clearly, people active in politics and the leaders of the Puerto Rican community expect that Spanish will be the major language in use in the community for as long ahead as anyone can see. As against the situation in some earlier immigrant groups, where dominant opinion in the city and in the group insisted on the need to learn English and relegate the immigrant tongue to a minority position, in the Puerto Rican group many leaders—and they are young people, for the entire group and its leaders too are young—expect and hope that Spanish will maintain a strong position in the group. The city government on its part encourages city employees to learn Spanish, and issues many announcements to the general public in both languages. Conceivably this will change, but Spanish already has a much stronger official position in New York than either Italian or Yiddish ever had. This is one influence of the closeness of the island, physically, politically, and culturally.

This closeness to the island is unquestionably a factor in another interesting characteristic of the Puerto Ricans in New York, the relative weakness of community organization and community leadership among them. The early group was so completely working class and below that it was understandable that professionals and businessmen would find little in common with the other Puerto Ricans, and tended to blend into the Spanish-language group in the city. This consisted not only of some immigrants from Spain but of immigrants from Cuba and other parts of Latin America. In 1930 New York had 137,-000 Spanish-speaking people, of whom only a third were Puerto Rican. It was understandable that those of higher status tended to understress their connection with a group of low status. As the Puerto Rican group grew in the city, something happened to the Spanish-speaking that is reminiscent of what happened to the high-status German Jews when the poor East European Jews arrived—the effort to maintain a separate image for themselves in the public mind failed. When the overwhelming majority of the Spanish-speaking in the city became Puerto Rican, the status of all the Spanish-speaking began to reflect the status of the new Puerto Ricans among them. While there is still some tendency for the upper-income and high-status Puerto Rican to identify himself as a Hispano, Spanish-speaking, this is declining. Under these circumstances, the growing size of the Puerto Rican group, and the fact that it now forms probably four-fifths of all the Spanish-speaking, has led to a recapture of some of the leadership elements that might have tried to separate themselves from the Puerto Rican group when it was smaller: it has also led to the acquisition of new leadership elements from the longer-settled, and perhaps better-educated, non-Puerto Rican Spanish-speaking in New York. The Spanish-speaking begin to act to some extent as if they all are in the same boat. Some of the leadership in the Puerto Rican group today comes from non-Puerto Ricans who have been in the city longer or have had more varied training and experience. Thus, Emilio Nuñez, the first Spanish-speaking city magistrate, appointed in 1951, was born in Spain. The five Spanish-speaking members of the executive board of the Skirt-makers' Union, Local 23 of the ILGWU, include one South American, one Mexican, one Cuban, and only two Puerto Ricans, though the Puerto Ricans make up by far the largest part of the Spanish-speaking membership.[27] *La Prensa,* an old and established Spanish daily, with originally little Puerto Rican emphasis, was a few years ago completely revamped as a tabloid to appeal directly to the Puerto Rican population.

The fact that a newspaper that was originally designed for another group, and that was owned by the Italian newspaper publisher and businessman Fortune Pope, was so easily modifiable into an organ of the Puerto Rican group is itself a sign of the relative weakness of what may be called indigenous organization among the Puerto Ricans. The other newspaper of the Puerto Rican group, much larger in circulation than *La Prensa, El Diario,* was owned by a Dominican, and edited by a New York newspaperman who formerly edited a newspaper in the (then) Ciudad Trujillo. Today both newspapers are owned by the transit operator O. Ray Chalk, who is also not a Puerto Rican. These newspapers do serve the community, in expressing its concerns, in supplying various services, in helping people find their relatives, in guiding their readers to find the agencies that might help them, in carrying community news and community items. But they are not the *creations* of the community or of groups within it. And this is what one sees in many other areas of Puerto Rican life.*

We have already referred to the weakness of Catholicism in Puerto Rico. Roman Catholicism is not a national church, as it is in Ireland and Poland. It sets the general frame of life by baptizing (most), marrying (less), and burying, and its calendar sets the holidays and festivals, but its impact on the people, in guiding their lives and molding their ideas, and in serving as a vessel for their social life, is relatively small. It is, as elsewhere in Latin America, a church for the women. In New York the Catholic Church is engaged in an energetic program to increase the number of Spanish-speaking priests, and to widen the circle of activity among the Puerto Ricans. Since the Puerto Ricans have spread so widely through the city, the Church has for the most part carried on its Puerto Rican work in established parishes. The Puerto Ricans have not created, as others did, national parishes of their own. Thus the ca-

---

* This situation may be changing. After this book was in press, the two newspapers were merged, and a new Spanish-language daily began publication.

pacities of the Church are weak in just those areas in which the needs of the migrants are great—in creating a surrounding, supporting community to replace the extended families, broken by city life, and to supply a social setting for those who feel lost and lonely in the great city. This is a task that smaller churches, with an active lay leadership, and a ministering group that is closer to and of the people, can do better.

Most of the Puerto Ricans in the city are Catholic, but their participation in Catholic life is small. It is interesting for example that there are but 15,000 Puerto Rican children in parochial schools in the New York Archdiocese, against almost ten times as many in the public schools, a much smaller percentage than for any other Catholic group in the city. There are only 250 Spanish-speaking priests in the Archdiocese of New York for the Puerto Rican population, and most of these—as many in Puerto Rico itself—have learned Spanish to minister to the group. In 1961, in 42 Catholic parishes in New York City with Spanish-speaking priests, there was only one Puerto Rican. And the proportion of the Spanish-speaking priests to the Catholic Puerto Rican population was still one-third or one-fourth what it was for other New York Catholics.[28]

As the problems of the first generation are overcome, as families become stabler, incomes higher, and the attachment to American middle-class culture stronger, Catholicism will probably also become stronger among the Puerto Ricans. But it does not seem likely that it will play as important a role among them as it plays in the European Catholic ethnic groups. For there is already well-established a strong rival to Catholicism among the Puerto Ricans, and if we were to reckon religious strength not by mild affiliation but by real commitment, it would be likely that there are not many less committed Protestants among the Puerto Ricans than there are committed Catholics.

Protestantism's history on the island dates from the American occupation, when some major denominations divided up the island and began work there. A 1947–1948 study of the island showed that about 82 per cent called themselves Catholic, that 6 per cent of the population belonged to the major Protestant denominations, 2 per cent to Protestant sects, and 2 or 3 per cent were Spiritualists.[29] The Mills–Senior–Goldsen 1948 study of New York Puerto Ricans showed about 83 per cent Catholic and slightly higher proportions of Protestants in the major denominations—9 per cent—and in the sects—5 per cent.[30] But the fervor of the Protestants seems greater than that of the Catholics; and the fervor of the members of the Pentecostalist and similar sects of the hundreds of the storefront churches that dot the Puerto Rican neighborhoods is even greater.

There are about 70 Spanish-language Protestant churches of major denominations in the city, and close to another 50 that have both English and Spanish services. Another 70 have some Spanish members. All told, there are about 14,000 Spanish-speaking members of major Protestant denominations in the city, about 10,000 in their own all-Spanish churches.[31] Attendance in the Spanish churches is high, evangelical zeal puts most Anglo-Saxon Protestantism to shame, and the willingness to spend money to support the church is also great.[32]

This is now largely an indigenous movement, staffed by Puerto Rican ministers. The Protestant church leaders of the city have been anxious to have the English-language churches also reach out to the surrounding Puerto Rican population. But for regular, denominational Protestantism, this is not an easy task. The strength of Protestantism is that it forms a community, and its weakness is that in forming a community it finds it difficult to reach out from its original ethnic or class base to attract other groups. The most catholic of the Protestant groups, the Protestant Episcopal Church, has been most successful in developing integrated churches of mixed native Protestant and Puerto Rican members, just as it is also this church that is most successful in developing churches that integrate white and colored members. Father James Gusweller's West Side Church of St. Matthew and St. Timothy is the best-known example of such an integrated church.

But the most vigorous and intense religious movements among the Puerto Ricans are the Pentecostal and independent Pentecostal-type churches. The 1960 study of the Protestant Council of New York located 240 such churches—there are certainly more than this. Their membership was conservatively estimated at about 25,000.[33] These tiny churches generally run services every day of the week. They demand of their members that they give up smoking and alcohol and fornication. They are completely supported by their memberships, and often a church of 100 members will support a full-time minister. The Pentecostal movement, which began in America, has for reasons that are not clear been successful in penetrating a number of Catholic areas, for example Italy and Chile. Two Catholic sociologists who have studied the Pentecostal churches in New York suggest that they derive their strength from Catholicism's weakness. Many migrants feel lost in the city; many search for a community within the Church, and the integrated Catholic parish, whose base is another ethnic group and whose priests are not Spanish, cannot give this. The preachers and ministers of the Pentecostal Church in New York are almost all Puerto Ricans. Though it was initially spread to the island by English-speaking evangelists, working through translators, the requirements for preaching and ministering make it possible for devout members to rise rapidly to such positions. "In the Catholic Church," one member told the investigators, "no one knew me." Here, if a stranger comes in, he is warmly greeted; if a member falls sick, he is visited; the tight congregation is one of the most important expressions of a community that is found among Puerto Ricans in New York.[34]

Some of the Pentecostal churches have grown beyond their storefront beginnings and are now quite large, but despite their growth they maintain the allegiance and support of the earlier days, and maintain a sense of community in the larger group.

(The "Jardin Botanicas" of the Puerto Rican districts evidence the strength of "Spiritualism," which to a few Puerto Ricans is a religion, but which is more akin to an occult science like astrology. The Botanica will sell, in addition to herbs prescribed by the practitioners, books on mysticism and other subjects, and religious pictures and objects, for this occultism is practiced or believed in, to varying degrees, by many who are nominally or also Catholic.[35])

Protestantism is an interesting if minority phenomenon among the Puerto Ricans; and there exists here a real field for competition between Catholicism and Protestantism in the city. It is impossible now to predict how things will come out. There are some potential areas for conflict. For example: Will Protestant social welfare agencies try to serve Puerto Ricans? Up to now this has been left to city agencies and to Catholic agencies. A third to a half of the clients of the family and child-serving agencies of Catholic Charities are now Puerto Ricans; since the Protestants have to take some responsibility for the Negroes, it is understandable that they have dragged their feet somewhat in staking out a claim to lost souls among the Puerto Ricans too. But according to the press releases of Billy Graham's three-day crusade to the Spanish-speaking of New York in 1960, 500,000 of New York's Spanish-American population are considered unchurched—which means that the religious organization of New York Protestantism considers most of the field available for sowing. If Protestant agencies should also make this claim, some serious headaches will arise for the public agencies (such as the New York City Youth Board) which distribute cases to private agencies, and help support them.

Aside from the storefront churches, organizational life is not strong among the Puerto Ricans. There are many social organizations, based on place of origin on the island, but they do not have the importance of the immigrant societies among earlier immigrants. It is understandable they should not; their functions for recreation and entertainment have been usurped by movies and television and other commercialized recreation, their practical functions—aiding the poor and the sick—are now in the hands of public and private agencies. One can always find functions for an organization if one is organizationally minded, but Puerto Rico, just as the rest of Latin America, has always been weak in spontaneous grass-roots organization. Probably the rise of organization has been inhibited too by the factors that have dispersed the population and prevented the development of a great center for the Puerto Rican population—housing shortage, slum clearance, and the availability of public housing. In 1948 only 6 per cent of the migrants belonged to Puerto Rican organizations, somewhat more men than women, and more of the older migrants than recent arrivals.[36] Compared to some other ethnic groups, this seems low.

If slum clearance has been a factor preventing the growth of certain kinds of organization among Puerto Ricans, it has also been the occasion for the birth of other kinds of organization, the groups that try to prevent the bulldozing of a neighborhood, or, in the cases of more selective renewal as on the West Side,* the weeding out of the "bad housing." The demolition of the houses that affront the neighborhood means precisely the demolition of those that house vast numbers of Puerto Ricans— families living in single rooms, families taking in migrant relatives, displaced children, and temporarily homeless friends. Ironically, "improving a neighborhood" means moving out those who are most crowded, have the least room, and whose resettlement offers the most difficult problem for themselves and city agencies. But in the defense of their threatened homes, an organization will often be created, and nascent leaders will become real leaders, developing experience in cooperating with and fighting with other groups and city agencies. In a New York neighborhood one may find out that a community exists only at the point where one is ready to destroy it, and it rises up to protect itself. More realistically, however, the threatened destruction is not what demonstrates that a community exists; it is rather that the threat creates a common interest where none existed before, and brings out people ready to take leadership to protect the threatened interest. Under such circumstances (as in the West Side Urban Renewal scheme), since one of the aims of the enterprise is to create neighborhoods and communities, one might sophisticatedly conclude that the aim has been effected in the fight to carry through the plan, and modify it to deal with the problems that everyone agrees are problems (overcrowding and antisocial elements).

There are probably many and subtle ways in which the relation to the island affects the organizational

---

* We refer to the West Side Urban Renewal Project, which will displace most of the present Puerto Rican population of the area from 87th to 97th Street, from Central Park West to Amsterdam Avenue.

life of Puerto Ricans in New York; but one clear impact is seen in the role of the Office of the Commonwealth of Puerto Rico in New York City. The Migration Division of the Department of Labor of the Commonwealth of Puerto Rico maintains offices in a number of cities of the mainland, the largest in New York, and this is for the Puerto Rican community of New York what the NAACP and the National Urban League are for the Negroes. It serves as an employment agency and an orientation office for new migrants; it represents Puerto Ricans and Puerto Rican interests on various city committees and organizations, formal and informal, private and government; it helps organize the Puerto Rican community where such organization seems necessary, as, for example, in the 1960 campaign to increase registration, in which it took a leading and active role. It is concerned with the way city agencies handle problems of special interest to Puerto Ricans, and will make its position known to them, and it cooperates in the elaborate exchange programs and conferences whereby New York tries to educate its personnel in the problems of their Puerto Rican clientele, and the Commonwealth of Puerto Rico tries to educate its people on the problems the migrants face in New York. It is also concerned with the public relations of the Puerto Ricans, supplying information and correcting misconceptions. It has been the chief agency in attempting to get Puerto Ricans to move to other cities besides New York, and its efforts have helped reduce the proportion of migrants who settle in the city from 85 per cent in 1950 to about 60 per cent, which is the figure for the last few years. (Jews had the same problem early in the century, when their organizations were worried about the huge concentration of Jews developing in New York City. The "Galveston Project" tried to get them to move elsewhere—it was by no means as successful as the Migration Division has been.)

Under the sociologist Clarence Senior (who in 1961 became a member of the New York City Board of Education) and now under Joseph Monserrat, it has been an efficient and effective organization, with a staff of great competence and skill, and it has drawn on some of the best people outside the Puerto Rican community to aid it in its work, just as every branch of the Commonwealth government has.

But it is again a special twist for New York's Puerto Ricans that its equivalent of NAACP and NUL, or of the Jewish community organizational complex, should be a *government* office, supported by *government* funds. It is understandable that we do not leave newcomers to New York to sink or swim any more: but it may very well be that it is because the Puerto Rican group has been so well supplied with paternalistic guidance from their own government, as well as with social services by city and private agencies, that it has not developed powerful grass-roots organizations.

But perhaps with greater income, more leisure, and the solution of their most pressing problems, the Puerto Ricans will find they want things for themselves that the Commonwealth and the city do not provide.

THE MOBILE ELEMENT

IN 1947 CLARENCE SENIOR SURVEYED THE EXPERIENCE OF Puerto Rican migrants in various parts of the world and came upon the interesting case of the Puerto Ricans of the island of St. Croix. This is one of the American Virgin Islands. Its native population consists of English-speaking Negroes, descendants of Africans imported to work on sugar plantations. St. Croix went into decline more than a century ago; it has long been a depressed island losing population (from 27,000 in 1835 to 11,400 in 1930). Since the United States acquired it in 1917, it has in effect lived off funds of the American government.

Under these circumstances, for this to have begun to attract Puerto Rican migrants in the later 1920's and 1930's is somewhat surprising; what is even more surprising is that they have been economically successful, and seem to be on the way to taking over the economic life of the island. They arouse the same resentment among the natives by their energy and competence that Jews and Chinese have aroused in lands which these peoples have penetrated. "The newcomers . . . ," it is reported, "work harder and produce more than the natives." They are preferred in the sugar fields, where they are asserted to be "more intelligent and more adaptable to new methods." They also do about 40 per cent more work in the fields than the natives. They form one-quarter of the population but own and run more than half of the 122 businesses on the island—despite their recent arrival, and in an impoverished state:

The Crucian reaction to this aspect of the invasion is strong but ineffectual. It varies from bitter jokes to half-hearted attempts to organize "buy Crucian" campaigns. Soon stores will display signs "English spoken here," runs one of the current stories. On every hand one hears the assertion that the Puerto Ricans are "clannish," that they hire only fellow Puerto Ricans, that they help each other in financial crises, that the larger and wealthier storekeepers will help newcomers start businesses in competition with the local people. Several Crucians interviewed were honest enough to confess that if they owned stores, and dared to do so, they would hire Puerto Ricans themselves because, as one civic leader said, "The Puerto Ricans have taught us how to work and produce." [37]

They also have one of the highest birth rates on record (66 per thousand against 20 per thousand for the Crucians); they do not seem to take well to the Crucian schools—there is a great deal of truancy, and there are very few of them in the local high school (some go back to Puerto Rico for secondary education).

Certainly the New Yorker reading this story of Puerto Rican migrants in another setting will have cause for musing and wonder, and may conclude that "success" and "failure" are relative matters, and depend on the challenge that is presented, and the grading for the contest. The challenge of New York City is one of the most severe in the world; the grading is the hardest; and a sizable degree of success in adjustment by Puerto Ricans in the city tends to be swamped in consciousness by the problems of a new migration.

It is also true that adjustment means inconspicuousness, and the well-adjusted Puerto Rican is not seen as a Puerto Rican; he tends to be only someone with a Spanish name. The successful and adjusted withdraw to Washington Heights and two-family or one-family houses in the Bronx and Queens. The newcomers, crowding the rooming houses of the West Side and Chelsea, are in some of the busiest sections of the cities, with a large and active previously settled population that is made all too aware of their presence, and they are also easily accessible to any reporter out on a story. There is no answer to this problem of distribution and the images it creates. But the Puerto Rican story is more complex, and the degree of success greater than appears on the surface.

The Puerto Ricans of St. Croix are very much like the Puerto Ricans of New York; from the evidence, the only important difference seems to be that fewer of them are white, more dark. And their relatives in New York have very much the same impulses to better themselves, and the same business-minded instincts. As against however the easy-going Crucian competition, here we have A & P and Macy's. Yet in the face of heavy competition and a high rate of small business mortality, the New York Puerto Ricans have shown themselves amazingly fertile in spawning small stores. In 1948, when Mills, Senior, and Goldsen looked around for dense Puerto Rican neighborhoods in the city, they located them by the number of grocery stores, the distinctive "Bodega." They found no less than 468, and the count was certainly incomplete.[38] The population has gone up two and a half times since, and the number of stores has probably kept pace.

The Puerto Rican migration division estimated a few years ago that there are 4,000 Puerto Rican-run businesses all told in the city. This is an amazing figure. It is considerably more, for example, than the much larger Negro population has established, even though, in terms of period of major migration, it is thirty years ahead of the Puerto Ricans. It suggests that one of the widely accepted reasons for the low participation of Negroes in small business—discrimination in loans—probably is not of primary importance, for it is not likely that the Puerto Rican, with his characteristically accented and poor English, impresses the banker or supplier any more than a Negro does. Two other factors seem to explain the difference: one is that the Puerto Rican, coming from a country where he is not of the lower caste, does have a business tradition, and while not many successful storekeepers have migrated to this country, many have eked out a living in times of unemployment by peddling one thing or another. A second reason is that he has a special function—supplying products to a group with special needs in food, records, books, herbs, and what have you. There is further the special bond of language.

What is the future of the Puerto Rican businessman? There is no question that his path is not easy. There is the competition of the chain stores, more effective as tastes change and as English becomes more common. And there is, helping the chain stores, as if they needed it, the public policy of wiping out large numbers of small businessmen in the areas of older housing. This is an unfortunate consequence of slum clearance and urban renewal, and could be added to the many considerations that already suggest that these policies should be changed. The destruction of Puerto Rican businessmen in East Harlem, the old Barrio, which has been almost entirely leveled for new housing projects, was prodigious. The losses on the West Side will ultimately be as great. But entrepreneurial drive is one of those aspects of human potentiality that is not easily destroyed, and a businessman will be able to do business under even the most adverse circumstances. One already sees such adaptations as the sprouting of Puerto-Rican owned "superettes" on the West Side which serve a partly non-Puerto Rican clientele.

There is as yet little that the Puerto Rican storekeeper supplies the rest of us. But again, the energy that leads to the Bodega and the small restaurant will unquestionably apply itself to the problem of finding something to sell. There was after all nothing in Greek food that served as the basis of the Greek restaurant industry, and the Chinese had to invent a few dishes before they could sell meals to the unenlightened barbarians. There may be nothing in Puerto Rican cuisine today that any of the rest of us want, but it is amazing how brief traditions are and how the need can be father to the invention. In twenty years we may see a Puerto Rican equivalent to the Pizza Parlor.

The 1950 census already showed that there were slightly more Puerto Ricans proportionately in the category "managers, officials, and proprietors" than there were in the Negro group. There were somewhat fewer professionals. But we must say something about the professional group among the Puerto Ricans. The overwhelming majority of the migrants to New York came to seek work and were poorly qualified in skill and education. They were superior to the average Puerto Rican, but an elementary school education in Spanish, while better than illiteracy, still does not open up many doors in New York. However, from the beginning, in the twenties, there was a sizable flow of Puerto Ricans who came here to study and who in the end settled here. These became the basis for an important part of the Puerto Rican professional group that is the leadership group in the Puerto Rican community today.

Even during the heavy migration of the forties and fifties a sizable proportion of the immigrants were well educated and came here for advanced study or for specific jobs—5 per cent of the migrants in 1958 had had four years of college. Puerto Rico and the mainland often form one job market for the educated Puerto Rican as they do for the less educated.[39] We can expect a good deal of movement back and forth, as the balance of opportunity for upper-level employment shifts between New York and Puerto Rico. The University of San Juan, for example, has grown to an enrollment of 17,000, and many of the students will in time end up here, just as some of the Puerto Ricans in the city's colleges and universities will end up there.

The opportunities for professional and other well-paying white-collar employment for Puerto Ricans in the city will certainly increase. There has, for example, been nothing equivalent among Puerto Ricans to the flow of Negroes into city and other government offices, and yet here are certainly opportunities for a group that will make up perhaps an eighth of the city in 1970. There is the whole area of trade with Latin America, which requires bilingual personnel of all types. Conceivably this area of employment will also increase as the American government devotes more attention to Latin America, and as Latin America (hopefully) becomes more prosperous.

Will Puerto Ricans meet discrimination as they strike out for better jobs? A great deal depends on the development of racial attitudes among New Yorkers. Puerto Ricans in the city were about 4 per cent colored according to the 1960 census, but many more than that bear some indications of the mixture of white and black that has been going on in the island for centuries.

One index of discrimination is low. Relatively few complaints of discrimination are filed by Puerto Ricans with the State Committee Against Discrimination. Between 1945 and 1958 there were 273 complaints, and in the last two years of this period they were running at the rate of 40 to 50 a year. Only 12 of the complaints in this entire period were over sales and clerical jobs, only 4 for jobs as craftsmen; all the rest were for jobs as service workers, operatives, and laborers.[40] One would think that there are enough Puerto Ricans going into professional and white-collar work, and they are sufficiently sensitive to slights and discrimination, to have produced more complaints than this if discrimination were a serious problem. On the other hand, the Puerto Ricans are much less aggressive in fighting for and demanding their rights than are Jews and Negroes.

The 1950 census already indicated a remarkable shift upwards in the occupations of the second generation of Puerto Ricans. In 1950, 37 per cent of Puerto Rican men were operatives, 28 per cent were service workers (see Table 5). These were the two great categories of employment—the semiskilled in the various factories, toy, plastics, printing, assembling and the like, and porters, kitchen workers, elevator operators, and other workers in the hotels, restaurants, and office buildings. But if one looked at the Puerto Ricans born in this country who were under 24 and at work—still a small group, but suggesting the shape of the future—there were radical declines in these categories, and there was an increase in the sales and clerical category from 9 per cent for the Puerto Rican-born to 24 per cent for the native-born. Of course this group is still too young to number many professionals or businessmen, but one can be sure the proportion of these in the second generation will also rise.

The changes among women are even more striking. In 1950, more than four-fifths of young Puerto Rican women migrants were working in factories (mostly clothing factories) and only 7 per cent were in clerical and sales. Among the young native-born, on the other hand, the proportion working as operatives dropped in half, and the number working in clerical and sales rose to 43 per cent! [41] There has been a great increase in the native-born in these ten years, and there has been a major change in the over-all employment figures; how big it is we shall not know until we have further detailed reports from the 1960 census.

LOWER INCOME

THE WAY WE TALK ABOUT POVERTY AND MISERY TODAY ALMOST determines how we interpret it: our rhetoric explains that society is at fault. It is interesting to look back at the great study of poverty conducted by Charles Booth in London toward the end of the nineteenth century. Booth in a rather unimaginative and matter-of-fact way went through the whole population of London, looking for those who were poor and miserable and finding out the reasons why. The huge mass of poverty in London 60 to 70 years ago contained remarkably few able-bodied men who were healthy, who had some modicum of education, who had some skill, and who were not mentally unbalanced.

This rather obvious conclusion is nevertheless one that seems to play little role in present-day discussions of poverty. It does not explain everything—the proportion of unemployed *does* go up and down in response to conditions that have nothing to do with the qualities of individuals. But for any individual, and for any group made up of individuals, such factors as education, health, and skill are very important in determining income; and for a society as a whole the level of health, education, and skill is not only related to income but probably related to the level of employment too.

We have spoken up to this point of the successful and the adjusted among the Puerto Rican migrants. It takes no discerning eye to see that there is a sea of misery among the newcomers.

As to its extent: Puerto Rican median family income was considerably lower than even nonwhite median family income—$3,811 as against $4,437—in 1960. This was 63 per cent of the median income for all New York families. Unemployment among the Puerto Ricans seems to be consistently higher than among nonwhites and whites. The census of 1950 showed, for men, 7 per cent of the non-Puerto Rican whites, 12 per cent of the Negroes, and 17 per cent of the Puerto Ricans unemployed; for women, 5 per cent of the non-Puerto Rican whites, 8.5 per cent of the Negroes, and 11 per cent of Puerto Ricans. A random sample of New York City households in 1952 showed 13 per cent of the Puerto Ricans unemployed, 6 per cent of nonwhites, 4 per cent of the non-Puerto Rican whites.[42] In 1960, 5 per cent of all New York males, 6.9 per cent of nonwhite males, and 9.9 per cent of all Puerto Rican males were unemployed.

In explaining misery among the Puerto Ricans, the high birth rate must be taken into account. While the birth rate among Puerto Ricans in the United States does not reach the heights of that in St. Croix, it was estimated in 1950 at 43 per thousand. The nonwhite birth rate was 29 per thousand, the white birth rate 17 per thousand.[43] By 1960 the crude birth rate had declined slightly, to 40 per thousand, but it was still twice the continental birth rate, and half again as much as the nonwhite birth rate.

These are crude figures, affected by the fact that so many of the Puerto Ricans are in the childbearing ages, so few of them are aged (in 1950 of 605,000 New Yorkers over 65, only 5,000 were Puerto Rican; and it was estimated that of 865,000 over 65 in 1960, only 18,000 would be Puerto Rican).[44] But even making adjustment for this factor of a disproportionate number of young people, the Puerto Rican birth rate is remarkably high. Puerto Ricans begin bearing children younger, and bear more of them. The 1950 analysis showed that for women between 15 and 19 the Puerto Rican rate was about five times the continental white rate (the Negro rate for this age group was almost as high); for women 20 to 24 it was almost twice the white rate, and a third higher than the Negro birth rate.[45] The early arrival of children and the large numbers of children mean that a family income that in 1950 was slightly less than that earned by Negroes must support more people.

We see the strain in a number of ways. For example, there have been a number of studies of adjusted

Puerto Rican families, families that are not on relief, that are not broken, that do not have any severe problems. It is interesting to note how many of these families have only one or two children.[46] The job at $50 a week, which manages to support such a small family in an apartment in the Bronx and which, compared with the $12 a week income that was left behind on the island, represents real advancement, is completely inadequate to support five children or more. All problems tend to pile up. The bigger family may not get into a good apartment or a housing project. The crowding in a small apartment may mean more illness and poor management of children.

One sees the impact of the large families in welfare statistics. Once again, the same $50 a week that means bare self-sufficiency with one child (and it may mean more, for a child or two can be left with a neighbor or a relative and thus permit the mother to add to family income) means the need to go to welfare for supplementation with a large family. One-half of all the families in the city receiving supplementation from the Department of Welfare are Puerto Rican. One-quarter of all the Puerto Rican children in the city are on some form of assistance. About one-seventh of all Puerto Ricans are on public assistance.

It requires special reasons to explain an incapacity to support oneself in New York. Some of these reasons are to be found in age, some in disablement. Puerto Ricans make no significant contribution of the aged and disabled to the welfare load. They do however contribute one-half of the home-relief cases and one-third of the aid-to-dependent-children cases. And when one reads that more than half of the home relief cases consist of six persons or more, one discovers that the special misfortune that consigns so many Puerto Ricans to the relief rolls is their large number of children.[47]

Health also plays a special role. The Puerto Rican is not happy about going on relief; no one is, but one must be aware that the prevailing degree of poverty coexists with a high value placed on the maintenance of dignity and self-respect. There is no shame in a woman with children and without a husband to support her going on relief; that is understandable. But there is a good deal of shame in a man being forced to go on relief. If however he suffers from an understandable and acceptable misfortune—he has had an accident, he is in ill-health and cannot work—then there is no shame in requiring public assistance. Now as a matter of fact there seems to be a higher degree of illness among Puerto Ricans. Many arrive with ills, many acquire them in the strain of transition. Dr. Beatrice Bishop Berle, who has made a subtle and understanding study of the health problems of a sample of eighty Puerto Rican families, reports,

. . . The data on the eighty Puerto Rican families in this study, the clinical impression of physicians who treat Puerto Rican patients, the high incidence of new cases of tuberculosis . . . and the high admission rate to mental hospitals . . . reported for Puerto Ricans suggest that the general susceptibility to illness is high among Puerto Ricans in New York City as compared to other segments of the population. . . .

But there is more to the story. Dr. Berle points out that Puerto Ricans come here to progress, to work and make a better life for them and their children:

In order to progress one must work, and in order to work one must have health. In New York, a man can no longer take pride in his biceps. He is expected to wield a pen or operate a complex machine if he is to be respected and progress. . . .

Under these circumstances, illness may be an aspect of lack of success and may therefore become a justification for failure. Failure is inevitable when the discrepancy between an individual's aspirations and the limited employment opportunities open to him due to lack of schooling or special skill cannot be reconciled. To prove illness so that one may be cared for then becomes a vital necessity.

A good hospital will exhaust a large battery of tests to prove that there is nothing wrong with such an individual. Each new doctor, each additional test, confirms the man or woman in his conviction that he is sick, and that he is not being helped. . . . [But such individuals] are actually sick since they are unable to carry on the activities of their daily lives in the environment in which they live. . . .

. . . occasionally, a sick man is made whole. Apparently this is a matter of luck or a result of a careful manipulation of the environment by interested persons. In a family, school, church, settlement house, trade union, or neighborhood, when a dedicated individual with imagination who can mobilize some social or economic resources establishes and maintains a relationship with a man in trouble, things begin to happen. As a young American Negro who had become a member of the council of a local Baptist church in the neighborhood put it: "For the first time in my life I felt I was somebody." [48]

Everything may contribute to breaking the circle of dependency: more education, more training, fewer children, fewer illnesses, better housing, dedicated people who are interested in you, etc., etc. Some times at the bottom of the scale things are too far gone for anything to break the circle. Here are the "multiproblem" families, afflicted simultaneously by a variety of miseries—a child who is a drug-addict, another who is delinquent, a father who is psychologically or physically unable to work, or perhaps is not there. Here are the families so vividly described in Julius Horwitz's *The Inhabitants,* a novel by a man who has worked as an investigator for the welfare department. (Eight thousand employees are required to service the 300,-000 people in the case load of the welfare department of the city.) Perhaps the worst misfortune of this bottom layer in New York is the need to deal with large numbers of harried city employees who have no contact with each other, or, in truth, with their clients, except for the specific malfunction which brought them into action. The schoolteacher or principal can do nothing about what goes on at home; the welfare investigator's role must be simply one of testing whether the family is qualified; the probation officer is supposed to keep in touch with his case, not the case's family, and can do nothing if the home in which the probationer lives is located in a tenement that is a center for drug addiction or thievery; the housing project employee (if the family is lucky enough to be in one) is concerned with financial eligibility, the payment of rent, and the maintenance of the physical property; the hospital hands out drugs and treatment, and so on and so on. And social workers and others now and then set up a joint project to see if out of the welter of bureaucratic confusion there can be fashioned an instrument that responds to families and individuals as full human beings.

The Puerto Rican has entered the city in the age of the welfare state. Here and there are to be found the settlement houses of an earlier period, in which a fuller and richer concern for the individual was manifested by devoted people from the prosperous classes. The job of such social workers today is largely to humanize and coordinate, often through arousing the people of a neighborhood to bring pressure on public authorities, the various agencies on which the poor are so dependent. But there are few such agencies and social workers who can stand outside the system and see what is wrong with it, and within each Puerto Rican community there flourish individuals—"interpreters" —who accompany the unfortunates on their round of the city agencies, and who claim to be more skillful in finding their way through the maze of regulations and requirements.

In New York City one of the greatest misfortunes of the unfortunates who cannot help themselves is the enormous difficulty of managing one of the most complex and ingrown bureaucracies in the world. An equal misfortune is the housing situation, which consigns those without sufficient resources and without energy to the frightful one-room furnished dwellings carved out of brownstones and apartment houses principally on the West Side of Manhattan. There are better living quarters, at cheaper rents, in the Bronx and Brooklyn. But when one is overwhelmed by so many misfortunes, the energy to take the subway to look for an unfurnished apartment, to get together the few sticks of furniture and the minimal kitchen equipment (the welfare department will pay), is often literally beyond the capacity of many families. And so they migrate dully from one of these awful dwellings to another scarcely better a few blocks away. On these lower levels, what are needed are rehabilitation programs on a scale that scarcely anyone dares propose. It may cost no more than what the many agencies now spend, but the difficulties of breaking through the encrusted barriers that assign functions to each agency are simply too great for a new and more effective arrangement.

Meanwhile, one generation on relief gives rise to another. One-quarter of the Puerto Rican children in the city are on public assistance. The culture of public welfare, which Horwitz has so brilliantly described, is as relevant for the future of Puerto Ricans in the city as the culture of Puerto Rico.

During the fifties, despite all this, there was not an exceptionally high rate of delinquency among Puerto Rican children.[49] But it takes a while to adapt to a new culture, and one may reasonably expect that the "Americanization" of the Puerto Ricans under conditions we have described will lead to somewhat higher rates of delinquency and crime in the future. Today, a good deal of Puerto Rican crime consists of crimes of passion involving members of the community, but once again, it is not unreasonable to expect that in the future more and more of this violence will be turned outward. Rates of admission to mental hospitals are higher than they are on the island, or for New Yorkers in general.[50] And the Midtown study of mental health showed a remarkably high rate of impairment for the Puerto Ricans in the East Midtown area. This is not one of the typical areas of Puerto Rican settlement; the authors suggest that this group, isolated from the main body of new migrants, may be under greater strain than Puerto Ricans in more characteristically Puerto Rican parts of the city,[51] yet the findings are consistent with other findings on rates of illness. The migration it seems has hit New York Puerto Ricans very hard. For some reason, the rate of suicide seems to be less than it is on the island.[52] It may have risen since this study was made in the late forties.

THE NEXT GENERATION:
FAMILY, SCHOOL, NEIGHBORHOOD

WHAT KIND OF EXPERIENCES DO THE CHILDREN MEET IN THEIR families, schools, neighborhoods? How are they growing up? [53]

A typical pattern of migration of families with children is for the father to migrate alone, stay with relatives and friends, find a job and living quarters, and then gradually bring over the rest of the family. Many families are consequently divided between Puerto Rico and New York, and when they are united, if ever, they show wide differences in degree of knowledge of English, assimilation, and the like. A second pattern of migration involves a woman with children—her husband has deserted her, or she has decided to leave home and go to New York, where jobs are plentiful, where the government is reputed to be "for the women and the children," and where relief is plentiful.

The Puerto Rican mother works here much more often than she does in Puerto Rico, but women still tend, if at all possible, to stay home to take care of the children. Fewer of them work than do Negro mothers.

The question then is what kind of care the children get from these mothers, many of whom have been married since what we could consider childhood. In Puerto Rico, despite rapid urbanization and industrialization, and many consequent social changes, it is perfectly clear how one raises children. The boys are praised for their manliness, taught to be proper males, and aside from requiring them to be respectful to their fathers (whether or not these still live with their mothers) are left to raise themselves. In radically different fashion, the girls are carefully watched, warned to keep their virginity—without which a proper marriage is inconceivable—and relatively early escape from this restrictive stifling atmosphere into marriage and motherhood.

But in New York both traditional patterns raise serious problems. If the boys are left to themselves, they find bad friends, may take to drugs, will learn to be disrespectful and disobedient. And even if a boy survives the streets morally, how is he to survive them physically, with cars and trucks whizzing by, and tough Negro and Italian boys ready to beat him up under slight provocation? If the girls are guarded, are raised in the house as proper girls should be, they become resentful at a treatment that their classmates and friends are not subjected to. In addition, guarding in Puerto Rico means to keep an eye on one's daughters in a community where everyone was known and you knew everyone. Here, since the streets are dangerous, it means keeping the girl literally in the house. And if the house is a furnished room or apartment, tiny and over-crowded, it seems cruel and heartless to do so (yet many Puerto Rican parents do).

The radical boy-girl disjunction does not work in New York City. To the mind of the migrant parent the social agencies and settlement houses are no great help and often seem nests of sin. To the social worker or young minister working in the slums the dancing and other co-educational activities seem to be inducting young boys and girls into proper American behavior patterns, to be teaching them how to relate to each other in ways that are not purely sexual and exploitative, and perhaps in a measure they do accomplish this. To the Puerto Rican (and often Negro) parents what goes on seems simply shocking invitations to premature pregnancy. Very often then the children who go to the centers and the church activities are the ones from the most disorganized families, where the effort to raise them in proper fashion has been given up, and they are allowed to run wild! [54]

In this confusing situation there are two possibilities. One is to give up. There is a widespread belief among migrant parents that the government prevents dis-ciplining of children, but this seems to be in part a ra-tionalization for the difficulty of making the adjustment to the great freedom of American children, for the Puerto Rican Commonwealth protects children as much as New York City does. The parents feel inadequate at handling the children (and one can sympathize with such feelings in a teen-age mother) and explain the inadequacy by the gov-ernment's responsibility for the children. Another sign of giving up is the frequency with which Puerto Rican parents express the desire that their children should be sent away someplace where they may learn discipline, manners, and respect.[55]

But a more typical reaction to this confus-ing new situation is a tightening of the screws, not only on the girls but on the boys too. Many cases of disturbed Puerto Rican boys that come to the attention of social agen-cies are cases of anxious concern by parents, overprotection, exaggerated fear of the streets—their physical and moral dangers.[56] What is exaggeration or what is realism in thinking of the New York streets is a difficult question. The Puerto Rican mother is not as well disciplined as the native American mother who, in her desire to see her child become independent, can steel herself to forget the dangers her children face in such a simple act as coming home from school. The overprotection of the boys is often a response, social workers feel, to dissatisfaction with the marital relationship. The pattern is of course a common and widespread one, and there is nothing especially Puerto Rican about it.

The screws will also be tightened on the girls. Even without a tighter discipline against the greater dangers, the same discipline here as in Puerto Rico is going to be felt as a serious deprivation. One also faces the change in the age of marriage. Half the girls in Puerto Rico will be married by 19 and freed from the stern parental supervision. But there is no place in Puerto Rican cultural and family patterns for the older working girls who will not get married at such young ages here, and who are expected to scurry home from work as fast as they did from school. When one social worker suggested to a Puerto Rican girl who was working that she get away from the traditionally strict supervision of her father by moving into a residence, the girl was shocked. "She seems to think that in Puerto Rico they would consider any girl who moves away from her family into a residence as someone who goes into a house of prostitution." [57]

Then another problem is created by the inevitable shift from the extended family in Puerto Rico to the smaller one in New York. The Puerto Rican mother expects to have someone around to relieve her in the care of her children—there will be a mother, a sister, an aunt, a *comadre,* and she will be living with her or close enough to be helpful. In New York this traditional pattern will often be found, but it is much more difficult to maintain. It cannot be arranged, for example, to have mother or sister move next door in the same housing project. Children become much more of a bother, much more of a strain. One is expected to take care of them completely on one's own, and without help. An anthropologist who has studied this matter feels that the more traditional Puerto Rican family in New York does a better job raising its children than the nuclear family of man and woman, for in the latter the mother is likely to feel resentment and strain.[58]

The changing city no longer provides the neighborhood that is exclusive to one ethnic group. And the city administration insists that in the low-rent housing under its management the groups be mixed as much as possible (20 per cent of the city's low-cost housing is now occupied by Puerto Ricans, and about a seventh of the Puerto Rican population now lives in them). And so the models for new conduct in rearing one's children vary; there are Negro, Jewish, and Italian models of child rearing and child discipline, as well as the American models of the welfare workers and the settlement houses, and a variety of sub-variants in each. What degree of discipline, what kind of punishment and rewards, what expectations should one have from one's children—the Puerto Rican mother is at a loss in deciding the right course.

We speak of the Puerto Rican mother, because on her falls the main task of child rearing, in part because so many of them manage homes without males present, or with males who take no particular responsibility for the children; and because in the traditional Puerto Rican home the father expects, aside from his demand for respect and obedience, to have little to do with the children. He also considers it beneath his dignity to participate in the management of the home, and considers it his prerogative to be off by himself whenever he wishes to be. But of course his traditional position is seriously challenged in America. Not only can the mother get relief and throw him out, not only can she get a job that pays as well as his does (she can often do this in Puerto Rico, too, today), but society does not prevent her from following an independent course. The women, many of the men grumble, are "spoiled" here; the women, on the other hand, will often express preference for a man raised in America who does not expect the same self-effacement from them. Nor are the courts or the police or the social workers sympathetic to the position of a traditional Puerto Rican male standing upon his dignity. His

world often falls apart—this is why there is so often a
descent into incapacity and into mental or physical illness.
          And then there is the role of the school in
the lives of the children. Even the least-schooled migrant
knows the value of education; Puerto Ricans universally
would like to see their children well educated, and hope
they will be professionals. But school is often a frustrating
experience. The shift to a new language has been peculiarly
difficult for the Puerto Ricans. We can only speculate about
the reasons why Jews and even Italians, coming into the city
at roughly the same ages, with much less formal knowledge
of English, should have made a rather better linguistic adjustment. Certainly the schools did much less to ease their
path./ Of course in the years of the heaviest Jewish and
Italian migration the school-leaving age was much lower,
children often began working at 12, and the problems that
the schools must today face (which are severer with the older
children) were reduced. In other words, the children who
could not learn English forty years ago got out before their
problems became too noticeable. But we can only guess at
the differences—no one seems to have gone back to see what
the schools did when whole districts were filled with Yiddish-
speaking and Italian-speaking children.

          ❘ Probably no public school system has spent
as much money and devoted as much effort to the problem
of a group of minority children as the New York public
school system has devoted to the Puerto Ricans. There are
now hundreds of special personnel to deal with parents, to
help teachers, to deal with special problems of students. The
magnitude of the problems is barely communicated by figures. "On October 31, 1958," reports the Board of Education, "of the 558,741 children in our elementary schools,
there were 56,296 children of Puerto Rican ancestry whose
lack of ability to speak or understand English represented
a considerable handicap to learning." [59]

          The numbers alone are enormous; there is
the additional problem of the rapid movement of the newcomers. On the West Side of Manhattan, one of the major
sections of entry for new migrants, the turnover in an area
containing sixteen schools was 92 per cent; which means

that each year the school confronts what is in effect a completely new student body.[60]

It is probably particularly difficult for the
adolescent boys to adjust to this situation. The pattern of
maintenance of male self-dignity makes it embarrassing to
speak English with an accent. Dr. Berle believes it is easier
for adolescent girls who have not had this emphasis in their
upbringing to adapt to the English language school. (Perhaps the Jewish tradition of self-ridicule—dignity there is
only for the old—stands them in good stead in new situations. One is astonished at the willingness of Jewish storekeepers to speak a most corrupt Spanish to deal with their
Puerto Rican clientele: in contrast to their customers they
are shameless.)

Meanwhile, there is a good deal of school-
leaving at the earliest possible age, and relatively small proportions today go into the academic high schools. The register for New York City schools in October 1960 showed that
18 per cent of the elementary school students, 17 per cent
of the junior high school students, and only 8 per cent of
the high school students were Puerto Ricans. The proportion in the academic high schools was 5 per cent.[61]

/ The other side of the coin is an impressive
amount of activity by young, educated Puerto Ricans to
raise the level of concern for education. For example, Puerto
Rican social workers, professionals, and teachers have set
up an organization, *Aspira,* devoted to working with students and their parents so that they will take all possible
advantage of educational opportunities. It runs workshops
in which plans to get through high school or into or through
college are worked out, it gives lectures on professional
opportunities, looks for money for scholarships, reaches
parents and community organizations. The young Puerto
Rican leaders also run an interesting annual youth conference that gives a revealing insight into the concerns and
struggles of the young people. This group clearly sees Puerto
Ricans as following in the path of the earlier ethnic groups
that preceded it, and speaks of them as models of emulation
rather than as targets for attack. Its identification is with
the Jews or Italians of forty years ago, rather than with the
Negroes of today. It has a rather hopeful outlook, which

emphasizes the group's potential for achievement more than the prejudice and discrimination it meets. One can only hope that this buoyant outlook will be better sustained by life in the city. It is a note in tune with the gentleness and gaiety of the Puerto Ricans themselves.

CULTURE, CONTRIBUTIONS, COLOR

THE YOUNG PUERTO RICAN LEADERS WOULD LIKE TO SEE A NEW Hispanic-American strand added to the culture of the city. They organize art shows and book fairs, and one feels they could make a contemporary Puerto Rican Educational Alliance hum with activity if they had more financial resources. They would like to see in the city a Spanish newspaper that was not a sensational tabloid. (As one Puerto Rican leader said, he would like to see a Spanish *Jewish Daily Forward*—this is the great Socialist daily that educated the Jewish immigrants.) Despite this spirit, one sees formidable obstacles in the path of establishing a high Hispanic-American culture among the Puerto Rican immigrants. The Nobel-prize-winning author of *Platero and I* and Pablo Casals, two great cultural figures of the Spanish-speaking world, have chosen to live in Puerto Rico; it is hardly imaginable that they could have found as congenial a setting in the Puerto Rican community of New York.

There are a few small groups in the city which give lectures, music and dance demonstrations, but the audiences for these are tiny. There is an occasional effort to try to do something about a Spanish theater or to mount a Spanish play, but as yet there is no regular living theater.

The Puerto Ricans, despite their numbers in the city, come from a small country, in which the Spanish cultural heritage has not been strong and has been affected by sixty years of contact with America to produce a certain amount of cultural schizophrenia; Puerto Rico can and does depend upon the cultural products of the whole Spanish-speaking world. And so Puerto Ricans read magazines and books printed in Spain and Latin America (as the Cuban *Bohemia,* which is popular among them) and see movies made in Latin America.

But there is a more general reason why we cannot expect any striking new cultural strands to be brought to the city by immigrants, regardless of their source. The fact is that all cultures, even in their homelands, become more and more alike under the impact of mass media. The Puerto Ricans, like many in Latin America, read the Spanish editions of the *Reader's Digest, Life,* and *Sexology* (relabeled in Spanish *Luz*), and the content carried by a different language comes more and more to parallel the common content of the most successful and widely distributed cultural products.

Under the impact of movies and television, the people, even if they could speak and say something distinctive, are dumb. The Yiddish stage and the theaters set up by other groups in the nineteenth century could flourish for a while because in the age of handicraft culture their products were almost as good as any others. It would have to take a striking degree of cultural self-consciousness on the part of Puerto Ricans to create a vital Spanish stage when there are thirty movie theaters showing Spanish-language movies. And by the time the more subtle and sophisticated cultural needs that might demand a stage or serious magazines are developed, the processes of assimilation will guarantee that the need will be met in the general cultural arena.

But if the prognosis for high culture is doubtful, New York's folk culture—and in time, one feels sure, its commercial culture—is already deeply affected by the Puerto Rican migration. In every area of Puerto Rican settlement little record stores carry a remarkable variety of Latin American music; the same records, and live music, pour from hundreds of rooms and apartment houses, and from small and large (and even internationally known) dance halls. As the group becomes larger and more self-conscious, the special Puerto Rican passion for music and dancing will mark the rather cold and sharp city more and more.

Indeed, if one spreads the word "culture" to include "ethos," one sees even more significant effects. The Puerto Ricans add to a rather tough and knowing cast of

New York characters a new type, softer and milder, gayer and more light-spirited. One hears little of these more positive elements of the Puerto Rican migration as yet, for the problems created by the mass migration take first place, both for the Puerto Ricans and the city.

Indeed, in speaking of the contribution of Puerto Rican migrants to New York City, one hears little of culture and rather more of the economic benefits of the migration. The Waldorf-Astoria and certain branches of the clothing industry, we are told, would not be able to manage without Puerto Rican labor. But then suppose for some reason there had not been this migration from the island? In part it would probably have been replaced by a somewhat greater migration of Negroes from the South; the Southern pool is not inexhaustible, but in proportion to the population of the cities, more of it has gone to Chicago, Detroit, and Philadelphia than has come to New York. Perhaps the two labor sources mutually complement each other, and where one is abundant, the other falls off.

But it is also possible there might have been a shortage of the lowest-priced labor in the city: in which case sections of the garment industry might have migrated to Pennsylvania and the South even faster than they did, and new factories based on cheap, semiskilled labor might have located elsewhere. The immovable industries (hotels and restaurants and laundries) would either have had worse service or charged more. There would have been other economic effects: for one consequence of the abundant quantity of cheap labor in the city was the fact the large parts of the housing stock were rapidly ruined by subdivision and overcrowding, and that the city had to invest more in welfare services. If one wants to argue the advantages of a migration on economic grounds, one must run the risk of the figure turning out against the migration rather than for it. This is not to say that there was a striking economic disadvantage to the Puerto Rican migration for the city; but it cannot be demonstrated that the city is better off as a result.

The Puerto Rican migration, it is true, responded to the supply of jobs in the city closely; but the fact that there was an inexhaustible and easily mobile supply of low-cost labor also affected the kinds of jobs that existed in the city.

A more significant Puerto Rican contribution to the city of New York, one suspects, will be in the area of attitudes toward color. There New York, as well as all America, does need improvement, and the Puerto Rican migration is likely to have interesting and varied effects on the city's attitudes. The Puerto Ricans introduce into the city a group that is intermediate in color, neither all white nor all dark, but having some of each, and a large number that show the physical characteristics of both groups. And second, they carry a new attitude toward color—an attitude that may be corrupted by continental color prejudice but it is more likely, since this is in harmony with the trends that are making all nations part of a single world community, that the Puerto Rican attitude to color, or something like it, will become the New York attitude.

The Puerto Ricans are not paragons of democratic color attitudes, but in contrast with American prejudices they show a very different picture. The upper classes in Puerto Rico, and the middle classes too, are almost entirely white. In the United States one knows that whatever the status of the Negro the dominant factor in his history is prejudice. In Puerto Rico one knows that whatever the status of the Negro he is what he is because of historical circumstances in which color prejudice has played little part. He was a slave, and when he was emancipated he was a landless laborer, and he has had no opportunity. And so he is poor, less educated, more frequently not legally married, and the rest. In the lower classes, where everyone is poor and without opportunity, there is no strong sense of difference based on color; intermarriage is common, and people are aware of color and hair and facial features as they are aware of any other personal and defining characteristics of an individual. They say he is darker or lighter the way we say he is blond or brunet, and personal taste in marriage and sexual partners may lead one, it appears, to someone of differing color almost as often as it will to someone of the same color. In Puerto Rico, in fact, there seems to be much less concern over color than there is in Jamaica, where among the Negro population that makes up almost the entire island there are subtle distinctions made in shade, and persons try to marry lighter than themselves. So indifferent is the lower class Puerto Rican to this aspect of people that one cannot detect any pattern in marriage—the more successful marrying lighter; darker men marrying lighter women; or what not.

Indeed, the mixture of races in Puerto Rico has been proceeding on a level that is almost without example in history. One effect of this mixture is that in every census there are less and less people who are definably Negro. In 1860 almost half the Puerto Ricans were listed in a census as Negro. By the end of the century only two-fifths, in 1950 only one-fifth.[62] Presumably this has happened only as a result of the fact that the traits which define a Negro are now distributed more widely through the population, because physical anthropologists take it as gospel that the hereditary genes do not change their proportions in a population unless the people carrying them reproduce less rapidly, and there is no evidence that Negroes reproduce less rapidly than whites in Puerto Rico. Perhaps, owing to poverty, they survive less. Another peculiar feature of the Puerto Rican racial distribution is that there seem to be less colored women than men, according to the best study of the physical anthropology of Puerto Rico. Why this should be so was as mysterious to the physical anthropologist making the study as it is to the lay observer.[63] It is also interesting that the proportion of colored Puerto Ricans in New York drops from census to census. Do the colored return to Puerto Rico? Or are the census takers' reactions to color changing?

There is color discrimination on the island, but it often reflects the attitude to the poor, the worker, the miserable. Father Joseph Fitzpatrick, the author of many subtle and insightful studies of the Puerto Ricans in New York, describes the matter as follows:

The traditional upper class always prided itself on being white and has always been very sensitive to the matter of color or racial characteristics. They became important factors in anyone's attempt to claim identity with a pure Spanish lineage. [In the 1940's, for example, the fraternities at the University of Puerto Rico and exclusive clubs in San Juan did not admit anyone who was clearly colored.] . . . The same attitude is found also among some of the poorer people who apparently seek distinction by identifying themselves as pure white. The author has been frequently surprised by the preoccupation with color of people in some of the poor mountain sections. "Look, Father, do you notice how white everyone is here!" is mentioned with a spontaneity and candor that is quite striking. These same people, however, will deny that there is racial prejudice or discrimination in Puerto Rico. They insist that the distinction is one of class, not color. People are excluded from social participation not because they are colored, but because they are lower class. . . .[64]

American color attitudes must have influenced some upper-middle-class Puerto Ricans. And yet the all-white social clubs of San Juan preceded the American occupation, because for them whiteness was a sign of pure (and legitimate) descent, and the all-white fraternities of the University reflected the same attitudes.

But what happens in New York? Here now only 4 per cent of the Puerto Ricans are clearly colored. In the forties, it seemed possible to look forward to a time when the Puerto Rican group would split, and the darker ones would be absorbed into the over-all American Negro community, just as West Indians and other colored immigrants of backgrounds very different from those of American Negroes were absorbed. And it was often pointed out that perhaps the Puerto Ricans clung to Spanish so strongly because this differentiated the colored among them from the lower caste in American life.

Mills and his colleagues argued in 1950 that the intermediate in color were least assimilated, most passionately attached to whatever identified them as Puerto Rican because they were not unambiguously white or colored.[65] Clearly, color was a problem for Puerto Ricans in New York, as it was for upwardly mobile ones of the island. And its psychological impact on individuals, the anxiety it created, was perhaps greater than any objective difference of treatment on the basis of it would warrant. For we think that the brown-skinned in New York are not subject to the kind of prejudice that Negroes are; indeed Puerto Ricans believe that they have opened up and can open up areas of the city in which Negroes have never lived. But personal problems are not only a reflection of reality but also of what one thinks reality is, and Puerto Ricans may feel their degree of color is more of a problem than it really is. It is perhaps suggestive of this problem that Dr. Berle reports a social worker's comment that every Puerto Rican drug addict he had dealt with was the darkest in his family.[66]

Father Fitzpatrick's study reveals that despite these problems and this anxiety, the newcomers still maintain the pattern of a single Puerto Rican community in which people mingle in social events of all kinds in disregard of the color marks that so affect American social behavior. Indeed, since we are without a Puerto Rican upper class or Puerto Rican upper-class institutions here, one could say that there is even less race prejudice among Puerto Ricans in New York than on the island.

Even more interesting: Father Fitzpatrick's study of marriages in the city shows a sizable proportion between persons of different color, and it would appear that at least a sixth of Puerto Rican marriages are what to American eyes would be "intermarriages."

There is unfortunately some evidence that when there are Americans at mixed social gatherings the Puerto Ricans present may be embarrassed at the mixture of color. As they mix more with Americans and become more middle class, this embarrassment may grow. But after fifteen years the break between colored and white Puerto Ricans has not occurred; the community is maintained; and if it continues as a single community in which color consciousness is not the cancer it is in American life, the Puerto Ricans may bring a greater gift to New York than any special cultural product.

The pressures of the attitudes of one-quarter of the population (Negroes and Puerto Ricans), who will soon be one-third of the population, will combine with the presence of the U.N. and the impact of the colored nations on American politics, and New York may be very different in ten years. Visitors from the Midwest are already startled by the numbers of social groups and couples of different colors to be seen on the streets; in some sections of New York, as on the West Side, the native white population is no longer even startled.

But all this is sheer speculation, as is the prediction of some expansive leaders of the Puerto Rican community that New York will become a bilingual city. (Indeed, it may soon be possible for Puerto Ricans to vote without being literate in English; and perhaps the school system may be tempted soon to take the radical step of seeing whether instruction in Spanish, for some grades, may not help solve some of its problems.) The Puerto Ricans are adapting to a city very different from the one to which earlier immigrant groups adapted, and they are being modified by the new process of adaptation in new and hardly predictable ways. In 1961 an Italian was replaced by a Puerto Rican as Democratic political leader in a district in East Harlem, and many saw Puerto Ricans entering the same path that Italians took forty years before. But it is a different city, and a different group, and one can barely imagine what kind of human community will emerge from the process of adaptation.

the Jews

A LEADING figure in Jewish community affairs relates that a Jew always eagerly asks, in any situation, "How many are Jews?" And when he gets an answer, he asks suspiciously, "How do you know?"

Self-consciousness, curiosity, pride—all these are Jewish traits; caution, timidity, fear—these are Jewish traits, too. But our interest for the moment is in the more mundane subject of figures.

The U.S. Census does not ask about religion. But sociologists, planners, journalists, and people in general are so interested in this question that it might have done so a long time ago except for, among other reasons, the strong opposition of certain Jewish organizations. At the same time, the Jewish community demands that such figures exist; so Jewish organizations have developed techniques for estimating the Jewish population. In 1957 the census did ask a question about religion, as a pretest for a possible question about religion in the 1960 census. Some information from this sample was released before the Jewish organizations that oppose official statistics on Jews had developed pressure enough to seal the returns. This abortive census study had at least the result of loosely corroborating the figures derived in less direct ways.

We know that somewhat more than a *quarter* of the population of New York City is Jewish; that about a *third* of the white and non-Puerto Rican part of the population of the city is Jewish; and that this huge concentration of Jews, the greatest that has existed in thousands of years of Jewish history, forms about two-fifths of all the Jews in the United States. The city and surrounding suburban counties together include about half of the nation's Jews,[1] and almost all the rest have once lived in the city, will at some time live there, or have parents or children who live there. New York is the headquarters of the Jewish group. The euphemistic use of the term "New Yorker" to refer to "Jew," which is not uncommon in the United States, is thus based on some reality.

There have been Jews in New York City since almost its beginning. The first group, which landed in 1654, were "Sephardic" Jews, as those originally from Spain and Portugal are called, and spoke Portuguese. But they were also "Dutch" Jews, for they had been driven from Spain and Portugal at the end of the fifteenth century and settled in Holland. They were also "Brazilian" Jews, having for some decades formed a large and important Jewish community in Brazil until the Portuguese, driving out the Dutch, had sent them on their way again. The synagogue these first Jews established is appropriately named Shearith Israel, "the Remnant of Israel," and in its latest physical form stands at Central Park West and 70th Street. There an ancient form of the Jewish service is carefully preserved and elegantly performed.

The special prominence of Jews in New York is, however, of much later origin. During the middle of the nineteenth century there was a sizable immigration of Jews from Germany. In 1880 there were perhaps 80,000 Jews in the city. Still, they were only 4 per cent of the population, which was then mainly Irish, German, and old-stock American, and they were mostly German-speaking (from Austria, Bohemia, and Hungary, as well as Germany itself). This largely German immigration became concentrated in business, particularly retail trade, and was economically quite successful. The German names of leading department stores in a dozen cities remind us of this wave of immigration. In the 1880's began the enormous migration from Eastern Europe, particularly from the Russian Empire, but also including sizable streams from pre-World-War Austria–Hungary and from Rumania. By 1910 there were a million and a quarter Jews in New York City. They then formed more than a quarter of the population, a proportion they have maintained ever since.

This great migration, which continued, except for the interruption of the First World War, until it was reduced by law in 1924, has stamped the character of New York. The city's Jews are descendants of the Yiddish-speaking, Orthodox and Socialist Jews of Eastern Europe. Despite a half-century of American life, which has made the grandchildren now coming to maturity very different from what their grandparents were, they retain much that recalls their origins.

By 1924 there were almost two million Jews in the city. The old German Jewish community, marked off in language, religion, culture, and occupation from the new immigrants, was a tenth part or less of New York Jewry. When we see the contrast between these two groups (the variations within each were of course also great), we must ask what made them in any sense a single group. The German Jews could have stood off from the East European, Yiddish-speaking Jews and insisted they had nothing in common. Indeed, in practice, tone, and theology, the Reform Judaism of the German Jews diverged from the Orthodoxy of the immigrants as much as the beliefs and practices of Southern Baptists differ from those of New England Unitarians.

Two wills make a group—the self-will that creates unity, and the will of others that imposes a unity where hardly any is felt. Conceivably this will of others had an effect on Jews, for since the 1870's anti-Semitism had been rising in the upper social circles to which the German

Jews felt closest. Perhaps German Jews feared that, regardless of what they thought and felt, non-Jews would identify them with the new immigrants. Whatever the reasons, they themselves sensed this identity. Out of a multitude of institutions and organizations, a consciously single Jewish community was formed by the time of the First World War.

The identification of the older group with the newer one took many forms. It was evident in the organization of charitable institutions to give immigrants money, guidance, training, and education so as to "Americanize" them. In 1917 a single Federation of Jewish Charities was formed to serve all Jews without discrimination. In 1906 wealthy German Jews founded the American Jewish Committee to defend Jewish interests, which meant, at that time, primarily the interests of East European Jews. Prominent Jews of the German group—Louis Marshall, Louis Brandeis, Jacob Schiff, Oscar Straus—were involved in the great strikes that created the powerful garment trades unions before the First World War. Both the bosses and the strikers were generally East European Jews, and German Jewish dignitaries served as mediators. Both communities cooperated in Jewish relief during the First World War, and elements of both helped create a Jewish state in Palestine. (Elements of both also opposed it.) Since 1920 the new groups that have arrived—Sephardic Jews from Greece and Turkey in the twenties, German refugees of the thirties, or displaced persons of the forties and fifties—have been met not by "German Jewish" or "East European Jewish" institutions, but by institutions that are simply "American Jewish."

What is this Jewish community? There is no organization that includes all Jews, though the United Jewish Appeal may come close in that it collects from very many. The neat division of "Protestant, Catholic, Jewish" makes it easy to think of Jews as a religious group, but whereas a single organization baptizes and keeps track of all Catholics (at least for statistical purposes), there is no central Jewish religious organization, except for a small coordinating group that links the rabbinical and congregational associations of the three Jewish denominations. In any case, most Jews in New York City belong to no synagogue or temple, and many of them are nonreligious, or even antireligious. And yet we know from experience that when asked, "What is your religion?" even *these* answer, "Jewish." [2]

If the category of religion does not define Jews well, neither does the category of national origin or culture, for Jews have come from a score of countries and speak many different languages. The Sephardic Jew has to learn Yiddish expressions just as the non-Jew does; his "Yiddish" is not a German dialect, but Spanish. Nor does a common sentimental commitment to a national homeland define Jews, for, despite the feeling of most Jews for Israel, many are violently opposed to the whole idea. And yet, despite the difficulty of finding the common denominator, there is really no ambiguity about being Jewish, even though people are Jewish in different ways.

There is first of all the fact that the over- whelming majority of American Jews *do* stem from a single culture—the Yiddish-speaking culture of Eastern Europe, which had a single, strongly defined religion, which we now call Orthodoxy but which was once only traditional Juda- ism, intensified by the isolation of the East European Jews from the surrounding world. This East European group had been stamped with a common character by common expe- riences: a strong governmental and popular anti-Semitism, and the development in response to it of a variety of ideo- logical movements, such as Socialism and Zionism, as well as the huge migratory movement that dispersed this group to the United States, Canada, Argentina, England, France, Israel, and South Africa. The worldwide migration of this vigorous people makes American Jews at home almost every- where they go, for other descendants of East European Jews, speaking or understanding Yiddish, will be found almost everywhere.

This dominant group created a Jewish sub- culture in which almost everyone knew and used a few Yiddish expressions, and which has served as the first stage in the assimilation to America of very different kinds of Jew- ish immigrants. But there is more to the creation of a Jewish community than the link with Eastern Europe and the crea- tion of a single American subculture. There is also, linking all Jews, the sense of a common fate. In part, the common fate is defined ultimately by connection to a single religion, to which everyone is still attached by birth and tradition if not by action and belief. In part, it reflects the imposition of a common fate by the outer world, whether in the form of Hitler's extermination or the mild differential behavior that is met in America today.

This "community," then, is a group that may never act together and that may never feel together, but that does know it is a single group, from which one can be disengaged only by a series of deliberate acts. Only a minority are "Jews" if we use some concrete defining index. Only a minority belongs to synagogues, is sent to Jewish schools, deals with Jewish welfare agencies, is interested in Jewish culture, speaks a traditional Jewish language, and can be distinguished by dress and custom as Jews. But, added together, the overlapping minorities create a community with a strong self-consciousness and a definite character.

The easiest way of identifying a Jew is to ask his religion. Regardless of the low rate of religious identification among the Jews in New York City, only rarely, as we have pointed out, will a person born of Jewish parents not answer "Jewish." The simplest answer to the question "Who is a Jew?" (which became a problem only because Jews broke with their traditional religion in the nineteenth century) is the return question, "Who is not a Jew?" For the purposes of those efficient fund-raising organizations which make it their business to keep tabs on Jews, only those who have converted are not Jews. There are remarkably few of them. So, linked by the strong arm of the Jewish communal organizations, even if resentfully, there is quite a range of individuals—Orthodox, Conservative, Reform, and secular Jews, self-conscious and proud Jews and hardly conscious and embarrassed Jews, Jews who know about their history and religion, and Jews who know less about it than any Christian minister.

There is then a reality to this notion of an American Jewish community, though it is not a reality that can be summed up in a simple definition. Aware of all the complexities of being Jewish, of all the groupings and subgroups within that category, and of all the ways in which Jews do not act as a group, we can still speak of it as a group.[3]

THE ECONOMIC BASE

OF COURSE, ONE OF THE REASONS WE CAN SPEAK OF THE JEWISH group is that in a number of ways it is sharply defined, special, and individual. As any casual observer knows, its economic characteristics are particularly striking.

Around the world, wherever they went, the Jews of Eastern Europe became in large proportions businessmen. Too, wherever they went, they showed a fierce passion to have their children educated and become professionals. In these respects, the Jews of England, the United States, Argentina, and South Africa are not very different. The opportunities were different, but in each case, arriving with no money and few skills, beginning as workers or tiny tradesmen, they have achieved remarkable economic success. Indeed, one of the probable reasons that the American Jewish Committee, the oldest of three major organizations interested in the civil rights of Jews (the others are the Anti-Defamation League of B'nai B'rith and the American Jewish Congress), opposed further analysis of the information gathered by the census in 1957 was that it feared anti-Semites could make use of figures on Jewish income.[4]

Income figures are difficult to interpret. One can point out that if Jews have higher incomes than non-Jews, it may be because they are concentrated on the Northeastern Seaboard, which has higher incomes than many other parts of the country; that they are concentrated in big cities, which have higher incomes than rural areas or small cities; that they are among the better educated, who have higher incomes than the less well educated; that they are in business and the professions to a higher degree than other people, and so forth. Presumably one might show that, all these factors taken into account, Jews have incomes no higher than those of other people. But then the factors of Northeastern concentration, urbanism, education, and occupation would have to be explained. Wherever studies have been made, Jews have been found to be moving out of the working class into the middle class at a surprising rate.

In New York, which once had a huge Jewish working class and in which the great Jewish labor movement arose, there are still large numbers of Jewish workers. Aside from garment workers, there are many Jewish painters, carpenters, bakers, glaziers, and other tradesmen, waiters, barbers, and taxicab drivers. In fact, the tone of New York as a "Jewish" city is communicated to visitors as much by workers as by businessmen and professionals. A study in 1952 showed that manual workers formed a *third* of Jewish employed males (but manual workers formed more than half of all New York City white males). A quarter of the Jewish males worked at white-collar occupations at the subprofessional level and as salesmen. But 15 per cent worked as professionals or semiprofessionals (as against 11 per cent of all white males in the metropolitan area), and 24 per cent were proprietors of their own businesses, managers or officials, as against 16 per cent of the white males of the metropolitan area. The differences between Jews and non-Jews are about the same for women's occupations. There are proportionately fewer manual workers and more clerical and sales workers among Jewish women than in the female population as a whole. But almost a quarter of all employed Jewish women in 1952 worked with their hands, in factories and in service occupations.[5]

Thus there is still a sizable Jewish working class in New York City, but very few Jews are casual laborers, service workers, or semiskilled factory workers. And the Jewish workers are for the most part old, of the immigrant generation. As they retire or die, they are not replaced by either their children or new Jewish immigrants. The unions are increasingly less Jewish. One huge local of the ILGWU which keeps records on the ethnicity of its members—Dressmakers' Local 22—reports a drop in the proportion of Jews from about 75 per cent in the 1940's to 44 per cent in 1958. And this is one of the most Jewish of labor unions. Among the men's clothing workers, there is now only a small percentage of Jews; among painters and carpenters too the percentage has dropped. Within the garment industry, Jews are now concentrated in the better-paying, more-skilled trades, and it is only these that young Jews enter. Just as Jews found when they entered the garment trades at the turn of the century that the designers and cutters were English and German, so today incoming Negroes and Puerto Ricans find that the designers and cutters are Jewish.

Yet Jewish labor leaders continue to dominate, even though they deal for the most part with non-Jewish workers. At the lower levels of leadership, they must make the same adaptation to foreign-language workers that Jewish peddlers and storekeepers have made to Puerto Rican customers on the Lower East Side. Thus, in the Skirtmakers' Union of the ILGWU, which is half Spanish-American and only a quarter Jewish (the Jews are divided between an East European and Sephardic group), there are four Spanish-speaking business agents, all of whom are Sephardic Jews. Their native language is basically the Spanish of fifteenth-century Spain! [6]

It will take quite a long time for the union leadership to reflect the new composition of the membership, for, at least in the garment unions, educated Jewish men, often with a background as socialist intellectuals, continue to provide a source of skilled leadership. For example, a new vice-president of the ILGWU, Henoch Mendelsund, perpetuates the old tradition of Jewish union leaders. He is one of the intellectuals and socialists who escaped from Hitler's Europe, and like other wartime and postwar refugees he began work in a garment shop.[7] Naturally, this kind of ideological background is rare among the newer workers in the industry, most of whom are from other ethnic groups.

The immigration from Hitler's Europe which supplied a few new Jewish labor leaders also supplied a sizable body of workers to the declining Jewish working class of the city. The 150,000 Jewish immigrants who came out of the displaced persons camps after the war were not, like earlier German refugees, highly educated professionals and businessmen. Most of them became workers. Some have already, like Jewish immigrants before them, become small businessmen (a few are wealthy). But most will remain workers, and, in the immigrant tradition, have transferred their hopes to their children. Scenes that were played out on the Lower East Side fifty years ago may now be seen again in the low-rent areas of Brooklyn and Bronx where these newest immigrants have settled. Jewish boys separate from their playmates and devote themselves to studies, heading for the academic and specialized high schools. This immigrant group is much too small to do more than slow down slightly the rapid disappearance of the Jewish working class—or the Yiddish press, which it has also stimulated. Furthermore, this group will be assimilated at a much more rapid rate than the Yiddish-speaking workers of fifty years ago, for it does not form a huge and dense concentration, and private organizations, families, and the government will help it move out of the working class.

Thus the Jewish working class is rapidly disappearing, though its unions and other institutions remain. The Workmen's Circle, a great fraternal order that supplied insurance benefits, Yiddish schools, social life, camps, and cultural activities, continues in existence, but despite its name many of its members today are small businessmen and white-collar workers.

In New York, as contrasted with cities where the Jewish community is smaller, there is a huge lower-middle class. Great numbers of Jewish women work in offices, and great numbers of Jewish men work in clerical jobs. One-seventh of the government employees in New York are Jewish. This is smaller than the Jewish proportion in the city, but much greater than the proportion of Jewish government employees in other cities. But even these occupations are probably in decline among Jews. Jewish secretaries are less common than they once were. And in view of the near-universal drive to college education among young Jews, this trend will probably continue.

The teaching force of New York is now, according to one informed guess, perhaps 50 per cent Jewish. A great majority of school principals are Jewish. This is in part a heritage of the depression, when Jewish college graduates found few other occupations that offered comparable income and security. The Board of Education has been forced to close the schools on Yom Kippur and Rosh Hashana, for it simply cannot depend on enough teachers showing up to take care of the children. (It was never induced to take this step by the large decline in pupil attendance on these holidays.) The very large number of Jewish teachers affects the character of New York schools. It is not easy to figure out what the impact of a largely Jewish teaching force is on students, compared with, for example, the largely Irish and German and white Protestant teaching force of thirty or forty years ago. Yet the groups are so different in their intellectual attitudes, cultural outlooks, and orientations toward education and college that some influence, one can be sure, must be felt. Whether, in their expectation of intellectual competence, the Jewish teachers overwhelm and discourage Negro and Puerto Rican migrant children, or encourage them to greater efforts, would be hard to say.

New York Jews can never become as completely a business and professional group as can Jews in cities where they form, say, only 5 per cent of the population. Yet Jews already constitute a majority of those engaged in many businesses and professions in the city (medicine, law, dentistry). Nor do they any longer meet discrimination in skilled trades or in white-collar and clerical employment, a situation that affected them very deeply in the 1920's and 1930's when they desperately needed such jobs. The wartime shortages took care of that. It is now only at the higher levels of the economy that discrimination arises. But it does arise there, and Jewish civil rights groups wonder what can be done about it.

In the great banks, insurance companies, public utilities, railroads, and corporation head offices that are located in New York, and in the Wall Street law firms, few Jews are to be found. One of the few things that strikes a Jew as unfamiliar in New York, so much a Jewish city, is the life of the junior executive of a great corporation as described recently by *Fortune* magazine, on the assumption, presumably, that such a life is typical in New York.[8] Jews find equally strange William H. Whyte's descriptions of the life of organization men. Not enough lead such lives to be familiar with their problems, for example, that of being "moved about" by the corporation. The Jewish businessman is traditionally a small businessman, in his own or a family-owned firm. He does not move about except to make sales or buy. The Jewish professional too is characteristically self-employed, a "free" professional—in part because the great private bureaucracies that employ professionals have in the past generally been closed to him. Rooted to his practice, he too does not move. This situation is changing somewhat, but very slowly. Where talent counts more than "appearance" or "type," Jews are employed more readily. Thus the Wall Street law firms that have always wanted to get the brightest law school graduates now have numbers of young Jews. And these firms are facing the prospect of having to take on their first, or first few, Jewish partners. The great banks and insurance companies, the corporations and public utilities, do not have a similar problem, so few are their Jewish executives.

Some interesting facts support these observations. An American Jewish Committee study of graduates of the Harvard Business School shows that the non-Jewish graduates proportionately outnumber Jewish graduates in executive positions in the leading American corporations by better than 30 to 1. John Slawson, the head of the Committee, has asserted, "Jews constitute less than one-half of 1 per cent of the total executive personnel in leading American industrial companies." This he compared with the fact the Jews form about 8 per cent of the college-trained in the country.[9] The Anti-Defamation League has studied employees making more than $10,000 a year (there were 6,100 of them) in seven insurance companies. While 5.4 per cent were Jewish, they were mostly engaged not in the home offices but in sales jobs—and these naturally reflect the population to which sales are made, as well perhaps as the belief that Jews make good salesmen. Even the relatively small numbers of Jews employed in home offices tend to be technicians—actuaries, physicians, attorneys, accountants. The ranks of general management are surprisingly free of Jews.[10] The Anti-Defamation League has also studied eight of the largest banks in the city. Of 844 vice-presidents and above, only 30 are Jews—less than 4 per cent. Four of the banks did not have a single Jewish officer.[11]

Obviously, in addition to discrimination, one must also reckon with taste and tradition among Jews, which may have had their origin in discrimination, but which may now lead a good number of Jews voluntarily to avoid huge bureaucratic organizations in favor of greater freedom in small companies, as independent entrepreneurs, and as self-employed professionals. Qualified observers feel, however, that regardless of tradition many Jewish youth would like a whack at the big corporations. For example, in a study of the values of college youth, little difference was found between Jewish and Christian students. Jews as well as non-Jews emphasized security and the opportunity to work with people, those organization-man values. Jews found adventure, the opportunity to exercise leadership, and other such traits associated with entrepreneurship no more attractive than non-Jews. Nevertheless, the study showed a higher proportion of Jews intending to go into free professions such as law and medicine and preferring, whether as professionals or businessmen, their own firms to other people's firms.[12]

Even if the absence of Jews from large corporations is partly a product of taste, we know enough of the linkage between these posts and social life, and of discrimination against Jews in the latter, to suspect that more than taste is involved. As the chairman of the board of a bank pointed out, "An active banker belongs to every damn club in town; it's part of the game." [13] However, the clubs he refers to have been closed to Jews, regardless of social standing or eminence, since the 1880's or thereabouts. It is for this reason that the American Jewish Committee is interested in the discriminatory practices of social clubs. If one's opportunities to reach the command posts of the economy are affected by club membership, and the clubs are closed, then so may be the command posts.[14]

Thus, for Jews business and the professions do not mean what they do for white Protestants and Catholics. They mean small business and free professions. This kind of career is more hazardous than that of the corporations, but it may also offer greater opportunities. The postwar period gave many opportunities to small businesses, and the tax structure was more favorable to the proprietor of a business than to the salary earner. But the organization man has status. An observer reports that in the bridge groups on the train to Larchmont, a Jew, when asked what he does, will say he is "in textiles" or "plastics" or is an "accountant," the non-Jew will say he is "with" General Electric or Union Carbide, and there is no question who outranks whom.

Jewish businessmen in large part are not as acculturated as Jewish professionals. Many have not gone to college, they are often self-made, even today they are often immigrants, and they may lack social polish or be aggressive and crude. For these reasons "succession," the problem of what their sons will do, is intense for them. When the father is an immigrant and not a college man, and not the sort of person one sees in the pages of *Fortune*, and the son has gotten a good education, there is great strain involved in his taking up the family business. Too, being a Jewish business it is likely to be of low status—a small clothing firm, an umbrella factory, a movie-house, a costume jewelry manufactory serving Negro or Puerto Rican trade. Though such a business supplied enough to send the children to college and support the family, it might not seem quite the right thing to a son with an expensive education. Thus very often the son of such a businessman goes into the professions, and the family business is regretfully sold or abandoned to partners.

For the Jewish businessman, who is culturally and socially bound to the Jewish community, who perhaps speaks with an accent and would not appreciate an exclusive club even if admitted, a life of associating with largely Jewish competitors, suppliers, and retailers is comfortable and cozy. To his son, who is perhaps a graduate of the Wharton School or Harvard Business School, such a life is not satisfying, even if the income is good. The son wants the business to be bigger and better, and perhaps he would rather be a cog in a great corporation than the manager of a small one. (The complex interplay between business and the professions for Jews has been subtly analyzed by the sociologists Judith Kramer and Seymour Leventman.)[15] He may not enjoy the tight Jewish community, with its limited horizons and its special satisfactions —he is not that much of a Jew any more. But the larger world portrayed in *The Organization Man* and *From the Terrace* is still closed to him, and perhaps for this very reason is glamorous and attractive. Wealth has been achieved by very sizable numbers of Jewish businessmen and professionals, but status may be the driving force of the third generation, as financial success was of the second. This, at any rate, is the conclusion of Kramer and Leventman.

In 1936, when anti-Semitism was becoming a major issue in American life, *Fortune* magazine examined Jewish wealth and financial influence. *Fortune* pointed out that financial institutions established by German Jews had given prominence to such families as the Lehmans, Warburgs, and Schiffs, but in top finance as a whole Jews were of minor significance, regardless of how awesome they looked to poor Jews or anti-Semites. In three branches of industry Jews were prominent in the mid-thirties: clothing manufacture, department stores, and entertainment. This was enough to support the illusion of Jewish economic significance. The ordinary American who bought at a Jewish-named department store, saw the movies of Goldwyn and Mayer, and had heard of Jewish bankers might presume Jewish financial power was extensive if he wished.

Since the late 1930's a general diversification has taken place. Merchandising, garment manufacturing, and entertainment maintain their importance, but to them has been added a sizable range of light manufacturing, and real estate and building. In the latter, especially, Jews play a prominent role, and important Jewish fortunes have been created. In the great office-building boom that has transformed Manhattan, most of the big builders have been Jews: Uris Brothers, Tishman, Erwin Wolfson, Rudin, Webb and Knapp (Zeckendorf). Perhaps the chief architect of New York office space has been Emery Roth. The Uris Brothers–Emery Roth style of space manufacturing is depressing to those who prefer more elegant structures, but it would be an error to suppose that unexciting, commercial design represents something characteristically Jewish, in taste or attitudes toward money. The finest of the postwar office buildings, Seagram's, which is perhaps the most lavish and expensive in use of space and detail, was erected by a company headed by a Canadian Jewish communal leader, Samuel Bronfman, and it was said to be his daughter's concern for good design that led to the choice of Mies van der Rohe and Philip Johnson as architects. Perhaps the efficient operations of the Urises and Tishmans, and the handsome gesture to the city of Seagram's, both owe something to the patterns of the Jewish family.

In other kinds of building Jews have also been prominent. The Levitts have given a word to the English language with their Levittowns. And in the vast apartment house boom in Manhattan, Queens, Brooklyn, and the suburbs, Jews have again done much of the building. As in the case of the office builders, a variety of trends is apparent: on the one hand, there are the efficient commercial operations which have transformed Queens and are transforming the East Side, to the distress of those who would prefer to see more low-income housing and better central planning and design. On the other hand, there are the nonprofit cooperatives, the only form of new building which can provide middle-income housing in Manhattan. The Amalgamated Clothing Workers of America, the International Ladies' Garment Workers' Union, and various groups of Jewish radicals and intellectuals experimented with co-op buildings in the twenties. Abraham Kazan, having managed the Amalgamated Co-ops successfully through the depression, played the major role in launching postwar co-ops in the city. The success of these led to other large cooperative developments, which have anchored large groups of middle-income citizens to the inner city and are now spreading to the outer city (the Jamaica race track is to be a huge cooperative community).

Real estate has attracted many Jews. The skill at financial operations that is thought to be a Jewish characteristic has apparently found full play in the huge land boom of postwar America. The acquisition of land sites, the accumulation of enough private and government money to put something profitable on them, the managing of short- and long-term credit and leases and leasebacks, the organizing of large new developments that include a variety of building types—in these, as well as in more mundane forms of real estate enterprise, Jews play a major role. William Zeckendorf of Webb and Knapp has done as much as any man to dramatize such operations. He assembled the site for the United Nations, bailed out Manhattantown and put up Park West Village on the Upper West Side, and built great new apartment developments at Kips Bay and the Lincoln Square area.[16]

The Jewish role in real estate, perhaps the biggest business in the city, is as extensive and various as real estate itself. There is no discernible "Jewish pattern," though skill in financial and business management, derived from a long history in business, has unquestionably served many Jews well in a field that is incredibly complex and laden with pitfalls. Jews can be attacked for all of real estate's social abuses, but they must also be given credit for much that has been accomplished. Some individual Jews are responsible for bad design and good design; for tenement exploitation and for nonprofit cooperatives; for the corruption of the idea of urban renewal (as in Sidney Unger's attempt to get special consideration from Manhattan Borough President Hulan Jack) and for some of its best examples (as in James H. Scheuer's development in Southwest Washington). The Levitts have tried to keep Negroes out of their towns (and even Jews, in one early Long Island development!), but Eichler in California was the only big builder in the country whose developments were from the beginning open to all, and Morris Milgram's Modern Community Developers have built successful interracial housing in Philadelphia and Princeton.

It would be a serious mistake to exaggerate the meaning of the ethnic identity of Jewish businessmen, but in two ways it is important. First, these men are part of the Jewish community. They are related to it by more than origins, for in fund-raising and spending for Jewish communal interests of all kinds they are prominent. At the least they lend their names; very often they are genuinely active in the Federation of Jewish Philanthropies, United Jewish Appeal, and other organizations that raise money for Jewish causes in the city and abroad.

Second—and this is much harder to document, being no more than a hunch—there is something in Jewish experience that combines with the pattern of opportunity offered by American society to determine in what areas Jews will become prominent. Jewish real-estate operators might have been just as skillful in managing the affairs of big investment banks and insurance companies. But these great institutions do not easily give place to new men from new groups. Their bureaucratic ladders of advancement are relatively impervious to Jewish ascent. And perhaps too it is more than the white Protestant preemption of certain sectors of the economy that is responsible for certain Jewish concentrations. One notices how often Jewish enterprises involve fathers and sons or groups of brothers—and one wonders whether the fact that the Jewish family is in certain ways "stronger" than the typical American (that is, the white Protestant) family has something to do with occupational patterns. And, as we have suggested, skills may be in some measure inherited. Knowledge of business is a transferable skill, one that in parts of Europe was largely a Jewish monopoly. This unquestionably gave some advantage to tradesmen, merchants, artisans (as Jews were) as compared with peasants, nobles, soldiers, priests (as non-Jews were). The Jewish concentration in the garment trades in this country had nothing to do with knowledge of cloth or clothing. Rather, it had something to do with the sudden rise of a new form of business enterprise—the manufacturing of ready-made clothing for the masses. It was because this was a new form of business enterprise involving very little capital that East European Jews could flow into it. The expansion of ready-made clothing in the American economy meant new jobs for immigrants, and entrepreneurial opportunities for those who could scrape together a bit of capital. Similarly, movies were a new field of business enterprise that originally required little capital. Perhaps, then, there is among Jews an accumulation of business acumen, supported by a relatively strong family system that permits mobilization of capital (even if in small sums), and that makes it possible to move into new areas with opportunities for great growth and high profits.

Jewish experience in real estate fits this pattern. Real estate in America is very different from what it has been in Europe. Land has never been held with sentimental attachment, and the first American farmers and tradesmen set the model of viewing land as capital, to be held only until a fat profit could be made on it. Real estate in the postwar boom years was, in a sense, an infant industry requiring ingenuity and small capital, like the garment manufacturing and the mass entertainments of early generations. Consequently, it joined these others as an important area in which East European Jews and their children have become prominent. In considering the pattern of Jewish wealth, it is worth speaking of one more phenomenon, less important certainly than the Jewish role in real estate but significant as representing the first important breakthrough of Jews in heavy industry. *Fortune* magazine has described the "egghead millionaires," young scientists who have found in the development of electronics and highly technical forms of manufacturing a way in which they can put their education and brains to work very profitably. The Bakalar brothers' Transitron Company, *Fortune* estimated in 1959, could be valued at $150,000,000—a finding which seems to have astonished the engineer-scientist Bakalar, if not the businessman brother.[17] These new companies reflect less the old Jewish business skill than the almost equally traditional Jewish investment in education. In orientation, culture, and outlook, these new scientists in business differ greatly from the traditional Jewish businessman. It is the difference between the Cadillac and the station wagon, Miami vacations and camping in the Sierras, the *Schmoos* on Seventh Avenue and the bull session in the Berkeley or Cambridge coffeeshop. They are very different worlds, yet they are as close as father and son.

THE PASSION FOR EDUCATION

EASTERN EUROPEAN JEWS SHOWED ALMOST FROM THE BEGINning of their arrival in this country a passion for education that was unique in American history. City College was largely Jewish by the turn of the century, which was as soon as there were enough Jews of college age to fill it; and Jews overflowed into the other colleges of the Northeast.[18] The Jewish tide in the city colleges has receded somewhat. From perhaps 85 per cent Jewish they have fallen to 65 per cent or less, but this is partly because the increasing prosperity of the Jewish community, its rising social status, and the greater availability of scholarships and other aids to education mean that more Jews can go to paying colleges,

THE JEWS

inside or outside the city. The emphasis on getting a college education touches almost every Jewish schoolchild. The pressure is so great that what to do about those who are not able to manage college intellectually has become a serious social and emotional problem for them and their families.

As larger numbers of Americans go to college, the concentration on higher education among Jews will become less distinctive. But for the time being the college-educated proportion is perhaps three times as large among Jews as in the rest of the population. In New York City, Jews constitute half of the college-educated. A study in 1955 showed that 62 per cent of Jews of college age were in college, as against only 26 per cent of the population as a whole.[19]

To admissions officers of good colleges, keeping Jewish students to some reasonable proportion of the whole has often been a problem, and they must have wondered how 3 per cent of the population could create such an impact. In the 1930's, medical schools set tight quotas limiting the entry of Jewish students. These practices were often kept secret, but we know a good deal of them. For example, the Cornell University Medical School, located in New York City, limited Jewish students to their proportion in the state of New York, that is, to about 1 in 7. Thus, of 80 places the Cornell school had in 1940, 10 were to be for Jews, 70 for non-Jews. But 7 of every 12 applicants were Jews. Thus 1 of 70 Jewish applicants and 1 of 7 non-Jewish applicants were admitted. So boys seeking entry to medical school took as a fact of life that bright Jews would be rejected in favor of much less bright non-Jews—and this even when both were undergraduates at Cornell and knew perfectly well how one another stood in class.[20]

In the last decade a number of important developments have changed this situation. First, a state law against discrimination in higher education was passed in 1948. Second, the number of applicants to medical schools has declined precipitously, from a peak of 4 for every place in 1948 to less than 2 for every place in 1960. In addition, the new Yeshiva University Medical School, named after Albert Einstein, and the New York State Medical School have opened. Qualified Jewish students have no problem getting into a medical school.[21]

The medical school problem has always been a special one, affecting relatively small numbers of students. Besides, the passion for medicine among Jewish boys is declining as opportunities open up in research, teaching, science, and engineering. Getting into the undergraduate college of one's choice is now the great Jewish (and middle-class) problem. The rising wealth of Jews permits many of them to pay tuition at the best schools; their emphasis on education leads them to take for granted that their children should go to the best schools; and since, in contrast to white Protestants, fewer of them have traditional ties to a variety of American colleges, they think first and foremost of getting into the best schools, which are the hardest to enter.

A study of high school graduates who had applied for Regents' Scholarships in New York State in 1958 showed a remarkable preference among Jews for Ivy League schools. In the city one-third of the Jewish high school graduates applied to Ivy League schools, as against a smaller percentage of white Protestant students, and very few Catholic students. In the suburbs the desire of Jewish students to go to these schools was even more marked. Three-fifths of the Jewish students in Nassau and Suffolk applied to Ivy League schools, but only one-quarter of the Protestant students did. In Westchester almost *three-quarters* of the Jewish students applied, against one-half of the Protestant students.

As far as could be seen, there was no discrimination by Ivy League schools against Jewish applicants. In fact, in the city a slightly *higher* percentage of Jewish than Protestant applicants were successful in getting into an Ivy League school. In Nassau and Suffolk, however, a higher percentage of Protestant students gained admission, and in Westchester 63 per cent of the Jewish applicants were admitted as compared with 89 per cent of the Protestants.[22] The proportion of Jewish students in the Ivy League schools rose from 15 per cent in 1949 to 23 per cent in 1955, and in the "Seven Sisters" (the female equivalents of the Ivy League) it rose from 10 to 16 per cent.[23] It is interesting that objections to Jewish students in these schools were much greater twenty and thirty years ago when they formed only tiny percentages of the student body. It was in 1922 that President Lowell of Harvard openly proposed a Jewish quota, and it was in 1945 that President Hopkins of Dartmouth openly defended a quota policy. The Jewish proportion of students in these colleges is now far greater than it was; yet the desirability of these schools has certainly not declined.

The quotas of the twenties are not to be ascribed to anti-Semitism and left at that. We have pointed out that more Jews than non-Jews once applied to the Cornell Medical School; probably the Jewish average grades were somewhat higher. A strict consideration of scholarship alone in admissions policy might have led to Cornell's becoming almost as Jewish as City College. It was sometimes argued that this could not have happened—that, after all, Jews are not such a large proportion of the population, and that the only reason so many applied was that they were discriminated against elsewhere and had to apply in large numbers to the few that accepted them. There is some truth in this, but unfortunately not enough. For certain colleges and universities may be particularly attractive to Jews, and there will be enough applicants to quite transform them.

Thus, the president of Bard College said a few years ago it was about 80 per cent Jewish. Close to New York, co-ed, and avant-garde, Bard has been very attractive to Jews. Similar colleges such as Bennington and Antioch have also attracted sizable Jewish enrollments, though nothing like the fantastic proportion at Bard, which a century ago was a preparatory institution for the Protestant Episcopal ministry.[24] The Cornell Medical School, Bard, and many other colleges were built up by Protestant clergymen and laymen who naturally equated "American" with "Protestant." Even though this Protestant tradition has accommodated itself to the increase of Catholics and Jews in America, it is unreasonable to expect that leaders of institutions founded and financed by Protestants would be content to see them become mostly Jewish.

Jews as well as non-Jews would be unhappy over such an outcome. Part of the attraction of such institutions is undoubtedly the chance they give to experience a wider range of American life than is possible in New York, and to be part of an institution traditionally connected with the major stream in American life. But these benefits are denied if the college becomes mostly Jewish. We come up against a problem similar to one we have met before in our discussion of Negro housing patterns. Some American Negroes, perhaps most, prefer communities in which they have white neighbors; most communities will accept almost no Negroes, and those that do tend rapidly to become all Negro. It is for this reason that various people have proposed "benign quotas," limitations on the proportions of Negroes in a development, so that both Negroes and whites may get whatever benefit there is to be gotten from a mixed community.

The Jewish defense organizations have assumed that if one treats every man as an individual, without any thought of his ethnic affiliation or religion, then such problems—in which the concentration of Jews in an institution takes away some of the things that made it attractive to begin with—will not arise. But as a matter of fact, being a Jew does have consequences for one's behavior, and we cannot expect Jews, just as we cannot expect members of any other group, to distribute themselves evenly over all possibilities. So the religion-blind acceptance policy suddenly wakes up to find that something has happened that no one wanted. But just what to do about it, no one knows. The long-range answer is that with the powerful acculturative processes of American life, Jews will become like everyone else, and Bard with its avant-garde character will attract as few of them as it would of any other group. But here it is 1963 . . . and one wonders whether the effect of social progress is to make Jews just like the upper-class Protestant denominations that they begin to approximate in wealth and occupation.

COMMUNITY, NEIGHBORHOOD, INTEGRATION

JOHN HIGHAM HAS POINTED OUT IN A FASCINATING HISTORY OF social discrimination against Jews in America that, owing to their rapid economic rise, Jews very early sought entry into the higher levels of society in large numbers. They thus presented a problem new to American society, and it responded by strict exclusion. After about the 1880's, Jews were excluded from social clubs, preparatory schools, "better" neighborhoods, the organized institutions of high society, and even the occupations associated with high status. This exclusion was greatest during the 1920's and 1930's, but the war against Hitler, the strengthening of equalitarian ideology, and probably the affluence of the postwar period led to relaxation of this system after 1945.[25] In New York City, only social and golf clubs and high society remain pretty rigorously closed to Jews. No residential areas in the city and only a few in the suburbs exclude Jews, although a number of Upper East Side luxury apartment houses are closed to them.[26] However, the breakdown of systematic exclusion has not been followed by "integration" of the Jewish community, and Jews are becoming more and more aware of a new "ghettoization."

Intermarriage, an important sign of integration, remains low among Jews. The 1957 sample census showed that about $3\frac{1}{2}$ per cent of married Jews were married to non-Jews, and the proportion is possibly even lower in New York, where the concentration of Jewish population, as compared with other communities, reduces the probability of intermarriage.[27] A sizable proportion of these intermarried couples—possibly about a third—consider themselves part of the Jewish community, and raise their children as Jews. The only studies that have surveyed intermarriage over a long period of time (those from New Haven) show no increase of it since 1930, although in this period the Jews of New Haven became much more acculturated and prosperous.[28] This pattern sharply distinguishes the Jews of the United States from those of other countries in which Jews have achieved wealth and social position, such as Holland, Germany, Austria, and Hungary in the twenties. There the intermarriage rates were phenomenally high.

Nor is there a strong tendency toward residential integration of Jews. In the thirties the following areas of New York City had very high Jewish proportions: the Lower East Side and Washington Heights in Manhattan; the Hunts Point, West Bronx, Morrisania, Fordham, and Pelham Parkway areas in the Bronx; and Brownsville, Coney Island, Brighton Beach, Manhattan Beach, Borough Park, Flatlands, East New York, Bensonhurst, and Williamsburg in Brooklyn. All of these were at least two-fifths Jews, and large sections within them were four-fifths and nine-tenths Jewish. These concentrations included both lower-class and middle-class Jews. When the great exodus to Queens, Long Island, and other suburban areas began after World War II, many observers assumed that Jews would cease to be concentrated. While many apartment houses and, in particular, cooperative developments began with a largely Jewish group of renters and co-op owners, many of the suburban small-homes developments were to begin with mixed. However, before long the mixed developments showed a strong tendency to become almost entirely Jewish or non-Jewish. What happened depended on a multitude of factors: a new synagogue might be built before a church, symbolizing the Jewish character of the development; perhaps a particularly good school system might attract an influx of Jews; perhaps the proportion of Jews to begin with (by sheer statistical accident) was too high to keep the non-Jews comfortable, or too low to keep the Jews comfortable.[29]

Most Jews would deny that they prefer an all-Jewish neighborhood, and most would agree that they are not comfortable in one with "too few" Jews. John Slawson of the American Jewish Committee reports:

"In a suburban city, part of the New York metropolitan area, where only 15 per cent of the population is Jewish, half of the group would like to live in neighborhoods that are at least 50 per cent Jewish; one-quarter would like to live in neighborhoods that are 75 per cent Jewish. When asked whether they would like more opportunity for contact with Christians, two out of ten said yes, two said no, and six said they did not care." [30]

Fifty per cent would strike most New York Jews as "just right." But 50 per cent, which is twice the proportion of Jews in the city, and three times their proportion in the metropolitan area, would strike most non-Jews as too much. It is probably not a stable proportion in home-owning developments (apartment-house areas are different). In some good suburban areas non-Jews have fled from incoming Jews. But this is pretty clearly not the only, nor even the most important, reason for Jewish concentration. Jews prefer to live with other Jews. Owing to these tendencies among Jews and non-Jews, a truly mixed neighborhood in the suburbs is hard to find, as many young Jewish families who have tried can testify.

In Manhattan, the great exception to most statements about New York City, residential areas are much more mixed, and aside from a concentration in Washington Heights (which is more like the other boroughs), Jews live pretty much everywhere. These are the young unmarried people, the young couples without children, the intellectuals and bohemians who are involved in New York's cultural life. They do not share the desire for self-segregation that characterizes many Jews in the other boroughs, and they have a high rate of intermarriage.[31]

The main point is that Jewish residential concentration is not confined to the immigrant generation or the poor. It is characteristic of the middle and upper-middle classes and of the third generation no less than the second. One of the areas of densest Jewish concentration in the city today is the Forest Hills–Rego Park area, which consists almost entirely of new apartment houses. It is two-thirds Jewish, compared with only 5 per cent in 1930. The Jewish concentration in some other new areas is hardly less striking. The Bayside–Oakland Gardens, Central Queens, and Douglaston–Little Neck–Bellerose areas are two-fifths Jewish or more, although almost no Jews lived in them in 1940. Since the Second World War, Jews have moved from one concentrated Jewish area only to create new ones—and largely out of their own desires.

This tendency survives even as the acculturation of Jews proceeds. In the new communities, Yiddish is hardly spoken, and Jewish culture is of no great interest. Nor is it possible to say that Jews have gathered in order to defend their religion. It is true that their concentration helps synagogues as well as nonreligious Jewish institutions. The social pressure of the group is felt on those who might resist participating; large, expensive synagogues and recreational-educational centers are made feasible; fund-raising is easier. But the religious institutions are so strong because they serve the social desire to remain separate to begin with.

It is true that among Orthodox Jews there is a religious reason for separation. The Jewish religious law was in the past elaborated consciously in order to make Jews different in dress, custom, and outlook, so that there would be less chance of conversion and assimilation. In part we see this process at work today, when, for example, Orthodox parents send their children to the "Yeshivas," Jewish parochial schools. These all-day schools have been growing rapidly in the past decade and a half, another sign of the segregation of the Jewish community. They enroll 8 per cent of the Jewish schoolchildren of the city, and the percentage may go higher.[32] The separation of the Hasidic groups is even more extreme. Living in Williamsburg, one of the oldest Jewish neighborhoods (but now largely Negro and Puerto Rican), and on Eastern Parkway, a much better and newer neighborhood (but one bordering the growing Negro neighborhood of Crown Heights), the Hasidim insist on a more complete separation than other Orthodox Jews. Not only do they have their own schools, more Orthodox than the ordinary Yeshiva, but they retain traditional peculiarities of dress and hair arrangement that marked off Jews from non-Jews in Eastern Europe centuries ago. In this group, one must wear Judaism on one's face in order to strengthen the Judaism of the heart. One of the reasons Hasidim live next door to Negroes in unconcern is because nothing in the modern world—the drive for respectability, fear of Negroes, or what other people think—affects them much.

But the overwhelming majority of Jews do not maintain any of these outward distinctions, and it is not for fear of the loss of religious faith that they congregate, join synagogues, and send their children to Jewish schools. More than a third of the Jewish children in the city and rather more in the suburbs are enrolled in part-time Jewish schools.[33] The teachers and principals of these schools do want to teach Jewish religion and culture, as an end in itself, in order to perpetuate Judaism. But the parents of these children do not want them to be any more religious or consciously Jewish than is necessary, and that often means just enough to make them immune to marriage with non-Jews. This fear of intermarriage is also one of the reasons that Jewish centers are so popular; they permit the teen-agers to get together.

This disapproval of intermarriage is remarkably strong, even among the native-born. At least through the third generation Jews tend to accept the notion that intermarriage is probably not good. Erich Rosenthal reports in the *American Journal of Sociology* on a study of a new middle-class Jewish concentration in Chicago (the situation is the same in New York):

When I asked Rabbi Breightman [a pseudonym]—as I asked all my informants—what his explanation is for the recent aggregation of the Jewish community on the North Side of Chicago, his reply was that the one thing that parents fear more than anything else and fear more than at any other time in history is amalgamation, the marriage of their children to "outsiders." While at one time the problem of Jewish identity was no problem for the individual who lived a distinctively Jewish life in his home, his synagogue, and the community, today there is little that marks the Jew as a Jew except Jewish self-consciousness and association with fellow Jews. If one were to depend on the religio-cultural rather than on the associational tie, then large-scale amalgamation would be the order of the day. To forestall this, the parents favor residence in a neighborhood that has such a high density of Jewish families that the probability of their children marrying a Jewish person approaches certainty.

Commenting on religious schooling, Dr. Rosenthal says,

It appears . . . that the basic function of Jewish education is to implant Jewish self-consciousness rather than Judaism, to "inoculate" the next generation with that minimum of religious practice and belief that is considered necessary to keep alive a level of Jewish self-consciousness that will hold the line against assimilation.[34]

The mere fact that Jews are clustered together may help explain why types of behavior associated with being Jewish that we might have expected to disappear are instead enduring. These include a strong family life, a low rate of alcoholism, and a high degree of political liberalism.

Studies have long shown that Jewish families break up less than non-Jewish ones.[35] (Once again, we separate the integrated fringe from the mass of middle-class Jews.) Rabbis rarely seem to find it necessary to warn their congregations against marital breakup, neglect of children, cocktail-partying, and the like. Although the powerful maternal overprotection that was one of the chief characteristics of the first immigrant generation is perhaps somewhat abated, Jewish parents still seem to hover more over their children and give them shorter rein for exploration and independence than other middle-class American parents. The results seem to be that there is more neurosis among Jews, but less psychosis.[36] The fault of Jewish family relations is in the strength of the tie that binds; but the radical disorders that result from the absence of such a tie are less common among Jews than non-Jews.

The study of alcoholism, one of the chief disorders that afflicts this country, has for a long time concentrated on those special groups—including Jews, Chinese, Italians—that show a lower rate of disorder even though they drink. Those who have studied this phenomenon among Jews (very few of whom are teetotalers) explain it by, among other things, the Orthodox religion, which requires a certain amount of ceremonial drinking at the Sabbath meal, Passover Seder, and other times, and also imposes a system of built-in self-control in many ways.[37] But this explanation loses force in that even as Orthodoxy has rapidly declined, particularly in the newer areas in which Jews live, alcoholism among Jews does not seem to have increased. Once again, the great exception is the "integrated" Jew, most common in Manhattan. Whatever the sources of the low rate of alcoholism among Jews—and certainly the surviving effects of Orthodoxy may be an important source—the Conservative and Reform Jews of the suburbs seem to have sustained the traditional pattern. At the elaborate Bar Mitzvah parties for thirteen-year-old boys that are held in middle-class Jewish areas, one finds a huge array of liquor, and everyone drinks before, during, and after the meal, but the alcoholic and semialcoholic are nowhere in sight.

Finally, in these well-to-do areas another old Jewish pattern holds up—liberalism in politics. The Jews of suburbia may have indulged themselves with a few votes for Eisenhower, but the vast majority continue their allegiance to the Democratic party. The surge of city dwellers into New York's suburbs has made them more Democratic, it is generally agreed. But, to be more subtle in the analysis, it is the surge of *Jewish* population that has made them more Democratic. Protestants and Catholics, as their income rises, do turn Republican. But only at stratospheric economic heights, perhaps, are a majority of Jews Republicans. Indeed, nowhere in the metropolitan area does one find such a phenomenon. Their aberrant political behavior is certainly one of the things that will serve to keep Jews somewhat separate and peculiar as their old practices disappear.

POLITICS

THE JEWS OF NEW YORK CITY HAVE HAD FOR THE PAST THIRTY years a kind of split political personality that can be matched only in such areas as the Southern cities that now vote Republican nationally and Democratic locally. No group in the city supports national Democratic candidates as strongly and consistently as the Jews; none except perhaps the white Protestants has been as uncomfortable about voting Democratic locally. The American Labor Party and the Liberal Party have developed in New York City partly in response to this Jewish dilemma.

Jews are not alone in their partisan irregularity in a city where the local machines have often been poor representatives of national Democratic administrations. But no other group is quite so irregular. The white Protestant old stock generally votes for Republicans locally and nationally. The Irish and Italians are torn between a traditional attachment to local Democratic organizations and an attraction, as a result of their own increased social mobility and the Democrats' interventionism in World War II, to the Republicans. The Negroes and Puerto Ricans, following in the path of other new immigrant groups, are solidly committed to the Democrats, both locally and nationally.

What attracts Jews is liberalism, using the term to refer to the entire range of leftist positions, from the mildest to the most extreme. The Jewish vote is primarily an "ideological" rather than a party or even an ethnic one. There is little question that Jews are moved, as other groups are, by issues that affect them alone, such as policy toward Israel. But it is impossible to test the effect of pro-Israel feeling on voting, for political candidates in New York City all profess an enthusiasm for Israel. Nor is it easy to test the pull of a Jewish versus a non-Jewish name in the city. In cases where the non-Jew is clearly identified with the "more liberal" position—as in the 1960 primary between Ludwig Teller, regular organization Democrat, and William Fitts Ryan, Reform Democrat, in the 20th Congressional District on the West Side—there has been little question that the Jewish name helped hardly at all with Jewish voters. The races between Franklin D. Roosevelt, Jr., and Jacob Javits for Attorney General in 1954, and between Robert F. Wagner and Javits for U.S. Senator in 1956, are not as simple to analyze, for in both cases there was some question as to who was more liberal. It was hard in either case to demonstrate a "Jewish" vote for Javits.[38] In 1932, when three liberal heroes, Franklin D. Roosevelt, Herbert Lehman, and Robert Wagner, Sr., were running for President, Governor, and Senator, Wagner pulled a higher vote in some Jewish districts than Roosevelt or Lehman even though he ran against a Jewish Republican candidate, George Z. Medalie.[39]

The Jewish liberal voting pattern has been of great persistence. The transformation of Jews from a working-class group (as they were in the time of Al Smith) to a middle-class group (as they are in the time of John F. Kennedy) has affected hardly at all their tendency to vote for liberal Democratic candidates. The Jewish vote for a national Democratic candidate has dropped only once in thirty years—in 1948, when Truman ran against Dewey. But then Jews defected not to Dewey, as one might expect of a business and professional community, but to Henry Wallace. The Jewish vote for Truman and Wallace was almost everywhere equal to the Jewish vote for Roosevelt in 1944.

At the same time, the candidates of the local Democratic organization have generally been unappealing. The same Jewish voters who turned out enthusiastically for Roosevelt in 1940 and 1944 were cold to O'Dwyer, running against La Guardia, in 1941, and they hardly warmed up by 1945, even though O'Dwyer, campaigning in uniform, no longer appeared to Jews to be clearly the favored choice of isolationists and Christian Frontiers.[40]

Upper-income Jews do not seem to be importantly differentiated from lower-income ones in voting habits. All economic levels were enthusiastically for Roosevelt, Lehman, and La Guardia in the 1930's and 1940's. If enthusiasm for Truman was considerably less, it was hardly a class matter—both upper- and lower-income Jews voted heavily for Wallace. Again, both upper- and lower-income Jews were fervently for Stevenson, and both, emerging from their Stevenson mania, decided that Kennedy was perhaps the heir of Roosevelt, and they voted for him more heavily than did the Irish Catholics!

The voting of ethnic groups, as Samuel Lubell pointed out long ago, is not simply a function of ethnic issues or candidates, though it is true that a group wants representatives, and almost any Jewish candidate gets some Jewish votes running against a non-Jew. Rather, ethnic tendencies in voting express the entire culture and traditions of the group. As Lubell said:

Ethnic groups do not now—if they ever did—act simply as cohesive voting blocs. Rather, their influence is exerted through common group consciousness, through the effect of common antecedents and cultural traditions which enable them to view developing issues from a common point of view.[41]

The Jewish commitment to the Democratic party is virtually complete today because the Democrats, since 1928, have nominated liberal candidates for the Presidency. East European Jews found the Democratic party much less attractive in the period from the Civil War to Alfred E. Smith, when its candidates were as likely to be conservatives like Alton Parker and John Davis as to be crusaders like William Jennings Bryan and Woodrow Wilson. Indeed, German Jews, coming to political maturity and consciousness in the period of the Civil War, were perhaps predominantly Republican. Their preference for the Republicans on the national level coincided with their local interests, since the Democratic party, in the hands of the Irish, had no room for them. Instead, Jews held office in the Republican party organization. In the 1870's and 1880's Greenpoint had Jewish Republican leaders, and there were Jewish Republican county leaders in Brooklyn before the end of the century. In the 1920's Meier Steinbrink and Samuel Koenig were Republican county leaders in Brooklyn and Manhattan.

Some East European Jews followed the German Jews into the Republican party, and some, like other immigrants, went into the Democratic party. But at least as many became strong Socialists. It was for this reason, as well as because the Irish held tenaciously to their posts, that Jewish progress in the Democratic party was slow.

Woodrow Wilson aroused some enthusiasm among Jews in 1912 and 1916. Henry Morgenthau, Sr., was chairman of the Democratic Financial Committee in 1912, Bernard Baruch was one of the President's advisers, Louis D. Brandeis became the first Jew to serve on the Supreme Court. But it was Al Smith who challenged the power of the Socialists on the East Side and taught Jews to vote for Democratic state and national candidates. In 1922, with Smith heading the Democratic ticket for Governor, four Jews—three Democrats and a Republican—went to Congress from New York City. Two years before, six Jews were elected to Congress from the city, but all except one were Republicans, and the sixth was a Socialist. It was in 1922 that Sol Bloom, Nathaniel Dickstein, and Emanuel Celler began their long service in Congress, in seats that became as safe as any in the South.[42]

If many Jews had entered the Democratic party, it is very likely that they could have dominated it. They formed, after all, one-quarter of the population from the early twenties on. In addition, Jews became citizens rapidly—much more rapidly, for example, than Italians—they were politically conscious, and they had a high rate of voting participation. But so much of their energy was devoted to the Socialist party that it was not difficult for the

Irish to maintain control of the Democratic party. Between 1933 and 1945, when Jews were drawn away from socialism by the New Deal, they still did not enter the local Democratic party on a massive scale, for this was the age of La Guardia, and Jews preferred the American Labor Party and Liberal Party and good government groups to the Democratic party clubs. But since the middle forties there has been less and less to keep Jews from becoming Democrats locally as well as nationally. Many have become active as Reform Democrats in the struggle against the regular party organization. In this conflict, Democrats who are identified closely with the liberal Northern wing of the party have sought to take over and reform the party organization in the city, so as to end the power of the old regular party leaders. Control is being shifted from the Irish and their junior partners, the Italians, who organized masses of regular voters from immigrant groups, to professionals and intellectuals who appeal to independent voters. The elections of the past ten years in New York have shown the greater effectiveness of their approach as compared to that of the traditional machine. The college man is taking over in politics as in business; inevitably many Jews are included. With white Protestants, they dominate the reform movement.

This newer generation of Jews in politics has of course very little in common with the Jews who were in the old Democratic machine. These did very well indeed with the old politics. They have received a high proportion of the judicial posts and nominations for the past thirty years. One-third of the Congressmen from the city, and rather more of the judges, State Senators, and Assemblymen are Jewish. Jews have in fact held more judicial and elective offices than their numerical strength in the organization would seem to warrant. Their prominence in this respect reflects their financial contributions to electoral campaigns, the large number of lawyers among them, and their high rate of voting participation, rather than strength on the clubhouse floor. Still, Jews do have an important place in the organization, and in the struggle between the organization and the Reform Democrats we see manifested the same social change that separates the Jewish businessman father from his college-trained son. The fathers are slow to realize that in the rich America of today the material reward of the job (in business or politics) is not as important as personal fulfillment. And in defending itself the organization has failed to see that its attackers are not merely a new wave of seekers after jobs but rather a group that hopes to change the nature of local politics.

How successful this new group will be in transforming the politics of the city, which has resisted many such movements in the past, we shall discover in the next few years.

But the reform movement in politics has already become one of those areas in city life in which people of different backgrounds, from different groups, come together not as representatives of groups, not to bargain for group rights and positions, but to work in a common task, as individuals. This happens often enough in New York business, but there the common end is gain. The fact that it happens in politics, where the common end is a general good, is a cause for satisfaction. This is after all the only real basis of "integration"—common work in which one's group characteristics are not primary and therefore of no great account.

Another great area of New York life in which this kind of integration proceeds is in the fields of cultural activity.

CULTURE AND THE FUTURE

THE GREATEST CITY IN THE RICHEST AND (PERHAPS) MOST powerful nation of the world must be a world cultural capital in which some things are done better than anywhere else in the world (for example, musical plays, postclassical ballet, abstract expressionist painting), in which almost everything in the sphere of culture can be found, in which new things are tried in every field, old things brought to a high degree of finish, and all kinds of cultural products are marketed to a vast audience—the people of the metropolitan area, the country, and the world. This must be so in great cities in great countries at the peak of their power; and if New York is culturally as exciting as any city in the world, this must be ascribed to America, and not to the composition of the population of New York. Even if all the Jews had gone to Argentina or Canada, New York would still be New York, and Buenos Aires and Montreal would only be pretty much what they are.

This we think is a fair statement of the larger truth against which we must view the participation of the various groups in New York's cultural life. And yet, the fact that the city *is* one-quarter Jewish; that Jews broke with the most orthodox and traditional of religions to become open to everything new; that they seized upon everything new because the old things were so often tied up with social snobbery, anti-Semitism, obscurantist conservatism—these facts must also be fitted into an understanding of the cultural life of New York.

New York was America's cultural center even when the German Jews arrived, but for the most part they were preoccupied with business, finance, and solid middle-class life. And when, before the First World War, New York's Greenwich Village became a center of revolt against genteel culture, drawing young rebels from all over the country, the bright young men of the first East European Jewish generation were too busy getting into City College and respectable professions to worry much about the avant-garde. The first link between the group in Greenwich Village and the East European Jews on the other side of the island came through interest not in avant-garde culture but in radical politics. The disgust with the older middle-class America that seized so many young people around the turn of the century and drove them to Chicago and New York met something in the young Jews. They too were against "capitalism." Both groups came together in the Socialist party and in Max Eastman's prewar magazine, *The Masses;* compared, however, with similar enterprises of later years —for example, *The New Masses* of the twenties and *Partisan Review* in the thirties—*The Masses* attracted only a small number of East European Jews.

This world of left-wing politics and avant-garde culture, which survives to the present day in New York, was the first important meeting ground for Jewish and non-Jewish cultural figures and bohemians. It has helped define Greenwich Village and has represented a phase in the career of American creators in many fields. The experience of this milieu has been very different for the Jewish and non-Jewish participants. For the young American from, say, the Midwest, Greenwich Village, whether as art, politics, or just off-beat living, meant a radical break with the past—with a Republican father, a conservative religious mother, and other relatives who could not conceivably understand what was going on. For the young Jewish radical or bohemian, the break was much less sharp. He had come from the Bronx or Brooklyn, or a Chicago or Detroit whose Jewish section was not very different; he went home now and then for the holidays or some family gathering. If he was a Communist, his father had been a Socialist (or vice versa), and regardless of his wild goings-on he could usually depend on a little financial help from anxious parents. The non-Jews in these circles were a million miles from home, the Jews but a subway ride away.

Thus, paradoxically, the non-Jews in New York's bohemia felt uprooted, alienated, alone, and the Jews (who were often envied for it) were by contrast rooted and at home. It is perhaps because for Jews the step to bohemia is not great or decisive that up to now the really creative figures in American culture have not been Jews as often as we might expect. It is difficult to count heads (the question is always, which heads), but in the avant-garde circles of the twenties, thirties, and forties Jews were very often the critics (and entrepreneurs), non-Jews the creators. This was so in literature, painting, music, and the theater.

But if Jews bulked larger among the critics than the creators, they bulked largest of all among the audience. Here, they made perhaps their most important contribution to New York's cultural life. Once again statistics are not available; but it is clear that neither tourists, the working-class masses, nor the small Protestant elite could have filled or could fill today the audiences for chamber and contemporary music, modern dancing, and poetry reading, or the subscription lists for avant-garde magazines. As they have become wealthier, Jews have also become patrons and collectors. Many descendants of the older German-Jewish immigration have played important roles in New York's cultural life as patrons, collectors, and organizers.

Their independence of old American traditions makes Jews a market for the new. They do not as often fill their homes with early American, but they are receptive to new painting, new household design, and new houses. In New York there are relatively few contemporary houses, but outside New York Jews have been among the most important patrons of advanced architecture. It is not uncharacteristic that two of the most striking and widely reproduced symbols of American architecture were commissioned by Jews—Frank Lloyd Wright's Bear Run house and his Guggenheim Museum.

Culture, whether high, middlebrow, or mass, is big business, one of the few big businesses in which Jews have been active and prominent for many years. They are producers of movies and television shows and agents for actors and performers. They have also been the creators of the single most valuable commodity the entertainment industry in New York handles, the Broadway musical. Whether Jews have influenced the character of musicals is another question; Kurt List, the music critic, made the intriguing point some years ago that it was no accident that a string of the most popular musicals by Jewish composers and lyricists (*Show Boat, South Pacific, The King and I*) had an interracial and intergroup theme.[43] *West Side Story* continues the tradition.

In the marketing of culture and entertainment, there is only one business, book publishing, in which Jews were not especially prominent. This is the most conservative of such fields, and for a long time, New York, the center of book publishing, had very few Jewish publishers and editors. Starting with the period of the First World War, some important publishing houses were founded by Jews, in particular, Alfred A. Knopf and Random House. Since the Second World War the Jewish role in publishing has increased in the city, as a result both of creation of new firms and changes in old ones. The rapid development of paperback book publishing in particular has given many opportunities to Jewish publishers and editors.

The involvement of Jews with the new has meant a special role for them too in another area which certainly affects New York's cultural life, that is, psychoanalysis. Psychoanalysis in America is a peculiarly Jewish product. This is not only because Freud and many of his early followers were Jews. At most, this reflected only some special aspects of the position of Jews in Central Europe. For the East Europeans who made up the greatest part of New York Jewry, and for the bourgeois German Jews of the nineteenth century and their descendants who made up a smaller part of the community, nothing could have been on the face of it more foreign than psychoanalysis. The East European Jew was blind to many kinds of psychological abnormality: for him there was only one kind of abnormality, the social one, and all his intelligence was applied to changing the abnormal social position of the Jew. Why then do large numbers of psychoanalysts and patients come from this group in the United States?

The explanation probably lies in the effects of secularism on Jews, who have been so rapidly divorced from traditional religion and who have accepted the possibilities of science and intellect so completely that a movement like psychoanalysis—even had its founder been a German anti-Semite—would have been irresistibly attractive. For here was a scientific form of soul-rebuilding to make them whole and hardy, and it was divorced, at least on the surface, from mysticism, will, religion, and all those other romantic and obscure trends that their rational minds rejected. And then too, it was also a new field with room for new people, which fact may explain why so many Jews became analysts. But it is primarily the complete secularization of the second-generation East European Jew in America that explains why so many became patients.[44]

We have spoken about education, politics, and culture as forming the stage on which work and productivity may overcome the significance of group affiliation; but at the same time we have pointed to tendencies among Jews that hold the group together and reestablish a tight, closed community in new middle-class settings. Obviously, a group stays together and maintains common institutions to further certain ends. And groups stay together too for no end but simply the simple human pleasure in forming smaller worlds in a big world. Jewish togetherness has a good deal of both aspects. Who else is to raise money for Israel if not the United Jewish Appeal, who else is to raise money for Jewish Old Age Homes if not the Federation of Jewish Philanthropies, who is to maintain the Jewish religion if not the synagogues and the temples? Around these tasks social circles are formed. And yet at the same time a good deal of this Jewish togetherness is simply frightened and unimaginative, and its only purpose is to maintain separateness.

Despite economic prosperity and liberalism, all is not well in the Jewish world—or perhaps because of them. When Jews were poor, it seemed reasonable that they should try to become rich; as they emerged from poverty, it seemed desirable that they should remain liberal and sympathetic to the needs of those who were still poor and deprived and those who came after them. But a hard look at the Jewish situation today reveals a number of disturbing elements. Jewish liberalism, it is true, supports the NAACP, CORE, the reform Democrats, freedom riders in the South, and a variety of liberal Democratic candidates who come to New York to refresh their campaigns with Jewish money. But what now supports Jewish liberalism? Many decent impulses, of course, and ties to old friends and early allegiances, but also, simply, an excessive timidity or fright. Reaction and conservatism are so staunchly opposed in part because there is always the fear that it hides anti-Semitism, even though there may scarcely be a hint of it. Perhaps it is unjust to regard as unwarranted strong Jewish concern for anti-Semitism at a time when it is scarcely to be detected as a significant force anywhere in the United States. After all, Hitler did kill six million Jews, and anti-Semites in Argentina have carved swastikas on the breasts of young Jewish women. And yet, where are the dangers to Jews in New York City, or in the United States? Nevertheless, large sums of money (compared at any rate to the sums raised for other causes) can be collected to fight anti-Semitism. When the American anti-Semite George Rockwell wanted to speak in New York City, Jewish groups and individuals (not all) put great pressure on the government to prevent him from opening his mouth legally. When young boys painted swastikas on Jewish synagogues, it became a matter for almost hysterical outbursts and elaborate studies—as if no one had written dirty words on appropriate walls before. A few years ago, the Police Commissioner of New York spoke out in irritation against Jewish policemen who were taking off Yom Kippur as a holiday when he needed every man to guard Khrushchev and Castro, who were attending a meeting of the U.N. General Assembly. Married to a Jewish woman, knowledgeable about New York and New York Jews, he said that he knew many of them were not planning to spend the day in the synagogue. The outburst against him by Jewish organizations was violent, and when he refused to apologize, he only scarcely retained his job. Such incidents, and they are common in the life of the city, lead one to reflect on the future of the Jewish community. What is it afraid of? What is it defending? Are these minor slights matters that should so deeply concern it?

The Jewish community is affected not only by the context of America in the sixties but by the context of Jewish history. But never in the Diaspora have Jews wielded such weight and power in a great city, and in such circumstances it is necessary to consider how the traditional parameters of Jewish history may, if only for some generations, have been altered. The defense of a minority group and its interests may legitimately be shrill and insistent when it is powerless and weak and there is no one to listen; thus much may be excused the Negroes. But the maintenance of this habit when conditions change may seem to those outside the group arrogance and hypocrisy.

Consequently, Jewish liberalism, which is sound enough perhaps from the perspective of an American nation that is still in many ways remarkably conservative and bound to old slogans, is, in the context of New York, not quite as sound as it should be. There is much self-congratulation on the struggles and successes of the past. Jewish socialists and intellectuals played a great and important role in the building up of the labor movement in the 1930's, but they seem to have been struck dumb by the problems raised for the city by the rise of a new proletariat of Negroes and Puerto Ricans. There is no question that these raise far more difficult problems of organization than Jews or other European immigrant groups. Nor is there any question that traditional labor organization itself is an insufficient answer at a time when poverty is so solidly based on lack of skills, training, and education and a heavy incidence of social problems. Yet one must acknowledge that the great tradition of social reform and social engineering that was identified with the Jewish labor unions and the Jewish labor movement in the city seems to have been unable to make any serious impact on this problem. The major social achievement of the Jewish labor movement since the end of the war has been the creation of the great middle-income cooperatives, and this is a real achievement, but it is one that benefits a largely Jewish middle class, and scarcely affects the conditions of the new proletariat.

In 1962 and 1963 a conflict between the NAACP and the International Ladies' Garment Workers broke into the open. Herbert Hill, the (Jewish) labor union expert of the NAACP attacked the ILGWU for discrimination against Negroes. The one attested case was of a Negro cutter who was denied entrance into the union. Just a few years before, a refugee Jewish DP who had arrived in the city, and who had great skill as a cutter, was denied entrance into the union as a full cutter, even though his family in this country included a number of employees of New York labor unions and made every effort to help him. Clearly the problem in the cutters' union was not simply racial discrimination. It was the job monopoly that is found in extreme form in many skilled unions. But even if one could dispute specific points in Herbert Hill's case, one could not dispute the fact that the Negroes and Puerto Ricans had not been brought into the trade union establishment in New York. And it was understandable that it was the Jewish, not the Irish and Italian, unions that were attacked first. More was expected from them. The attack was supported by Jewish writers, sympathetic indeed to the Jewish unions, who nevertheless could look back on their own radical youth and see that something had gone out of the Jewish labor movement in New York.[45]

Consider another area that reveals something of the life of the Jewish group in the city. On the West Side of Manhattan there has existed since the 1920's a large and prosperous Jewish community. Much of the life of the area was and is concentrated in the great synagogues. Jewish religious and political ideals were merged in such liberal rabbis as Stephen S. Wise and Mordecai Kaplan. Since the Second World War, the area has changed. Many Jews moved out, many Negroes and Puerto Ricans moved in. There have been difficult problems, but not different from those in other great American cities. The major attempt to deal with these problems has been through urban renewal—the rebuilding of the area so as to reduce the low-income and increase the middle- and high-income population. This movement has been supported by all the middle-class groups and institutions of the area, who of course would like to see less crime and disorder and crowding and dirt around them. The West Side's solution has been no worse than that of other cities, and perhaps even better, for the largest of these projects will incorporate a considerable number of low-income families. And yet one cannot help but feel that somewhat more enlightened and imaginative solutions could have emerged from the Jewish group of the West Side and from the synagogues. Two of these have already followed their flocks across Central Park to the more expensive and exclusive East Side. As for the rest, if there have been prophetic voices, they have not made themselves heard.

The real achievement of the Jews in America has been the generations of energetic and gifted young people they have supplied to the arts, to radical politics, to the labor movement. Many of these young people were able in the twenties and thirties and forties to find challenging and satisfying environments that were formally or *de facto* Jewish. Even while considering themselves free from all Jewish ties, they worked among Jews in the theater, in political activity, in the unions. One wonders about the supply of such young people in the future—will they emerge from this comfortable middle-class group? One also wonders where they will go. They certainly find little in the formal

Jewish community of the day that attracts them. Neither the synagogues and temples, nor the charitable and philanthrophic work, nor the fund-raising for Israel and defense seems sufficiently vital and relevant for the most gifted young people who are emerging from the community. This is at any rate one conclusion that might be drawn from a remarkable symposium conducted by the magazine *Commentary* in 1961. Nor does that other community that was scarcely less Jewish, that of the radical movements and the unions, engage them much.[46]

But these are the best of the young people, one assumes, those that are repelled by what is increasingly called "the gilded ghetto." What of the rest? Are they likely to find this new ghetto even as stimulating as the ghettoes of the past? When the Jews lived on the Lower East Side and in other working-class areas, they led a separate life. But they were intensely curious about everything going on in the outer world, eager to participate in it and to master whatever had to be mastered for this participation. When the Jews were thus most Jewish, when they took their Jewishness for granted, they looked forward to a time when all barriers would be down and they could participate freely in the labor movement, business, politics, culture, and social life. The ideology of the working-class Jews was not separation but the fullest involvement in society; Jewish culture and religion, they felt, could take care of itself.

Now that so many of these barriers are down, and Jews have become less Jewish and more prosperous, there are tendencies to caution and withdrawal. A satisfying pattern of Jewish middle-class life has not yet emerged. This failure in Jewish life reflects the general unease of American middle-class life, as well as the specific Jewish dilemma of finding, in this amorphous society, a balance between separation and the loss of identity.

the Italians

WHEN the Chinese, confident that they were the only civilized people, were confronted by Italian Jesuits in the seventeenth century, and discovered that another people could write, and were even more competent than themselves at clock-building and calendar-making, they decided they would have to add to the number of known civilized nations. They consequently added the Italians, the first Western civilized people with whom they had contact, and the Jews, who had written the book that the Jesuits were trying to propagate.

Thus, to Chinese writers of the early modern period, the Chinese, Jews, and Italians were linked by a peculiar accident as the three civilized nations. Historical accident has again linked them more recently, for in the late nineteenth and early twentieth centuries these three peoples —so different in size, character, and history—became the great migrating nations. In each case, the migrants were impoverished, had commercial skill that marked them off in many places where they settled, and showed a surprising strength of family, which served both to advance and to limit them.

Italian immigrants, from Genoa, Venice, and other cities, had settled in a number of countries in the early nineteenth century. In New York there were musicians, opera singers, and impresarios (including Mozart's librettist, Lorenzo da Ponte), political émigrés (including, for a while, Garibaldi), humbler sellers of cheap statuary, street musicians with monkeys, and some workers.[1] However, mass migration from Italy did not begin until the 1870's. Then it became modern history's greatest and most sustained movement of population from a single country.

This migration was a proletarian one, made up of peasants and landless laborers, large numbers of craftsmen and building workers, and much smaller numbers of professional people. It began as Italian workmen from the North made a seasonal migration to France, Switzerland, and Germany to get jobs. Italian workers preceded and followed the French and British flags into North Africa, making Tunis, for example, more Italian than French. Just as they labored on the railroads and tunnels of Central Europe, so they worked on the (first) Assuan Dam, the Suez Canal, Tunisian and Algerian railways, and the ports of Algiers and Tunis. They came as stonecutters, masons, and unskilled laborers, but they remained to become merchants, professional people, and—where opportunity offered, as in Tunis—farmers.

These migrations throughout Europe and the Mediterranean basin were soon eclipsed by migrations overseas. By 1885 more Italians were going across the Atlantic than to the nearer countries. Between 1860 and 1900 Italian immigration transformed the economy of Argentina, where many settlers of Spanish descent had disdained manual labor. A great stream of Italian laborers and farmers put the broad plains under plow, laid a railroad network, and built the city of Buenos Aires, largely along Italian lines. Almost half the immigrants to Argentina between 1857 and 1926 were Italians. The role of Italians in Brazil was also great, though in that enormous country they formed a much smaller proportion of the population. More than a third of all the immigrants to Brazil between 1884 and 1941 were Italians, and they were the single most numerous immigrant group.[2]

In the nineteenth century, Argentina, Brazil, and Uruguay underwent serious crises attendant on rapid development, and the flow of Italian immigrants was deflected, ever more heavily, to the United States. There, the pioneers' task was already done. Only in one state, California, did Italian immigration coincide with early growth, and there Italians played an important role in the creation of vineyards and production of wine (just as they did in Argentina), in fishing, and in growing and marketing produce.

In New York and the other industrial and commercial cities of the Northeast, where the great mass of the Italian immigrants settled, the story was different. The energy and hard work that achieved wealth and social position for Italians in Argentina could in the United States achieve only a moderately comfortable workingman's existence. The challenge of an underdeveloped country, which made traders and merchants of Italian emigrants in North Africa and South America and attracted professional people from Italy, was not to be found. The Italians arrived in New York with only a small complement of trained and even literate people.

Another significant change accompanied the shift of Italian migration from Argentina and Brazil to the United States. After 1900 emigration from Southern Italy and Sicily increased, and became almost as numerous as that from the Northern and Central parts of the country. And whereas emigrants from Northern and Central Italy continued for the most part to go to countries where their relatives had become established, to Latin America, the new streams of immigrants from the South headed for the United States.

Thus, the great mass of the Italians of New York are of South Italian origin, different in culture and outlook from the first Italians who came to the city. The distinction between North and South Italian that is embedded in the early official immigration statistics of the

United States is not an expression of American prejudices and stereotypes alone. Indeed, Italian government statistics had long made the same distinction. "Wherever Italians might go," wrote Dr. Leonard Covello, the most subtle and perceptive writer on the Italo-Americans, "they were already divided into two groups." [3] The statistics reflected the disdain of the Northern and Central Italians and the Southern gentry for the South Italian and Sicilian peasant. South Italians were considered inferior, hardly civilized.

They were in fact illiterate, having been totally neglected by incredibly reactionary monarchical regimes. Their horizon was limited to their own village; all outside of it were seen as foreigners. Indeed, the South Italian even called all those outside of his own family *"forestieri"*—"strangers." [4] The South Italian had survived regimes that were as destructive as natural disasters; and he accepted natural disasters—earthquakes, floods, droughts —as part of the common course of events. Perhaps this helps explain his extraordinary suspiciousness of everyone and everything outside his family of blood relatives.

In any case, the South has been seen as the problem area of Italy for a hundred years, and like some such areas in other places, it has produced a great and fascinating literature that has made its problems familiar to intellectual Americans.

Of 2,300,000 Italian immigrants to the United States between 1899 and 1910, 1,900,000 were South Italians.[5] Of these, less than half of 1 per cent were in the professions, only 15 per cent were in skilled occupations, and 77 per cent were farm workers or laborers—that is, without any skill of value in an urban, industrial setting. By contrast, three times as many North Italians were professionals, and 66 per cent were laborers. North Italians had on the average twice as much money as South Italians when they came in, and slightly more than the average immigrant. More than half of the South Italian immigrants over fourteen were illiterate, but only 12 per cent of the North Italians.[6] This difference was reduced when, after the First World War, adult immigrants were required to show literacy.

Coming from the land, unskilled and illiterate, the South Italians at first worked as common laborers on railroad and other construction projects throughout the Northeast. They replaced the Irish, who also had arrived unskilled and illiterate, but in contrast to the Irish, the Italian men generally came alone, and in many cases with no intention of staying. The Italian migration had one of the smallest proportions of women and children, one of the highest proportions of returning immigrants.[7]

In 1880, according to the census, there were only 44,000 Italians in the country, 12,000 of them in New York. New York was the largest settlement from the beginning, and as the number of Italians in the country grew, New York continued to hold about one-quarter of them. In the first great decade of migration, the 1880's, 268,000 Italians came, but so many returned that only 183,000 were numbered in 1890. This pattern was repeated for the next two decades. In the nineties, 604,000 Italians entered the country, but only 484,000 were enumerated in 1900. In the first decade of the nineteenth century, 2,104,000 came, but only 1,343,000 persons of Italian birth were enumerated in 1910. The pattern then began to change. Between 1910 and 1920, 1,110,000 immigrants arrived, and in 1920 there were 1,610,000 persons of Italian birth in the country. By the 1920's the immigration was a permanent one. Men came with their families, or hoped to bring them soon, and returned to Italy only for visits or in their old age. The immigration continued at flood tide until cut off by the quota act of 1924, and 455,000 entered during the twenties. In 1930 there were 1,790,000 persons of Italian birth in this country, the largest number ever shown in a census. As many Italian immigrants as the stringent laws allow still enter this country. During the 1950's between 15,000 and 20,000 Italians entered each year,[8] of whom probably a third settled in the New York metropolitan region.

In New York in 1890 there were 75,000 Italian-born persons and 40,000 of Italian parentage, together less than 5 per cent of the city's population. By 1900 the total had increased to 220,000, still only 6 per cent of the population. In the next decade it increased to 11 per cent of the population, and in 1920 to 14 per cent. In 1917, 30 per cent of the children in the public schools of the city were of Italian parentage. Considering the high birth rate of the Italian population in the 1910's and 1920's, the Italian population of the city—that is, those born in Italy, their children and grandchildren—must by 1930 have been at least a sixth of the city.[9] They make up perhaps the same proportion today, and thus rank second in size only to the Jews among ethnic groups in the city.[10]

THE COMMUNITY

WHEN A WELL-KNOWN SOCIOLOGIST STUDIED AN ITALIAN SEC-tion of Boston just a few years ago, he titled his study *The Urban Villagers*.[11] The two keys to understanding the role of Italians in America are the Italian neighborhood and the Italian family. Italians adapted to American society, took on new occupations, became politically significant, but still today, three generations after the founding of the first big Italian settlements in New York, the traditional bounds of neighborhood and family determine in large measure the accomplishments of American Italians.

From the beginning, the village-mindedness of the Southern Italians was striking to American observers. When the immigrants settled in the blocks of New York or in the small industrial communities around the city, they tended to congregate with others from the same province or even village.[12] Illiteracy seriously hampered the development of these diverse settlements into a single ethnic group, for differences in dialect, which in turn engendered mutual suspicion, tended to endure in the absence of widespread written communication. The Italian press was hampered not only by the illiteracy of its clientele but also by the existence of a great gap between the ordinary spoken language and the official language of the press. This contrasted, for example, with the Jewish situation. After Ab Cahan created the *Daily Forward,* literary and difficult Yiddish all but disappeared from the daily Yiddish press. In any case the dialectical differences within Yiddish were minor compared with those in Italian, and the Jews attached less importance to them than did the Italians, for whom they had great symbolic and emotional meaning.

The first Italian neighborhoods proved remarkably stable. Areas that were Italian in 1920 remain so, somewhat attenuated, today. East Harlem, which sent La Guardia to Congress in the twenties and Marcantonio in the 1940's, sent Santangelo in the late fifties and early sixties. However, this East Harlem community is now closely ringed by mostly Negro and Puerto Rican housing projects, and the district that elected Santangelo did not exist in 1962. The North Bronx Italian sections developed (as did similar areas in Queens) when Italians went to the end of the subway lines and beyond, seeking cheap land on which to build houses and raise vegetables and goats. These sections are still heavily Italian, and help elect Representative Paul Fino from the Bronx. Staten Island, which also was attractive to Italians forty years ago because it offered a semirural life, remains heavily Italian. It was the first borough to have an Italian borough president. Even the Italian section of Greenwich Village remains solidly established despite a dozen waves of artists and Bohemians. Indeed, there is no more striking evidence of the strength of Italian communities than the tenements of the South Village, which, regardless of the bizarre Bohemian activities in the basements and storefronts, are still largely Italian. While the Jewish map of New York City in 1920 bears almost no relation to that in 1961, the Italian districts, though weakened in some cases and strengthened in others, are still in large measure where they were.[13]

Nor are these old Italian neighborhoods only shells of their former selves, inhabited exclusively by the older people. Many of the married sons and daughters have stayed close to their parents. Even the trek to the suburbs, when it does occur among Italians, is very often a trek of families of two generations, rather than simply of the young. And it is striking how the old neighborhoods have been artfully adapted to a higher standard of living rather than simply deserted, as they would have been by other groups, in more American style.[14] Tenements that once housed eight families now house half as many. The old houses are rebuilt on the inside (there is always a great amount of skilled building and crafts labor in an Italian community), new furniture is brought into the old apartments, new cars line the streets, and even the restaurants reflect quality and affluence, for they serve not only friends and relatives who come back to the neighborhood but also those who never moved away, and who now have an income far greater than the cost and quality of their housing would suggest.

Pleasant Avenue (now Paladino Avenue) in old Italian East Harlem and Prince and Thompson Streets in downtown Manhattan are very different from what they once were. They are less crowded and more comfortable, but they still reflect the surprising endurance of the Italian neighborhood in the city. The conservative village is in part recreated in an urban environment. When Salvatore Cotillo, the first Italian elected to the State Assembly from East Harlem, left to take his seat in Albany, he had never before, since arriving in New York as a boy, ventured beyond the borders of the city! [15]

Because the desire for the new and the fashionable in housing is so restrained among Italians by attachment to the old neighborhood, even old neighborhoods that are quite unfashionable (because they are adjacent to docks, railroad yards, and factories) remain fully occupied, resisting the social consequences if not the outer appearance of blight. For example, there is such a community just across the East River from the United Nations, north of the Long Island Railroad yards. The industrial side of the Hudson River is also heavily Italian. Thus Italians occupy inlying areas that have been by-passed in the push to develop distant suburbs; in the shadows of the skyscrapers they enjoy quiet and convenient neighborhoods.

Powerful as the Italian village culture was, however, it could not, when transferred to the United States, sustain the absolute power of the father and the unquestioning humility of the children. Instead, the children, finding a serious gap between themselves and their parents, tended to create groups of their own, with something of their own values, code, and morality. Thus, to the structure of the Italian-American neighborhood was added a group known variously as the "boys," the "fellows," the "club," the "gang." In it boys gathered around the corner store, outside of the crowded tenements, and horsed around, talked, and whistled at girls. This phenomenon was not confined among immigrant groups to Italians, but it seems to have been especially characteristic of them. W. F. Whyte's vivid description in *Street Corner Society* of the life of these corner boys is drawn from an Italian slum.[16] A possible explanation is that in Italian culture there is a strong emphasis on male exhibitionism, strength, and sexual potency. The exhibition needs a proper audience, which might be found among the circle of family and relatives who gather daily or at least on Sunday, and among the street corner boys who gather nightly. The boys would withdraw from this society at marriage, almost embarrassed to be deserting the gang even for so compelling a reason. (A very few deserted the boys to train for careers.) But a little while after marriage they would be back among their old friends. Then the nightly gatherings might be moved to an apartment, where the women could talk separately in another room.[17] In older age, the group might organize a club. Every Italian neighborhood is marked by storefronts behind which men chat, play cards, and drink coffee, free from intrusion by strangers.

"Free from strangers" is again the motif. Even today in Italian neighborhoods strangers are conspicuous. A non-Italian newcomer encounters a tight net of friendship and blood relation that binds the community and excludes outsiders until they are found to be "all right." And yet Italian neighborhoods supplied the best settings for bohemia. Oddities that did not affect the group could easily be ignored. Italians of the immigrant and second generations, who still dominate most of the old neighborhoods, do not subscribe to an abstract morality. Concern for odd or immoral behavior is limited to one's own family; the rest of the world, as long as it poses no threat, may be ignored. Emphasis on outer appearances—the "middle-class look"—develops relatively slowly among Italian Americans, probably not until the third generation. What is important is not the appearance of streets and houses, but the inner quality, where relatives and friends are welcome, and a good table is set. Thus it has been possible for Italians to look tolerantly on the oddballs, and to go about their business without being bothered. But perhaps this characteristic of the Italian neighborhood accounts less for its attractiveness to bohemians than the supply of cheap housing and small, low-priced restaurants that serve wine!

The tight little Italian neighborhood can accommodate a special group that really doesn't participate in its life, just as an Italian village can live comfortably with tourists; but it rigidly resists invasions of new immigrant groups, who have their own form of community existence. In New York, of course, these new groups are Puerto Rican and Negro. When they move into Italian neighborhoods there is, at the least, a good deal of resentful talk. The boys' gangs respond in tough fashion. And the Italian community—whether of renters or homeowners—moves away slowly, if at all. This has been the case in East Harlem, in Bushwick in Brooklyn, and elsewhere.[18]

The little circles of kinfolk and townfolk, gathered in a neighborhood, were the base of the American Italian community. In the early days, when Italians were the laborers and building workers of New York, they worked in groups under a leader from the same village, or someone known to one of the group. These were *padroni,* who supplied squads of laborers, took the pay, and divided it among the workers—a necessary function when employers and workers could not speak each other's language. In 1897 it was estimated that two-thirds of the Italian labor in New York was controlled by the *padroni.*[19] At that time Italians formed roughly three-quarters of building labor in the city (the Irish had made up the same proportion only ten years before). By 1900 they formed almost the entire force building the New York subways.

The *padroni* often exploited the workers. Their contracts with employers gave them far too much of the workers' return, they lied in describing jobs, and the workers had no redress. In any case, the workers—illiterate, fearful of government, and docile before men of prominence —did not dream of bringing the *padroni* to justice. Aware of the evil, the Italian government tried to set up independent agencies that would arrange jobs for Italian workmen; it got little support from the *prominenti* (leaders) in New York's Italian community, who themselves very often had been *padroni.* Thus, among the immigrants, money that might have improved the miserable standard of living or financed workers' institutions as in other ethnic groups instead went to a small number of wealthy dignitaries, either *padroni* or "bankers"—the shopkeepers and travel agents who kept and transmitted money for the immigrants. The illiterate workers preferred to use these kinfolk for saving money or sending it to Italy. Once more they were exploited, until state laws were passed to control these immigrant banks and bankers.

Italian government representatives and socialist and anarchist groups tried in various ways to ameliorate the lot of the Italian workers but were helpless against the *padroni* and the bankers. In the village community there was neither a tradition of self-help nor an expectation of improvement. The Italian immigrants did not assume that their children were as good as anybody else's. Thus, the most proletarian of immigrant groups played little role in the labor movement.[20] Furthermore, the Italian building-trades workers were sometimes excluded from unions, which the Irish dominated.[21] Many Italian common laborers were organized in the Hod Carriers, the first union to have an Italian president, but this union became *padronismo* on a larger scale and was a scandal to the labor movement. Dominic D'Allessandro, who had worked in a bank before becoming a labor organizer, skillfully maneuvered himself into the presidency of the Hod Carriers in 1909 and thereafter ran the union as a private fief. There was no convention from 1911 to 1941.[22] Whatever material advantages this union brought to Italian workers, it did little to develop in them any sense of independence and competence.

The Italian workers hesitated to strike against kinfolk who were *padroni* or employers, or to organize against Italians who became union leaders. The difference in station intimidated them, and in any case, many at first looked forward to returning to Italy and did not want to lose wages in a strike or risk trouble in a union fight in order to improve a long-run position. Furthermore, having come from the land, they had no knowledge of trade-unionism or radical movements. Italian girls scabbed in the great strike of the waistmakers in 1909–1910. It took careful work by the International Ladies' Garment Workers' Union, with the aid of such men as Salvatore Ninfo and Fiorello La Guardia, to develop powerful Italian locals within that union after 1910.[23]

To the business union-minded Irish leaders of the building trades, the Italians were cheap labor under-cutting the market; to the socialist-minded Jewish leaders of the garment trades, they were deficient in class consciousness. Their own leaders were often the spiritual brethren of the narrow-minded and selfish *galantuomi* of the South Italian small town, and they lorded it over the workingman in New York as the gentry lorded it over the peasant in Southern Italy. There were many outstanding leaders of Italian labor and many outstanding Italian radicals—for example, Ettor and Giovanitti, who led the Lawrence strike for the IWW in 1912, and Carlo Tresca, who was for many years a leading radical editor. Salvatore Ninfo, August Bellanca, Luigi Antonini, and others organized and led powerful locals in the Jewish-dominated garment-trades unions. But the influence of radical and labor leaders in the Italian community was small. It was impossible to establish a socialist Italian daily. The leading newspaper of the Italian community was (and remains) *Il Progresso Italo-Americano,* which was founded by Carlo Borsatti, a former *padrone.* He was succeeded as editor by a wealthy businessman, Generoso Pope. This newspaper and the Italian press in general were opposed to unions in the years when Italian workers might have been creating powerful ones.[24] This was in marked contrast to the Yiddish press, of which the most important paper was the Socialist *Forward.*

The family- and community-based Italian settlements were incapable of creating group-wide institutions such as the Jewish community built. Indeed, while the Jews were founding the Hebrew Immigrant Aid Society, the Educational Alliance, and other institutions to help immigrants off to a good start, the leaders of the Italian community were sabotaging efforts of the Italian government and a few farsighted Italian individuals to set up similar institutions. At a time when money was desperately needed for the Italian Home, a social agency launched by the consul to aid the immigrants, Borsatti's *Il Progresso* was raising large sums from the immigrants and their mutual aid societies for a monument to Columbus.[25] This was the kind of communal enterprise the Italian *prominenti* favored; statues to Columbus, Mazzini, Verrazzano, Garibaldi, and Verdi went up in rapid succession, all gifts of American Italians to the city of New York. (Again by contrast, the larger, more prosperous, and better organized Jewish community has still not built a statue to any of its famous men in the city.)

This pattern has characterized the Italian community of New York to the present day. It can make great efforts for a noble gesture, but it has been incapable of creating institutions that work steadily for common ends. Thus, in the twenties, the Italians of New York raised the grand Casa Italiana at 117th Street and Broadway. Wealthy Italians of the city, and particularly those who had made fortunes in erecting fine buildings—the Paterno brothers and Anthony Campagna—gave generously. But it has not become a significant cultural center for the New York Italian community. And while this campaign was going on, the Italian lawyer and sociologist John H. Mariano could write, after pointing to the enormous neglected educational, health, and social needs of Italian youths: "Altogether in New York City there are thirty-seven welfare agencies catering exclusively to Jewish-speaking children, eleven catering exclusively to Irish children, four to German children, three to Greek, one to Spanish. There is in existence an Italian Child Welfare Committee, an organization affiliated with the Catholic Big Brothers." [26] Robert F. Foerster, the great scholar who chronicled the Italians' emigration, also mused about their individualism: "Musical as few people have been, the Italians have never developed much interest in choir singing." And the love of grandeur:

. . . the municipal expenditures in Italy are, to an unusual extent, munificent rather than provident and every town wants a statue to some *valoroso concittadino*. . . . Much of the life of Italians in their foreign settlements is organized about this trait. Many a mutual aid society has come into existence largely because of the chance offered for pomp and paraphernalia, and has been held together by its picnics, excursions, and parades. Through the narrow streets of such a colony a funeral procession may take its way, an endless succession of carriages smothered in flowers, followed by an endless line of men marching single file, plumed, decorated in uniform, carrying gorgeous banners —is it for the deceased or the living? [27]

Mutual aid societies did flourish, as in other immigrant communities. Workingmen and small shopkeepers showed a capacity to cooperate in the days before relief and social insurance, in confronting the accidents of an industrial society. But once again, the social strength of the neighborhood could not be developed on a larger scale. There were no less than 2,000 Italian mutual benefit societies in New York City in 1910.[28] While large numbers of these were banded together in the National Order of the Sons of Italy, it never developed beyond the city and state level to become a strong national organization. It had nothing like the strength of B'nai B'rith or the great Croatian and Slovenian benefit societies. Indeed, in 1961 when Italians everywhere were agitated by the representation of Italian criminals in the television program "The Untouchables," they had in effect to create a protest organization. They had none of the size and resources of the American Jewish Committee, the American Jewish Congress, the Anti-Defamation League, or the National Association for the Advancement of Colored People.

FAMILY INFLUENCES

IT IS IMPOSSIBLE TO DIVIDE THE COMMUNITY, NEIGHBORHOOD, and peer-group from the family in their impact on immigrant and second-generation Italian Americans. The set of qualities that seems to distinguish Italian Americans includes individuality, temperament, and ambition, all of which, however, are restricted by the culture and outlook of the family and neighborhood. This produces a tension, the most satisfying resolution of which is some form of worldly success that is admired by one's family and the friends of one's childhood. Perhaps the ideal is the entertainer—to give him a name, Frank Sinatra—who is an international celebrity, but still the big-hearted, generous, unchanged boy from the block. That form of individuality and ambition which is identified with Protestant and Anglo-Saxon culture, and for which the criteria of success are abstract and impersonal, is rare among American Italians. A good deal of this Italian-American orientation can be explained by looking at the family.

Edward C. Banfield has named the characteristic outlook of a small southern Italian village "amoral familism." [29] According to this outlook, one owes nothing to anyone outside one's family, and effort should advance only the family. The picture of such a life has been shown also in Verga's *The House by the Medlar Tree,* in Carlo Levi's *Christ Stopped at Eboli,* and in many novels of Italian-American life, such as Michael DeCapite's moving *Maria.* But the fullest and most vivid description of how this outlook has been carried to America is in Leonard Covello's *The Social Background of the Italo-American School Child.* "It is impossible," Covello writes, "to imagine the *contadino* [peasant] in South Italy contributing to the Red Cross." [30] He gives vivid examples of the universal acceptance of the notion that morality is limited to family members. Perhaps the most striking is the case of the old woman who saw a village boy stealing fruit from a tree. She ignored this. But after she saw him do it a second time she severely reprimanded the boy. Why? Because the first time he was stealing from someone who was not part of his family, a "stranger," and this was all right.[31]

The content of this moral code remained basically the same among Italian immigrants to America. One should not trust strangers, and may advance one's interest at the cost of strangers. Also, one does not interfere with strangers' business. One therefore tolerates the breaking of law by others (leaving aside the fact that it might be dangerous to do otherwise). "You be a gentleman, I'll be a gentleman," is the way this outlook is expressed in America today.[32] Obviously it has a good deal in common with contemporary American morality. But whereas for America in general this self-serving and anticommunal ethic breaks with something in the American past, for the Italian American it is continuous with the past. For him it is rather the old American universalistic and abstract morality that is alien. The Italian peasant village and the contemporary American metropolis thus converge to some extent in a common ethical outlook.

But there remains the difference that the contemporary American ethic values *self*-advancement, whereas the Italian variant still values *family* advancement. Thus, even in the case of Italian gangsters or racketeers, there is a surprising degree of family stability and concern with children, brothers, sisters, and other relatives. For example, the important group of Italians with illegal business connections who were discovered accidentally in a conclave at Apalachin, New York, were on the whole good family men; in fact, the Apalachin conference itself resembled nothing so much as a great family picnic. Indeed, it is impossible to understand Italians in crime without the setting of the family and neighborhood. Perhaps this accounts in part for the Italian-American superiority in organized crime. The "natural" succession in the management of criminal enterprise from the Italians to the newest slum-dwellers, the Negroes and Puerto Ricans, has not taken place in the city, and one reason may be that the Italian family and neighborhood provide connections of a closeness and dependability that the other groups cannot match.*

Of course, Italians have the advantage of better political connections, but that is not a satisfactory explanation by itself. In early 1960 a *New York Post* reporter, Ted Poston, investigated Adam Clayton Powell's charge that the New York police favored Italian and Jewish policy bankers in Harlem over Negro ones. He found indeed that Italians were driving Negroes out of business, but one reason was the Negroes' own style. As one player told him, the Negro policy banker gets a flashy car and flashy woman, and this annoys the customers, particularly when he has to scratch around in his pockets to pay off on a hit. The Italian banker has a conservative car and family life, a situation reassuring to the customers.[33]

---

* We should point out something that perhaps hardly needs to be pointed out: that when we talk of the relationship between Italians and crime we speak of only a minute fraction of American Italians. It seems quite true that many or most of the people engaged in organized crime (that is, crime organized as a business) are first- and second-generation Italians; but even if their numbers run into the thousands, this is still an insignificant part of some 6,000,000 Americans of Italian origin.

Obviously the relationship between Italians and crime cannot be explained simply on the ground that Italo-Americans have maintained the strong family of the Italian village. Other explanations include the characteristic Southern Italian peasant's attitude to government officials (they are "thieves," and in Southern Italy they were); the complementary attitude to laws (which help the "thieves" in their work); and the fact that while social mobility among Italians was slow, the desire for material goods and sensual satisfactions was strongly felt and uninhibited by a Puritanical religion. There is too the fact that one common American channel to success—education—was narrowed for American Italians by the peculiar constitution and outlook of the family and neighborhood.

It is hard to determine how much the structure of the family helps us understand crime, education, and social mobility among American Italians. That the family is "strong" is clear. Divorce, separation, and desertion are relatively rare. Family life is considered the norm for everyone; bachelors and spinsters are few, much fewer than among the Irish. The Italian family resembles in some ways the Jewish one, in its strength, its heightened and uninhibited emotional quality, and even in some of its inner alliances. Thus, there is a strong tie between mother and son. But while the Jewish father is often ignored by this mother-son alliance, the Italian father is feared, for great emphasis is placed on male strength, and violent behavior is not unusual.

Both the Jewish and the Italian mother overfeed and overprotect the children. This is perhaps one reason why the rate of alcoholism is low among both groups, but probably more important is the fact that in both cultures wine is drunk early in family settings. Both mothers want to keep their children close. But the Jewish son, despite his dependence and neurosis, finds it easier to leave home than the Italian son. This is perhaps because accomplishment for the Italian son is felt by the parents to be meaningless unless it directly gratifies the family—for example, by maintaining the closeness of the family or advancing the family's interests through jobs and marriage. The

Jewish parents can be gratified symbolically by the accomplishment of a son who may be removed from or even indifferent to them. To draw a distinction from cultural anthropology, the Italian family seems to be more interested in a child's being than his becoming, and the latter is sacrificed to the former.[34]

But the social explanations for the differences are as convincing as the psychological. The Jewish child never has to face the conflict between departure from the family and individual achievement as clearly as the Italian child does, for the Jewish child is part of a whole group that is changing simultaneously its occupations, way of life, and dwelling places. Mobility for Italians has to be individual mobility, because the group moves slowly and is conservative in its outlook and habits; Jewish mobility is a mass phenomenon. Conceivably the Italian family nurtures a confident and self-reliant personality by its warmth and dependability and by early gratification of the child's desires (but studies show that there is a good deal of inconsistency in this gratification, which may not be so comforting to the child). But the society of his childhood is ready to punish him if he does seek to leave upon growing up and it is painful to leave in any case because so few do. An Italian-American novel published in 1961 (*A Cup of the Sun,* by Octavia Waldo) describes the problem of a young Italian American of great sensitivity who wants to become an artist or writer. She is as isolated in her community as she would be in a small Midwest town. She must go *away* to school, and she knows she will never have anything to come back to. Her development separates her decisively from the friends with whom she grew up.

There are distinctive solutions to this problem of expressing individualism while staying with the group. One can become a local lawyer, staying in the neighborhood and active in politics, or a local doctor, or a local businessman. Or one may become that special variant of a local businessman, a racketeer, who is a celebrity yet a resident of the old neighborhood block, where connections to the police, the local political powers, and the customers are available. But to enter a larger society—Wall Street, Madison Avenue, Washington—has been a challenging and difficult task, and it is only in the past ten or fifteen years that any sizable numbers of Italians have deserted the hearth and neighborhood to try. Even now, the proportion is not large.

But perhaps the chief factor in restricting the movement of second-generation Italian Americans has been their attitude to schooling. The South Italian immigrants came from villages in which schools were only for the children of the *galantuomi,* and the peasant's child (should his parents have the strange idea of sending him) was unwelcome. Education was for a cultural style of life and professions the peasant could never aspire to. Nor was there an ideology of change; intellectual curiosity and originality were ridiculed or suppressed. "Do not make your child better than you are," runs a South Italian proverb.

Nor, despite a strong desire for material improvement, did the Italian family see a role for education in America.[35] One improved one's circumstances by hard work, perhaps by a lucky strike, but not by spending time in a school, taught by women, who didn't even beat the children. Parents felt that the children should contribute to the family budget as soon as possible, and that was years before the time fixed by the state for the end of their education. Truancy and drop-outs were a constant problem, and were often abetted by the parents, who wanted the children to help out in the shop or store. And aside from these parental attitudes, the general isolation of the Italians as a result of their slow assimilation meant that the children, when forced out of the close, familiar family and into school, were ill at ease. They had not been raised for new adventures. Under this (from an American viewpoint) topsy-turvy system of values, it was the "bad" son who wanted to go to school instead of to work, the "bad" daughter who wanted to remain in school instead of helping her mother. Such behavior made the "bad" ones strangers to their families. For the children of the South Italian peasants in New York to get college educations in the 1920's and 1930's was a heroic struggle. (The situation was different among North Italians and South Italians not of peasant background. From these groups, most college-trained professionals were drawn until recently.)[36]

To New York's public school administrators of twenty and thirty years ago the great burden was the "Italian problem," just as today it is the Negro and Puerto Rican problem. The two periods have some things in common, such as the language difficulty of Italian and Puerto Rican children, and the disdain, even contempt, of many teachers and administrators for the children. But there are also striking differences. The problems of present-day Negro and Puerto Rican children often stem from the weakness of the family, in which a single overburdened and resentful parent is unable to maintain an ordered home life for the child. By contrast, the problems of the Italian children stemmed from a too strong, too rigorously ordered family, which did not value education.

Leonard Covello, one of the great educators of New York City, has described the whole educational history of the New York Italian in his autobiography, *The Heart is the Teacher*. He came to an overcrowded tenement in East Harlem from a Southern Italian town. He attended elementary school and left high school when all his friends did. The influence of a neighbor's daughter, and later of settlement house workers and Protestant missionaries, sustained him in returning to high school and going through Columbia University on scholarships. When his father heard that he was involved in sports in school, he told him to go to work—why should he go to school to be a strong man? (Many Negro parents today are also suspicious of anything other than the three R's, but Covello's parents weren't enthusiastic about those, either.)

Covello became a foreign-language teacher in DeWitt Clinton High School. Italian was not then one of the foreign languages taught, and Covello felt (aside from the significance of Italian as a major language) that teaching it might do much to enhance the self-image of the Italian boys (the problem was largely with the boys, interestingly enough, just as it is today with Negro boys). Covello, one of the first teachers of Italian background in the city high schools, and Salvatore Cotillo, the first elected Assemblyman—who were both from East Harlem—fought for this change and got the Board of Education to admit Italian to the high school curriculum in 1922.

Covello later became principal of the new Benjamin Franklin High School in East Harlem. He continually studied the educational problems of Italian children, gave a course to teachers at the School of Education of New York University on the background of Italo-American children, and worked on his own major study of this problem. In the later forties, Covello saw the Italian problem in the schools give way to the Negro and Puerto Rican problems, just as Italian laborers and other workers in the least skilled jobs were being replaced by these new groups. He then became the adviser on education problems to the New York office of the Migration Division of the Commonwealth of Puerto Rico, and has since energetically devoted his enormous talents and experience to that problem.

For two long generations, for immigrants and second generation alike, the burden of Southern Italian culture prevented Italo-Americans from making effective use of the public school system in New York. The effects of this heritage, while they are no longer particularly visible in the elementary and high schools, may be seen in the city colleges. Eleven per cent of the graduates of Hunter College in 1960 were of Italian name, and 6 per cent of the graduates of City College. These proportions are less than one would expect on the basis of the city population of Italian origin. The difference in Italian enrollment between Hunter and City College reflects the role of Catholicism in the process of Italian adaptation to American norms of high education. There are more Italian girls in Hunter because of the sequence of Catholic presidents there and because, in accordance with the Catholic preferred practice, Hunter is not coeducational. Priests and other religious advisers therefore suggest Hunter for girls. City College and Brooklyn College, with their radical traditions, are less favored. Around Queens College there has for many years centered a struggle in which Catholic elements have attempted to increase their influence on the administration, for Catholics feel that Queens, which began as a very liberal institution in a borough of homeowners—many of them Italian, German, and Irish Catholic—should reflect the attitudes of its community somewhat more strongly.

With respect to the Italian graduates of City College, another interesting point is that the majority of boys take degrees as engineers. The background of South Italians does not incline them toward the more intellectual and speculative college curricula; education is seen, when its importance is finally understood, almost exclusively as a means of preparing for a profession—teaching for the girls, engineering or the free professions for the boys. American Catholicism too encourages such practical pursuits, and in the third generation, the influence of Catholicism among Italian Americans has become formidable. From a collection of village cults with a distinct and marked character that made Italian immigrants very different from Irish or German Catholics, the religion of Italian Americans has slowly become incorporated into the large and efficient structure of American Catholicism. Thus, the proportion of Italian Americans enrolled in parochial schools steadily increases; the student body of Fordham University, for example, has become half Italian. This new appeal of the Catholic universities is another factor reducing the Italian proportion in the free city colleges.

RELIGION

THE ITALIAN NEIGHBORHOOD AND THE ITALIAN FAMILY, IN THE first decades of heavy Italian migration, offered strong barriers to the organizational and intellectual influence of Catholicism. There was much discussion, from the 1880's on, of the "Italian problem" in the Church: the fact that there were few priests, that many of these were of poor quality, that few Italians observed the sacraments, and that many departed from the Church.[37] In the first two decades of this century Protestant groups conducted mission churches in an energetic effort to convert Italians. Norman Thomas, the Socialist leader, was the pastor of one such church in East Harlem before World War I, and at that time there were almost 300 Italian Protestant missionaries engaged in full-time work among the American Italians.[38] Fiorello H. La Guardia was himself Protestant, as were such other important Italian political figures as Ferdinand Pecora and Charles Poletti. All this reflected the weakness of Catholicism among Italian Americans up until about the 1940's.

This situation is now changing. As Italians emerged from the grip of neighborhood and family which had maintained the peculiar cast of South Italian culture, they did not enter directly into an unmodulated and abstract Americanism. By the 1950's the American temper, as reflected in the age of suburbia and Eisenhower, emphasized the fact that every man must have a religion, and the Catholic was indeed one of the best and most American. Thus, the Italian migrant to the suburbs, who had perhaps never taken the village-type church of the dense ethnic neighborhood seriously (though his wife and perhaps his children had), found in the new, ethnically mixed Roman Catholic church of the suburbs an important expression of his new status as a middle-class American, just as his Jewish neighbor who had ignored the Orthodox church in the old neighborhood could not ignore the Conservative synagogue or Reform temple of the suburbs.

In particular, the rising Italian middle class, which adopts American Roman Catholicism as a symbol of its new status, also adopts the parochial school. The public schools, headed by Dr. Covello's Benjamin Franklin High School, dominated the educational life of East Harlem; this is not the case in the heavily Italian areas of New Jersey and Long Island. There the parochial school, whatever the heavy sacrifices necessary to maintain it, is strongly favored, while the American Italian population, as part now of a general American Catholic group, maintains pressure on the public schools to reflect the cultural orientations of American Catholicism. (Thus, for example, when an issue developed in 1961 in a Long Island suburb over corporal punishment in the public schools, it was, one might see in the papers, those with the Jewish names who opposed such punishment, and those with Italian names who favored it.)

This new suburban Catholicism is stronger than the Catholicism of the old neighborhood. It also operates as a special variant of the melting pot for the American-Italian group. In the old neighborhoods there was antagonism between Irish and Italian Catholics. It began over jobs in construction and influence in the Irish-run unions. It was maintained by cultural differences between the celibate, hard-drinking Irish, and the more sensual, wine-drinking Italians. It was expressed in Italian resentment over the Irish monopoly of municipal politics and jobs and also in Italian antagonism to an Irish-run church. The care of Italian souls was largely—almost always on the upper levels, but also often in the parishes—in Irish hands. Italians responded with indifference to religious observances in the case of most of the men, or, in the case of the most upwardly mobile, with a change of allegiance to Protestantism.

However, as mobility of Italians has become a large-scale phenomenon since World War II, the Catholic Church has assimilated this rising group into the new American Catholicism. The Irish and Italians, who often contended with each other in the city, may work together and with other groups in the Church in the suburbs, and their separate ethnic identities are gradually being muted in the common identity of American Catholicism. Protestantism was a symbol of rising social status among Italians thirty and forty years ago. Today, a more significant symbol of rising social status is marriage with a girl of Irish descent, who has gone to a good Catholic school, and who seems to young Italians to represent the older American society as much as Protestantism did a generation ago. The social pages of the *New York Times* often report such marriages.

Not that all is as yet peace between Italians and Irish in the Catholic Church. The hierarchy of the Church remains overwhelmingly Irish. In the New York Archdiocese, of thirteen auxiliary bishops, only one, Joseph M. Pernicone, is of Italian origin. Even he, the lone Italian bishop in the American Church, was not appointed until 1954. In Brooklyn, where there are very likely more Catholics of Italian than Irish origin, there are no Italian bishops.

The number of Italian priests, too, remains small. Today, as Italians are finally becoming integrated into American Catholicism, with respect to their degree of observance, their support of parochial schooling, and their replacement of the cultural outlook of neighborhood and family by that of the Irish-American church, their integration lags in one respect—they do not provide large numbers of priests. Perhaps this will change, but it seems likely that one reason for the small weight of Italians in the Catholic Church—aside from the influence of the superlative organizational and bureaucratic skills of the Irish—is the fact that so few of them enter the Church and are available for further advancement. Here the old weight of South Italian culture makes itself felt. A man is supposed to be a man, and celibacy has always been something of a problem for the South Italian culture, which tends to see sexual needs as imperative and almost incapable of suppression or moderation. Celibacy is apparently no great problem for the American Irish. Very many of them—as do the Irish in Ireland—marry late, or not at all. (Of second-generation Irish men in the New York metropolitan area, aged 14 to 24, 8 per cent are married; of second-generation Italian men in the same age group, 14 per cent are married. Of those aged 25 to 44, 72 per cent of the Irish men and 80 per cent of the Italian men are married. Of those over 45, 17 per cent of the second-generation Irish men are still unmarried, against 10 per cent of the Italian men.) If one is to be celibate anyway, then an important consideration in contemplating a career in the Church need not affect one's decision. Among Italian Americans the South Italian assumption that sex is important and hardly controllable has under the circumstances of American life become transformed into the very similar point of view of American mass culture, and this too leaves little room for celibacy.

Despite the relative paucity of priests of Italian origin, Catholicism is now firmly rooted among the Italian Americans, and its impact will be reflected more effectively, we believe, in their moral and social attitudes in the future. In time, the American hierarchy may take on more of an Italian cast than it has today.

OCCUPATIONS

THE SLOW CHANGE THAT HAS CHARACTERIZED ITALIAN AMERIcans in the location of their neighborhood and the character of the family-based culture may also be seen when we consider their occupational history. The first-generation men were principally workers. Three-quarters of them were to be found, in 1950, in the categories of skilled, semiskilled, and unskilled workers. Two-thirds of the second-generation men were still workers. Among the women, the first generation was highly concentrated among factory operatives. In the second generation, two-fifths were employed as clerical and salesworkers, but the largest single category among the native-born Italian-American women was still factory workers, principally in the garment industry. The gap between first and second generation among Italians, in the occupations pursued, and in the income earned, was smaller than that for the other major European immigrant groups. (See Tables 6, 7, and 8, comparing the occupational distributions of first- and second-generation immigrants in the New York metropolitan area from Italy, the U. S. S. R., and Ireland.)

Indeed, in the sphere of economy, as in that of residence and family, differences between first and second generation among Italians are likely to be less important than the differences between second and third generation. In all these fields these differences are only beginning to emerge now, in the period since the Second World War. As late as the thirties and the forties most Italian professionals came from either the small North Italian group or the small part of the South Italian immigrant group that was of non-peasant background. Today, the grandchildren of the immigrants are moving into the professions and the higher white-collar fields. The mass media and advertising in particular have a good deal of glamour, and names of Italian origin are evident in these fields.

The pattern whereby, among Jews, the children of storekeepers and small businessmen went to college and became professionals, is being repeated, on a smaller scale and a generation later, among Italian Americans. Despite their peasant background, their lack of commercial experience, their educational limitations, the first generation of Italian immigrants showed a strong inclination for business enterprise, and established many thousands of stores, restaurants, wholesale food concerns, produce-handling firms, small contracting businesses, trucking and moving concerns (moving in New York is almost an Italian-American monopoly), clothes manufacturing factories, and the like. The business spirit was much stronger among Italian immigrants than, for example, among Irish immigrants. This network of small businesses has been expanded and maintained by the second generation, but since it is small business, often founded by parents with little education and social status, it does not very often attract the better-educated sons, just as in the case of Jewish small business. But Jewish small business was on a much greater scale than Italian small business, and many more Jewish enterprises have grown so that the father's socially lowering enterprise (such as dealing in junk) has become socially more respectable (such as dealing in scrap), as well as financially more rewarding.

The great bureaucracies of government and business have also been attractive to the second and third generation of Italian Americans. But whereas the great corporations could potentially draw from large numbers of college-trained Jews who have up to now found entrance into the executive hierarchy difficult (this has become a great matter of concern to Jewish defense agencies), as yet relatively few Italian Americans seek these jobs. It is hard to know whether there is discrimination against Italian Americans in the corporations, and in the country clubs and city clubs that are linked with their higher echelons. There are no Italian defense agencies and other community organizations to draw attention to such matters, even to the extent of formulating some general community opinion as to what the facts are. Perhaps Italian Americans, since there are relatively few of them, are treated more as individuals when they seek these higher jobs. There is evidence in studies of prejudice that in the thirties and forties Italian Americans came near the bottom of the list of American preferences. But today one-quarter of the population of New York City is Puerto Rican and Negro, and these raise on their shoulders, as they take over the dirty work, those who had the dirty work before them.

This great change in the bottom economic group of the city in the last twenty years has unquestionably raised the status of Italians and reduced the prejudice they may expect. The image of Italian Americans has also undoubtedly been affected by the more favorable image of Italy and things Italian since the end of the war. (In the past, Italians attempting to improve their social position would indicate they were linked to some noble or old family in Italy, rather than identify themselves with the generally low-status Italian-American group. Today, the entire group must benefit from the admiration and warm feeling felt by Americans for the culture and style of living of present-day Italy.)

But just what will happen when Italians join Jews in large numbers in attempting to enter the desirable places in American business life and society is hard to predict. Perhaps by that time the American corporation will see itself, as its propaganda so often pictures it, as a truly public institution, bound to the same criteria of selection that today affect the government service—freedom from bias, and the requirement at the same time to represent and reflect all parts of the American population.

POLITICS

IN 1950, AS UNPLEASANT SCANDALS WERE ABOUT TO BREAK, Mayor William O'Dwyer, Democrat, resigned shortly after being elected to his second term as mayor of New York, and sought refuge in Mexico as our Ambassador. A remarkable race for the mayoralty then developed. Vincent Impellitteri, president of the City Council, wished to succeed O'Dwyer, but Democratic leaders decided to give the party's nomination to Judge Ferdinand Pecora, who had had a far more distinguished record. Impellitteri, who had the support of a large part of the machine, then decided to run as an independent. Both men had been born in Sicily, but while Impellitteri was a good son of the Church, Pecora had in his youth become active in a Protestant Episcopal church in his neighborhood. The third major candidate, Edward Corsi, had also been born in Italy, but he represented an earlier stage of New York Italian life. He came from Central Italy, not the South. His father had been a member of the Italian Chamber of Deputies. He had become part of that able group of Italian Americans in East Harlem who had made up a sort of Italian-American intelligentsia. He had in the twenties edited *The New American,* one of the few efforts to create a serious Italian-American publication in English. He had been a settlement house director in East Harlem and an active Republican, and had risen to the post of Commissioner of Immigration under Hoover.

Yet a fourth major Italian-born figure played an important role in this campaign—Frank Costello, long reputed to be one of the country's major entrepreneurs and organizers of gambling and other illegal activities. Costello was not running for office. But were it not for the fact that Mayor O'Dwyer could never explain satisfactorily why he had attended a meeting with some Tammany leaders in Costello's apartment before he ran for mayor in 1945, he might not have had to depart for Mexico, and this remarkable election, which gave opportunities to three other Italian Americans, might never have taken place. The principal problem of the campaign, for both Pecora and Impellitteri, was to convince the electorate that the other was more deeply implicated in relations with underworld figures, and for Corsi, to convince the electorate that both were equally implicated.

The campaign illustrates three major themes that have characterized the Italian-American role in New York City politics.

First, despite the evidence of this campaign, the Italian Americans were slow and late in gaining an important place in the considerations of party leaders. Impellitteri had been, only five years before, the first Italian American to be placed on a citywide Democratic ticket. The formula for ticket balancing now requires that an Italian American fill one of the three major posts for which the entire city votes, but until 1945 this was not so. In 1941 O'Dwyer ran against La Guardia, McGoldrick, and Newbold Morris. La Guardia's appeal was varied and rich, and his Italian-American background was no particular source of strength in the three mayoralty elections that he won. If it had been, it would not have taken the Democratic party leaders three unsuccessful campaigns to come up with an Italian-American candidate for comptroller or president of the City Council.

The Italians were late in arriving at the forefront of the New York political scene because, despite their numbers, they had relatively few men of wealth and education. Through the twenties La Guardia was the only

Congressman of Italian background from the city—and, as we have already suggested, he was in no sense chosen by party leaders as a "representative" of his ethnic group (this was the nature of Impellitteri's political rise).[39] La Guardia's personal gifts made it possible for him to win elections ten years before the Italian Americans, in the course of their slow ascent, achieved recognition. But in the forties this began to change. Generoso Pope and Frank Costello became powers in the affairs of New York City's Democrats. The number of Italian-American Assemblymen and judges rose. In 1949 Carmine DeSapio became the first Tammany leader of Italian background.

A second major theme in the Italian-American role in New York politics is involvement with crime. Daniel Bell has brilliantly analyzed the relationship between crime, American life, and politics.[40] He points out that each ethnic group trying to achieve wealth and recognition, to find a place on the American scene, has, in sequence, produced underworld figures. The early Irish gangsters were succeeded by the Jews, and Arnold Rothstein, "Czar" of the New York underworld in the 1920's, was as closely linked to Democratic judges in Jimmy Walker's day as Frank Costello was fifteen years later. After the middle thirties, the most prominent gangsters in New York were of Italian origin, though their careers had begun in the 1920's.

But the matter, as Bell points out, is not so simple, because the role of crime in each community has varied with the other sources of wealth and prominence that were available to it. The Irish controlled the political machines and city administrations, and Irish wealth developed in construction, contracting, trucking, and public utilities, on the basis in part of this political link. There was no major role for strong-arm men and underworld elements, though Irish thugs helped control the polls. Jewish wealth developed somewhat more independently of political power in the garment industry, merchandising, and building, and offered opportunities to the large numbers of Jewish lawyers, of whom a relatively small proportion went into politics. Jewish gangsters became involved with Jewish wealth as industrial racketeers in the garment industry, but they played no important function, and were finally driven out.

Opportunities for wealth and prominence came slow and late to Italian Americans. Meanwhile, gambling, drugs, and the waterfront succeeded industrial racketeering and bootlegging as the major sources of illegal wealth. Into this field, as the older groups withdrew, the new group moved. By the time of the Kefauver investigations in the early 1950's, a large part of the gambling and other illegal industries had fallen almost completely into the hands of Italian Americans. And in their hands they apparently remain, because the Negroes and Puerto Ricans have not shown the ability to capture them.

The link between the illegal businessmen and the politicians was complex. The politicians of course needed money; and political protection was on the whole more important to illegitimate than to legitimate businessmen. Other elements were mixed in. There was ethnic pride, which motivated a Frank Costello as much as it did a businessman who had not become rich as a bootlegger. There was a desire to help out relatives and friends. There was the fact that bootleggers, politicians, lawyers, judges, and policemen had all grown up on the block together, and had never lost touch. How was one to sort out the influences, and decide the significance of the fact that judges and ex-bootleggers and gamblers all sat around the same table to raise money for an orphan's home?

In 1952, the New York State Crime Commission held hearings in New York City on the links between politicians and criminals. Here is a bit of testimony on which anyone trying to unravel the relationship among crime, politics, and the Italian community may muse. Francis X. Mancuso, who had been a judge of the Court of General Sessions and a Tammany district leader, is testifying:

"Do you know Frank Costello?"
"I do, sir."
"How long have you known him?"
"About thirty-five years or so. His people come from the same town my people come from. They know each other. I may say there is intermarriage in the family; my first cousin married his first cousin."

"There has been some notoriety about a meeting supposedly attended by you with Costello and Mr. Pope [Generoso Pope, publisher of Il Progresso Italo Americano, in the sand and gravel business], and the present county leader [Carmine DeSapio] at the Hotel Biltmore."

"That's right."

"You were at that meeting?"

"Yes, sir."

"All four of you?"

"Four: Mr. Pope, Sr., Costello, Judge Valente—Louis Valente, DeSapio, and myself—five. I have no present recollection of the precise date; either the year '46 or '47."

"Can you relate it to nominations or elections of any particular official?"

"No. Just shortly after the first World War Gene Pope was interested in raising funds for orphan children of Italy—or the destitute children. He wanted to form a committee for the purpose of raising funds, and that was the prime object of the meeting." [41]

Obviously, the investigators thought the fine hand of Mr. Costello, who had received the gratitude of Thomas A. Aurelio in 1943 for helping with his nomination to the Supreme Court of New York, might again be involved in judicial nominations. Yet the people at the meeting would have been pretty much the same whether the purpose was to discuss judicial nominations or raise money for the poor children of Italy. The vulnerability of Italian-American political figures to charges of links with criminals will remain great as long as substantial wealth in the Italian-American community is derived from illegitimate enterprises.

Mr. Impellitteri won the election. This illustrates the third theme of Italian-American politics in New York—the emergence of the smooth, affable, middle-class, good Catholic as a representative of the group. It would be hard to prove it was this image that won the election for Impellitteri. Yet it is interesting to contrast New York's second Italian-American mayor with its first. La Guardia was a Protestant, his mother was from Trieste and of an Italian Jewish family, his father was from Foggia in Apulia, and he had been raised and educated in the Far West. This background made him as untypical a representative of New

York's Italians as one can imagine. La Guardia was in fact the last white Protestant mayor of New York—and we do not use this designation in a simple demographic or classificatory sense. He made more appointments from the old-stock, Anglo-Saxon population of the city than any other mayor since John Purroy Mitchel.[42] Like Mitchel, he represented Reform, and in his day Reform meant the white Anglo-Saxon Protestant elements in New York's population, allied with Jews.

After representing the East Harlem district in Congress through most of the twenties, La Guardia lost to a Tammany candidate, James J. Lanzetta, in 1932, when he was at the height of his national prominence. This surprise has been analyzed by La Guardia's biographer, Arthur Mann:

Jimmy Lanzetta, born and raised in East Harlem and educated as an engineer and a lawyer at Columbia University, was thirty-eight, a Catholic, and the uptown hope of Tammany Hall. Witty and affable, good looking and hard-working, he had no public philosophy and entered politics by making himself known to the district family by family and by pleasing the local leaders.

. . . .

. . . Lanzetta challenged La Guardia's popularity among the Italo-Americans. Their fathers held the Mayor in awe, named their children after him, and tipped their hats in deference to him. He was still their village *Signore*. But in a decade the sons and daughters of the immigrants came of voting age and "these youthful iconoclasts do not hold the great La Guardia in the same veneration as do their elders."

The Italo-Americans were only part of La Guardia's district; he also lost votes among the Puerto Ricans. He held only the Jewish vote.[43]

La Guardia's loss to Lanzetta in 1932 presaged the development of Italian political opinion. When La Guardia defeated O'Dwyer in 1941, he did worse in the Italian districts than in the city as a whole. O'Dwyer got 57 per cent of the vote in the Italian districts and 50 per cent of the votes in the city. In 1945, when Newbold Morris ran against O'Dwyer and Jonah Goldstein with La Guardia's support, he did worse in the Italian areas than anywhere in the city. He got 11 per cent of the vote there as against 18 per cent in the city as a whole.[44]

The rejection of La Guardia symbolized the fact that there had never developed among the Italian-American proletarian group a generalized ideology in support of liberalism and progressivism. Roosevelt got the Italian votes in his early elections, as he got votes from all low-income groups. However, when he spoke out against Mussolini's attack on France in 1940—"the hand that held the dagger has plunged it into the back of its neighbor"—the Italian Americans became probably the most anti-Roosevelt of all low-income groups. In 1944 he got only 41 per cent of the vote in Italian districts of the city, while getting 61 per cent in the city as a whole.[45] Because there had never developed a strong socialist, liberal, or labor tradition and ideology, because the leaders of the community were generally conservative businessmen, because the community press expressed their opinion, it was relatively easy for the pro-Roosevelt feeling in the community to be overcome. The vacuum of ideology of the socialist and liberal type was filled in part with a vague sort of national feeling. Except for a handful of radicals and socialists, almost everyone in the Italian community supported Mussolini, or at least did not oppose him.[46] The vacuum was also in part filled by the ideological outlook of small homeowners, which many Italian Americans were or aspired to be; this involved opposition to high taxes, welfare programs, and the like. The comptroller of the city in Wagner's first two administrations, Lawrence Gerosa, exemplified this point of view perfectly. He was against "frills" in the building of schools (art, murals), in favor of a conservative financial policy, and without any views on the general problems of the city. Such views are hardly necessary when one's major concern is the neighborhood and its homeowners.

One aspect of this conservatism can unquestionably be traced to insecurity. The Italian American is still uncertain about his acceptance, concerned about his image, and consequently many—in a style similar to that of other second generations—become more American than the

Americans, more nationalist than the Mayflower descendants. This, combined with the need, in the war and early postwar years, to dissociate oneself from any suspicion of support of an enemy nation, makes it all the easier for the Italian American to adopt the political outlook of the conservative nationalist, the present-day descendant of the old-time isolationist.

Holding this point of view (which is not very different from that held by the small-town dwellers of the Midwest), it is understandable that Italian Americans should find the Republican party, and the conservative wing of the Democratic party, ever more congenial.[47] This is occurring at a time when New York Italians are producing a number of singularly able political leaders. Both responding to and reflecting their political base, these leaders have not been notably articulate or adventurous in their views of the great issues of state, and this has generally cost them the good opinion of the liberals, but as with conservatives elsewhere, they have shown a keen understanding of the ways and uses of power. Carmine DeSapio was far and away the most competent politician the New York Democrats produced in the postwar era. Significantly, the middle-class reformers, while able to destroy him, were quite incapable of replacing him. The immediate result was not a transfer of power but a vacuum.

Mayor Wagner's running mate in the 1961 primary and election campaigns was Paul R. Screvane, who thereafter emerged as a distinct political power in the city. Reared in the Bronx, Screvane began life as a truck driver in the City Sanitation Department, rose from private to lieutenant colonel during World War II, became Sanitation Commissioner at the age of 42, was appointed Deputy Mayor at 46, and the same year was elected president of the City Council. As with many Italian leaders, Screvane combines a high level of vitality and administrative ability with a plain manner and a sure sense of public opinion. One may see develop in New York City, and in the state, the situation we see in Massachusetts and Rhode Island, where competent Italian political leaders have come near to establishing a political hegemony.

In moving from the age of La Guardia and Poletti to the age of Impellitteri and Gerosa, the Italian Americans have moved from the working class to (in increasing measure) the middle class, from the city to the suburbs, and from secularism to Catholicism. Young Italian intellectuals do not find this a very congenial atmosphere. But there are as yet not enough of them to develop any steady criticism of the style of Italian-American life; and the few who might do this have neither the organs nor the audience that would make such an enterprise worthwhile. If they are novelists, they celebrate the rich content of the old proletarian, city life. They know this is disappearing, and is being replaced by a new middle-class style, which is American Catholic more than it is anything that may be called American Italian. But it is still too new to have found anyone to record it, to criticize it, and perhaps transcend it.

the Irish

Nᴇᴡ ʏᴏʀᴋ used to be an Irish
city. Or so it seemed. There were sixty or seventy years
when the Irish were everywhere. *They* felt it was their town.
It is no longer, and they know it. That is one of the things
bothering them.

The Irish era began in the early 1870's,
about the time Charles O'Conor, "the ablest member of
the New York bar," [1] began the prosecution of Honorable
William March Tweed. It ended in the 1930's. A symbolic
point might be the day ex-Mayor James J. Walker sailed for
Europe and exile with his beloved, but unwed, Betty.

Boss Tweed was the last vulgar white Prot-
estant to win a prominent place in the city's life. The Protestants who have since entered public life have represented
the "better element." Tweed was a roughneck, a ward
heeler, a man of the people at a time when the people still
contained a large body of native-born Protestant workers
of Scotch and English antecedents. By the time of his death

217

in the Ludlow Street jail this had all but completely changed. The New York working class had become predominantly Catholic, as it has since remained. The Irish promptly assumed the leadership of this working class. "Honest John" Kelly succeeded Tweed as leader of Tammany Hall, formalizing a process that had been steadily advancing. In 1868 the New York diarist George Templeton Strong had recorded, "Our rulers are partly American scoundrels and partly Celtic scoundrels. The Celts are predominant, however, and we submit to the rod and the sceptre of Maguires and O'Tooles and O'Shanes. . . ." [2] But the American scoundrels disappeared, and soon Strong was writing only of the city's "blackguard Celtic tyrants." [3] A note of helplessness appears: "we are to Papistical Paddy as Cedric the Saxon to Front de Boeuf." [4]

In 1880 Tammany Hall elected the city's first Irish Catholic mayor, William R. Grace of the shipping line. This ascendancy persisted for another half century, reaching an apogee toward the end of the twenties when Al Smith ran for President and Jimmy Walker "wore New York in his buttonhole."

The crash came suddenly. In June 1932 Smith was denied the Democratic renomination. The Tammany delegates left Chicago bitter and unreconciled. Two months later Mayor Walker resigned in the face of mounting scandal, and decided to leave the country with his English mistress. A few days before his departure, Franklin Roosevelt had been elected President. The next man to be elected Mayor of New York City would be Fiorello H. La Guardia. Next, a Jewish world heavyweight champion. DiMaggio became the new name in baseball; Sinatra the new crooner. So it went. The almost formal end came within a decade. In 1943 Tammany Hall itself, built while Walker was Mayor at the cost of just under one million dollars, was sold to Local 91 of the International Ladies' Garment Workers' Union. Tammany and the New York County Democratic Committee went their separate ways. The oldest political organization on earth was finished. So was the Irish era.

This is not to say the Irish have disappeared. They are still a powerful group. St. Patrick's Day is still the largest public observance of the city's year. On March 17 a green line is painted up Fifth Avenue and a half-million people turn out to watch the parade. (In Albany the Legislative Calendar is printed in green ink.) The Irish have a position in the city now as they had before the 1870's, but now, as then, it is a lopsided position. "Slippery Dick" Connoly and "Brains" Sweeney shared power and office with Tweed, as did any number of their followers. But, with few exceptions, they represented the *canaille*. With the coming of the Gilded Age, middle-class and even upper-class Irish appeared. For a period they ranged across the social spectrum, and in this way seemed to dominate much of the city's life. The Tweed ring was heavily Irish, but so was the group that brought on its downfall. This pattern persisted. The Irish came to run the police force *and* the underworld; they were the reformers and the hoodlums; employers and employed. The city entered the era of Boss Croker of Tammany Hall and Judge Goff of the Lexow Committee which investigated him; of business leader Thomas Fortune Ryan and labor leader Peter J. McGuire; of Reform Mayor John Purroy Mitchel and Tammany Mayor John F. "Red Mike" Hylan. It was a stimulating miscellany.

All this is past. The mass of the Irish have left the working class, and in considerable measure the Democratic party as well. But the pattern of egalitarian politics which they established on the whole persists, so that increasingly the Irish are left out. Their reaction to this is one of the principal elements of the Irish impact on the city today.

THE GREEN WAVE

THE BASIS OF IRISH HEGEMONY IN THE CITY WAS ESTABLISHED by the famine emigration of 1846–1850. By mid-century there were 133,730 Irish-born inhabitants of the city, 26 per cent of the total population. By 1855, 34 per cent of the city voters were Irish.[5] By 1890, when 80 per cent of the population of New York City was of foreign parentage, a third of these (409,924 persons of 1,215,463) were Irish, making more than a quarter of the total population.[6] With older stock included, over one-third of the population of

New York and Brooklyn at the outset of the Gay Nineties was Irish-American.

The older stock went far back in the city's history. Ireland provided a continuing portion of the emigration to North America during the seventeenth and eighteenth centuries. Much of it was made up of Protestants with English or Scottish antecedents, but there were always some Celtic Irish of Protestant or Catholic persuasion. The city received its first charter from Governor Thomas Dongan, afterwards Earl of Limerick. In 1683 Dongan summoned the first representative assembly in the history of the colony, at which he sponsored the Charter of Liberties and Privileges granting broad religious freedom, guaranteeing trial by jury, and establishing representative government. He was nonetheless suspected of plotting a Catholic establishment, and with the Glorious Revolution of 1688 the Catholics of New York were disfranchised.

This was a basic event. The Catholic Irish were kept out of the political life of the city for almost a century. It began a long tradition of denying rights to Irish Catholics on grounds that they wished to do the same to English Protestants. To this day the most fair-minded New York Protestants will caution that Irish Catholics have never experienced the great Anglo-Saxon tradition of the separation of church and state, although indeed they have known nothing but.

At the first New York Constitutional Convention in 1777, John Jay even proposed that Roman Catholics be deprived of their civil rights and the right to hold land until taking an oath that no Pope or priest could absolve them from sin or from allegiance to the state.[7] This proposal was rejected, but Jay did succeed in including a religious test for naturalization in the constitution which remained in force until superseded by a federal naturalization statute in 1790.[8] It was not until 1806 that a similar oath required for officeholders was repealed, permitting the first Irish Catholic to take his seat in the Assembly.

After the Revolution Irish emigration began in earnest. Writing in 1835, de Tocqueville reported: "About fifty years ago Ireland began to pour a Catholic population into the United States. . . ." He estimated that with conversions the number of Catholics had reached a million (which was three times the actual amount.)[9]

In 1798 another of the native Irish revolts took place, and failed. In its aftermath came the first of a long trail of Irish revolutionaries, Catholic and Protestant, who disturbed the peace of the city for a century and a quarter. These were educated professional men who had risked their lives for much the same cause that had inspired the Sons of Liberty in New York a generation earlier. In general they were received as such. A few such as Dr. William J. MacNeven and Thomas Addis Emmet, became prominent New Yorkers. Emmet served in 1812 as the state's Attorney-General. Mr. Justice Story described him as "the favorite counsellor of New York." [10]

In the early nineteenth century a sizable Irish-Catholic community gathered in New York. By the time of the great migration it was well enough established. Charles O'Conor, John Kelly, and W. R. Grace were all native New Yorkers. For some time prior to the potato famine the basic patterns of Irish life in New York had been set. The hordes that arrived at mid-century strengthened some of these patterns more than others, but they did not change them nearly so much as they were changed by them. They got off the boat to find their identity waiting for them: they were to be Irish-Catholic Democrats.

There were times when this identity took on the mysteries of the Trinity itself; the three were one and the one three. Identity with the Democratic party came last in point of time, but it could have been received from the hands of Finn MacCool for the way the Irish clung to it.

THE DEMOCRATIC PARTY

TAMMANY WAS ORGANIZED IN NEW YORK A FEW WEEKS AFTER Washington was inaugurated at Federal Hall on April 30, 1789. The principal founder was one William Mooney, an upholsterer and apparently by birth an Irish Catholic. Originally a national organization, from the first its *motif* was egalitarian and nationalist: the Sons of St. Tammany, the American Indian chief, as against the foreign ties of the societies of St. George and St. David (as well, apparently, of the Sons of St. Patrick), or the aristocratic airs of the

Sons of the Cincinnati. Its members promptly involved themselves in politics, establishing the New York Democratic party. (Until recently Tammany officially retained the Jeffersonian designation "Democratic-Republican" party. Far into the twentieth century the Phrygian cap of the French Revolution was an important prop in Tammany ceremonies; it will be seen atop the staff of Liberty in the New York State seal, contrasting with the crown at her feet.) The original issues on which the New York political parties organized concerned the events of the French Revolution. Jefferson and his Democratic followers were instinctively sympathetic to France. Hamilton, Jay, and the Federalists looked just as fervently to England. This automatically aligned the Irish with the Democrats: the French Revolution had inspired the Irish revolt of 1798, and the French had sent three expeditions to aid it. The Federalists reacted with the Alien and Sedition Acts of 1798, designed in part to prevent the absorption of immigrants into the Jeffersonian party, but which only strengthened their attachment to it. In 1812 the Federalists bitterly, but unsuccessfully, opposed the establishment of more-or-less universal white suffrage, certain it would swell the immigrant Irish vote of New York City.[11]

So it did, and in no time the Irish developed a powerful voting bloc. In the 1827 city elections, a prelude to the contest between John Quincy Adams and Andrew Jackson, the Irish sided mightily with Jackson, himself the son of poor Irish immigrants, and thereupon entered wholeheartedly into the politics of the Jacksonian era. By 1832 the Whig candidate for President found himself assuring a St. Patrick's Day dinner that "Some of my nearest and dearest friends (are) Irishmen." [12]

The contest for the "Irish vote" became an aspect of almost every New York election that followed. A week before the election of 1884 a delegation of Protestant clergymen waited on the Republican candidate James G. Blaine, at the Fifth Avenue Hotel, to assure him, in the words of Reverend Samuel D. Burchard, ". . . We are Republicans and don't propose to leave our party, and identify ourselves with the party whose antecedents have been rum, Romanism, and rebellion." [13] Blaine, who had been making headway with the Irish, lost New York by 1,077 votes, and thereby the election, which ended the Republican rule of post-Civil War America.

By this time the New York City Irish were not only voting for the Democratic party but thoroughly controlled its organization. Apart from building their church, this was the one singular achievement of the nineteenth-century Irish. "The Irish role in politics was creative, not imitative." [14]

New York became the first great city in history to be ruled by men of the people, not as an isolated phenomenon of the Gracchi or the Commune, but as a persisting, established pattern. Almost to this day the men who have run New York City have talked out of the side of their mouths. The intermittent discovery that New York did have representative government led to periodic reform movements. But the reformers came and went; the party remained. The secret lay in the structure of the party bureaucracy which ever replenished and perpetuated itself. It is only in the past decade, when the middle class at length discovered the secret and began themselves to move into the party bureaucracy that the character of the New York City government has begun to change. Even here, the party complexion persists: of the twenty-six members of the City Council, twenty-four were Democrats in 1963.

In politics, as in religion, the Irish brought many traits from the Old Country. The machine governments that they established in New York (as in many Northern cities) show a number of features characteristic of nineteenth-century Ireland. The exact nature of the relationship is not clear: much that follows is speculative. But the coincidence is clear enough to warrant the proposition that the machine governments resulted from a merger of rural Irish custom with urban American politics. "Politics," in Charles Frankel's words, "is a substitute for custom; it becomes conspicuous wherever custom recedes or breaks down." [15] But in nineteenth-century New York events did not permit one system gradually to recede as the other slowly emerged. The ancient world of folkways and the modern world of contracts came suddenly together. The collision is nicely evoked by the story of Congressman

Timothy J. Campbell of New York, a native of Cavan, calling on President Grover Cleveland with a request the President refused on the ground that it was unconstitutional. "Ah, Mr. President," replied Tim, "what is the Constitution between friends?" [16]

There were four features of the machine government which are particularly noticeable in this context.

First, there was an indifference to Yankee proprieties. To the Irish, stealing an election was rascally, not to be approved, but neither quite to be abhorred. It may be they picked up some of this from the English. Eighteenth-century politics in Ireland were—in Yankee terms—thoroughly corrupt. George Potter has written,

The great and the wealthy ran Ireland politically like Tammany Hall in its worst days. Had they not sold their own country for money and titles in the Act of Union with England and, as one rogue said, thanked God they had a country to sell? . . . A gentleman was thought no less a gentleman because he dealt, like merchandise, with the votes of his tenants or purchased his parliamentary seat as he would a horse or a new wing for his big house.[17]

But the Irish added to the practice, from their own social structure, a personal concept of government action. Describing the early period of Irish self-government, Conrad M. Arensberg relates that

. . . At first, geese and country produce besieged the new officers and magistrates; a favourable decision or a necessary public work performed was interpreted as a favour given. It demanded a direct and personal return. "Influence" to the countryman was and is a direct personal relationship, like the friendship of the countryside along which his own life moves.[18]

Second, the Irish brought to America a settled tradition of regarding the formal government as illegitimate, and the informal one as bearing the true impress of popular sovereignty. The Penal Laws of eighteenth-century Ireland totally proscribed the Catholic religion, and reduced the Catholic Irish to a condition of *de facto* slavery.

Cecil Woodham-Smith holds with Burke that the lawless-
ness, dissimulation and revenge which followed left the
Irish character, above all the character of the peasantry,
"degraded and debased."

His religion made him an outlaw; in the Irish House of
Commons he was described as "the common enemy," and
whatever was inflicted on him he must bear, for where could
he look for redress? To his landlord? Almost invariably an
alien conqueror. To the law? Not when every person connected with the law, from the jailer to the judge, was a
Protestant. . . .
      In these conditions suspicion of the law, of
the ministers of the law and of all established authority
"worked into the very nerves and blood of the Irish peasant," and since the law did not give him justice he set up
his own law. The secret societies which have been the curse
of Ireland became widespread during the Penal period . . .
dissimulation became a moral necessity and evasion of the
law the duty of every God-fearing Catholic.[19]

This habit of mind pervaded Tammany at its height. City
Hall as such was no more to be trusted than Dublin Castle.
Alone one could fight neither. If in trouble it was best to see
The McManus. If the McMani were in power in City Hall
as well as in the Tuscarora Regular Democratic Organization of the Second Assembly District Middle—so much the
better.
      Third, most of the Irish arrived in America
fresh from the momentous experience of the Catholic
Emancipation movement. The Catholic Association that the
Irish leader Daniel O'Connell established in 1823 for the
purpose of achieving emancipation is the "first fully-fledged
democratic political party known to the world." Daniel
O'Connell, Potter writes, "was the first modern man to use
the mass of a people as a democratic instrument for revolutionary changes by peaceful constitutional methods. He
anticipated the coming into power of the people as the decisive political element in modern democratic society."[20]
The Irish peasants, who had taken little part in Gaelic Ireland's resistance to the English (that had been a matter for
the warrior class of an aristocratic society) arrived in America with some feeling at least for the possibilities of politics,

and they brought with them, as a fourth quality, a phenomenally effective capacity for political bureaucracy.

Politics is a risky business. Hence it has ever been the affair of speculators with the nerve to gamble and an impulse to boldness. These are anything but peasant qualities. Certainly they are not qualities of Irish peasants who, collectively, yielded to none in the rigidity of their social structure and their disinclination to adventure. Instead of letting politics transform them, the Irish transformed politics, establishing a political system in New York City that, from a distance, seems like the social system of an Irish village writ large.

The Irish village was a place of stable, predictable social relations in which almost everyone had a role to play, under the surveillance of a stern oligarchy of elders, and in which, on the whole, a person's position was likely to improve with time. Transferred to Manhattan, these were the essentials of Tammany Hall.

By 1817 the Irish were playing a significant role in Tammany.[21] Working from the original ward committees, they slowly established a vast hierarchy of party positions descending from the county leader at the top down to the block captain and beyond, even to building captains. Each position had rights and responsibilities that had to be observed. The result was a massive party bureaucracy. The county committees of the five boroughs came to number more than 32,000 persons. It became necessary to hire Madison Square Garden for their meetings, and to hope that not more than half would come. The system in its prime was remarkably stable. Kelly, Richard Croker, and Frank Murphy in succession ran Tammany for half a century. Across the river Hugh McLaughlin ran the Brooklyn Democratic party and fought off Tammany for better than forty years, from 1862 to 1903. He was followed shortly by John H. McCooey, who ruled from 1909 until his death a quarter century later in 1934. Ed Flynn ran the Bronx from 1922 until his death in 1953.

The stereotype of the Irish politician as a beer-guzzling back-slapper is nonsense. Croker, McLaughlin, and *Mister* Murphy were the least affable of men. Their task was not to charm but to administer with firmness and predictability a political bureaucracy in which the prerogatives of rank were carefully observed. The hierarchy had to be maintained. For the group as a whole this served to take the risks out of politics. Each would get his deserts—in time.

In the intraparty struggles of the 1950's and 1960's no one characteristic divides the "regular" Democratic party men in New York City from the "reform" group more than the matter of taking pride in following the chain of command. The "reform" group was composed overwhelmingly of educated, middle-class career people hardened to the struggle for advancement in their professions. Waiting in line to see one's leader seemed to such persons slavish and undignified, the kind of conduct that could be imposed only by a Boss. By contrast, the "organization" regulars regarded such conduct as proper and well-behaved. The reformers, who tend to feel superior, would have been surprised, perhaps, to learn that among the regulars they were widely regarded as rude, unethical people. As Arensberg said of the Irish village, so of the political machine, "Public honour and self-satisfaction reward conformity." [22]

It would also seem that the term "Boss" and the persistent attacks on "Boss rule" have misrepresented the nature of power in the old machine system. Power was hierarchical in the party, diffused in the way it is diffused in an army. Because the commanding general was powerful, it did not follow that the division generals were powerless. Tammany district leaders were important men, and, right down to the block captain, all had rights.

The principle of Boss rule was not tyranny, but order. When Lincoln Steffens asked Croker, "Why must there be a boss, when we've got a mayor and—a council and —" "That's why," Croker broke in. "It's because there's a mayor *and* a council *and* judges—*and* a hundred other men to deal with." [23]

At the risk of exaggerating, it is possible to point to any number of further parallels between the political machine and rural Irish society. The incredible capacity of the rural Irish to remain celibate, awaiting their turn to inherit the farm, was matched by generations of assistant corporation counsels awaiting that opening on the City Court bench. Arensberg has described the great respect for rank in the Irish peasantry. Even after an Irish son had taken over direction of the farm, he would go each morning to his father to ask what to do that day. So was respect shown to the "Boss," whose essential demand often seemed only that he be consulted. The story goes that one day a fellow leader of Thomas J. Dunn, a Tammany Sachem, confided that he was about to be married. "Have you seen Croker?" Dunn asked. In 1913, when Governor William Sulzer refused to consult the organization on appointments, Murphy forthwith impeached and removed him. Rival leaders fought bitterly in the courts for the privilege of describing their club as the *"Regular"* Democratic Organization.

The narrow boundaries of the peasant world were ideally adaptable to precinct politics. "Irish familism is of the soil," wrote Arensberg. "It operates most strongly within allegiances to a definite small area." [24] Only men from such a background could make an Assembly district their life's work.

The parallel role of the saloonkeeper is striking. Arensberg writes of the saloonkeeper in Ireland:

. . . the shopkeeper-publican-politician was a very effective instrument, both for the countryside which used him and for himself. He might perhaps exact buying at his shop in return for the performance of his elective duties, as his enemies charge: but he also saw to it that those duties were performed for the very people who wished to see them done. Through him, as through no other possible channel, Ireland reached political maturity and effective national strength.[25]

Among the New York Irish, "the saloons were the nodal points of district organization. . . ." [26] It used to be said the only way to break up a meeting of the Tammany Executive Committee was to open the door and yell "Your saloon's on fire!" At the same time a mark of the successful leaders was sobriety. George Washington Plunkitt, a Tammany district leader, related with glee the events of election night 1897 when Tammany had just elected—against considerable odds—the first mayor of the consolidated City of New York.

Up to 10 P.M. Croker, John F. Carroll, Tim Sullivan, Charlie Murphy, and myself sat in the committee-room receivin returns. When nearly all the city was heard from and we saw that Van Wyck was elected by a big majority, I invited the crowd to go across the street for a little celebration. A lot of small politicians followed us, expectin' to see magnums of champagne opened. The waiters in the restaurant expected it, too, and you never saw a more disgusted lot of waiters when they got our orders. Here's the orders: Croker, vichy and bicarbonate of soda; Carroll, seltzer lemonade; Sullivan, apollinaris; Murphy, vichy; Plunkitt, ditto. Before midnight we were all in bed, and next mornin' we were up bright and early attendin' to business while other men were nursin' swelled heads. Is there anything the matter with temperance as a pure business proposition?[27]

As a business proposition it all worked very well. But that is about as far as it went. The Irish were immensely successful in politics. They ran the city. But the very parochialism and bureaucracy that enabled them to succeed in politics prevented them from doing much with government. In all those sixty or seventy years in which they could have done almost anything they wanted in politics, they did very little. Of all those candidates and all those campaigns, what remains? The names of two or three men: Al Smith principally (who was a quarter English, apparently a quarter German and possibly a quarter Italian), and his career went sour before it ever quite came to glory.

In a sense, the Irish did not know what to do with power once they got it. Steffens was surely exaggerating when he suggested the political bosses kept power only on the sufferance of the business community. The two groups worked in harmony, but it was a symbiotic, not an agency relationship. The Irish leaders did for the Protestant establishment what it could not do for itself, and could not do without. Croker "understood completely the worthlessness of the superior American in politics." [28] But the Irish just didn't know what to do with their opportunity. They never thought of politics as an instrument of social change —their kind of politics involved the processes of a society that was not changing. Croker alone solved the problem. Having become rich he did the thing rich people in Ireland did: he bought himself a manor house in England, bred horses, and won the Derby. The King did not ask him to the Derby Day dinner.

THE ROMAN CATHOLIC CHURCH

THE STORY GOES THAT IN THE LAST DAYS OF ONE OF HIS CAM-
paigns Al Smith was on a speaking tour of the northern
counties of the state. Sunday morning he and all but one of
his aides got up and trekked off to Mass, returning to find
the remaining member of the party, Herbert Bayard Swope,
resplendent in his de Pinna bathrobe and slippers, having
a second cup of coffee, reading the Sunday papers. As the
Catholics stamped the snow off their feet and climbed out
of their overcoats, Smith looked at Swope and said, "You
know, boys, it would be a hell of a thing if it turned out
Swope was right and we were wrong."

That sums it up. The Irish of New York,
as elsewhere, have made a tremendous sacrifice for their
church. They have built it from a despised and proscripted
sect of the eighteenth century to the largest religious organization of the nation, numbering some 43,851,000 members in 1963. This is incomparably the most important thing
they have done in America. But they have done it at a price.

In secular terms, it has cost them dearly in
men and money. A good part of the surplus that might have
gone into family property has gone to building the church.
This has almost certainly inhibited the development of the
solid middle-class dynasties that produce so many of the
important people in America. (Thomas F. O'Dea speculates
that the relative absence of a Catholic *rentier* class has much
inhibited the development of Catholic intellectuals.)[29] The
celibacy of the Catholic clergy has also deprived the Irish of
the class of ministers' sons which has contributed notably to
the prosperity and distinction of the Protestant world.
These disadvantages have been combined with a pervasive
prejudice against Catholics on the part of Protestants that
has not entirely disappeared.

The Catholic Church does not measure its
success by the standards of secular society. Many of its finest
men and women disappear from the great world altogether.
This is well understood and accepted by Catholics. What
troubles a growing number of persons within the Church is
the performance of the great bulk of Catholics who remain
very much a part of the world in which they live. For a

Church notably committed to the processes of intellect, the performance of Catholic scholars and writers is particularly galling. In the words of Professor O'Dea, formerly of Fordham:

> The American Catholic group has failed to produce . . . both qualitatively and quantitatively an appropriate intellectual life. It has failed to evolve in this country a vital intellectual tradition displaying vigor and creativity in proportion to the numerical strength of American Catholics. It has also failed to produce intellectual and other national leaders in numbers appropriate to its size and resources.[30]

It is notorious that Catholics have produced hardly a handful of important scientists. But this seems to be true of Catholics everywhere. The failure of the American Catholics seems deeper than that. Neither have they produced a great poet, a great painter, a great diplomatist. None of the arts, none of the achievements that most characterize the older Catholic societies seem to prosper here. "Is the honorable adjective 'Roman Catholic' truly merited by America's middle-class-Jansenist Catholicism, puritanized, Calvinized, and dehydrated . . . ?"[31] asked the Protestant Peter Viereck. What he perhaps really wanted to know is whether Irish Catholics are Roman Catholics.

It is impossible to pull the terms apart in the reality of American life. Thus *Time* magazine was apparently not conscious of having said anything odd when it referred, in 1960, to "The City's Irish-Catholic population, 1,000,000 strong and predominantly Roman Catholic. . . ." Since the early nineteenth century the American Catholic Church has been dominated by the Irish. This is nowhere more true than in New York, the preeminent Catholic city of the nation.

Obviously, the Irish Church in America was established in the nineteenth century in the sense that parishes were organized and the churches built at that time. But it is also apparent that certain essential qualities of the religion itself derive from the world that followed the French Revolution. The English in the seventeenth and eighteenth centuries practically destroyed the Irish Church. The *faith* remained, but the institution practically disappeared; Catholics had almost no churches, few clergy, hardly any organization. Mass was said in the mountains by priests who were practically fugitives. The Irish Church did not even have a seminary in Ireland until Pitt established May-nooth in 1794—to obviate the training of Irish priests in revolutionary France.

The Church that grew from this beginning was something different from the historical Roman Catholic Church, not in theology, although there was a distinct Jan-senist flavor, but in culture. It was a church with a decided aversion to the modern liberal state. This aversion began with the French Revolution (the Irish hierarchy had been trained in France and gave refuge to any number of émigré French clerics) and was confirmed by the events of Italian unification. It was a church that was decidedly separatist in its attitude toward the non-Catholic community, which for long, in America as in Ireland, was the ascendant commu-nity. It was a church with almost no intellectual tradition. Ireland was almost the only Christian nation of the middle ages that never founded a university. With all this, as Kevin Sullivan writes, "Irish Catholicism, in order to hold its own in a land dominated by an English Protestant culture, had developed many of the characteristics of English sectarian-ism: defensive, insular, parochial, puritanical. . . ." [32]

It emphatically did not, however, acquire the English fondness for royalty. In a passage which Father C. J. McNaspy has said "speaks volumes," de Tocqueville noted that Father Power, the pastor at the time of St. Peter's, the first Catholic Church in New York, "appears to have no prejudice against republican institutions." [33] This was surely because the Irish had no great fear of republican institutions, which far from disestablishing their church had had the effect of raising it to equality with Protestant churches. Moreover, republicanism had raised Irishmen to a kind of equality with Protestants: one man, one vote.

Beginning with Bishop John Hughes, who came to the city in 1838, the New York Catholic Church became anything but passive in asserting this equality. In 1844, when the good folk of Philadelphia took to burning Catholic Churches, Hughes issued a statement that "if a single Catholic church were burned in New York, the city would become a second Moscow." [34] None was burned.

Accepting republicanism did not entail accepting liberalism. From the first the Irish Catholic clergy of New York have been conservative. The Revolutions of 1848, which involved European liberals in a direct physical attack on the Papacy, produced a powerful effect on the American hierarchy. Bishop John Hughes of New York put his flock on guard against the " 'Red Republicans' of Europe," as he called them. At this point the Church began to find itself in conflict not only with primitive, no-Popery Protestants who burned convents, but also with liberal, educated, post-Calvinist Protestant leadership. An early episode involved the Hungarian revolutionary Kossuth. As Hughes reported to Rome in 1858, "The enthusiasm and admiration in which Kossuth was held by the American people were almost boundless." Dreading the influence such liberalism might have on Catholics, Hughes denounced Kossuth prior to his appearance in New York City, with the result, the Bishop felt, that the visit was a failure.[35]

The divergence between liberal Protestant and Catholic views in New York grew when Catholics generally declined to support the movement for the abolition of Negro slavery. In July, 1863, the New York Irish rioted against the newly enacted draft. For four bloody, smoke-filled days the mobs ranged the city. They attacked Negroes everywhere, lynched some, and burned a Negro orphanage. Strong's diary records absolute revulsion:

The fury of the low Irish woman . . . was noteworthy. Stalwart young vixens and withered old hags were swarming everywhere, all cursing the "bloody draft" and egging on their men. . . . How is one to deal with women who assemble around the lamp post to which a Negro had been hanged and cut off certain parts of his body to keep as souvenirs? . . . For myself, personally, I would like to see war made on Irish scum as in 1688.[36]

In the post-Civil War period, when much Protestant energy turned to the issues of social reform, the Catholic Church continued to remain apart and, in the view of many, opposed. The New York diocese was notably alert to the perils of socialism. One widely popular priest, Father Edward McGlynn, was temporarily excommunicated in a controversy that followed his support of Henry George who

ran for mayor in 1897. (George had made headway by linking his single tax proposal to the problems of Irish land
reform.) Bishop Corrigan even tried to get *Progress and
Poverty* placed on the Index of Prohibited Books, although
without success other than to have George's theories declared "false." [37]

These developments strengthened the sep-
aratist tendencies in the Church, although again, the basic
decisions had been made prior to the great migration. Foremost of these was the decision to establish a separate school
system.

In New York City, as elsewhere, education
was largely a church function in the early days of the republic. In 1805 a Free School Society was formed, "for the education of such poor children as do not belong to, or are not
provided for, by any religious society." [38] Its first address to
the public proclaimed that ". . . it will be a primary object,
without observing the peculiar forms of any religious society,
to inculcate the sublime truths of religion and morality
contained in the Holy Scriptures." [39] That year the state
legislature established a fund for the support of common
schools which was distributed in New York City to the
trustees of the Free School Society and "of such incorporated
religious societies in said city as now support, or hereafter
shall establish charity schools. . . ." [40] Under this system
Catholic schools, along with Baptist, Methodist, Episcopal,
Reformed Dutch, German Lutheran, and Scotch Presbyterian ones, among others, received state aid.

In 1823 it developed that the Baptist schools
were padding their enrollment books and requiring teachers to turn over part of their salaries. In the upshot, the
distribution of state aid was turned over to the City Common Council, which thereafter channeled most of the public
funds to the Free School Society, renamed the Public School
Society. By 1839 the Society operated eighty-six schools, with
an average total attendance of 11,789.[41]

As the Society was strongly Protestant, most
Protestants could accept this development, but Catholics did
not. They persisted with their own schools. By 1839 there
were seven Roman Catholic Free Schools in the city "open
to all children, without discrimination," with more than

5,000 pupils attending.[42] (Thus parochial school attendance equaled almost half the average attendance of the "public" schools, a proportion not far different from that of today.) Nonetheless, almost half the children of the city attended no school of any kind, at a time when some 94 per cent of children of school age in the rest of the state attended common schools established by school districts under direction of elected officers.

This situation prompted the Whig Governor William H. Seward to make this proposal to the legislature in his message for 1840:

The children of foreigners, found in great numbers in our populous cities and towns, and in the vicinity of our public works, are too often deprived of the advantages of our system of public education, in consequence of prejudices arising from difference of language or religion. It ought never to be forgotten that the public welfare is as deeply concerned in their education as in that of our own children. I do not hesitate, therefore, to recommend the establishment of schools in which they may be instructed by teachers speaking the same language with themselves and professing the same faith.[43]

Instead of waiting for the rural, upstate legislature to ponder and act upon this proposal of an upstate Whig governor, the Catholics in the city immediately began clamoring for a share of public education funds.[44] The Common Council declined on grounds that this would be unconstitutional. In October, 1840, the Bishop himself appeared before the Council, even offering to place the parochial schools under the supervision of the Public School Society in return for public aid. When he was turned down, tempers began to rise.

In April, 1841, Seward's Secretary of State John C. Spencer, *ex officio* superintendent of public schools, submitted a report on the issue to the State Senate. This was a state paper of the first quality, drafted by an authority on the laws of New York State (who was also de Tocqueville's American editor). Spencer began by assuming the essential justice of the Catholic request for aid to their schools:

It can scarcely be necessary to say that the founders of these schools, and those who wish to establish others, have absolute rights to the benefits of a common burthen; and that any system which deprives them of their just share in the application of a common and public fund, must be justified, if at all, by a necessity which demands the sacrifice of individual rights, for the accomplishment of a social benefit of paramount importance. It is presumed no such necessity can be urged in the present instance.[45]

To those who feared use of public funds for sectarian purposes, Spencer replied that all instruction is in some ways sectarian: "No books can be found, no reading lessons can be selected, which do not contain more or less of some principles of religious faith, either directly avowed, or indirectly assumed." The activities of the Public School Society were no exception to this rule: "Even the moderate degree of religious instruction which the Public School Society imparts, must therefore be sectarian; that is, it must favor one set of opinions in opposition to another, or others; and it is believed that this always will be the result, in any course of education that the wit of man can devise." As for avoiding sectarianism by abolishing religious instruction altogether, "On the contrary, it would be in itself sectarian; because it would be consonant to the views of a peculiar class, and opposed to the opinions of other classes."

Spencer proposed to take advantage of the diversity of opinion by a form of local option. He suggested that the direction of the New York City school system be turned over to a board of elected school commissioners which would establish and maintain general standards, while leaving religious matters to the trustees of the individual schools, the assumption being that those sectarians who so wished would proceed to establish their own schools.

A rivalry may, and probably will, be produced between them, to increase the number of pupils. As an essential means to such an object, there will be a constant effort to improve the schools, in the mode and degree of instruction, and in the qualification of the teachers. Thus, not only will the number of children brought into the schools be incalculably augmented, but the competition anticipated will produce its usual effect of providing the very best material to satisfy the public demand. These advantages will more than compensate for any possible evils that may be apprehended from having schools adapted to the feelings and views of the different denominations.[46]

The legislature put off immediate action on Spencer's report. But Catholics grew impatient. When neither party endorsed the proposal in the political campaign that fall, Bishop Hughes made the calamitous mistake —four days before the election—of entering a slate of his own candidates for the legislature. Protestants were horrified. James G. Bennett in the *New York Herald* declared the Bishop was trying "to organize the Irish Catholics of New York as a district party, that could be given to the Whigs or Locofocos at the wave of his crozier." The Carroll Hall candidates, as they were known, polled just enough votes to put an end to further discussion of using public funds to help Catholics become more active citizens.

At the next session of the legislature the Public School Society was, in effect, disestablished. Spencer's proposal for an elected Board of Education in New York City was adopted. Each city ward was to have elected commissioners, inspectors, and trustees to run the common schools in its area. But the Protestants, foreseeing the numerical supremacy of the Catholics, blocked Spencer's proposal for local option on religious instruction. "In a word, the Protestants disliked secularism, but they disliked the Pope more. . . ." [47] The 1842 law provided that "No school . . . in which any religious sectarian doctrine or tenet shall be taught, inculcated, or practised [*sic*], shall receive any portion of the school moneys to be distributed by this act. . . ." Thus the sectarian position that the Spencerian analysis would describe as "non-sectarian" won out. New York became the first of the original thirteen states to prohibit the teaching of religion in public schools. The New York Catholic Church thereupon set about establishing its own school system. In 1850 Hughes declared, "the time has almost come when it will be necessary to build the schoolhouse first, and the church afterward." [48]

Along with the great effort of building and operating parish facilities and charitable institutions, the Church proceeded to establish a vast private school system.

But it seems clear that the high intellectual tradition was slighted. In the New York dioceses today, for every fifteen students in Catholic schools, there is but one in a Catholic college.

Monsignor John Tracy Ellis has suggested that development of the parochial schools swamped an incipient Catholic intellectual movement which stemmed from the educated offspring of the Maryland gentry and was powerfully reinforced in the 1840's by the conversion of prominent Protestants, corresponding to the Oxford movement in England. A century later Richard Cardinal Cushing of Boston was to tell a CIO convention ". . . in all the American hierarchy, resident in the United States, there is not known to me one Bishop, Archbishop or Cardinal whose father or mother was a college graduate. Every one of our Bishops and Archbishops is the son of a working man and a working man's wife." [49]

It seems clear that the prestige of the Church declined as it became more Irish. In 1785 the dedication of St. Peter's, with hardly 200 parishioners, could command the presence of the Governor of New York and the President of the Continental Congress. Rome itself was not seen as the traditional threat to Anglo-Saxon liberties. But as the Irish question got in the way, some of this sympathy and esteem disappeared. The Irish were the one oppressed people on earth the American Protestants could never quite bring themselves wholeheartedly to sympathize with. They would consider including insurgent Greece within the protection of the Monroe Doctrine, they would send a warship to bring the rebel Kossuth safe to the shores of liberty, they would fight a war and kill half a million men to free the Negro slaves. But the Irish were different.

THE WILD IRISH

"THE IRISH," WROTE MACAULAY, ". . . WERE DISTINGUISHED by qualities which tend to make men interesting rather than prosperous. They were an ardent and impetuous race, easily moved to tears or laughter, to fury or to love." [50] His words evoke the stage Irishman, battered hat in hand, loquacious and sly, proclaiming "Faith, yer Honor, if I'd of known it was Hogan's goat . . ."

There was little in Gaelic culture, "exclusive, despotic, aristocratic," as Sean O'Faolain described it,[51] to evoke the stage Irishman, but by the nineteenth century Gaelic culture had all but disappeared. The peasant Irish character that remained did have within it contrasting impulses to conformity and to fantasy, to the most plodding routine and the wildest adventure. This was overlaid with a kind of fecklessness with which the Celts survived the savagery of the English in eighteenth-century Ireland. Thus there was some truth in the caricature. The peasants who poured into America brought with them little by way of an Irish culture but a definite enough Irish character. It is not surprising then that in America they learned to act as they were expected to act. Within weeks of landing they were marching in the Mulligan Guards. Within a generation the half-starved people who had produced Blind Raftery were eating meat twice a day and singing about the "Overhauls in Mrs. Murphy's Chowder."

Prior to the great immigration, the Irish community in New York was reasonably symmetrical. There was a base of laborers and artisans surmounted by levels of tradesmen, professional men, entrepreneurs, and even aristocrats. The top layers were a mixture of Celt and Saxon, Catholic and Protestant. The first president of the Friendly Sons of St. Patrick, organized in New York in 1784, was a Presbyterian. Speakers at today's session of the Friendly Sons can recount the mercantile triumphs of their first members. "As you undoubtedly know," a Fordham professor told a recent meeting, "most of the founders of your society were merchants, who formed the aristocracy of New York in olden days."

With each successive shipload of famine stricken peasants, the Irish community became more unbalanced. The "wild Irish," as Henry II had called them, in just the sense Americans would describe the wild Indians, poured into the city to drink and dance and fight in the streets. These were not merchant adventurers. They were Paddies for whom the city had shortly to provide paddy wagons. They felt neither relation to nor respect for the business leaders of their colony. Rather than waiting until they might be asked to join the Friendly Sons of St. Patrick, in perhaps two or three generations, they founded the Ancient Order of Hibernians. St. Patrick was a Briton, a peer of St. David, St. Andrew, and St. George. Hibernians were plain Irish Catholics.

The result was the Protestants ceased being Irish. For a while they became "Ulster Irish" and took to celebrating the Battle of the Boyne. (Orange Day riots in New York began in the 1830's. That of 1871 killed fifty-two persons and wounded hundreds.) But before long the Protestant Irish blended into the composite native American stock that had already claimed the Scots.

These developments robbed the New York Irish of middle-class leadership at the very moment they most needed it. Just when it was important for the enterprising among them to start going into the counting houses, the signs went up that "No Irish need apply."

The detachment of the Protestants from the Irish community was unquestionably hastened by the rise of nativism. In 1834 Samuel F. B. Morse published in the New York *Observer* a dozen letters which subsequently appeared as a book entitled *Foreign Conspiracy Against the Liberties of the United States.* He propounded the existence of a conspiracy between the Holy Alliance and the Papacy to gain control of the nation.

Morse ran for mayor of New York in 1841 on the Native American ticket, in the same election with Bishop Hughes' Catholic candidates. The Know-Nothing party, which emerged from this, almost won the 1854 state elections. It disappeared after 1856; most of its members went into the new Republican party—and helped confirm the allegiance of Irish Catholics to the Democrats.

Toward the end of the nineteenth century the cultural and religious separation of the Irish Catholics from Protestant New York was intensified when the groups split on just that issue that had originally established a bond of sympathy between them: British rule in Ireland.

In the days of the American Revolution, the Irish and the American causes seemed very much the same. At Valley Forge Washington ordered grog for the entire army on St. Patrick's Day. As much as 40 per cent of his men appear to have been of Irish or Scotch-Irish stock. In the century and a quarter that followed, America came repeatedly to the brink of war with England. While Anglo-American hostility prevailed, Irish nationalism and American patriotism were easily reconcilable. But as the nineteenth century passed, each successive crisis with England was somehow resolved, and, as new empires emerged in Europe and Asia, England and America drew closer together. Irish nationalists in America, who in 1776 had been looked upon by George Washington as stalwart patriots, were looked upon by Woodrow Wilson in 1916, when the last Irish revolution began, as traitors. Wilson, to be sure, was Ulster Presbyterian.

The cruel part of this history is that by 1916 Irish nationalism in America had little to do with Ireland. It was a hodgepodge of fine feeling and bad history with which the immigrants filled a cultural void. Organized campaigns for Irish freedom, centered in New York, began early in the nineteenth century and grew more rather than less intense. "Indeed," Thomas N. Brown writes, "it was the ruling passion for many of the second and third generation who knew only of America." [52]

. . . Irish nationalism was the cement, not the purpose of Irish American organization. Essentially they were pressure groups designed to defend and advance the American interests of the immigrant. Nationalism gave dignity to this effort, it offered a system of apologetics that explained their lowly state, and its emotional appeal was powerful enough to hold together the divergent sectional and class interests of the American Irish. This nationalism was not an alternative to American nationalism, but a variety of it. Its function was not to alienate the Irish immigrant but to accommodate him to an often hostile environment.[53]

For the Irish, nationalism gave a structure to working-class resentments that in other groups produced political radicalism. A group of Irish managed to combine both. Elizabeth Gurley Flynn, whom Theodore Dreiser described as "An East Side Joan of Arc," was part of an Irish socialist movement that was active in New York at the turn of the century. Her autobiography begins with a chapter "Paddy the Rebel," which captures some of the atmosphere of the Irish-American home in the 1890's.

The awareness of being Irish came to us as small children through plaintive song and heroic story. . . . We drew in a burning hatred of British rule with our mother's milk. Until my father died at over eighty, he never said *England* without adding, "God damn her!" Before I was ten I knew of the great heroes—Robert Emmet, Wolfe Tone, Michael Davitt, Parnell and O'Donovan Rossa, who was chained hand and foot, like a dog, and had to eat from a tin plate on the floor of a British prison.[54]

Flynn notes that her second-generation father felt much more strongly about Ireland than her mother, who was born there.

The nineteenth-century Irish discovered they were Celts, locked in ageless struggle with Saxons. The most bizarre notions evolved from this discovery: hardly credible, were it not a time when American cotton farmers were organizing tournaments and civilized Scotsmen were appearing in kilts. But somehow the contrast between Irish reality and pretense was more pitiful than ludicrous. The proceedings were, as George Templeton Strong declared, "full of gas and brag and bosh." [55] Referring to an exiled leader of the 1848 revolt, Thomas F. Meagher, Strong noted: " 'Meagher of the Sword' they call that commonplace decent attorney-at-law. 'Tis he will sheathe that battle axe in Saxon gore.' " [56]

The speeches were grand; the rallies grander. One hundred thousand persons attended a Fenian gathering in Jones' Wood in New York in 1866—against the wishes of the Archbishop! The Fenians hoped to free Ireland by capturing Canada. From their New York headquarters they raised an army, and prepared for the invasion, with the full regalia of a modern government-in-exile.

They pledged their lives and honor and beseeched the intercession of the Saints:

By the old rebel Pike
By the waving sunburst
By the immortal shamrock
By the sprig of fern　　　　　　We beseech thee to hear us,
By the bayonet charge　　　　　　O'Toole[57]
By the Irish hurrah

Nothing came of it. A thousand men or so marched into Canada. And marched right out again. In the one battle of the whole fiasco, eight Irishmen were killed. With what contempt did Strong record: "Their raid into Canada is a most ridiculous failure. . . . Had there been an Old John Brown among them they would have failed less ignominiously, at least. But there are no Celtic John Browns, and there never will be, I think." [58]

Strong was mistaken. The Celtic John Browns did appear. The foremost of them, Eamon de Valera, like Old John Brown himself, was born in New York.

The Irish issue all but dominated English politics in the last third of the nineteenth century. Then, as earlier, many of the Irish leaders were Protestants. The principal Irish objectives were land reform and home rule. By 1914 it appeared these had all but been obtained, despite the obstinate stupidity of the Conservative party. But in the meantime a far more intransigent group had grown up, the Sinn Fein party, dedicated to the establishment of a Gaelic, Catholic republic. It received much of its inspiration and money from Irish-Americans.

In 1869 the New York Irish established a secret society, *Clan-na-Gael*, dedicated to a radical, violent course in Ireland. This remained a vigorous, nationwide organization for half a century, led in the New York area by a Fenian exile, John Devoy, and a Tammany judge, Daniel Cohalan. During much of this time the Irish issue seemed to dominate New York as well. During the middle years of the century the arrival of Irish patriots in the port were occasions for great public celebrations. The exiles enhanced a tendency, apparent from the time of O'Connell, for Irish-Americans to be more extreme in their attitudes toward England than were the native Irish.

At the turn of the century, when an Anglo-American *entente* was becoming evident, a number of German- and Irish-Americans began to work together against it. When World War I came, this collaboration became an earnest, perilous affair. "A comparison of such Irish papers as *The Gaelic-American* and the *Irish World* with the

German-language press indicates how closely they followed a common propaganda line," writes Carl Wittke.[59] The fateful move was that of *Clan-na-Gael,* which actively participated with the Germans and Sir Roger Casement in plotting and financing the uprising in Dublin in Easter Week, 1916. It was at best a minority act, despite all the provocations to revolt. In the curious words of a recent Irish-American historian:

The age-old hope of securing Irish Independence *through physical force* had been abandoned by most Irishmen and was cherished chiefly by some stout-hearted men of the I.R.B. [Irish Republican Brotherhood] who would stage the rising of 1916. The uncertain solution in the Irish national test tube could be precipitated only by the blood of heroes who were not afraid to die in order that a nation might live.[60]

The Easter Rebellion established the leaders of Irish-American nationalism as among those who wished to see Germany defeat England. This position was barely tolerated in America in 1916. In the election campaign that year such Irish were scorned by both sides as "hyphenated Americans." President Wilson came to regard Cohalan as little better than a traitor, refusing even to enter the same room with him.[61] The efforts of Irish-Americans, in which the Catholic hierarchy took part, to obtain Wilsonian self-determination for Ireland at the peace conference, received little sympathy and no real help from the Wilson administration.

After the war, in a sequence that was to become familiar, Irish affairs went from insurrection, to independence, to civil war, to neutrality. When Irish bases were refused even American forces during the Second World War, Ireland was off America's conscience for good, if indeed she had ever been on it.

The shame of it from the point of view of the New York Irish was that Irish nationalism went sour just when they themselves were becoming almost a symbol of American nationalism. Just when issues of Irish-American newspapers were being banned from the mails as seditious, "Wild Bill" Donovan was leading the Fighting Sixty-Ninth into the Argonne and George M. Cohan was proclaiming to all the world: "I'm a Yankee Doodle Dandy . . . Born on the Fourth of July."

> Red, White and Blue,
> I am for you,
> Honest you're a grand old flag.[62]

The Irish-American character had formed, and no longer needed Irish nationalism to sustain itself. This is not to say that most Irish-Americans had such a character, but the *image* had jelled and in the manner of such things began to verify itself.

The Irish-American character was not very different from that which Macaulay described, save in two respects: it was urban and it was egalitarian. Where the Irish had been wild, they now became tough. Where they had been rebellious, it now became more a matter of being defiantly democratic. In the words of Thomas Beer, "an infinitely pugnacious, utterly common and merry animal." [63]

Picture John Morrissey: heavyweight champion of the world, Member of Congress, principal owner of the Saratoga race course, proprietor of gambling houses, husband of a famous beauty, and a leader of the "Young Democracy" that helped overthrow Tweed. In 1875 a respectable enough Mayor named Wickham, who had been elected by the new Tammany group, posted a man in his anteroom at City Hall to receive the calling cards of visitors. Shortly thereafter, Morrissey, having no card, was refused admittance to the Mayor's office. As recounted by Morris R. Werner:

A few days later, a friend met John Morrissey in City Hall Park. He was dressed in a swallowtail coat, patent leather boots, white kid gloves, and he carried a light coat over his arm. In his other hand was a thick book. His friend, John B. Haskin, said: "Hello, John, what's up now? Going to a wedding?" "No," answered Morrissey, "not so bad as that. I've just bought a French dictionary to help me talk to our dandy Mayor. I'm going in full dress to make a call, for that is now the style at the Hotel Wickham," pointing to the City Hall. "No Irish need apply now," Morrissey added.[64]

Fifteen thousand people followed him to his grave.

Let it be said that the Irish gave style to life in the slums:

Boys and girls together, me and Mamie Rorke,
Tripped the light fantastic on the sidewalks of New York.

They became the playboys of this new Western World. "None can Love Like an Irishman" was a favorite song of Lincoln's day. By the turn of the century it had become equally clear that none could run like them, nor fight like them, nor drink as much, nor sing as well. When it came to diving off the Brooklyn Bridge or winning pennants for the Giants, it took an Irishman. And who could write such bittersweet songs as Victor Herbert? Or enjoy life like "Diamond Jim" Brady? All was "bliss and blarney."

Much was forgiven them. Their failures, as they themselves said of their principal one, were "A good man's weakness." A certain compassion pervaded even their wrongdoing. Jimmy Walker was nothing so much as P. T. Barnum in a speakeasy: predatory, not evil. At their best such Irish had a genius for getting through to the people: no one in the history of New York has ever been able to explain state government to the voters in the way Al Smith did. Nor have they ever quite forgotten the compliment he paid their intelligence.

By degrees the Irish style of the gaslight era became less and less Irish, more and more the style of the American city. Al Smith came close to being for the people of the Lower East Side of America what Lincoln had been for the Frontier. Better still, what Jackson had been—two Irishmen, a century apart. When the comic strips began, the principal urban characters—Maggie and Jiggs, Moon Mullins, Dick Tracy—were Irish. When the movies began to fashion a composite picture of the American people, the New York Irishman was projected to the very center of the national image.

For whatever reason, perhaps because of the influence of New York Jews in the film industry, when Hollywood undertook to synthesize the Christian religion, they found it most easy to do in the person of an Irish priest: Pat O'Brien as Father Duffy in the trenches. When it came to portraying the tough American, up from the

246

streets, the image was repeatedly that of an Irishman. James Cagney (a New Yorker) was the quintessential figure: fists cocked, chin out, back straight, bouncing along on his heels. But also doomed: at the end of the movie he was usually dead. The contrast with Chaplin tells worlds.

By the time the New York journalist, John O'Sullivan, coined the phrase "Manifest Destiny" as a compact apologetic for American expansionism, the Irish were seasoned nationalists. Their exploits, or their accounts thereof, in the Mexican and Civil Wars established the American institution of the "Fighting Irish." Thomas Beer recalled,

This dummy figure of the Irishman had become deeply sacred with Americans; in 1898 a group of young journalists went hunting the first trooper to reach the blockhouse on San Juan Hill, assuring each other . . . that he would be a red-haired Irishman and warmly disappointed when he proved an ordinary American of German ancestry. . . . Nineteen years later, another group of journalists went hunting a red-haired Irishman who fired the first shot of the American Expeditionary Force in France.[65]

Success went to their heads; it also undermined the character of many. It is to be noted, as Beer does, that "The Irish were at once established as a tremendously funny, gay, charming people and concurrently were snubbed." [66] There was a touch of Sambo in the professional Irishman: he was willing to be welcomed on terms that he not forget his place. There was also more than a bit of mucker in the man-of-the-people pose. Derision of the hifalutin all too easily shaded into contempt for intelligence and learning, particularly on the lace-curtain fringe. The Irish were flirting with the peril Whitehead pointed to in his remark that in the conditions of the modern world the nation that does not value trained intelligence is doomed.

This was painfully manifest in the Irish-American response to the extraordinary flowering of Irish literature in the late nineteenth century. The emigrant Irish may have brought with them a certain peasant respect for learning—"Isle of Saints and Scholars"—but two generations in the slums of New York killed it, if it ever existed. Instead of embracing and glorying in the new literature, the New York Irish either ignored it, or if they were respectable enough, turned on the Irish authors, accusing them of using bad language!

The Ancient Order of Hibernians raged and rioted when the Abbey Theatre brought the new playwrights to America. John Quinn, a New York lawyer, and an important patron of the Irish writers, showed an early copy of the *Playboy* to John Devoy, the Fenian journalist so dedicated to a dynamite-and-blood solution of the land question. Quinn later wrote Cohalan that for weeks and weeks in his paper "Devoy railed at the *language* of the *Playboy* as foul, un-Irish, indecent, blasphemous, and so on. . . ." [67] The Irish-Americans' reaction to the new literature was, of course, not very different from that of many or most of the native Irish.

Reilly and the 400 was fun, but it was not *Riders to the Sea*. When it emerged that the American Irish did not see this, their opportunity to attain a degree of cultural ascendancy quite vanished. After that began a steady emigration from the Irish "community" of many of the strongest and best of the young. This migration was as devitalizing in America as it was to the Irish nation overseas.

The image changed. At the turn of the century Ireland stood for brave things. The painter John Sloan was Scot by descent, but preferred to think otherwise: "I'm an Irishman," he would say. "Therefore I'm agin the government. . . ." But as time passed, the rebel receded, the policeman loomed larger. "We wur once the world's dramers af freedom," says the drunk old woman in Anthony West's *The Native Moment*, "—what are we now?"

There are, of course, no statistics or measures of this kind of movement, but the impression is overwhelming. Excepting those with a strong religious vocation, the sensitive, perceptive children of the American Irish born early in the twentieth century found little to commend itself in the culture to which they were born.

Of all the New York Irish to live with this and write about it, foremost was Eugene O'Neill. Only toward the end of his life was he able to do so. *Long Day's Journey Into Night* recounts the agony of his family, "the four haunted Tyrones," headed by the actor father. (The O'Neills were the Earls of Tyrone.) Throughout one feels the rending insufficiency for the sons of the "gas and brag and bosh" of their father's Irishness.

EDMUND
Sits down opposite his Father—contemptuously
Yes, facts don't mean a thing, do they? What you want to believe, that's the only truth!
Derisively
Shakespeare was an Irish Catholic, for example.

TYRONE
Stubbornly
So he was. The proof is in his plays.

EDMUND
Well he wasn't, and there's no proof of it in his plays, except to you!
Jeeringly
The Duke of Wellington, there was another good Irish Catholic!

TYRONE
I never said he was a good one. He was a renegade but a Catholic just the same.

EDMUND
Well, he wasn't. You just want to believe no one but an Irish Catholic general could beat Napoleon.[68]

One of O'Neill's last plays, *A Touch of the Poet*, recounts the final defeat of Major Cornelius Melody, an Irish officer, late of Wellington's army. Descended to running a tavern near Boston, he is scorned by the Yankees and mocked by the Irish, neither of whom accept him as a gentleman. Melody returns from his crisis broken, a bogtrotter once more. He has killed his horse and dropped his English accent.

. . . Me brins, if I have any, is clear as a bell. And I'm not puttin' on brogue to tormint you, me darlint. Nor play-actin', Sara. That was the Major's game. It's quare, surely, for the two av ye to object when I talk in me natural tongue, and yours, and don't put on airs loike the late lamented auld liar and lunatic, Major Cornelius Melody, av His Majesty's Seventh Dragoons, used to do. So let you be aisy, darlint. He'll nivir again hurt you with his sneers, and his pretendin' he's a gintleman, blatherin' about pride and honor, and his showin' off before the Yankees, and thim laughin' at him, prancing around drunk on his beautiful thoroughbred mare—For she's dead, too, poor baste.[69]

Melody rises and makes for the bar to drink with the Irish laborers he had scorned. From within he shouts a toast: "Here's to our next President, Andy Jackson! Hurroo for Auld Hickory, God bless him!" Melody was now, like the rest, an Irish Catholic Democrat—at peace with a world that would have it no other way.

"THERE ARE SOME OF US LEFT"

ON THE SURFACE, THE "IRISH" IN IRISH-AMERICAN IS FAST fading. "Sweet Rosie O'Grady" has become simply one of the old songs about the old-fashioned American girl. If any recognize the wild notes of "Garryowen," it is most likely as the charging call of the U.S. Seventh Cavalry, and the association is more with the battle of the Little Big Horn River than with the gay times of old on the banks of the Shannon.

Unquestionably, however, an Irish identity persists. It would seem that it now identifies someone as plain as against fancy American. In an urban culture, Irishness has come to represent some of the qualities the honest yeoman stood for in an earlier age, notably in the undertone of toughness and practicality. "Be more Irish than Harvard," Robert Frost told the young President in 1961.

Ethnic identity being mostly a matter of where one came from, it loses much of its content in the Middle and Far West where most persons came from the Eastern Seaboard in the character of Yankees, or Southerners, or whatever. New York being the first stop in America, however, most white New Yorkers continue to identify themselves as originating somewhere in Europe. Asked, "What are you?" a New Yorker replies, "Italian," or "Greek," or "Jewish." Most Irish still answer, "Irish." For one thing, it is probably an advantage to do so. The more amiable qualities of the stage Irishman have persisted in tradition. The Irish are commonly thought to be a friendly, witty, generous people, physically courageous and fond of drink. There is a distinct tendency among many to try to live up to this image.

The problem with perpetuating this Irish type is that it is essentially proletarian and does not jibe with middle-class reality. Like Southern hospitality, the Irish temperament has become a tradition—valid enough, perhaps, but requiring constant reinforcement. Hence names acquire importance. The Maguires and O'Tooles and O'Shanes are continually reminded by others that they are Irish and are therefore less likely to forget (it normally being a pleasant thing to tell a man he is Irish). But the vast numbers of Irish Blacks and Whites, Longs and Shorts, Smiths and Joneses, not to mention the Comiskeys, Nagles, and Costellos, seem to lose their Irish identity more easily. In addition, there is a fairly strict rule of patrimonial descent: to be an Irish-American writer, an Irish last name is required. A kind of cultural rule also obtains: Henry James was pure New York Celt, but is hardly regarded as an Irish-American author.

The three additional factors working toward a decline of Irish identity in America are the decline of immigration, the fading of Irish nationalism, and the relative absence of Irish cultural influence from abroad on the majority of American Irish.

The native Irish continue to emigrate (the population today is not half the prefamine level), but most of the immigrants settle in England. A trickle of Irishmen arrives in New York, but it is barely sufficient to keep the County associations alive and to provide talent for and interest in the sporting events that are centered at Gaelic Park in the Bronx. A handful of declining Irish papers continues to be published, and the Ancient Order of Hibernians manages to keep an organization together, if only to arrange the St. Patrick's Day parade. But the first-generation immigrants are a declining, rather isolated group. A fair indication is the disparate course of development between the Jewish and Irish summer resorts in the Catskills. As the Jews have become more prosperous, their recreation centers in Sullivan County have developed into fabulous pleasure domes. By contrast, the Irish colonies in Greene County to the north seem to be dying out.

In truth, most of the recent immigrants are rather a disappointment to the American Irish, just as is

Ireland itself to many Americans who go back. Neither the people nor the land fits the stereotype. Few sights are more revealing than that of a second- or third-generation Irish-American tourist sitting down to his first meal, boiled in one iron pot over the open peat fire, in his grandparents' cottage. Embarrassment hangs just as heavy over the Fifth Avenue reviewing stand of the St. Patrick's Day parade. The sleek, porcine judges and contractors, all uneasy bravado, simply don't know what to make of the smallish, dour Irish officials and emissaries gathered for the occasion. Neither do the guests from Eire seem to know quite what to make of the "O'Donnell Abu," Fighting 69th, "Top O'the Marnin" goings-on. In Dublin, March 17th is a holy day, the parade is like as not devoted to the theme of industrial progress; and until recently the bars were closed.

Modern-day Ireland has little to commend itself to the average Irish-American. Where the American granddaughters of Calabrian peasants are blossoming forth in Roman chic, there is no contemporary Irish manner to emulate. Even the most visible Irish contribution to the New York scene, the Irish saloon, is vanishing, decimated by prohibition and now unable to compete with the attractions of television and the fact that Italians can cook. A very considerable body of Irish traits and speech habits has become so thoroughly absorbed in New York culture as no longer to be regarded as Irish. No one, for example, any longer thinks of Halloween as another of those curious days on which all the Irish in town get drunk. The result is fewer and fewer opportunities for Irish-Americans to associate themselves with their past.

Fewer and fewer need to do so in order to sustain their own identity. This is nowhere more evident than in the plight of the American Irish Historical Society. This group was founded in New York in 1897 "to make better known the Irish chapter in American history." There was certainly a case to be made that the Irish had been slighted, and the Society set out to right this imbalance with some vigor. But little came of it. The membership was basically not interested in history; it was the imbalance of the present, not the past, that concerned them. When this was righted, the purpose of the Society vanished. Its *Journal,* which had inclined to articles by aspiring judges beginning "While we know that an Irishman was in Columbus' crew on his first voyage to the New World . . . ," has long ceased publication. The Society continues to occupy a great tomb of a mansion on Fifth Avenue, with a fine library that few seem interested in using, and splendid meeting rooms where no one evidently wants to meet.

The establishment of the Irish Free State and later the Republic of Eire, despite the Ulster issue, has substantially put an end to the agitation for Irish independence which contributed so much to the maintenance of Irish identity in America. As Whitehead said of Protestantism, so of Irish-American nationalism; "Its dogmas no longer dominate; its divisions no longer interest; its institutions no longer direct the patterns of life." [70] On the contrary, the more militantly Irish circles in America have become alarmed about the unorthodox behavior of the Irish government on issues such as admission of Red China to the United Nations. The *American Mercury* has published an article on the imminent possibility of a Communist takeover in Ireland. The Brooklyn *Tablet* carries long pleas from Irish-Americans for ideological aid to "an Ireland subject to the seductive siren call of the Left and the domination of an alien and atheistic ideology." [71]

Ironically, it is precisely those persons who were most attached to the Irish cause and the Irish culture of the nineteenth century who are having the most difficulty maintaining such attachments in the present time. Ireland has not ceased to influence America. Contemporary American literature can hardly be understood save in the context of Shaw, Wilde, Yeats, O'Casey, Joyce, and the like. Contemporary Irish authors appear almost weekly in *The New Yorker.* But those who would most value their Irishness seem least able to respond to such achievements. Irish writers have been Irish indeed. Protestants, agnostics, atheists, socialists, communists, homosexuals, drunkards, and mockers, they have had but few traits that commend themselves to the Catholic middle class. "A common drunk," Honorable James A. Comerford of the Court of Special Sessions exclaimed in announcing that the playwright Brendan Behan would not be marching in the 1961 St. Patrick's Day parade in New York.

In the coming generation it is likely that those persons who have the fewest conventional Irish attachments will become the most conscious of their Irish heritage. This is already evident in writers such as Mary McCarthy and John O'Hara: things Irish are to be found throughout their work. It would seem that any heightened self-consciousness tends to raise the question of racial origin and to stir some form of racial pride. Irish authors abound in the bookstores around Fordham. In Greenwich Village there is a distinct Irish strain, compounded of the literary and political traditions. Songs of the Irish Revolution have taken their place in the repertoire of the balladeers and are listened to rapturously by emancipated young Irish-Americans.

Irish consciousness would seem to be holding its own in the upper reaches of the business as well as the intellectual sphere. The Society of the Friendly Sons of Saint Patrick can hardly ever have been more prosperous than today, as it approaches the third century of its existence. The annual dinners, strictly adhering to a format that seems to have been fixed about the time Victor Herbert was president, are splendid affairs, moving in ponderous array from the Boned Diamondback Terrapin à la Travers with Bobadillia Amontillado, through the Chicken Forestière and Heidsieck Brut, to the demitasse, H. Upman Belvederes, and brandy. They leave no doubt that even if the Protestants have rather disappeared, the Society remains, as it began, an organization of well-fed merchants. Perhaps the principal innovation of the past century is a middle course of boiled bacon, Irish potatoes, and kale, a wistful reminder of those far-off cabins in Roscommon. No one touches it.

Indications are that the Irish are now about the most evenly distributed group in New York in terms of economic and social position. (See Table 8.) They are perhaps a bit heavy on the extremes: rather more than their share of the men on the Bowery and on Wall Street, but generally about the right proportions. In this respect they are unique among the major ethnic groups in New York.

Their distribution within class strata is not nearly so even. O'Faolain has reminded us that the ancient Irish had a powerful distaste for commerce; through history the Irish were by preference lawyers and soldiers and priests, and the pattern rather persists in the New World. The Irish are well represented in Wall Street law firms. In one of the largest the Irish partners were recently considering whether a quota should be imposed. But they have shown relatively little talent as merchants, and most of those that did so have been quite overwhelmed by Jewish competition.

The principal Irish businesses in the city still tend to be family affairs, founded by working men and involving the organization of manual labor in forms that may begin small and grow larger. Thus in 1850, Michael Moran, just off the boat, began as a mule driver on the Erie Canal at 50¢ a day. Ten years later he put down $2,700 for half-interest in a towboat hauling barges from New York to Albany. Today his descendants operate the largest tugboat fleet in the world, with only two competitors left in New York Harbor. The *Sheila,* and *Moira,* and *Kevin,* and *Kathleen Moran's* greet one and all as the great ships move in and out of the harbor.[72]

The Irish, in a sense, have never strayed far from the docks, where they established a singularly dispiriting regime of political, business, and trade-union corruption. They quickly enough got into the businesses of digging ditches and hauling freight, and Irish contractors have eviscerated, built up, knocked down, and again built up a good deal of New York City. Whether their firms will survive the rationalization process that appears to be going on in this industry remains to be seen. Considerable Irish fortunes were made in real estate speculation—a peasant attachment for land which O'Neill describes in his portrait of the elder Tyrone—but these seem not to have produced much in the way of continuing enterprise.

The Irish have done well in businesses such as banking, where there is stress on personal qualities and the accommodation of conflicting interests, and not a little involvement in politics. In 1850, at Bishop Hughes' suggestion, the directors of the Irish Emigrant Society, founded in 1841, established the Emigrant Industrial Savings Bank. As time passed, the bank became more active, and the charitable society less so until, in 1936, the Society went out of existence. But the bank remains, on its original site behind City Hall, the fourth-largest savings bank in the nation and still very much an Irish affair. The Irish have also done well on Wall Street. James V. Forrestal, the son of an immigrant, was president of Dillon, Read & Co. before he entered the Roosevelt Administration.

The Irish talent for political bureaucracy seems to have carried over into the world of business organization. The Irish have been content to get in the long lines of the giant corporations and for some time have been popping up in the front ranks as their turn came. In the long run, their patience may prove as important a commercial asset as Jewish daring or Yankee rigor.

For the moment, however, the relevant question is not how the Irish have succeeded, but why they have not succeeded more. The English and Dutch who preceded them in New York are now almost entirely middle- and upper-class. The Germans who accompanied them are predominantly middle-class. The Jews who followed them are already predominantly middle-class and soon will be exclusively so. If the majority of the Irish have climbed out of the working class, it has been only to settle on the next rung. Oscar Handlin has put it candidly that, just as the movement of Jews out of the ranks of unskilled labor was exceptionally rapid, that of the Irish was "exceptionally slow." [73]

A clue might be found in a cover story of *Life* magazine in 1947 on the "Peoples of New York." The Irish were not included among the major groups in the city but were relegated to a small block between the Rumanians and the Arabs. The picture was that of a cop, and the caption read "Once the victims of a violent prejudice, New York's many Irish are now thoroughly assimilated. Many of them become politicians or members of the city's police force." [74] Instead of profiting by their success in the all-but-despised roles of ward heeler and policeman, the Irish seem to have been trapped by it. As with the elder Tyrone, they seem almost to have ruined their talent by playing one role over and over until they could do little else.

For Tyrone, as for his sons, so also for the race: drink has been their curse. It is the principal fact of Irishness that they have not been able to shake. A good deal of competent enquiry has still not produced much understanding of the Irish tendency to alcohol addiction. It would seem, in the words of Charles R. Snyder, that

Irish country culture appears to be an "ideal type" case of a deeply embedded tradition of utilitarian drinking. There is also a tradition of convivial social drinking in which drunkenness is common, but there is an extensive body of tradition which tends to orient individuals toward drinking for the effect of alcohol as a generalized means of individual adjustment.[75]

It seems to be agreed (but with less persuasiveness) that the Irish culture was "such as to create and maintain an immense amount of suppressed aggression and sexuality." [76] The question may still be asked why drinking becomes addictive, and why the pattern persists in the New World. Aspects of the culture, particularly the suppressed sexuality, survive, of course. It may also be, as Roger J. Williams suggests, that the problem is at least in part heredity.[77]

Whatever the explanation, the fact itself is indisputable. In a study of a group on the Bowery, Straus and McCarthy found 44 per cent of the whites to be Irish.[78] A dominant social fact of the Irish community is the number of good men who are destroyed by drink. In ways it is worse now than in the past: a stevedore could drink and do his work; a lawyer, a doctor, a legislator cannot.

In New York the Irish are competing with groups whose alcoholism rates are as phenomenally low as theirs is high. Studies almost invariably find the Irish at one end of the spectrum and the Jews at the very opposite. Meyer found "alcoholism is 74 times as important a cause of psychoses among men of Irish descent as it is among those of Jewish descent." [79] The Italians are well down on the scale. In 1947 Donald D. Glad reported the following incidence of inebriety in New York State based on first admission for alcohol psychoses per 100,000 population of each ethnic group:

Irish	25.6
Scandinavian	7.6
Italian	4.8
English	4.3
German	3.8
Jews	0.5[80]

It is evident enough that Irish drunkenness has given competitors a margin in business and the professions—it may even have tended to keep the Irish out of some of the professions. It is probably also true that it partially accounts for the disappearance of the Irish from organized crime. Gambling and related activities are among the largest business activities in New York and certainly among the most profitable. With their political power, even if declining, the Irish ought to have a share of control in them, but the Southern Italians, with Jewish connections, have completely taken over. Bookmaking, policy, and drugs are complex, serious, exacting trades. They are not jobs for heavy drinkers.

The relative failure of the Irish to rise socially seems on the surface to be part of a general Catholic failure. This hypothesis, with regard to Catholics, was put by a Notre Dame sociologist, John J. Kane:

There may be some kind of lower middle or lower class orientation among them to education and occupation which tends to anchor Catholics in the lower socio-economic groups and which limits those who do achieve higher education to certain fields which appear to offer more security albeit less prestige and income. It may also be that leadership, even outside the purely religious field, is still considered a clerical prerogative, and the same seems equally true of scholarship. It seems that Catholics creep forward rather than stride forward in American society and the position of American Catholics in the mid-twentieth century is better, but not so much better than it was a century ago. Neither is it as high as one might expect from such a sizable minority with a large educational system and reputed equality of opportunity in a democracy.[81]

Such evidence as is available supports this hypothesis. In Detroit Gerhard Lenski found white Catholics to have the least positive attitude toward work of any of the major groups (Jews, white Protestants, Negro Protestants and Catholics). Where Catholic attitudes were positive, it was, in contrast with Protestants, toward the less demanding, and hence less rewarding, positions. Positive attitudes toward work came close to being nonexistent (6 per cent of the sample) among middle-class Catholics with Catholic education. In striking contrast, 28 per cent of the middle-class Catholic males with a *public* education had a positive attitude.[82] The evidence also underlines the concentration of Catholics in certain activities. Kane found that in a sample of American Catholics in *Who's Who in America* 48.6 per cent were lawyers or priests. Bosco D. Cestello found in a sample of Catholic businessmen in the same directory that 25 per cent were in finance, two-thirds more than the national proportion, while only 7.7 per cent, barely a quarter the national average, were in trade.[83]

The curious distribution of even successful Catholics—getting ahead as bankers before making much progress as merchants—raises the question whether the relative poor showing of Catholics in the business world is not primarily a poor Irish showing. The Italians and Poles and Puerto Ricans have not really been settled long enough to make it clear what their performance in normal circumstances will be. In time they may produce a Catholic business class that is quite up to average. But clearly, the Irish have not done so.

In New York this failure may well be related to the Irish success in politics. It is perilous to speculate in such matters, but a case can be made that contrary to the general impression politics is not a lucrative calling. This case is more confirmed than contradicted by the periodic scandals that reveal the large amounts of graft and benefactions passed between politicians and various legitimate and illegitimate businessmen: the politicians are often as not on their way to jail. The secret of the long tenure of many of the better known Irish politicians is that they were honest men by any standards, and certainly by the American standards of their time.

THE IRISH

The equally relevant fact in a city like New York, with constantly changing neighborhoods, is the extreme difficulty of passing on political power from one generation to the next and in that way establishing prosperous family dynasties. The problem of Tammany leaders is not much different in this respect from that of champion prize fighters. A few Irish district leaders today are sons of old leaders, but they are rarely of the old breed. The *New York Times* recently ran a striking photograph of "The Clan Finn," the rulers of Greenwich Village from the 1870's to 1943. On the wall of the Huron Club, a three-story brick and stone edifice ("Pitched it up in an afternoon himself, he did.") hung a portrait of old "Battery Dan" Finn. Back stiff as a North River pile, and a head that must have been fashioned of cast iron. His eyes look straight ahead. Standing before the portrait is his son, "Sheriff Dan." Homburg and high collar, with the vast jowls of a prosperous official in an age when Luchow's and Tammany Hall shared Union Square. His eyes are glazed rather. Next to him is his son, "Bashful Dan." Gray flannels, hair and chin receding. Eyes downcast. "Bashful Dan" inherited his post in 1935. Eight years later Carmine G. DeSapio took it away from him.

The small potatoes of political success have become even less nourishing over the years. Swarms of Irish descended on the city government after the Civil War and began successions of low-grade civil servants. Here, as with the top-rank politicians, there was little cumulative improvement from one generation to the next. The economic rewards in America over the past century have gone to entrepreneurs, not to *fonctionnaires,* and hence, in that measure, not to the Irish of New York.

Even were the Irish rising faster socially and economically than seems to be the case, the first impression would be one of decline. People *disappear* into the lower-middle class, to emerge, if ever, only years or generations later, in the upper reaches of achievement. In the interval, they are outdistanced in the areas of popular achievement, which are particularly visible in an age of mass media. This has been painfully obvious for the Irish in New York, which is the center of the nation's entertainment industry and thereby the center of most of the popular arts. The past thirty years have been a time of steady decline for the Irish. The Irish fighters and ballplayers have gone down before Negroes and Italians. The Irish crooners have been driven out by Italians. Most of the popular comedians are Jewish. The best of the musicians are Negro.

A similar, if more complex, process is at work in the trade-union movement. The most important of the working-class leaders of the city, from Gompers to Dubinsky, have emerged from the Jewish Socialist tradition (Peter McGuire and George Meany excepted). This tradition, however, has about played out; the Jews have left the working class, and Jewish liberals have largely turned their interests elsewhere. During all this time the bulk of the trade-union leadership, notably in the craft unions, has been Irish. This leadership continues with a diminished, but by no means vanished ethnic base. Of late the leadership has even been revived by the influence of Catholic ideological movements, symbolized in New York by the Association of Catholic Trade Unionists and the various church-related labor schools. It is likely that Irish influence in this area will continue for some time.

In their classic stronghold, the police force, the Irish have been forced to set up a society to protect their interests. For some time ethnic groups in the New York police, as in many of the city bureaucracies—as in the life of the city generally—have maintained fraternal organizations. The Italians were first to organize on an ethnic basis within the Police Department. In the 1930's they were followed by Jews, the white Protestants, the black Protestants, the Puerto Ricans, and the Poles. For a long while, the Irish were so dominant that it would have seemed ludicrous for them to organize. But by 1952 it was obvious that those days were passing; the Irish still had a majority of the force, but no longer a majority of the police academy, and so they set up the Emerald Society and took their place among the other minorities.

Turning lower-middle class is a painful process for a group such as the Irish who, as stevedores and truck drivers, made such a grand thing of Saturday night. Most prize fighters and a good many saloon fighters die in the gutter—but they have moments of glory unknown to accountants. Most Irish laborers died penniless, but they had been rich one night a week much of their lives, whereas their white-collar children never know a moment of financial peace, much less affluence. A good deal of color goes out of life when a group begins to rise. A good deal of resentment enters.

The cumulative effect of this process has been to produce among a great many Irish a powerful sense of displacement. It is summed up in a phrase they will use on hearing an Irish name or being introduced to another Irishman. "There are some of us left," they say. One could be in Connaught in the seventeenth century.

THE PARTY OF THE PEOPLE

THE SENSE OF DISPLACEMENT IS NOWHERE MORE ACUTE THAN in politics.

The basic cause of the decline of the political power of the Irish has been their decline as a proportion of the population. Where they accounted for a third of the population of the city in 1890, they are probably no more than one-tenth today. In 1960 there were 312,000 first- or second-generation Irish in the city, and a considerably larger number of older stock.[84] But like their English and Scotch predecessors, much of the old Irish stock has moved to the suburbs. Some, of course, have dispersed throughout the country. Many of the Irish who remain in the city have become Republicans, thus splitting the Irish vote, and of those who remain Democrats, a great many have been at odds with the prevailing ideology within their party. The result, inevitably, has been the rapid waning of Irish political power.

At first glance the Irish appear to be doing well enough, but only because they are passing out of political power. They have most of the very top jobs. But they have fewer and fewer of the bottom ones, a fact which means that in time they will lose the top ones. Seven of the last nine mayors of New York have been Irish, if one counts the latest, Robert F. Wagner, who is half Irish. Recently an Irish-Catholic Democrat from Brooklyn was chief judge of the Court of Appeals, the highest judicial post of the state. (He was succeeded by an Irish-Catholic Democrat from Buffalo.) A Manhattan Irish Democrat retired recently as Chancellor of the State Board of Regents. A third of the New York delegation to the 1960 Democratic convention was Irish. In the city itself, as of 1961, the chief justice of the City Court and the Chief City Magistrate were Irish, but Italians and Jews predominated in the city courts. In 1959, of sixty-three State Supreme Court judges from New York, less than a quarter were Irish. During the Harriman administration in Albany, 1955–1958, New York City Jews received two jobs for every one given the Irish.

Nine of the nineteen Congressmen elected from New York City in 1962 were Irish, but only a fifth of the sixty-five Assemblymen were. Al Smith was the last Irish officeholder who could command a large vote in New York politics. Since he left office in 1928, only one Irish Catholic, James M. Mead of Buffalo, has been elected Senator or Governor. A series of Irish candidates were put up against Dewey with no success. It was not until 1954, when for the first time in memory the Democrats nominated a state ticket with no Irishman on it, that they won back the governorship. In 1962 James B. Donovan, the Democratic candidate for Senator, managed even to lose his home borough of Brooklyn to the Republican Jacob K. Javits.

Within the Democratic party the death of Edward J. Flynn of the Bronx in 1953 marked the end of Irish political leadership. Although the Irish continued with a majority of the county leaders, the initiative and leadership of the party passed almost entirely to the Italian leader Carmine DeSapio. In the great primary contest of 1961 over the mayoralty nomination, DeSapio was beaten, and with him most of the Irish that had survived. By 1963 the county leader in Manhattan was Armenian, Brooklyn and Queens had Jewish leaders, with only the Bronx and Staten Island lingering in Irish hands.

As stated, the principal cause of the decline of Irish political power in New York City is the decline of Irish population. In the suburbs, to which many Irish have moved, they retain a good deal of power. Westchester, Nassau, and Suffolk all had Irish Democratic county leaders as of 1963. In the city, where the Irish established a system of popular rule, they no longer rule now that they account for only some 10 or 12 per cent of the populace. But this is not the whole story. The ideological displacement of the Irish in the Democratic party has also been a major cause of their decline in New York.

The emergence of Irish political conservatism in recent years may seem to call for more explanation than is needed. The main thrust of Irish political activity has always been moderate or conservative in New York, but until recently it has not been articulately so. There is a well-known story about the Tammany Fourth of July fête at which a reporter asked why "Mister" Murphy had not joined in singing "The Star-Spangled Banner." "Maybe," came the reply, "he didn't want to commit himself." The functioning urban politician does not commit himself; he negotiates with the commitments of others. This came naturally to the Irish, who were the least encumbered with abstract notions about municipal ownership and trade-union rights.

Tammany conservatism has been greatly reinforced by the political developments which from the beginning of the Irish era to the present have kept the New York Democratic party isolated from that party in the rest of the country. Tammany stood for sin in a party wedded to virtue. This was never better expressed than by the Midwesterner speaking for Grover Cleveland at the Democratic convention in 1884. "They love Cleveland for his character," said the speaker, turning to the New York City delegation, "but they love him also for the enemies he has made." Tammany did not support the original nomination of a single successful Democratic Presidential candidate between the Civil War and the Second World War. The ideas behind the programs of Cleveland and Wilson and Roosevelt largely passed them by.

Indifference began to turn to opposition about the time of the First World War. A great many New York Irish were bitter about Wilson's refusal to give American support to Irish independence, and the election returns showed it. Wilson's league became for them a symbol of American toadying to British imperialism. Cohalan organized five hours of testimony by the Friends of Irish Freedom before the Senate Foreign Relations Committee in the hearings on the Treaty of Versailles. The League was denounced as "an abomination," "a perversion of American ideals." [85] Many New York Irish Democrats entered the 1920's alienated from their party on what was then the fundamental issue of foreign policy.

The rejection of Al Smith, first by his country and then by his party, was the breaking point for many. The New York Irish gave their hearts to Smith, who was an Irish figure whatever his ancestry. He was in no sense a product of the slum, but rather a representative of a distinct New York urban culture that to this day asserts its own manner of speech and dress in a society otherwise overwhelmed by Brooks Brothers. Smith had not the slightest qualms about the adequacy of his education: it was hyperbole, and perhaps a sense of mockery, that led him to tell the New York State Assembly that he was a graduate, not of Yale, but of the Fulton Fish Market. He was the greatest state governor of his generation, perhaps of the century, but he was such without the pomposity of Good Government. He talked out of the side of his mouth, and mispronounced words. When he declared, "No matter how you slice it, it's still baloney," he seemed to strip the establishment of all the pretense and posture designed to keep the Irish and such in their places.

The bitter anti-Catholicism and the crushing defeat of the 1928 campaign came as a blow. The New York Irish had been running their city for a long time, or so it seemed. They did not think of themselves as immigrants and interlopers with an alien religion; it was a shock to find that so much of the country did. Worse yet, in 1932, when the chance came to redress this wrong, the Democrats, instead of renominating Smith, turned instead to a Hudson Valley aristocrat with a Harvard accent who had established his reputation by blocking Murphy's nomination of "Blue-eyed Billy" Sheehan for the U.S. Senate, and was soon to enhance it by getting rid of Jimmy Walker.

The main effect of the New Deal in the upper reaches of the Irish community in New York was to reveal to its members that while they had been rising socially and economically, the Democratic party as a whole remained an organization of the masses. It rarely occurred to the Irish to stop being Democrats because they had become bankers, or whatever. The party was an ethnic and religious alliance, as much as an economic one. (In DeSapio's day, for example, the chairman of the board of the New York Stock exchange, a distinguished broker, son of an Irish policeman, regularly attended the Tammany Dinner.) Irish businessmen hated Roosevelt much as did other businessmen but with the special twist that they felt it was their own political party, overcome by alien influences, that was causing the trouble.

A distinctive quality of the anti-New Deal Irish during the 1930's is that they tended to identify the subversive influences in the nation with the old Protestant establishment. The well-to-do Irish felt it was Harvard, as much or more than Union Square, that was out to socialize America. The lower ranks of the New York Irish were powerfully attracted by Father Coughlin and his notions about social justice, Jews, and Wall Street bankers.

Al Smith openly endorsed the Republican candidate for the Presidency in 1936. In a major address to an enthusiastic New York City audience he accused Roosevelt of preparing the way for a Communist-controlled America. The feeling of displacement is painfully evident. He told a Chicago audience that Jeffersonian Democrats were "out on a limb today, holding the bag, driven out of the party, because some new bunch that nobody ever heard of in their life before came in and took charge of things and started planning everything." [86]

When Jim Farley broke with Roosevelt in 1940, the Irish conservatives became even more united in opposition. Farley had hoped to succeed Roosevelt, only in the end to be pushed aside. For the Irish conservatives the Third Term became a racial insult as well as a constitutional affront. Farley's account of those years is bitter:

What few people realize is that the relationship between Roosevelt and me had been basically political and seldom social. Strange as it may seem, the President never took me into the bosom of the family, although everyone agreed I was more responsible than any other single man for his being in the White House. Never was I invited to spend the night in the historic mansion. Only twice did I ever make a cruise on the presidential yacht. Both cruises were political. Never was I invited to join informal White House gatherings. My appearances there were for official social functions or for informal dinners followed by exploration of political and patronage problems. Mrs. Eleanor Roosevelt once said, "Franklin finds it hard to relax with people who aren't his social equals." I took this remark to explain my being out of the infield.[87]

Apart from his great talent, Farley was, after all, a man of honor and decorum in private life as in politics. He broke with Roosevelt on what he regarded as an issue of principle—only to find it interpreted as the inevitable incompatibility of landlord and tenant. He later wrote:

What particularly irked me were the background articles emphasizing my quote humble unquote beginnings. I am an American of Irish descent. I have known many people of Irish descent. Fat, thin, tall, short—loquacious, taciturn, ebullient, and morose—but never in my life have I met a "humble" one. It just doesn't run in the strain. The fact is that I have met few men of Irish descent who were not their own figurative secretaries of state. Whatever else they may lack, it isn't opinions or the willingness to fight for them. As to authenticity as Americans, while the Mayflower passenger list will be combed in vain for their names, sixteen Kelleys, seventeen Murphys, and hundreds of others of old sod ancestry have won the Congressional Medal of Honor—enough to assure even the unfairminded that the credentials of Americans of Irish descent are in order.[88]

The record would certainly support Farley's contention, but, if so, why bring it up? It was one thing to make a fuss over Irish performance in the Mexican War, when they were still new to the country and the nation for the first time faced a Catholic enemy. But a century later to carry on in the same way about, for example, the flyer Colin Kelly betrayed a curious defensiveness on the part of the Irish themselves.

Mixed with this defensiveness was a measure of aggression on the subject of Communism. The Irish revolutionary tradition contributed its portion of recruits to American radicalism. William Z. Foster, who organized the great steel strike of 1919, turned from the IWW to the Communist party, ran as the Communist candidate for President in 1924, 1928, and 1932, and then became head of the Communist party, was the son of Irish revolutionary exiles. The chairman of the Communist party in America as of 1961 was Elizabeth Gurley Flynn. But none of these counted as Irish so far as the Irish were concerned because they had ceased to be Catholic. For the mass of the Irish who stayed within the Church, the reaction to the Russian revolution was as uniform as it was intense. In June 1919 the *Catholic World* declared:

The excesses of the Bolshevik revolution are . . . not the exaggeration of otherwise worldly tendencies. They are the absolute subversion of all moral principles, the destruction of religion, and the overthrow of civilization.

The Catholic reaction was notably different from that of the New York Jews. In September, 1920, *The American Hebrew* declared that the overthrow of Russian Czarism "was largely the outcome of Jewish thinking, of Jewish discontent, of Jewish effort to reconstruct." If there had been an initial "destructive" phase to Bolshevism, this had been supplanted by a "constructive phase" which was itself "a conspicuous expression of the constructive genius of Jewish discontent." [89] In the years that followed, the gulf, if anything, widened. On the issues of recognition of the Soviet Union, the Spanish Civil War, wartime collaboration with Russia, and postwar cooperation, the New York Catholics were profoundly at odds with a significant portion of the New York Jews. The Catholics kept seeming to get the worst of it. Russia was recognized, became our wartime ally, and seemed destined to be our postwar friend. The Communist influence in New York, in politics, in education, and in the trade-union movement, was abundantly evident.

This was not an easy period for the Catholic Irish. Disdained on the left as reactionaries, they were not really welcomed by the Protestant establishment, whose interests they sought to preserve. Even today if Catholics are admitted to have been profoundly right about Russian Communism, the suspicion is widely shared among non-

Catholics that they were right for the wrong reasons. Two decades ago it was not even clear they were right.

The fact seems to be that non-Catholics did not pay very much attention to speeches of the kind in which Monsignor Fulton J. Sheen, in 1941, denounced "the colossal wastage of taxes to pay professors who would destroy America by teaching Russian Bolshevism," and went on to tell the Friendly Sons of St. Patrick:

It is not to the point to say, as some newspapers do, that only 3 per cent of the professors, and 20 per cent of the students are disloyal to their country. Why is it you will not find a single Communist teaching in Manhattan College? Why none in Fordham? Why none in St. Patrick's Parochial School?

This climaxed with the announcement that "The professors in certain universities and colleges in New York City are the most learned professors in the world—because they are the 'best red.' " [90]

This kind of anti-Communism for a long period suffered from a characteristic Irish-Catholic failing. It was felt to be enough to know and to say that Communism was morally wrong. But nothing much was offered by way of specific advice to those who struggled in the world of day-to-day events.

The crisis came in the years immediately after the Second World War when evidence began to accumulate about the true nature of the Communist conspiracy—only to have the evidence, seemingly, ignored. Alger Hiss and William Remington and the Rosenbergs seemed proof enough for anybody—but not for a good number of persons in the Protestant-Jewish intellectual elite. To many Irish Catholics these innocents seemed to grow more arrogant as their failings proved more serious. The country seemed filled with persons who, in Irving Kristol's description, "prefer to regard Whittaker Chambers and Elizabeth Bentley as pathological liars, and who believe that to plead the privilege of the Fifth Amendment is the first refuge of a scholar and a gentleman. . . ." [91] This is the context in which the New York Irish turned overwhelmingly to the support of Senator McCarthy.

A clue to the nature of McCarthy's influence on the New York Irish is that he did not bring out the worst in them. New York Communism was primarily a Jewish affair, but Irish anti-Communism in the postwar period never became anti-Semitism. Even when it looked like anti-Semitism, and Jewish groups became disturbed—42 of the 47 employees suspended or refused clearance at Fort Monmouth after the McCarthy hearings, were Jewish —this was not the Irish-Catholic reaction. At best, the Irish position at this time rested on profoundly responsible religious convictions. At its worst, Irish anti-Communism was not directed at Communism at all. From start to finish, McCarthy got his largest response from the New York Irish when he attacked the institutions of the white Anglo-Saxon Protestant establishment. It was Harvard University and the State Department and the United States Army that seemed to be subverting the country. The faculty of Franklin Delano Roosevelt's college was riddled with Reds. Dean Gooderham Acheson would not turn his back on spies in the Foreign Service. George Catlett Marshall was a front man for traitors. Eventually McCarthy's aides began proposing that the biggest threat of Communism to the nation came from the Protestant clergy, and the Senator himself intervened to put an end to the "real threat" to American security, the British blood trade with Red China. The Irish Catholics, and they had many supporters, could not believe the men running the country could be blind to the Communist threat that seemed so clear to them. There had to be a more sinister explanation. No action was too drastic to uncover it.

The Catholic hierarchy in New York left little doubt that it supported McCarthy. In 1954, despite the opposition of the Democratic city administration, the Senator was invited to address the annual communion breakfast of the Police Department Holy Name Society of the New York Diocese. He received a tumultuous reception as he explained that an educator under Communist discipline with a "captive audience" was "ten times as dangerous" as even a traitor in an atomic plant.[92] Among some liberals there was a reaction almost of terror: the Fascists had won over the police! Preparations were actually discussed for an underground opposition in the event of a coup d'état.

McCarthy let the Irish down. He ended up a stumblebum lurching about the corridors of the Senate where it had been decided he was no gentleman. This left the Irish to defend a reputation that had become, in practical terms, indefensible. Yet the Irish achieved a strong temporary advantage from the McCarthy period that may or may not prove of permanent value. In the era of security clearances, to be an Irish Catholic became *prima facie* evidence of loyalty. Harvard men were to be checked; Fordham men would do the checking. The disadvantage of this is that it put the Irish back on the force. It encouraged their tendency to be regular rather than creative.

The agitation against Communists in government produced valuable results. But once the issue of Communist subversion at home was settled, the problem remained of what to do about Communist aggression abroad. Here the Irish had little to contribute. They had so committed themselves to the issue of internal conspiracy that they seemed to have no resources left for positive thinking. They remained with the FBI while Harvard men continued to run foreign policy—with an increasingly evident assist from the sons of Lower East Side radicals. When the "twenty years of treason" came to an end and Eisenhower installed his cabinet of "nine millionaires and a plumber," the plumber (appointed Secretary of Labor) was the Irish Catholic. Apart from a few persons such as Thomas B. Murray of the Atomic Energy Commission, the principal area of foreign affairs in which Irish Catholics have so far played a creative anti-Communist role has been in the international labor movement under the leadership of an Irish plumber from the Bronx, George Meany of the AFL-CIO, and even here the influence of the State Department and Jewish intellectuals has been much in evidence.

During the New Deal and, later, the McCarthy period, a great many New York Irish began voting Republican. Certainly a majority voted for Eisenhower. They were easily convinced that Stevenson was soft on Communism. It was Farley who said that "to send Governor

Stevenson to negotiate with Mr. Khrushchev is to send the cabbage patch to the goat." [93]

The crisis for the conservative Irish came in 1960, when, for the second time, an Irish Catholic ran for President. It turned out that for many the estrangement from the Democratic party had gone too deep to be overcome by more primitive appeals. Alfred E. Smith, Jr., announced he was voting for Nixon. In fashionable Greenwich, Connecticut, the grandson of John H. McCooey of Brooklyn turned up ringing doorbells for the straight Republican ticket. Kennedy probably got little more than a bare majority of the Irish vote in New York City. The students at Fordham gave him as much, but it appears it was the Jewish students in the College of Pharmacy who saved that ancient Jesuit institution from going on record as opposed to the election of the first Catholic President of the United States.

For some time a considerable number of New York Irish have been enrolling as well as voting Republican, but they have not made much progress in the Republican party organization. Reversing earlier roles, the Jews and Italians are keeping the Irish out of things. Barely an eighth of the New York delegation to the 1960 Republican convention was Irish.

Contrary to appearances, within the New York Democratic party, Irish fortunes probably took a turn for the better during the cataclysmic events of the 1961 mayoralty primary and election campaigns. The estrangement between the Irish organization leaders and the growing Jewish and Protestant liberal middle class, which intensified during the McCarthy period, became open warfare after Stevenson's defeat in 1952, which turned the attention of the latter group to local politics. Manhattan erupted in a series of Democratic primary fights in which the liberals set out to unseat the old guard Irish incumbents.

One by one the Irish district leaders were defeated. When this process had about run its course, the reformers turned on the leader of Tammany itself, Carmine DeSapio, accusing him of being a boss, which was of course his proper function in the traditional system. The Tammany leader's position was, as always, ideologically indefensible. Unfortunately for DeSapio, it was also ecologically untenable: middle-class voters were pouring into his district and had begun to operate within the regular party system. Forced to choose between increasingly hostile forces, Mayor Robert F. Wagner came down on the side of the reformers, whereupon DeSapio in the classic manner set out to deny him renomination. As agreed by all involved, the essential power of the Democratic party organization was not to elect its candidates, but to choose them. Historically, no one could get the Democratic nomination without the support of the organization. The issue was of such central importance that the Irish county leaders of Brooklyn and the Bronx, along with the lesser figures in Queens and Richmond, joined DeSapio in a solid organization front.

Except for the Negro areas of the city, the primary contest that followed was bitter and pitiless in contrasting the appeals of the traditional, neighborhood-oriented party organization with the modern, mass-media-oriented, liberal establishment. "If Wagner wins," said one party leader, "you can close down every clubhouse in the city." Wagner won overwhelmingly.

It may be that the Wagner victory put an end to the Irish political system itself in New York, just as La Guardia in the 1930's had broken the hold of the Irish on the system. Wagner's victory was a triumph of middle- and upper-class political initiative, organization, and leadership over the traditional, conservative, working-class party. It was uniquely a victory of public opinion experts, communication specialists, and theoreticians allied with a haute bourgeoisie whose liberalism and genuine concern for the poor of the city were nonetheless combined with something very like old-fashioned Tory will-to-power. Tammany disciplined the masses and enabled them to rule. With that discipline broken, it is likely New York will revert to the normal municipal condition of rule by the centers of economic power in alliance with the communications media. Organized crime is likely to persist as one such center and may even grow more important. There are indications that the powerful political machines of the Tammany variety were the one social force capable of controlling organized crime —certainly the decline of Tammany was accompanied by the rise of Costello and the like—and it may well be that the future will see the liberal middle class and the criminal syndicates sharing power in a pattern that was already to be perceived during La Guardia's ascendancy.

If this should happen, the Irish have a role to play, for they have in significant numbers joined the middle and upper classes. A number of new Irish faces appeared in the ranks of the reformers, indistinguishable in most respects from their Jewish and Protestant counterparts, and helped perhaps by a tradition of being "politicians." Sharing the honors of primary day with Robert F. Wagner of Yale was James S. Lanigan of Harvard, who defeated DeSapio for district leader in Greenwich Village. The Irish liberals lack, for the moment at least, an ethnic constituency, but they are not less sensitive to the changed style of politics. "The old-line political club," said one reformer, "is concerned with individuals, getting a job for this one or doing a favor for that one. In our modern society, politicians have to deal with the problems of whole groups of people, and we reformers are concerned more with groups than with individuals." This was said by Peter P. Meagher, running for district leader on the West Side of Manhattan against the son of The McManus.

CITY OF GOD AND MAN

THE FUTURE OF THE IRISH IN NEW YORK POLITICS WILL BE profoundly affected by events within the Catholic Church, which is, and for a generation at the very least, will remain, essentially an Irish Catholic Church. If New York, like Washington or Paris, had no great cathedral on a main thoroughfare, it is not likely that 120,000 marchers and more would turn out on St. Patrick's Day. The great parade is no longer an *Irish* affair; it is even questionable whether a majority of the marchers are, in fact, Irish. The parade is rather an annual display of the size of the New York Catholic Church, whose priests and hierarchy on the whole are quite conscious of their Irish origins. The center of interest on the line of march is not the reviewing stand at 66th Street so much as the steps of St. Patrick's Cathedral, where Cardinal Spellman accepts the homage of his flock. This Catholic Church is now entering a new phase both for the clerics and the laity. Two items will evoke the period that is passing.

Some time prior to the 1928 campaign the *Atlantic Monthly* published a statement by an Episcopalian layman directed to Al Smith which, citing papal encyclicals and canon law, challenged the compatibility of Smith's religion with his loyalty to the United States Constitution. It was clear to Smith's advisers, who gathered to discuss it, that the Governor would have to answer this challenge, but Smith himself was most reluctant. Hurt and dismayed, he said to Judge Joseph M. Proskauer (as reported by his daughter):

Joe, . . . to tell you the truth . . . I don't know what the words mean. I've been a Catholic all my life—a devout Catholic, I believe—and I never heard of these encyclicals and papal bulls and books that he writes about. They have nothing to do with being a Catholic, and I just don't know how to answer such a thing.[94]

According to Reinhold Niebuhr's version of the meeting, which may be more accurate in spirit, Smith simply entered the room and asked all present, "Will someone tell me what the hell a Papal Encyclical is?" [95]

On the clerical side, a Catholic sociologist recently looked into Cardinal Cushing's remarks about the social origins of the parents of American Catholic hierarchy. He found the Cardinal was substantially correct about the absence of college graduates, but not so much in his impression that the American Bishops are the sons of working men and working men's wives. Only 5 per cent of the fathers of some 133 prelates studied in 1957 had graduated from college, and 65 per cent had not even gone to high school. But only 17 per cent of these men remained unskilled laborers. The largest single group, 27 per cent, became the owners of small businesses. Over half were either small businessmen, clerks, salesmen, foremen, or minor executives.[96]

All this is passing. It is hard to conceive an American Catholic of the future becoming a candidate for President of the United States without having acquired a fairly sophisticated understanding of Catholic dogma on the subject of relations of church to state. Nor is it likely that henceforth the prelates of the American Church will be drawn so preponderately from the lower-middle class. But the one social characteristic of the present New York Church which does not seem likely to change during the next generation is its Irishness. Of the eighteen bishops in the New York area, in 1961, one was Chinese, one was Italian, and the rest were Irish.[97] And in contrast to the police academy and the legislature, in the seminaries the Irish are holding their own.

The Catholic Church in New York during the remainder of this century will be characterized by an increasingly articulate and inquiring laity, ministered to by a steadily more sophisticated, predominantly Irish clergy. But the role of the Church in the life of the city is as yet uncertain. It will be determined by two sets of events: first, the course of Catholic education and intellectual life; second, the attitude of the Church toward social change.

There is nothing in the history of organized religion comparable with the effort of the American Catholic Church to maintain a complete, comprehensive educational system ranging from the most elementary tutelage to the most advanced disciplines. The effort absorbs so much of the energies and resources of the faithful as to prompt the remark of a New York Jesuit that a Catholic diocese is a school system here and there associated with a church. Lately, however, the strain on resources has become all but intolerable while serious misgivings have arisen as to the value of the end product.

Encouraged by the growing proportion of educated Catholics and much stimulated by the renaissance of Catholic thought in Europe, American Catholic intellectual life is going through, in the words of one nun, "an orgy of self-criticism." [98] (Fortunately, as Reverend Gustav Weigel, S.J., writes, "non-Catholics have politely and wisely kept out of the debate.")[99] The most widely discussed statement of the issue appeared in 1955 in the Fordham quarterly *Thought*. It was written by Monsignor John Tracy Ellis.[100] Msgr. Ellis began with Denis Brogan's statement that . . . "In no Western society is the intellectual prestige of Catholicism lower than in the country where, in such respects as wealth, numbers, and strength of organization, it is so powerful." [101] "No well informed Catholic," said Monsignor Ellis, "will attempt to challenge that statement." He listed as causes: First, the deep anti-Catholic bias inherited from seventeenth-century England, which has discouraged Catholic intellectuals and fostered "an overeagerness in Catholic circles for apologetics rather than pure scholarship." Second, the fierce problem of settling the immigrants which has preoccupied the Church until this generation. Third, the native American anti-intellectualism: "In that —as in so many other ways—the Catholics are, and have been thoroughly American. . . ." With no encouragement at home, and no well-established intellectual tradition to draw on from Ireland and Germany abroad, the American seminaries became unintellectual, and so also their products. Even the revival of scholastic philosophy was the work of non-Catholic institutions such as the University of Chicago.

Monsignor Ellis was particularly concerned with the studies that showed the abysmal performance of Catholics and Catholic institutions in scientific work. Two years earlier, Reverend Joseph P. Fitzpatrick, S.J., of Fordham, in the presidential address of the American Catholic Sociological Society, had said, on the same subject, "If this is true for the physical sciences, I would not hesitate to assert that it is more true of the social sciences." He suggested this was more than simply a matter of pedagogy; it had to do with the Catholic mind in a much wider sense:

. . . there is one state of mind, fairly common, that is confident in the possession of the ultimate answers to life's mysteries and does not see the need of seeking anxiously for the proximate answers also. There is another state of mind, also common enough, which is convinced that God saved the world without science; therefore prayer, sacrament and sacrifice are the things to be concerned about.[102]

Father Weigel has put the matter even more succinctly. In a paper presented to the Catholic Commission on Intellectual and Cultural Affairs, the group that has stimulated much of this discussion, he declared: "The postulate of all scholarly investigation is the nagging existence of mystery. The training of not a few young Catholics makes them believe that there is no mystery." [103] While at Fordham, Thomas F. O'Dea spoke out severely on the matter of the Catholic preoccupation with apologetics:

The great Protestant and secular thinkers of America are not just men who made mistakes, like the "adversaries" of the scholastic manual. They have positive things to say to those American Catholics who have neglected the search itself. The partial segregation of Catholic life from that of the general community adds difficulties in that respect, but further defensiveness concealed under lethargic self-satisfaction is hardly an adequate response to the situation. We repeat: to be an intellectual means to be engaged in a quest, and if to be a Christian has come to mean to have the whole truth that matters—albeit in capsule form—in advance (to know, for example, that "Plato had an erroneous theory of human nature," that "Comte held God knows what, which is absurd") without ever having been introduced to a genuine philosophical experience, then we are hopelessly lost.[104]

To be sure, not every professor at Fordham holds this view, but the proposition fits the observed facts. Apart from a spate of half-apologetic articles on "Great Catholic Intellectuals" there has been surprisingly little dissent. On the other hand, this is an argument that disproves itself: the act of asserting the lack of Catholic intellectual standards is the first step of establishing them. The Catholic world is in fact astir with intellectual aspiration that carries with it the possibility of great achievement.

It is possible, even likely, that such a development will come quickly. Over the past half century there has been no lack of artists and intellectuals born and raised in Catholic, especially Irish-Catholic, environments, but the greater part of them have rejected this environment as one hostile to their aspirations to scholarly or aesthetic excellence. If this atmosphere were to change, as it is now changing, it is possible to envision an almost sudden emergence of a Catholic intellectual class, encouraged by the Church and sustained by the increasing relevance of religious doctrine to the intellectual concerns of the present age.

Whether this happens will depend largely on the quality of the education Catholics receive in the coming generation. The criticism of Catholic intellectual standards inevitably involved the quality of Catholic elementary and secondary schools as well as the colleges and universities. Despite evidence that parochial schools get a good quality student, the end results have simply not been good enough. Moreover, evidence exists that some of the better Catholic students have been avoiding competition in the tougher non-Catholic schools, with a resulting isolation that feeds on itself. In a study of New York City high school students who applied for state scholarships, it was found that while 34 per cent of the Jews and 28 per cent of the Protestants in the group were seeking admission to Ivy League schools, only 8 per cent of the Catholics had submitted similar applications.[105] Without question, Catholic education came to a moment of crisis by the early 1960's.

There are three elements to this crisis. First, the Catholics have a large and rapidly growing population. Second, it is the teaching of the Church and the wish of most of the laity that Catholic children should be educated in Catholic schools. Third, if this education is to meet their rising intellectual and social requirements, the already crushing cost will grow much greater; this leads to an increasingly adamant demand that in one form or another there be an end to the double taxation of the Catholic population for the cost of education.

The best available estimate of religious backgrounds in New York City identifies 48.6 per cent of the total population in 1952 as Roman Catholic. Only 27.1 per cent of the population was actually affiliated with a Catholic Church—but this figure, according to Leland Gartrell, the author of the study, would account for more than half the persons with religious affiliation in the city (some 50 per cent having no affiliation).[106] It is unquestionably a growing group. Dr. Ronald A. Barrett, a Catholic sociologist, has recently shown that in the 1950–1959 decade American Catholic population increased twice as fast as the general population, accounting for 41.1 per cent of the total United States population growth during that period.[107]

The cost of the Catholic school system in New York City is by any standards staggering. In 1960 in the dioceses of Brooklyn and New York (excluding those parts outside the city) there were some 360,000 students in Catholic elementary and secondary schools. This was 37 per cent of the enrollment of the public schools: a proportion hardly changed from the days of Bishop Hughes. On top of this the dioceses maintain eighteen colleges and universities, with some 30,000 students. The operating expenses of the city public schools came to $650,000,000 in 1960, on top of which was the cost of the city colleges. The Catholic population of the city, barely a median income group, pay their share of the taxes that support the public schools in addition to the full cost of the Catholic education system.

The Catholics manage this by sacrifice and by what appears to be a high level of managerial efficiency. (The cost per pupil of Catholic elementary schools in New York is not one-third that of the public schools.) But there is a limit to such possibilities, and when that limit is reached, as it almost surely has been in some respects, the disparity in costs creates a difference in quality as well. In a period of rising intellectual expectations, this fact has led inevitably to active dissatisfaction with the existing arrangement under which Catholic schools are denied all but marginal public assistance.

Ironically, the crisis was precipitated by the election of President John F. Kennedy, which created a serious possibility that a program of federal aid to education would be enacted. For the President there was no apparent constitutional or political way to include aid to Catholic elementary or secondary schools in his program. But the New York Catholic Church, having been left out at the beginning of the era of state aid in the 1840's, was determined not to be excluded from the era of federal aid which seemed about to begin. Cardinal Spellman did not even wait for the new President to be inaugurated before denouncing in the strongest terms a proposal for federal aid prepared by advisers to the President-Elect, and later adopted by him. ". . . It is unthinkable," said His Eminence, "that any American child be denied the federal funds allotted to other children which are necessary for his mental development because his parents choose for him God-centered education." [108] Months later the vote of Democratic Congressman James J. Delaney of Queens killed the administration proposal in the House Rules Committee. Thereafter a stalemate ensucd, with the Cardinal becoming if anything more adamant. In 1962, at the 18th annual Archdiocesan Teachers Institute, he declared that it would be a "terrible crime" to exclude parents, children, and supporters of Catholic schools from the benefits of help from the national government. To do so, he said, would mean the "eventual end" of parochial schools: "we cannot compete with the federal government support and subsidy of the public schools alone." [109]

In the early 1960's elements of the New York Catholic Church seemed to be entering electoral politics for the second time in its history—but on the same issue. A series of Democratic congressional primary contests occurred in which the school aid issue was raised by militant Catholic groups. The New York State Federation of Citizens for Educational Freedom, a nonsectarian group but overwhelmingly Catholic, began endorsing candidates for office. In the 1962 elections this organization came out strongly for the Republican candidate for Governor and the Democratic candidate for United States Senator.[110]

The prospects for the Church are at best doubtful. The basic problem is that Catholics have failed to persuade any significant number of non-Catholic opinion leaders of the justice of their case. The history of the 1840's has vanished for Catholic and non-Catholic alike. In New York Catholic spokesmen have not yet been able to couch the issue in terms that have appeal, even perhaps meaning, for many Jewish or Protestant leaders, nor have they succeeded in providing Catholics in public and party office with any very coherent understanding of the problem. This is itself a measure of Catholic isolation from the liberal, secular tradition of the city that is epitomized by the *New York Times,* but this isolation is breaking down. At the same time Catholics appear to be making some progress with their case among the public generally, and increasingly opinion leaders such as Walter Lippmann have been concluding that the national deadlock over federal aid to education can be broken only by including Catholic schools.

If an accommodation is reached on the school issue, there is likely to be some diminishment of

Catholic defensiveness of the kind that led Heywood Broun to call the New York Irish "the cry babies of the Western world." This defensiveness takes the most painful and destructive forms, as in the continuing controversy over discrimination against Catholic scholars at Queens College.

Catholic defensiveness can be particularly destructive on the issue of Communist subversion and American loyalty. New York Catholics have been prone to think they have learned something when the leader of Tammany Hall informs a communion breakfast of the Sanitation Department Holy Name Society that "there is no Mother's Day behind the Iron Curtain." [111] When a number of the leading universities of the nation announced their opposition to the loyalty oath provisions of the National Defense Education Act of 1958 all over the country, as one disgusted Catholic scientist put it, "Catholic newspapers . . . proudly displayed front-page stories in which they told how Catholic students in Catholic colleges virtually demanded loyalty oaths. . . ." [112] This is at best a curious posture for members of a church whose principal effort in American society is to limit the role of the state in education.

The announcement in 1961 by the head of the John Birch Society that half his membership was Catholic—whether true or not—caused a stir in Catholic circles, as did in general the rise of the radical right in the post-Eisenhower period. Elements within the Church appeared to realize how uncritical and remote from reality large sections of lay opinion had become. There followed a series of lucid and eloquent statements denouncing extremist organizations and expounding the bases of effective anti-Communism, but whether the minds of those concerned had been conditioned beyond the reach of appeals to reason remained to be seen.

The excesses of Catholic militancy are producing a reaction among the laity as well. There is a suggestion of anticlericalism in the New York air. A student writer for *The Fordham Ram* recently devoted his column to ridiculing the Brooklyn *Tablet,* the official weekly of the Brooklyn Diocese, with this description of a typical issue:

Well then you come to the editorial page and look at the cartoon. Usually you got some guy in a dark suit with 'Out-

sider' written on him. Then there's a mountain with a building on it, and there's light coming out from behind it. This
is generally a church or Truth or something. Then you got
a rowboat between the man and the building, and it's
marked 'Penance' or 'Hard Work' or something and the
oars have 'Guidance' written on them. Well all this is too
deep for me. I like straight from the shoulder talk. None of
this symbolism.

. . . .

I look at the letters section and see that people who write
in are all against something. Generally it's Queens College.
Once in a while a college kid complains about the 'Tablet's'
editorials or point of view. And they pull him apart like a
broken accordion. Usually the poor sap says, 'How can an
adult newspaper be so stupid?' Well they never answer his
question, but they knock him because he spelled a word
wrong or mentioned Shakespeare or somebody.[113]

Although New York has for long been a
center of clerical conservatism in the Catholic Church, it is
also a center of Catholic intellecual activity that tends to
"liberal" views in about the same proportion and along the
same lines as intellectual opinion generally. The isolation
of the Catholic community is rapidly breaking down as the
great issues of the 1930's and 1940's recede. The passing of
the Franco regime in Spain, already an object of strong
criticism by the Spanish Catholic Church, will remove a
time-honored source of misunderstanding, bitterness, and
bona fide hostility. The expulsion of Communism from the
power centers of American life has been acknowledged in
most Catholic circles, while the appearance of Communism
in Latin America must give Catholics pause in their assumptions about the process of Marxist subversion: no Protestant country has yet gone Communist. Increasingly, the
prospect is that the various elements of Catholic opinion—
liberal, conservative, radical—will merge with corresponding elements in non-Catholic groups, at one and the same
time expanding the area of Catholic influence while diminishing the influence of the Catholic bloc.

The strong likelihood, therefore, is that the
future will see Catholic opinion become increasingly varie-
gated, reflecting the widely divergent views of a community

that spans a broad social and ethnic spectrum. The development of Catholic social policy will almost certainly strengthen and hasten this process.

In 1962, some seven years after his widely read assessment of Catholic intellectual life, Monsignor John Tracy Ellis turned his attention to a potentially more dangerous situation: that the emergence of an intellectually trained and vigorous Catholic laity would bring with it "the curse of anti-clericalism." Already there was to be encountered "severe criticism of bishops and priests among the intellectuals and professional people."

This represented, of course, an almost entirely new situation for the American Catholic Church, reflecting the increased numbers of highly educated Catholics, but also the increasing intellectual stature of the Church itself. Whereas in the past a disgruntled Catholic intellectual, in Protestant-secular America, at a certain point would simply leave the Church, there now emerged the possibility of remaining Catholic but becoming an anticlerical!

Monsignor Ellis spoke with great feeling of the only solution he could envisage:

. . . the laymen must be freed to speak and to act without hindrance on the vital problems that press for solution outside the realm of doctrine. If they are not given such freedom the superior training and education of which they are the recipients in rapidly mounting numbers will have been —insofar as the Church is concerned—largely wasted, and the Church itself will be exposed to the very real threat of having the laymen's repressed zeal and frustrated ambitions for the Mystical Body turned into a disillusionment and embitterment that will breed in our land the kind of spirit that has poisoned the relations of clergy and laity in so much of western Europe and in Latin America.[114]

The prospects for dissension within the Catholic community are strongest in the area of social policy, although here the structure most likely will be that of liberal clergy *and* laity alike combining in opposition to their conservative counterparts. Since the time of *Rerum Novarum* (1891) Catholic social doctrine has been opposed to many of the most cherished economic doctrines of American conservatism. However, this fact has, as it were, only gradually emerged. (It may be speculated that semantics is in part to blame: Catholic spokesmen have used the term "liberal" to refer to *laissez-faire* economics of the Manchester school, and have generously denounced same. However, Catholic and non-Catholic audiences alike would seem generally to have understood the term in its contemporary American reference to essentially non-*laissez-faire* views.) With the promulgation of the papal encyclical *Quadragesimo Anno* (1931), and more drastically, with *Mater et Magistra,* the American Catholic Church found itself committed to a systematic social doctrine that was almost certainly far to the left of the social thinking of most American Catholics, clergy and laity alike.

       Mater et Magistra came as a distinct surprise to many. Reinhold Niebuhr, in a perhaps patronizing but authentic tone, noted in an editorial in *Christianity and Crisis* that the reaction of non-Catholics, secular and Protestant, had "been generally one of amazement that a church which they considered 'reactionary' should come out so clearly for such modern 'liberal' policies as social insurance, the whole philosophy of the 'welfare state' and aid to underdeveloped countries." The reaction of some conservative Catholics was disbelief bordering perilously (for a Catholic) on irreverence, as in the celebrated gibe "Mater sì, Magistra no" which appeared in the conservative *National Review.* The first reaction to the later encyclical of John XXIII, *Pacem in Terris,* was even more unusual. *The Commonweal* described the general attitude as follows: "Of all of the responses that Pope John's encyclical, *Pacem in Terris,* could have been expected to arouse, perhaps none has been more startling than the general paralysis which has gripped American Catholics in the face of its implicit 'opening to the left.' For once it seems impossible to find any significant support for an important part of a major encyclical."

       It is almost inevitable that American Catholicism will face a crisis of commitment as a result of the social doctrine set forth by Pope John XXIII. American Catholics, notably in areas such as New York, have not much thought of their religious obligations in terms of social action. A 1959 study of a Bronx parish, for example, found parishioners regarded the roles of Civic Leader, Social

Leader, Recreational Leader, and Reformer to be the least important functions of a priest. The role of Administrator, for one, ranked well ahead.[115] More seriously, even were the Catholic community to commit itself fully to the social objectives of Catholic doctrine, the question remains as to how successful would be the outcome.

The function of Catholic education has been primarily pastoral (or has been widely regarded as such). Educators such as Professor John J. O'Brien have presented the thesis "that the present *social* result of past American Catholic decisions in the field of education has been to establish a system of schools which have, . . . tended to encourage the development in their students of certain qualities which render them more or less ineffective in any effort to reconstruct American society along lines consonant with Catholic principles." He described these qualities as "negativism, a faulty operational perception of the order of virtues, provincialism, and a certain moral-intellectual arrogance." [116] Strong meat, but hardly to be avoided in a conservative communion suddenly confronted with a radical and not particularly congenial mission. What is here reflected, of course, is not simply the difficulties which Catholics must face, but also the sense of urgency and purpose which such a mission can arouse. Clearly, such conflict can produce much good as well as much anguish.

Although the bulk of Catholic intellectuals will almost certainly associate themselves with the main body of American liberal opinion, Catholics are likely to have their most significant impact on conservative thought. American conservatism has for a century been notably inarticulate. Whatever Catholic doctrine might be, the generation of Irish Catholics now being educated has been steeped in conservative social feeling both at home and in their formal education. This sets them apart from any large group in America outside the South, save possibly the less numerous German Catholics. If the education of these Catholics is good enough, they will have the opportunity to create a sustained and comprehensive body of conservative opinion in the United States based on the Catholic doctrine of the rights and responsibilities of the individual, the limitations on the power of the state, and the transcendent purpose of the social order, combined with a scholastic respect for intellect.

Had John Fitzgerald Kennedy lived out his time he might profoundly have altered the course of the Irish-American world. Among his incomparable powers was an ability to bring together the sacred and profane streams of American public life that have somehow, for example, made foreign affairs genteel but domestic politics coarse. Out of such a consummation might have emerged a new American style, combining as did he himself the tribal vigor of ward politics with the deft perceptions of the chancelleries.

But he is gone, and there is none like him. Although he may yet emerge as the first of a new breed, all that is certain is that he was the last of an old one. The era of the Irish politician culminated in Kennedy. He was born to the work and was at every stage in his life a "pro." He rose on the willing backs of three generations of district leaders and county chairmen who, like the Good Thief, may in the end have been saved for their one moment of recognition that something special had appeared among them. That moment was in 1960 when the Irish party chieftains of the great Eastern and Midwestern cities, for reasons they could probably even now not fully explain, came together to nominate for President the grandson of Honey Fitz.

It was the last hurrah. He, the youngest and newest, served in a final moment of ascendancy. On the day he died, the President of the United States, the Speaker of the House of Representatives, the Majority Leader of the United States Senate, the Chairman of the National Committee were all Irish, all Catholic, all Democrats. It will not come again.

Beyond
the Melting Pot

THE idea of the melting pot is as old as the Republic. "I could point out to you a family," wrote the naturalized New Yorker, M-G. Jean de Crèvecoeur, in 1782, "whose grandfather was an Englishman, whose wife was Dutch, whose son married a French woman, and whose present four sons have now four wives of different nations. *He* is an American, who leaving behind him all his ancient prejudices and manners, receives new ones from the new mode of life he has embraced. . . . Here individuals of all nations are melted into a new race of men. . . ." [1] It was an idea close to the heart of the American self-image. But as a century passed, and the number of individuals and nations involved grew, the confidence that they could be fused together waned, and so also the conviction that it would be a good thing if they were to be. In 1882 the Chinese were excluded, and the first general immigration law was enacted. In a steady succession thereafter, new and more selective barriers were raised until, by the National Origins Act of 1924, the nation formally adopted the policy of using immigration to reinforce, rather than further to dilute, the racial stock of the early America.

This latter process was well underway, had become in ways inexorable, when Israel Zangwill's play *The Melting Pot* was first performed in 1908. The play (quite a bad one) was an instant success. It ran for months on Broadway; its title was seized upon as a concise evocation of a profoundly significant American fact.

Behold David Quixano, the Russian Jewish immigrant—a "pogrom orphan"—escaped to New York City, exulting in the glory of his new country:

. . . America is God's Crucible, the great Melting Pot where all the races of Europe are melting and reforming! Here you stand, good folk, think I, when I see them at Ellis Island, here you stand in your fifty groups with your fifty languages and histories, and your fifty blood hatreds and rivalries, but you won't be long like that brothers, for these are the fires of God you've come to—these are the fires of God. A fig for your feuds and vendettas! German and Frenchman, Irishman and Englishman, Jews and Russians—into the Crucible with you all! God is making the American.

. . . .

. . . The real American has not yet arrived. He is only in the Crucible, I tell you—he will be the fusion of all the races, the coming superman.[2]

Yet looking back, it is possible to speculate that the response to *The Melting Pot* was as much one of relief as of affirmation: more a matter of reassurance that what had already taken place would turn out all right, rather than encouragement to carry on in the same direction.

Zangwill's hero throws himself into the amalgam process with the utmost energy; by curtainfall he has written his American symphony and won his Muscovite aristocrat: almost all concerned have been reconciled to the homogeneous future. Yet the play seems but little involved with American reality. It is a drama about Jewish separatism and Russian anti-Semitism, with a German concertmaster and an Irish maid thrown in for comic relief. Both protagonists are New Model Europeans of the time. Free thinkers and revolutionaries, it was doubtless in the power of such to merge. But neither of these doctrines was dominant among the ethnic groups of New York City in the 1900's, and in significant ways this became less so as time passed. Individuals, in very considerable numbers to be sure, broke out of their mold, but the groups remained. The experience of Zangwill's hero and heroine was *not* general. The point about the melting pot is that it did not happen.

Significantly, Zangwill was himself much involved in one of the more significant deterrents to the melting pot process. He was a Zionist. He gave more and more of his energy to this cause as time passed, and retreated from his earlier position on racial and religious mixture. Only eight years after the opening of *The Melting Pot* he was writing "It was vain for Paul to declare that there should be neither Jew nor Greek. Nature will return even if driven out with a pitchfork, still more if driven out with a dogma." [3]

We may argue whether it was "nature" that returned to frustrate continually the imminent creation of a single American nationality. The fact is that in every generation, throughout the history of the American republic, the merging of the varying streams of population differentiated from one another by origin, religion, outlook has seemed to lie just ahead—a generation, perhaps, in the future. This continual deferral of the final smelting of the different ingredients (or at least the different white ingredients) into a seamless national web as is to be found in the major national states of Europe suggests that we must search for some systematic and general causes for this American pattern of subnationalities; that it is not the temporary upsetting inflow of new and unassimilated immigrants that creates a pattern of ethnic groups within the nation, but rather some central tendency in the national ethos which structures people, whether those coming in afresh or the descendants of those who have been here for generations, into groups of different status and character.

It is striking that in 1963, almost forty years after mass immigration from Europe to this country ended, the ethnic pattern is still so strong in New York City. It is true we can point to specific causes that have served to maintain the pattern. But we know that it was not created by the great new migrations of Southern Negroes and Puerto Ricans into the city; nor by the "new" immigration, which added the great communities of East European Jews and Italians to the city; it was not even created by the great migration of Irish and Germans in the 1840's. Even in the 1830's, while the migration from Europe was still mild, and still consisted for the most part of English-speaking groups, one still finds in the politics of New York State, and of the city, the strong impress of group differentiation. In a fascinating study of the politics of the Jacksonian period in New York State, Lee Benson concludes: "At least since the 1820's, when manhood suffrage became widespread, ethnic and religious differences have tended to be *relatively* the most widespread sources of political differences." [4]

There were ways of making distinctions among Welshmen and Englishmen, Yorkers and New Englanders, long before people speaking strange tongues and practicing strange religions came upon the scene. The group-forming characteristics of American social life—more concretely, the general expectation among those of new and old groups that group membership is significant and formative for opinion and behavior—are as old as the city. The tendency is fixed deep in American life generally; the specific pattern of ethnic differentiation, however, in every generation is created by specific events.

We can distinguish four major events or processes that have structured this pattern in New York during the past generation and whose effects will remain to maintain this pattern for some time to come—to be replaced by others we can scarcely now discern. These four formative events are the following:

First, the shaping of the Jewish community under the impact of the Nazi persecution of the Jews in Europe and the establishment of the state of Israel; second, the parallel, if less marked, shaping of a Catholic community by the reemergence of the Catholic school controversy; third, the migration of Southern Negroes to New York following World War I and continuing through the fifties; fourth, the influx of Puerto Ricans during the fifteen years following World War II.

THE JEWS

DEVELOPMENTS WITHIN THE JEWISH COMMUNITY HAVE HAD the most immediate significance. A fourth of the city is Jewish; very much more than a fourth of its wealth, energy, talent, and style is derived from the Jews. Over the past thirty years this community has undergone profound emotional experiences, centered almost entirely on the fact of Jewishness, has been measurably strengthened by immigration, and has become involved in vast Zionist enterprises, the rationale of which is exclusively Jewish. There are two aspects of these developments as they affect melting pot tendencies, one negative, the other positive.

The negative aspect has prevented a change that might otherwise have occurred. Prior to the 1930's Jews contributed significantly to the ethnic pattern of New York politics by virtue of their radicalism. This kept them apart from the Catholic establishment in the Democratic party and the Protestant regime within the Republican party but did give them a distinct role of their own. At the time of *The Melting Pot* there were, to be sure, a great many Democratic and Republican Jewish merchants and businessmen. Most East Side Jews probably voted the Tammany ticket. But indigenous Jewish politics, the politics of the *Jewish Daily Forward,* of the Workmen's Circle, and the needle-trades unions were predominantly socialist. The Russian Revolution, in which Russian Jews played a prominent role, had a strong attraction for a small but important number of their kinsmen in New York. It would appear, for example, that during the 1930's most Communist party members in New York City were Jewish.[5] It must be stressed that the vast majority of New York Jews had nothing whatever to do with Communism. Some of the strongest centers of anti-Communist activity were and are to be found within the New York Jewish community. Nonetheless there was an ethnic cast to this form of political radicalism in New York, as there had been to the earlier Socialist movement.

Both Socialism and Communism are now considerably diminished and both have lost almost entirely any ethnic base. But just at the moment when the last distinctly Jewish political activity might have disappeared, a transcendent Jewish political interest was created by the ghastly persecutions of the Nazis, the vast dislocations of World War II, and the establishment of the State of Israel. These were matters that no Jew or Christian could ignore. They were equally matters about which little could be done except through politics. From the beginnings of the Zionist movement a certain number of New York Jews have been involved on that account with the high politics of the nation. Since the mid-1930's, however, this involvement has reached deeper and deeper into the New York Jewish community. They are the one group in the city (apart from the white Protestant financial establishment) of which it may fairly be said that among the leadership echelons there is a lively, active, and effective interest in who will be the next U.S. Secretary of State but one . . . or two, or three.

In a positive sense, events of the Nazi era and its aftermath have produced an intense group consciousness among New York Jews that binds together persons of widely disparate situations and beliefs. A pronounced religious revival has occurred. Among those without formal religious ties there is a heightened sense of the defensive importance of organized Jewish activity. Among intellectuals, the feeling of Jewishness is never far from the surface.

Now, as in the past, the Jewish community in New York is the one most actively committed to the principles of racial integration and group tolerance. But open housing is something different from the melting pot. There is no reason to think that any considerable portion of the Jewish community of New York ever subscribed to Israel Zangwill's vision of a nonreligious, intermarried, homogeneous population, but it surely does not do so today. To the contrary, much of the visible activity of the community is aimed in directions that will intensify Jewish identity: Jewish elementary and secondary schools, Jewish colleges and universities, Jewish periodicals, Jewish investments in Israel, and the like. In the meantime, Jewish politicians make more (or at least not less) of the "Jewish" vote.

This is not to say the Jewish community of New York has been *created* or *maintained* by these events of the thirties or forties: that would be too narrow a view of Jewish history, and would ignore the group-making characteristics of American civilization. But the Jewish community was *shaped* by these events. Moving rapidly from working-class to middle-class occupations and styles of life, many alternative courses of development were possible. Within the frame set by these large social movements, the historical drama shaped a community intensely conscious of its Jewishness. Religion plays in many ways the smallest part of the story of American Jews. In New York City in particular the religious definition of the group explains least. Here the formal religious groups are weakest, the degree of affiliation to synagogues and temples smallest. In a city with 2,000,000 Jews, Jews need make no excuses to explain Jewishness and Jewish interests. On the one hand, there is the social and economic structure of the community; on the other, ideologies and emotions molded by the specific history of recent decades. Together they have shaped a community that itself shapes New York and will for generations to come.[6]

THE CATHOLICS

OUTWARDLY, EVENTS SINCE WORLD WAR I HAVE BROUGHT Catholics, notably the Irish Catholics, ever closer to the centers of power and doctrine in American life. But following a pattern common in human affairs, the process of closing the gap has heightened resentment, among some at all events, that a gap should exist. Here, as in much else concerning this general subject, it is hardly possible to isolate New York events from those of the nation generally, but because New York tends to be the center of Catholic thinking and publishing, the distinction is not crucial. The great division between the Catholic Church and the leftist and liberal groups in the city during the period from the Spanish

Civil War to the era of McCarthy has been narrowed, with most elements of city politics converging on center positions. However issues of church-state relations have become considerably more difficult, and the issue of government aid to Catholic schools has become acute.

Controversy over church-state relations is nothing new to the American Catholic Church. What is new, however, and what is increasingly avowed, is the extent to which the current controversy derives from Catholic-Jewish disagreements rather than from traditional Catholic-Protestant differences. Relations between the two latter groups have steadily improved: to the point that after three centuries of separation Catholics in the 1960's began increasingly to talk of the prospects of reestablishing Christian unity. In general (there are, of course, many individual exceptions) the dominant view within Protestant and Catholic circles is that the United States is and ought to be a Christian commonwealth, to the point at very least of proclaiming "In God We Trust" on the currency and celebrating Christmas in the public schools. However, as this *rapprochement* has proceeded, within the Jewish community a contrary view has arisen which asserts that the separation of church and state ought to be even more complete than it has been, and that the "Post-Protestant era" means Post-Christian as well, insofar as government relations with religion are concerned.

The most dramatic episode of this development was the decision of the United States Supreme Court on June 25, 1962, that the recitation of an official prayer in the New York school system was unconstitutional. The case was brought by five parents of children in the public schools of the New York City suburb of New Hyde Park. Two of the parents were Jewish, one a member of the Ethical Culture Society, one a Unitarian, and one a nonbeliever. Before it concluded, however, the principal protagonists of the Catholic-Jewish controversy in New York City were involved. The attorney for the Archdiocese of New York, for example, argued in the Supreme Court for a group of parents who supported the prayer. The response to the decision could hardly have been more diametrical. Cardinal Spellman declared, "I am shocked and frightened. . . ." The New York Board of Rabbis, on the other hand, hailed the decision: "The recitation of prayers in the public schools, which is tantamount to the teaching of prayer, is not in conformity with the spirit of the American concept of the separation of church and state. All the religious groups in this country will best advance their respective faiths by adherence to this principle." The American Jewish Committee, the American Jewish Congress, and the Anti-Defamation League of B'nai B'rith strongly supported the Court. Only among the Orthodox was there mild disagreement with the Supreme Court decision.

Although the argument could certainly be made that the American Catholic Church ought to be the first to object to the spectacle of civil servants composing government prayers, and although many Catholic commentators noted that the decision strengthened the case for private Church-sponsored schools, the general Catholic reaction was most hostile. The Jesuit publication *America,* in an editorial "To our Jewish Friends," declared that Jewish efforts to assert an ever more strict separation of church and state were painting the Jewish community into a corner, where it would be isolated from the rest of Americans.

Significantly, Protestant reaction to the decision was mixed. The Brooklyn *Tablet* took the cue, stating that the crucial question raised by the decision was "What are the Protestants going to do about it? For, although this is a national problem, it is particularly a Protestant problem, given the large Protestant enrollment in the public schools. Catholics have been fighting long—and sometimes alone—against the Church-State extremists. May we count on Protestants to supply more leadership in this case? If so, we pledge our support to join efforts against the common enemy: secularism." [7]

The subject of aid to Catholic schools is only one aspect of the more general issue of church-state relations, and here again the ethnic composition of New York City tends to produce the same alignment of opposing groups. There are elements within the Jewish community, again the Orthodox, that favor public assistance for religious schools, but the dominant view is opposed. In 1961 the New York Republican party at the state level made a tentative move toward the Catholic position by proposing a Constitutional amendment that would have permitted state construction loans to private institutions of higher learning, sectarian as well as secular. Opposition from Jewish (as well as some Protestant) groups was pronounced, and the measure was beaten at the polls.

The situation developing in this area could soberly be termed dangerous. An element of interfaith competition has entered the controversy. As the costs of education mount, it becomes increasingly difficult to maintain the quality of the education provided by private schools deprived of public assistance. It is not uncommon to hear it stated in Catholic circles that the results of national scholarship competitions already point to the weakness of Catholic education in fields such as the physical sciences. The specter is raised that a parochial education will involve sacrifice for the students as well as for their parents.

There is understandably much resentment within Catholic educational circles at the relative crudity of most such observations. At the same time this resentment is often accompanied by an unmistakable withdrawal. In a thoughtful address calling for more meticulous assessment of the qualities of Catholic education, Bishop McEntegart of the Diocese of Brooklyn went on to state that "Judgment on the effectiveness of an educational system should be something more profound and more subtle than counting heads of so-called intellectuals who happen to be named in Who's Who or the 'Social Register.' " [8]

Whether the course of the controversy will lead Catholics further into separatist views of this kind is not clear. But it is abundantly evident that so long as Catholics maintain a separate education system and the rest of the community refuses to help support it by tax funds or tax relief, a basic divisive issue will exist. This will be an ethnic issue in measure that the Catholic community continues to include the bulk of the Irish, Italian, and Polish population in the city, at least the bulk of those affiliated with organizations taking a position on the issue. If, as may very well happen, the Catholics abandon elementary and even secondary education to concentrate on their colleges and universities, the larger issue of church-state relations will no doubt subside.

But it is not the single issue of school aid, no matter how important and long-lived it is, that alone shapes the polarization between the Jewish and the emerging Catholic community. There have been other issues in the past—for example, the struggle over the legitimacy of city hospitals giving advice on birth control, which put Jews and liberal Protestants on one side and Catholics on the other. There are the recurrent disputes over government censorship of books and movies and magazines that have become freer and freer in their handling of sex and sexual perversion. This again ranges Jewish and Protestant supporters of the widest possible freedom of speech against Catholics who are more anxious about the impact of such material on young people and family life. One can see emerging such issues as the rigid state laws on divorce and abortion.[9]

Many of these issues involve Catholic *religious* doctrine. But there exists here a situation that is broader than a conflict over doctrines and the degree to which government should recognize them. What is involved is the emergence of two subcultures, two value systems, shaped and defined certainly in part by religious practice and experience and organization but by now supported by the existence of two communities. If the bishops and the rabbis were to disappear tomorrow, the subcultures and subcommunities would remain. One is secular in its attitudes, liberal in its outlook on sexual life and divorce, positive about science and social science. The other is religious in its outlook, resists the growing liberalization in sexual mores and its reflection in cultural and family life, feels strongly the tension between moral values and modern science and technology. The conflict may be seen in many ways—not least in the fact that the new disciplines such as psychoanalysis, particularly in New York, are so largely staffed by Jews.

Thus a Jewish ethos and a Catholic ethos emerge: they are more strongly affected by a specific religious doctrine in the Catholic case than in the Jewish, but neither is purely the expression of the spirit of a religion.

Each is the result of the interplay of religion, ethnic group, American setting, and specific issues. The important fact is that the differences in values and attitudes between the two groups do not, in general, become smaller with time. On the contrary: there is probably a wider gap between Jews and Catholics in New York today than in the days of Al Smith.[10]

NEGROES AND PUERTO RICANS

A CLOSE EXAMINATION OF CATHOLIC-JEWISH RELATIONS WILL reveal some of the tendency of ethnic relations in New York to be a form of class relations as well. However, the tendency is unmistakably clear with regard to the Negroes and Puerto Ricans. Some 22 per cent of the population of the city is now Negro or Puerto Rican, and the proportion will increase. (Thirty-six per cent of the births in 1961 were Negro or Puerto Rican.) To a degree that cannot fail to startle anyone who encounters the reality for the first time, the overwhelming portion of both groups constitutes a submerged, exploited, and very possibly permanent proletariat.

New York is properly regarded as the wealthiest city in the nation. Its more affluent suburbs enjoy some of the highest standards of living on earth. In the city itself white-collar wages are high, and skilled labor through aggressive trade union activity has obtained almost unprecedented standards. Bricklayers earn $5.35 an hour, plus 52¢ for pension, vacation, and insurance benefits. Electricians have a nominal twenty-five hour week and a base pay of $4.96 an hour plus fringe benefits.[11] But amidst such plenty, unbelievable squalor persists: the line of demarcation is a color line in the case of Negroes, a less definite but equally real ethnic line in the case of Puerto Ricans.

The relationship between the rise of the Negro-Puerto Rican labor supply and the decline of industrial wages is unmistakable. In 1950 there were 246,000 Puerto Ricans in the city. By 1960 this number had increased by two and one-half times to 613,000, or 8 per cent. In 1950 the average hourly earnings of manufacturing production workers in New York City ranked tenth in the nation. By 1960 they ranked thirtieth. In the same period comparable wages in Birmingham, Alabama, rose from thirty-third to tenth. In 1959 median family income for Puerto Ricans was $3,811 as against $6,091 for all the city's families (and $8,052 for suburbs of Westchester). In 1962 average weekly earnings of manufacturing production workers were 19 per cent higher in Birmingham than in New York City, 15 per cent higher in New Orleans, and almost 10 per cent higher in the nation as a whole.

These economic conditions vastly reinforce the ethnic distinctions that serve to separate the Negro community and the Puerto Rican community from the rest of the city. The Negro separation is strengthened by the fact that the colored community is on the whole Protestant, and much of its leadership comes from Protestant clergy. Thus the Negroes provide the missing element of the Protestant-Catholic-Jew triad.

Housing segregation, otherwise an intolerable offense to the persons affected, serves nonetheless to ensure the Negroes a share of seats on the City Council and in the State Legislature and Congress. This power, as well as their voting power generally, has brought Negro political leaders to positions of considerable prominence. Following the 1961 mayoralty election, Mayor Wagner appointed the talented Harlem leader, J. Raymond Jones, as a political secretary through whom he would deal with all the Democratic party organizations of the city. Puerto Ricans have only begun to make their influence felt, but they are clearly on the way to doing so.

Their fate gives them an interest in the same issues: the housing of the poor in a city of perpetual housing shortage; the raising of the wages of the poorly paid service semiskilled occupations in which most of them work; the development of new approaches to raising motivation and capacity by means of education and training in the depressed areas of the city. They live adjacent to each other in vast neighborhoods. And they cooperate on many specific issues—for example, in fighting urban renewal programs that would displace them. But there are deeply felt differences between them. The more Americanized group is also more deeply marked by color. The furtive hope of the new group that it may move ahead as other immigrants have without the barrier of color, and the powerful links of language and culture that mark off the Puerto Ricans, suggest that, despite the fact that the two groups increasingly comprise the proletariat of the city, their history will be distinct.

Thus the cast of major characters for the next decades is complete: the Jews; the Catholics, subdivided at least into Irish and Italian components; the Negroes; the Puerto Ricans; and, of course, the white Anglo-Saxon Protestants. These latter, ranging from the Rockefeller brothers to reform district leaders in the Democratic party are, man for man, among the most influential and powerful persons in the city, and will continue to play a conspicuous and creative role in almost every aspect of the life of the metropolis.

THE ROLE OF POLITICS

THE LARGE MOVEMENTS OF HISTORY AND PEOPLE WHICH TEND to reinforce the role of the ethnic groups in the city have been accompanied by new developments in political life which similarly strengthen ethnic identities. This is a complicated matter, but we can point to a number of elements. First, there is some tendency (encouraged by the development of genuine ethnic-class combinations) to substitute ethnic issues in politics for class issues. Second, there has been a decline in the vigor and creativity of politics in New York City, which seems to make New York politicians prefer to deal in terms of premelting pot verities rather than to cope with the chaotic present. Third, the development of public opinion polling would seem to have significantly strengthened the historic tendency of New York political parties to occupy the same middle ground on substantive issues, and indirectly has the effect of strengthening the ethnic component in political campaigns. As competing parties and factions use substantially the same polling techniques, they get substantially the same information about the likes and dislikes of the electorate. Hence they tend to adopt similar positions on political issues. (In much the same way, the development of marketing survey techniques in business has produced standardized commercial products such as cigarettes, automobiles, detergents, and so forth.) For the time being at least, this seems to have increased the importance of racial and ethnic distinctions that, like advertising, can still create distinctions in appearance even if little or none exist in fact. Everything we say in this field is highly speculative, but the impression that the political patterns of the city strengthen the roles of ethnic groups is overwhelming.

It is not easy to illustrate the substitution of ethnic appeals for class appeals. To the extent it occurs, those involved would hope to conceal it, always assuming the practice is deliberate. The basic fact is that for the first half of the twentieth century New York was a center of political radicalism. Faced with fierce opposition, some at least of the left wing discovered that their best tactic was to couch class appeals in ethnic terms. In such manner Vito Marcantonio, a notorious fellow traveler, flourished in the United States Congress as an Italian representative of the Italians and Puerto Ricans of East Harlem. In response to such tactics, the traditional parties have themselves employed the ethnic shorthand to deal with what are essentially class problems. Thus much was made in terms of its ethnic significance of the appointment of a Puerto Rican as a City Commissioner responsible for the relocation of families affected by urban renewal projects, but behind this significance was the more basic one that the slum-dwelling proletariat of the city was being given some control over its housing. In much the same way the balanced ticket makes it possible to offer a slate of candidates ranging across the social spectrum—rich man, poor man, beggar man, thief— but to do so in terms of the ethnic groups represented rather than the classes. In a democratic culture that has never much liked to identify individuals in terms of social classes, and does so less in the aftermath of the radical 1930's and 1940's, the ethnic shorthand is a considerable advantage.

This is of course possible only because of the splintering of traditional economic classes along ethnic lines, which tends to create class-ethnic combinations that have considerable significance at the present time in New York. The sharp division and increasing conflict between the well-paid Jewish cutters in the International Ladies' Garment Workers' Union and the low-paid Negro and Puerto Rican majority in the union have been widely publicized. One Negro cutter hailed the union before the State Commission for Human Rights and obtained a favorable decision. Similar distinctions between skilled and unskilled workers are common enough throughout the trade unions of the city. At a higher level, not dissimilar patterns can be found among the large law firms and banks, where Protestant-Catholic-Jew distinctions exist and are important, even if somewhat less so than in past times.

From time to time the most significant issues of class relations assume ethnic form. Reform movements in New York City politics have invariably been class movements as well. Citing a study of Theodore Lowi, showing that reform in New York City has always meant a change in the class and ethnic background of top city appointees, James Q. Wilson summarized the phenomenon as follows:

> The three "reform" mayors preceding Wagner favored upper-middle-class Yankee Protestants six to one over the Irish as appointees. Almost 40 per cent of the appointees of Seth Low were listed in the Social Register. Further, all four reform mayors—Low, Mitchel, La Guardia, and Wagner—have appointed a much larger percentage of Jews to their cabinets than their regular organization predecessors.
>
> In fact, of course, the problem posed by the amateur Democrats is not simply one of ethnic succession. Militant reform leaders in Manhattan get angry when they hear this "explanation" of their motives, for they reject the idea that ethnicity or religion ought to be considered at all in politics. Although most amateur Democrats are either Jewish or Anglo-Saxon and practically none are Catholic, it is not their entry into politics so much as it is their desire to see a certain political ethic (which middle-class Jews and Yankees happen to share) implemented in local politics.[12]

The 1961 Democratic primary fight, which ended with the defeat of Carmine DeSapio and the regular Democratic organization, was a mixture of class and ethnic conflict that produced the utmost bitterness. In the mayoralty election that followed, the Democratic State Chairman, Michael H. Prendergast, in an unprecedented move, came out in support of an independent candidate, a conservative Italian Catholic, Lawrence E. Gerosa, against Mayor Wagner, who was running for reelection with the support of the middle-class reform elements within the Democratic party. In a bitter *cri de coeur*, almost inevitably his last statement as an acknowledged political leader, Prendergast lashed out at what he regarded as a leftwing conspiracy to take over the Democratic party and merge it with the Liberal party of David Dubinsky and Alex Rose, in the process excluding the traditional Catholic leadership of the city democracy. He declared:

> The New York Post lays the whole plot bare in a signed column entitled "One Big Party?" in its September 27 issue. Every Democrat should read it. "The first prerequisite of the new coalition," James A. Wechsler writes, "is that Mayor Wagner win the election." He goes on to say that the new "troops" which Messrs. Dubinsky and Rose will bring to this alliance will have to fight a "rear-guard action" on the part of "Catholics of Irish descent" who, Mr. Wechsler declares, "take their temporal guidance from Patrick Scanlan and his Brooklyn Tablet propaganda sheet.

. . . .

> It's time to call a spade a spade. The party of Al Smith's time was big enough for Democrats of all descent. The Democratic party of today is big enough for Americans of every race, creed, color or national origin.

Although much larger issues were at stake, it was natural enough for a traditionalist in politics such as Prendergast to describe the conflict in ethnic terms. And in justice it must be said that the ethnic elements of the controversy were probably much more significant than Prendergast's opponents would likely admit.

Apart from the reform movement represented by the Committee for Democratic Voters (which has yet to wield any decisive power over city—or statewide political nominations), the level of political creativity in New York politics has not been high over the past several decades. The almost pathetic tendency to follow established patterns has been reinforced by the growing practice of

THE ROLE OF POLITICS

nominating sons and grandsons of prominent public persons. The cast of such men as Roosevelt, Rockefeller, Harriman, Wagner, and Morgenthau seems almost bent on recreating the gaslight era. In this context the balanced ticket and the balanced distribution of patronage along ethnic lines have assumed an almost fervid sanctity—to the point indeed of caricature, as in the 1961 mayoralty contest in which the Republican team of Lefkowitz, Gilhooley, and Fino faced Democrats Wagner, Screvane, and Beame, the latter victors in a primary contest with Levitt, Mackell, and Di Fede. It will be noted that each ticket consisted of a Jew, an Italian Catholic, and an Irish Catholic, or German-Irish Catholic in the case of Wagner.

The development of polling techniques has greatly facilitated the calculations—and perhaps also the illusions—that go into the construction of a balanced ticket. It should be noted that these techniques would apply equally well, or badly, to all manner of social and economic classifications, but that so far it is the ethnic information that has attracted the interest of the political leaders and persons of influence in politics. Here, for example, is the key passage of the poll on the basis of which Robert M. Morgenthau was nominated as the Democratic candidate for governor in 1962:

The optimum way to look at the anatomy of the New York State electorate is to take three symbolic races for Governor and two for the Senate and compare them group by group. The three we will select for Governor are Screvane, Morgenthau, and Burke.* We select these because each represents a different fundamental assumption. Screvane makes sense as a candidate, if the election should be cast in terms of an extension of the Wagner-Rockefeller fight. This could have the advantage of potentially firming up a strong New York City vote, where, in fact, the election must be won by the Democrats. On the other hand, a Rockefeller-Screvane battle would make it more difficult to cast the election in national terms of Rockefeller vs. Kennedy, which, as we shall also see, is a critical dimension to pursue. A Morgenthau-Rockefeller race is run mainly because it

* Paul R. Screvane, President of the City Council, an Italian Catholic; Robert M. Morgenthau, United States Attorney for the Southern District of New York, a Jew; Adrian P. Burke, Judge of the Court of Appeals, an Irish Catholic.

represents meeting the Rockefeller-Javits ticket on its own
grounds of maximum strength: among Jewish and liberal-
minded voters, especially in New York City. Morgenthau is
the kind of name that stands with Lehman, and, as we shall
see, has undoubted appeal with Jewish voters. The question
of running a moderately liberal Jewish candidate for
Governor is whether this would in turn lose the Democrats
some conservative Catholic voters who are not enchanted
with Rockefeller and Javits to begin with, but who might
normally vote Republican.

The third tack that might be taken on the Governorship
is to put up an outstanding Irish Catholic candidate on the
assumption that with liberal Republicans Rockefeller and
Javits running, the Catholic vote can be moved appreciably
over to the Democratic column, especially in view of Rockefeller's divorce as a silent but powerful issue. Here, Court
of Appeals Judge Adrian Burke, who far outstripped the
statewide ticket in 1954 might be considered typical of this
type of candidate.

Let us then look at each of these alternatives and see how
the pattern of the vote varies by each. For it is certain that
the key Democratic decision in 1962 must be over the candidate for Governor first, and then followed by the candidate
for U.S. Senate. We also include the breakdowns by key
groups for Bunche and Murrow against Javits.*

Here some fascinating and revealing patterns emerge
which point the way sharply toward the kind of choice the
Democrats can make optimally in their selection of Gubernatorial and Senatorial candidates for 1962 in New York:

—By area, it appears that the recent Democratic gains in
the suburbs are quite solid, and a range of from 40 to 43
per cent of the vote seems wholly obtainable.

—By race and religion, we find equally revealing results.
The Protestant vote is as low as it was for Kennedy in 1960,
when the religious issue was running strong.

—By contrast, the Catholic vote remains relatively stable,
with a slight play for Burke above the rest, and with Bunche
and Murrow showing some weaknesses here. (The relative

* Ralph J. Bunche, United Nations official, a Negro; Edward R.
Murrow, Director, United States Information Agency, a white Protestant; Jacob K. Javits, United States Senator, a Jew.

† Each figure gives the percentage of total vote that the proposed
candidate received in the specified category. Thus, 35 per cent of the
business and professional vote were recorded as saying they would
vote for Screvane against Rockefeller.

KEY GROUP BREAKDOWNS †

	Democratic Candidates for Governor Pitted Against Rockefeller			Democratic Candidates for U.S. Senate Against Javits	
	Screvane %	Burke %	Morgenthau %	Bunche %	Murrow %
Statewide	47	43	49	47	46
By Area					
New York City (43%)	61	54	61	57	55
Suburbs (16%)	41	41	43	42	40
Upstate (41%)	35	35	40	40	40
By Occupation					
Business and Professional (14%)	35	22	30	57	33
White Collar (19%)	36	44	51	50	44
Sales and Service (8%)	49	49	54	42	42
Labor (34%)	56	53	57	34	52
Small Business, Shopkeeper (5%)	38	41	41	42	36
Retired and other (13%)	39	30	39	52	43
By Ethnic Groups					
White USA (29%)	35	37	36	36	40
Irish (9%)	44	49	44	48	36
English-Scotch (7%)	42	26	33	34	34
German (16%)	29	34	39	42	41
Italian (13%)	59	53	53	45	55
By Religion and Race					
White Protestant (37%)	27	27	29	35	32
White Catholic (37%)	51	54	51	42	48
White Jewish (18%)	70	56	82	71	61
Negro (8%)	70	55	68	93	74
Sex by Age					
Men (49%)	47	40	48	47	43
21–34 (15%)	42	39	40	43	34
35–49 (16%)	53	39	54	43	54
50 and over (18%)	48	43	51	55	42
Women (51%)	47	48	50	47	49
21–34 (15%)	56	56	58	55	45
35–49 (18%)	50	52	59	53	58
50 and over (18%)	39	35	36	37	41
By Union Membership					
Union Member (25%)	66	61	65	49	57
Union Family (11%)	56	59	57	52	47
Nonunion (64%)	38	35	42	45	40
By Income Groups					
Upper Middle (22%)	33	20	32	40	27
Lower Middle (64%)	47	47	52	45	48
Low (14%)	63	61	62	66	61

percentages, however, for a James A. Farley* race against Javits show Farley with 30 percent Protestant, a relatively lower standing; 58 percent of the Catholics, a very good showing, but with only 36 percent of the Jewish vote, a very poor result; and 67 percent of the Negro vote, only a fair showing).

The really volatile votes in this election clearly are going to be the Jewish and Negro votes. The Jewish vote ranges from a low of 56 percent (for Burke); 61 percent for Murrow (against Javits); 70 percent for Screvane (against Rockefeller); a very good 71 percent for Bunche (against Javits); and a thumping 82 percent for Morgenthau (against Rockefeller). Here the conclusion is perfectly obvious: by running a Lehman type of Jewish candidate against Rockefeller, the Jewish vote can be anchored well up into the high 70's and even into the 80's. By running an Irish Catholic candidate against Rockefeller, the Jewish vote comes tumbling precipitously down into the 50's. What is more, with Javits on the ticket, with strong appeal among Jews, any weakness among Jews with the Gubernatorial candidate, and the defection of the Jewish vote can be large enough to reduce the city vote to disastrously low proportions for the Democrats.

The Negro vote is only slightly less volatile. It ranges from a low of 55 percent (for Burke, again); to 68 percent for Morgenthau, not too good (an indication that Negroes will not automatically vote for a Jewish candidate, there being friction between the two groups); 70 percent for Screvane (who carried over some of the strong Wagner appeal among Negroes); 74 percent for Murrow, a good showing; and an incredibly high 93 percent for Bunche.

> *Observation:* The conclusion for Governor seems self-evident from these results. A candidate who would run in the Wagner image, such as Screvane, would poll a powerful New York City vote, but would fade more upstate and would not pull in a full measure of the Jewish swing vote. An Irish Catholic candidate would not do appreciably better than Screvane upstate (a pattern that has been repeated throughout New York's modern political history, with Kennedy the sole exception in 1960), but with good appeal in the suburbs, yet with a disastrous showing among Jews and Negroes in New York City. A Lehman-type Jewish candidate, such

* James A. Farley, former Postmaster General, an Irish Catholic.

as Morgenthau, by contrast, would appeal to a number of Protestants upstate (as, indeed, Lehman always did in his runs), would hold well in the suburbs, and could bring in solidly the pivotal Jewish vote in New York City.

The first choice must be a Jewish candidate for Governor of the highest caliber. (*sic.*)

There are two things to note about this poll. In the first place, the New York Jews did *not* vote solidly for Morgenthau, who lost by half a million votes. A week before the election Morgenthau headquarters received a report that a follow-up poll showed that 50 per cent of New York City Jews who had voted for the Democratic candidate Averell Harriman in 1958 were undecided about voting for Morgenthau four years later. An analysis of the vote cast in predominately Jewish election districts shows that Rockefeller significantly improved his performance over 1958, when he had run against Averell Harriman, another white Protestant. In important areas such as Long Beach, Rockefeller went from 37.2 per cent in 1958 to 62.7 per cent in 1962, which is sufficient evidence that a Jewish name alone does not pull many votes. It could also confirm the preelection fears of the Democrats that the notoriety of their search for a "Lehman type of Jewish candidate" had produced a strong resentment within the Jewish community. The following are returns from predominantly Jewish districts:

	Rockefeller			Javits		
	1962	1958	Dif.	1962	1956	Dif.
NEW YORK CITY						
Bronx AD 2, School 90	27.2	20.5	+6.7	41.9	19.2	+22.7
3	21.6	18.7	+2.9	44.0	17.5	+26.5
5	26.4	19.8	+6.6	39.9	21.4	+18.5
Queens AD 7 School 164	43.8	36.5	+7.3	66.5	32.0	+34.5
SUBURBS						
Jericho (part)	50.7	34.4	+16.3	60.7	36.1	+24.6
Long Beach (part)	62.7	37.2	+25.5	66.2	34.3	+31.9
Harrison (part)	71.3	69.6	+1.7	71.4	64.6	+6.8
New Rochelle Ward 4	57.8	58.8	−1.0	57.1	55.8	+1.3

These returns, which are typical enough, reveal an important fact about ethnic voting. Class interests and geographical location are the dominant influences in voting behavior, whatever the ethnic group involved. In urban, Democratic Bronx, the great majority of Jews vote Democratic. In suburban, Republican Westchester, the next county, the great majority of Jews vote Republican. But within that over-all pattern a definite ethnic swing does occur. Thus Rockefeller got barely a fifth of the vote in the third Assembly district of Democratic Bronx, while he got almost three-quarters in Harrison in Republican Westchester, *but he improved his performance in both areas* despite the fact that his 1962 plurality was lower, statewide, than 1948. Similarly, Rockefeller got as little as 8.8 per cent of the vote in the predominately Negro third ward of Democratic Albany, and as much as 76 per cent in upper-middle-class, Republican Rye in Westchester, but generally speaking, Rockefeller appears to have lost Negro votes in 1962 over 1958.

A second point to note is that while the poll provided detailed information on the response to the various potential candidates classified by sex, occupational status, and similar characteristics of the persons interviewed, the candidates proposed were all essentially ethnic prototypes, and the responses analyzed in the commentary were those on the ethnic line. These are terms, howsoever misleading, which are familiar to New York politics, and with which New York politicians prefer to deal.

THE FUTURE

WE HAVE TRIED TO SHOW HOW DEEPLY THE PATTERN OF ETHNicity is impressed on the life of the city. Ethnicity is more than an influence on events; it is commonly the source of events. Social and political institutions do not merely respond to ethnic interests; a great number of institutions exist for the specific purpose of serving ethnic interests. This in turn tends to perpetuate them. In many ways, the atmosphere of New York City is hospitable to ethnic groupings: it recognizes them, and rewards them, and to that extent encourages them.

This is not to say that no individual group will disappear. This, on the contrary, is a recurring phenomenon. The disappearance of the Germans is a particularly revealing case.

In terms of size or the achievements of its members, the Germans ought certainly to be included among the principal ethnic groups of the city. If never quite as numerous as the Irish, they were indisputably the second largest group in the late nineteenth century, accounting for perhaps a third of the population and enjoying the highest reputation. But today, while German influence is to be seen in virtually every aspect of the city's life, the Germans *as a group* are vanished. No appeals are made to the German vote, there are no German politicians in the sense that there are Irish or Italian politicians, there are in fact few Germans in political life and, generally speaking, no German component in the structure of the ethnic interests of the city.

The logical explanation of this development, in terms of the presumed course of American social evolution, is simply that the Germans have been "assimilated" by the Anglo-Saxon center. To some extent this has happened. The German immigrants of the nineteenth century were certainly much closer to the old Americans than were the Irish who arrived in the same period. Many were Protestants, many were skilled workers or even members of the professions, and their level of education in general was high. Despite the language difference, they did not seem nearly so alien to the New York mercantile establishment as did the Irish. At the time of their arrival German sympathies were high in New York. (George Templeton Strong was violent in his support of doughty Prussia in its struggle with imperial, tyrannical France.) All of this greatly facilitated German assimilation.

In any event, there were obstacles to the Germans' becoming a distinct ethnic bloc. Each of the five groups we have discussed arrived with a high degree of homogeneity: in matters of education, skills, and religion the members of the group were for the most part alike. This homogeneity, as we have tried to show, invested eth-

nicity with meaning and importance that it would not otherwise have had. But this was not so with the Germans, who
were split between Catholics and Protestants, liberals and
conservatives, craftsmen and businessmen and laborers.
They reflected, as it were, an entire modern society, not
simply an element of one. The only things all had in common were the outward manifestations of German culture:
language for a generation or two, and after that a fondness
for certain types of food and drink and a consciousness of
the German fatherland. This was a powerful enough bond
and would very likely be visible today, except for the impact of the World Wars. The Germanophobia of America
during the First World War is, of course, notorious. It had
limits in New York where, for instance, German was *not*
driven from the public school curriculum, but the attraction of things German was marred. This period was followed, in hardly more than a decade, by the Nazi era, during which German fascism made its appearance in Jewish
New York, with what results one can imagine. The German
American Bund was never a major force in the city, but it
did exist. The revulsion against Nazism extended indis-
criminately to things German. Thereafter, German Americans, as shocked by the Nazis as any, were disinclined to
make overmuch of their national origins.

Even so, it is not clear that consciousness
of German nationality has entirely ceased to exist among
German-Americans in the city, or elsewhere. There is evidence that for many it has simply been submerged. In New
York City, which ought logically to be producing a series
of Italian and Jewish mayors, the political phenomenon of
the postwar period has been Robert F. Wagner.

It is even possible that the future will see a
certain resurgence of German identity in New York, although we expect it will be mild. The enemy of two world
wars has become an increasingly powerful and important
ally in the Cold War. Berlin has become a symbol of resistance to totalitarianism; Germany has become an integral
part of the New Europe. Significantly, the German Americans of the city have recently begun an annual Steuben Day
Parade, adding for the politicians of the city yet another
command performance at an ethnic outing.

Despite this mild German resurgence, it is a good general rule that except where color is involved as well the specifically *national* aspect of most ethnic groups rarely survives the third generation in any significant terms. The intermarriage which de Crèvecoeur described continues apace, so that even the strongest national traditions are steadily diluted. The groups do not disappear, however, because of their *religious* aspect which serves as the basis of a subcommunity, and a subculture. Doctrines and practices are modified to some extent to conform to an American norm, but a distinctive set of values is nurtured in the social groupings defined by religious affiliation. This is quite contrary to early expectations. It appeared to de Crèvecoeur, for example, that religious as well as national identity was being melted into one by the process of mixed neighborhoods and marriage:

. . . This mixed neighborhood will exhibit a strange religious medley, that will be neither pure Catholicism nor pure Calvinism. A very perceptible indifference even in the first generation, will become apparent; and it may happen that the daughter of the Catholic will marry the son of the seceder, and settle by themselves at a distance from their parents. What religious education will they give their children? A very imperfect one. If there happens to be in the neighborhood any place of worship, we will suppose a Quaker's meeting; rather than not shew their fine clothes, they will go to it, and some of them may attach themselves to that society. Others will remain in a perfect state of indifference; the children of these zealous parents will not be able to tell what their religious principles are, and their grandchildren still less.

Thus all sects are mixed as well as all nations; thus religious indifference is imperceptibly disseminated from one end of the continent to the other; which is at present one of the strongest characteristics of the Americans.[13]

If this was the case in the late eighteenth century, it is no longer. Religious identities are strongly held by New Yorkers, and Americans generally, and they are for the most part transmitted by blood line from the original immigrant group. A great deal of intermarriage occurs among nationality groups of the three great religious groups, of the kind Ruby Jo Kennedy described in New Haven, Connecticut under the general term of the Triple Melting Pot,[14] but this does not weaken religious identity. When marriages occur between different religions, often one is dominant, and the result among the children is not indifference, but an increase in the numbers of one of the groups.

Religion and race seem to define the major groups into which American society is evolving as the specifically national aspect of ethnicity declines. In our large American cities, four major groups emerge: Catholics, Jews, white Protestants, and Negroes, each making up the city in different proportions. This evolution is by no means complete. And yet we can discern that the next stage of the evolution of the immigrant groups will involve a Catholic group in which the distinctions between Irish, Italian, Polish, and German Catholic are steadily reduced by intermarriage; a Jewish group, in which the line between East European, German, and Near Eastern Jews is already weak; the Negro group; and a white Protestant group, which adds to its Anglo-Saxon and Dutch old-stock elements German and Scandinavian Protestants, as well as, more typically, the white Protestant immigrants to the city from the interior.

The white Protestants are a distinct ethnic group in New York, one that has probably passed its low point and will now begin to grow in numbers and probably also in influence. It has its special occupations, with the customary freemasonry. This involves the banks, corporation front offices, educational and philanthropic institutions, and the law offices who serve them. It has its own social world (epitomized by, but by no means confined to, the *Social Register*), its own churches, schools, voluntary organizations and all the varied institutions of a New York minority. These are accompanied by the characteristic styles in food, clothing, and drink, special family patterns, special psychological problems and ailments. For a long while political conservatism, as well as social aloofness, tended to keep the white Protestants out of the main stream of New York politics, much in the way that political radicalism tended to isolate the Jews in the early parts of the century. Theodore

Roosevelt, when cautioned that none of his friends would touch New York politics, had a point in replying that it must follow that none of his friends were members of the governing classes.

There has been a resurgence of liberalism within the white Protestant group, in part based on its growth through vigorous young migrants from outside the city, who are conspicuous in the communications industry, law firms, and corporation offices of New York. These are the young people that supported Adlai Stevenson and helped lead and staff the Democratic reform movement. The influence of the white Protestant group on this city, it appears, must now grow as its numbers grow.

In this large array of the four major religio-racial groups, where do the Puerto Ricans stand? Ultimately perhaps they are to be absorbed into the Catholic group. But that is a long time away. The Puerto Ricans are separated from the Catholics as well as the Negroes by color and culture. One cannot even guess how this large element will ultimately relate itself to the other elements of the city; perhaps it will serve, in line with its own nature and genius, to soften the sharp lines that divide them.

Protestants will enjoy immunities in politics even in New York. When the Irish era came to an end in the Brooklyn Democratic party in 1961, Joseph T. Sharkey was succeeded by a troika (as it was called) of an Irish Catholic, a Jew, and a Negro Protestant. The last was a distinguished clergyman, who was at the same time head of the New York City Council of Protestant Churches. It would have been unlikely for a rabbi, unheard of for a priest, to hold such a position.

Religion and race define the next stage in the evolution of the American peoples. But the American nationality is still forming: its processes are mysterious, and the final form, if there is ever to be a final form, is as yet unknown.

Tables

COUNTRY OF ORIGIN OF THE FOREIGN WHITE STOCK, NEW YORK CITY, 1960
(All figures are in thousands)

COUNTRY	NUMBER	COUNTRY	NUMBER
Total: Foreign Stock	**3,785**	**Total: Foreign Stock**	**3,785**
United Kingdom	175	U.S.S.R.	564
Ireland (Eire)	312	Lithuania	31
Norway	37	Finland	10
Sweden	28	Rumania	62
Denmark	10	Greece	56
Netherlands	9	Italy	859
Switzerland	11	Portugal	5
France	35	Other Europe	59
Germany	324	Asia	103
Poland	389	Canada	66
Czechoslovakia	58	Mexico	7
Austria	220	Other America	204
Hungary	97	All other	10
Yugoslavia	20	Not reported	23

SOURCE: *United States Census of Population, 1960, New York*, Table 79.

2

**POPULATION OF NEW YORK CITY, 1900–1960,
BY NATIVITY, RACE, AND FOREIGN WHITE
STOCK BY MAJOR COUNTRIES OF ORIGIN**
(All figures are in thousands; all percentages of total city population)

	1900	1920	1940	1960
Total population	3,437	5,620	7,455	7,783
Foreign-born white	1,261	1,992	2,080	1,464
Per cent	*37*	*35*	*28*	*19*
Native white of foreign and mixed parentage	1,372	2,303	2,752	2,159
Per cent	*40*	*41*	*37*	*28*
Native white of native parentage	737	1,165	2,146	2,431*
Per cent	*21*	*21*	*29*	*31*
Puerto Rican-born and children, white				588
Per cent				*8*
Negro	61	152	458	1,088
Per cent	*2*	*3*	*6*	*14*
Other races	7	8	19	53
Per cent	—	—	—	*1*

Foreign white stock, by country (foreign-born, plus native white of foreign and mixed parentage)

	1900	1920	1940	1960
England, Scotland, and Wales	181	171	217	175
Per cent	*5*	*3*	*3*	*2*
Germany	762	608	498	324
Per cent	*22*	*11*	*7*	*4*
Ireland	692	621	518	311
Per cent	*20*	*11*	*7*	*4*
Russia†	241	1,006	927	564
Per cent	*7*	*18*	*12*	*7*
Poland†			413	389
Per cent			*5*	*5*
Italy	219	807	1,095	859
Per cent	*6*	*14*	*15*	*11*

3

NEW YORK CITY, TOTAL AND NEGRO POPULATION, 1900–1960

	Total Population (In thousands)	Negro Population (In thousands)	Per cent
1960	7,782	1,088	14
1957	7,795	948	12
1950	7,892	748	9
1940	7,455	458	6
1930	6,930	328	5
1920	5,620	152	3
1910	4,767	92	2
1900	3,437	61	2

SOURCE: "Negroes in the City of New York: Their Number and Proportion in Relation to the Total Population, 1790–1960," Florence M. Cromien, Commission on Intergroup Relations, City of New York, 1961.

* We have deducted for native-born white for the year 1960 the Puerto Rican white group, and placed the latter in a separate category, in order to permit the major elements of the population in 1960 to emerge more clearly.
† Foreign white stock from Russia and Poland, in New York City, is largely Jewish.

SOURCES: Walter Laidlaw, *Population of the City of New York, 1890–1930*, New York: Cities Census Committee, 1932, pp. 247, 263, 268; *Census Tract Data on Population and Housing*, New York: Welfare Council Committee on 1940 Census Tract Tabulations, 1942, p. 5; *United States Census of Population, 1960, New York*, Tables 21, 72, 79; *Census Tract Statistics, New York City, 1960*.

4

CHANGES IN OCCUPATIONAL DISTRIBUTION OF NEGROES 1940 (NEW YORK CITY)—1960 (NEW YORK STANDARD METROPOLITAN STATISTICAL AREA)

	Male (Per cent)		Female (Per cent)	
	1940	1960	1940	1960
Professional, technical, and kindred	4	4	4	7
Managers, officials, proprietors	5	4	1	1
Clerical, sales, and kindred	11	15	3	17
Craftsmen, foremen, and kindred	8	11	—	1
Operatives and kindred	20	25	14	21
Private household workers	3	1	64	25
Service workers, excluding private household workers	37	18	11	16
Laborers	13	11	—	—
Occupation not reported	1	12	1	12
Total employed, in thousands	88	272	81	231

SOURCES: *United States Census of Population, 1940,* Vol. III, *The Labor Force—New York,* Table 13; and *United States Census of Population, 1960, New York,* Table 122.

NOTE: The best comparison one can make for these two years is between New York City in 1960 and the New York Standard Metropolitan Statistical Area in 1960. While figures for occupation for nonwhites are available for 1960 for New York City, they reflect by the peculiarly heavy concentration of nonwhites aside from Negroes in professional, technical, and managerial occupations. Note too the large percentages in occupation not reported for 1960, and these also affect the comparability of occupation figures for 1944 and 1960.

5

OCCUPATIONAL DISTRIBUTION OF PUERTO RICANS (OF PUERTO RICAN BIRTH AND OF PUERTO RICAN PARENTAGE) IN NEW YORK CITY, 1950

	Male (Per cent)	Female (Per cent)
Professional, technical, and kindred	3	5
Managers, officials, and proprietors	5	1
Clerical, sales, and kindred	10	9
Craftsmen, foremen, and kindred	11	1
Operatives and kindred	37	72
Private household workers	—	1
Service workers, excluding private household workers	28	6
Laborers	5	1
Occupation not reported	1	1
Total employed, in thousands	50	35

SOURCE: *United States Census of Population, 1950*, Puerto Ricans in Continental United States, Table 5.

6

OCCUPATIONS OF IMMIGRANTS FROM ITALY AND THEIR CHILDREN, NEW YORK–NORTHEASTERN NEW JERSEY STANDARD METROPOLITAN AREA, 1950

	Male (Per cent)		Female (Per cent)	
	Immigrants	Children of Immigrants	Immigrants	Children of Immigrants
Professional, technical, and kindred	3	6	2	5
Managers, officials, and proprietors	13	10	4	2
Clerical, sales, and kindred	6	17	8	40
Craftsmen, foremen, and kindred	24	22	2	2
Operatives and kindred	24	29	77	44
Private household workers	—	—	1	—
Service workers, excluding private household workers	14	6	4	4
Laborers	14	9	—	—
Occupation not reported	1	1	1	1
Total employed, in thousands	197	370	52	177

SOURCE: *United States Census of Population, 1950, Nativity and Parentage,* Table 22.

7

OCCUPATIONS OF IMMIGRANTS FROM THE U.S.S.R. AND THEIR CHILDREN, NEW YORK–NORTHEASTERN NEW JERSEY STANDARD METROPOLITAN AREA, 1950

	Male (Per cent)		Female (Per cent)	
	Immigrants	Children of Immigrants	Immigrants	Children of Immigrants
Professional, technical, and kindred	9	19	8	16
Managers, officials, and proprietors	32	27	12	8
Clerical, sales, and kindred	14	28	28	63
Craftsmen, foremen, and kindred	16	10	2	1
Operatives and kindred	23	12	40	8
Private household workers	—	—	2	—
Service workers, excluding private household workers	4	3	6	3
Laborers	2	1	—	—
Occupation not reported	2	1	1	1
Total employed, in thousands	130	217	30	81

SOURCE: *United States Census of Population, 1950, Nativity and Parentage,* Table 22.

8

OCCUPATIONS OF IMMIGRANTS FROM IRELAND AND THEIR CHILDREN, NEW YORK–NORTHEASTERN NEW JERSEY STANDARD METROPOLITAN AREA, 1950

	Male (Per cent)		Female (Per cent)	
	Immigrants	Children of Immigrants	Immigrants	Children of Immigrants
Professional, technical, and kindred	3	10	9	15
Managers, officials, and proprietors	8	11	3	3
Clerical, sales, and kindred	13	26	16	58
Craftsmen, foremen, and kindred	20	18	1	2
Operatives and kindred	20	15	11	10
Private household workers	—	—	24.5	2
Service, excluding private household workers	23	14	34	9
Laborers	11	6	1	—
Occupation not reported	1	1	—	1
Total employed, in thousands	59	139	31	76

SOURCE: *United States Census of Population, 1950, Nativity and Parentage,* Table 22.

Notes

INTRODUCTION

1. David M. Ellis, James A. Frost, Harold C. Syrett, and Harry J. Carman, *A Short History of New York State*, Ithaca: Cornell University Press, 1957, p. 338.

2. Ellis *et al.*, *ibid.*, p. 64.

3. Robert Ernst, *Immigrant Life in New York City, 1825–1863*, New York: King's Crown Press, 1949.

4. Eleventh Census: 1890, Part I, pp. clvii, clxix.

5. Huthmacher describes the formation of the "old stock" element in Massachusetts as follows: "Some types of newcomers assimilated rapidly with the descendants of the state's original inhabitants. This was the case especially with hundreds of thousands of Englishmen from Great Britain and Canada who came to settle during the nineteenth century. Like the natives in cultural traditions, they found adjustment to their new surroundings comparatively easy. . . . By the First World War, moreover, they had advanced far up the economic scale. By that time, indeed, British and Canadian immigrants and their sons were hardly distinguishable from the remaining Yankees in social, occupational, or neighborhood status, and they were generally considered old-stock inhabitants of the Commonwealth." Pp. 5–6, *Massachusetts People and Politics, 1919–1933*, by J. Joseph Huthmacher, Cambridge, Mass.: Harvard University Press, 1959.

6. For the best estimate, though now more than ten years old, see Neva R. Deardorff, "The Religio-Cultural Composition of the New York City Population," *Milbank Memorial Fund Quarterly*, Vol. 33, No. 2, April, 1955, pp. 152–160.

THE NEGROES

1. *Bulletin, Department of City Planning*, New York City, November 22, 1954 and September 1958.

2. *U.S. Census of Population, 1960, New York*, Table 98.

3. This sketch of the history of Negroes in New York City draws from many sources, but the principal ones are Oscar Handlin, *The Newcomers*, Cambridge, Mass.: Harvard University Press, 1959; James Weldon Johnson, *Black Manhattan*, New York: Alfred A. Knopf, 1930; and Claude McKay, *Harlem: Negro Metropolis*, New York: E. P. Dutton, 1940. See, too, the memoirs of James Weldon Johnson, *Along My Way*, New York: Viking Press, 1933.

4. Johnson, *Black Manhattan*, pp. 146, 158.

5. McKay, *op. cit.*, p. 63.

6. The discussion on changes in income and occupation in this and subsequent paragraphs is based on "Family Income and Expenditure in New York City, 1935–6 Vol. I, Family Income," Washington: 1941, *Study of Consumer Purchases: Urban Series*, Bulletin #643, p. 20; *Discrimination and Low Incomes*, Studies under the direction of the New York State Commission Against Discrimination by the New School for Social Research, Aaron Antonovsky and Lewis L. Lorwin, Eds., State of New York Interdepartment Committee on Low Incomes, 1959 (multigraphed), Chap. III, "Minority Groups and Economic Status in New York State," by Gladys Engel Lang; and *U.S. Census of Population, 1960, New York*, Tables 124 and 139. On occasion our discussion is based on figures for the New York Metropolitan Area, if New York City figures are not available; or on figures for nonwhites, instead of Negroes, if figures by race are not available. However, New York's nonwhites are more than 95 per cent Negro, so there is hardly any possibility of serious error.

7. These unemployment figures are from a National Urban League Report, *New York Times*, March 5, 1961.

8. *U.S. Census of Population, 1960, New York*, Tables 73, 77.

9. *U.S. Census of Population, 1960, New York*, Table 133.

10. Claude McKay wrote twenty years ago: 99 per cent of the community commerce in the Puerto Rican section of the Negro quarter is "done by Puerto Ricans and other members of the Spanish-speaking community. Yet they started moving into Harlem in considerable numbers only about 1925, twenty years after the Negroes had established themselves there." (*Harlem, op. cit.*, pp. 89–90.)

11. See, for a good discussion of this entire problem, Robert H. Kinzer and Edward Sagarin, *The Negro in American Business*, New York: Greenberg, 1950.

12. See, for example, *New York Amsterdam News*, November 5, 1960, p. 2, "All-Negro Financed Apt. Building Planned."

13. See, on the slave background, E. Franklin Frazier,

Black Bourgeoisie, Glencoe, Ill.: The Free Press, 1957, p. 165 and elsewhere.

14. McKay tells the following interesting story: Negroes opened up many small stores, candy and cigar stores, as fronts for the numbers. At one point, there was a police crackdown, and the owners of these stores began to use them for their legitimate purpose. "The experience has taught many that it is even more advantageous to run such stores legitimately, without the numbers business." (*Op. cit.,* p. 90.)

15. *New York Citizen-Call,* August 6, 1960.

16. Ira De Augustine Reid, *The Negro Immigrant, His Background Characteristics, and Social Adjustment, 1899–1937,* New York: Columbia University Press, 1949, pp. 235 and 247.

17. *Ibid.,* p. 111; McKay, *op. cit.,* p. 252.

18. Johnson, *Black Manhattan, op. cit.,* p. 153.

19. McKay, *op. cit.,* pp. 127, 132, 143 ff.

20. Reid, *op. cit.,* p. 121.

21. Paule Marshall, *Brown Girl, Brownstones,* New York: Random House, 1959, p. 173.

22. Kinzer and Sagarin, *op. cit.,* p. 11.

23. G. Franklin Edwards, *The Negro Professional Class,* Glencoe, Ill.: The Free Press, 1959, p. 25; Gary S. Becker, *The Economics of Discrimination,* Chicago: University of Chicago Press, 1957, p. 73.

24. Less than 3 per cent of the metropolitan area's doctors and less than 1 per cent of its lawyers were Negro in 1960 (*U.S. Census of Population, 1960, New York,* Table 129).

25. *Jobs, 1960–1970: The Changing Pattern,* New York State Department of Labor, 1960.

26. James B. Conant, *Slums and Schools,* New York: McGraw-Hill, 1961.

27. *The Negro Wage-Earner and Apprenticeship Training Programs,* National Association for the Advancement of Colored People, 1960; and *Apprentices, Skilled Craftsmen and the Negro: An Analysis,* New York State Commission Against Discrimination, 1960.

28. See, for example, *The Employment of Negroes as Driver Salesmen in the Baking Industry,* New York State Commission Against Discrimination, 1960; and in *Discrimination and Low Incomes, op. cit.,* Chap. VII, "Discrimination in the Hiring Hall," by Gladys Engel Lang.

29. *The Negro Wage-Earner and Apprenticeship Training Programs,* p. 15.

30. *The Banking Industry: Verified Complaints and Informal Investigations,* New York State Commission Against Discrimination, 1958.

31. *Employment in the Hotel Industry,* New York State Commission Against Discrimination, 1958.

32. See *Non-white Employment in the U.S. 1947–1958,* New York State Commission Against Discrimination, 1958.

33. Figures supplied by the Board of Education, New York City.

34. *U.S. Census of Population, 1960, New York,* Tables 73, 77.

35. See Aaron Antonovsky and Melvin J. Lerner, "Negro and White Youth in Elmira," Chap. V in *Discrimination and Low In-*

comes, op. cit., and in particular their review of the literature, pp. 145–146; and Aaron Antonovsky, "Looking Ahead at Life: A Study of the Occupational Aspirations of New York City Tenth Graders," New York State Commission Against Discrimination, 1960 (mimeographed), which somewhat contradicts the general findings of high aspirations among Negro youth.

36. Richard L. Plaut, "Increasing the Quantity and Quality of Negro Enrollment in College," *Harvard Educational Review*, Vol. 30, No. 3, Summer, 1960, p. 273.

37. Personal interview.

38. Frederick D. Patterson, "Negro Youth on Democracy's Edge," *Reference Papers on Children and Youth, Golden Anniversary White House Conference on Children and Youth*, p. 103. On the general difficulty of finding qualified Negro candidates for medical schools, see Dietrich C. Reitzes, *Negroes and Medicine*, Cambridge, Mass.: Harvard University Press, 1950. ". . . leaders in the field of medical education have indicated it would be possible to place immediately at least 200 more Negroes in white medical schools, if qualified applicants could be found." P. 9

39. See *Toward Greater Opportunity: A Progress Report . . . dealing with . . . recommendations of the Commission on Education*, Board of Education in the City of New York, 1960; and Nathan Glazer, "Is Integration Possible in New York Schools?" *Commentary*, Vol. 30, No. 3, September, 1960, pp. 185–193; "Special Census of School Population, October 31, 1960," Board of Education of the City of New York.

40. Speech by Harold Siegel, executive director of the United Parents Associations, as reported in the *New York Times*, May 16, 1961.

41. "The Open Enrollment Program in the Elementary Schools, Progress Report, School Year 1960–61," Board of Education of the City of New York. We are indebted to Will Maslow of the American Jewish Congress for a special tabulation of school population, and an analysis of the Board of Education's integration efforts.

42. *U.S. Census of Population, 1960, New York*, Table 109.

43. *Fact Book on Youth in New York City*, Community Council of Greater New York, 1956, p. 62. For comparable figures from other cities (New York seems to be one of the very highest), see *Illegitimacy and its Impact on the Aid to Dependent Children Program*, Bureau of Public Assistance, U.S. Department of Health, Education and Welfare, 1960, p. 13.

44. *Babies Who Wait*, Citizens' Committee for Children of New York, Inc., 1960, p. 7.

45. *U.S. Census of Population, 1960*, New York, Tables 106, 107. For the general background of Negro family life, see the classic work of E. Franklin Frazier, *The Negro Family in the United States*, Chicago: University of Chicago Press, 1939; for a recent perceptive review, see Hylan Lewis, "The Changing Negro Family," in Eli Ginsberg, Ed., *The Nation's Children*, New York: Columbia University Press, 1960, Vol. I.

46. Indeed, one must seriously consider to what extent even the Negro middle class escapes the burden of these problems. See on the matter of Negro middle-class personality Abram Kardiner and Lionel Ovesey, *The Mark of Oppression*, New York: Norton, 1951.

47. Martin Deutsch, *Minority Group and Class Status as Related to Social and Personality Factors in Scholastic Achievement*, Monograph No. 2, Society for Applied Anthopology, 1960. See, too, Antonovsky, "Looking Ahead at Life," *op. cit.*, on problems created by absent or inadequate male figures.

48. Annual Report, 1958, Department of Correction, City of New York, Appendix, xxxvii.

49. See the valuable material on growth of New York Negro sections, and degree of segregation, in Davis McEntire, *Residence and Race*, Berkeley, Calif.: University of California Press, 1960. See, too, on the general patterns affecting the housing of Negroes, other books in this series: Nathan Glazer and Davis McEntire, Eds., Studies in *Housing and Minority Groups*; Eunice and George Grier, *Privately Developed Interracial Housing*; Chester Rapkin and William G. Grigsby, *The Demand for Housing in Racially Mixed Areas* (same place, publisher, year).

50. "Negroes in The City of New York," Commission on Intergroup Relations, City of New York, 1961.

51. *Population of New York State: 1960*, Report No. 1. New York State Commission Against Discrimination, 1961.

52. Howard Brotz, *The Black Jews of Harlem*, New York: The Free Press, 1964.

53. I accept here the argument of Will Herberg in *Protestant, Catholic, Jew*, New York: Doubleday, 1955. The discussion of the Negro problem in Protestant churches is often carried on under the general heading of the inner-city church, the urban church. See Frank S. Loescher, *The Protestant Church and the Negro*, New York: Association Press, 1948. There is need for a more up-to-date survey of this problem.

54. See Bernard Roshco, "The Integration Problem and Public Housing," *The New Leader*, July 4–11, 1960, pp. 10–13; and statements on this question by the New York City Housing Authority.

55. John Albert Morsell, *The Political Behavior of Negroes in New York City*, unpublished doctoral dissertation, Columbia University, 1950, is a good history and analysis of Negroes in New York politics to the mid-forties; see pp. 90 ff. for figures on registering and voting.

A most valuable study of contemporary Negro politics in Northern cities, concentrating on Chicago, is James Q. Wilson's *Negro Politics*, Glencoe, Ill.: The Free Press, 1960.

On the character of Negro participation in politics in New York as contrasted with Chicago, Wilson writes:

In New York, Negroes are more evidently aggressive than in Chicago. In New York, the Negro press and civic leaders level a steady stream of criticism against the city regarding school segregation, inadequate school facilities, alleged police brutality, slum conditions in Harlem and various discriminatory acts. Legal suits against the city seeking the correction of alleged racial injustices are more common in New York than Chicago. The number and strength of voluntary associations dealing with race issues are higher in New York. Negroes holding public offices in New York are more likely to take strong—and often public—stands on race issues. (Pp. 98–99.)

56. *The First Ten Years, 1949–59*, Committee on Civil Rights in Manhattan, New York; and "Restaurant Bias Held Overstated," *New York Times*, June 9, 1960.

57. "Powell Says City Limits Negro Jobs," *New York Times,* April 5, 1960. Wilson points out that Negroes have been much more successful in getting appointments in New York than in Chicago.

58. Wilson, *op. cit.,* p. 46.

59. Once again, the Chicago contrast is interesting:

In New York City, in contrast to Chicago, a large number of voluntary organizations have a vested interest in liberal causes. Most often these groups reflect the existence of a sizeable bloc of Jewish citizens who tend to proliferate well-staffed organizations with a commitment to social equality and integration goals. New York is a city with a large number of Jews, and hence has a strong group of such associations as the Anti-Defamation League, the American Jewish Committee, the Jewish Labor Committee, the American Jewish Congress, and so on. It is also a city which is the site of the national headquarters of a host of liberal associations of all kinds. . . . (Wilson, *op. cit.,* p. 151.)

60. See "Negro-Jewish Relations in the North," by Will Maslow (a paper read at the annual meeting of the Association of Jewish Community Workers, January 11, 1960); the Negro press since then has given many other indications of this feeling.

61. "The Harlem Ghetto: Winter 1948," James Baldwin, *Commentary,* Vol. 5, No. 2, February, 1948, pp. 165–170; "Candor about Negro-Jewish Relations," Kenneth Clark, *Commentary,* Vol. 1, No. 4, February, 1946, pp. 8–14.

62. Richard Simpson, "Negro-Jewish Prejudice: Authoritarianism and Some Social Variables as Correlates," *Social Problems,* Vol. 7, No. 2, Fall, 1959, pp. 138–146.

63. Wilson, *op. cit.,* pp. 152–153.

64. Indeed, these things might again, in a curious if understandable psychological reaction, be held against the *Post.* Its liberalism becomes suspect just because it is making an effort—what is it trying to get from us? The *New York World Telegram* and the *Journal-American,* tending to appeal to white Protestant and Catholic readerships more than the more Jewish-oriented *Post,* and making no effort to be liberal, are also less suspected or attacked. As an extreme form of this attack on the *Post:* "Even the self-consciously liberal *New York Post* has only two Negro reporters," John Aigner writes in a column in the *Citizen-Call,* May 21, 1960. Aigner is white, but represented as well as he could the Negro militant mood.

65. It scarcely mattered what one said to defend him, even if one was a minister: "Calling Negroes the 'most ruthless' judges of our own race, Rev. X pointed out that he 'admires Jack' for 'sticking to his guns.'" *New York Amsterdam News,* "Jack Repeats Charge Before More Ministers," January 30, 1960.

66. Note how "American" is the listing of ethnic and racial groups by order of preference among Negro college students— Jews are far below "American white (North)," below French, English, and Italian, and just above such inferior breeds in the American outlook as Hindus, Chinese, Japanese. See Alvin Eboine and Max Meenes, "Ethnic and Class Preferences Among College Negroes," *Journal of Negro Education,* Vol. 29, No. 2, pp. 128–132, 1960. This study is based on a Howard University sample.

67. See James Baldwin, *Notes of a Native Son,* Boston: Beacon Press, 1955; James Baldwin, "A Negro Assays the Negro

Mood," *New York Times Magazine*, March 12, 1961; *The Fire Next Time*, New York: Dial, 1963; and letter of Lorraine Hansberry to the *New York Times Magazine*, March 26, 1961.

68. *The Newcomers*, Cambridge, Mass.: Harvard University Press, 1961, p. 105. His chapter, "Forms of Social Action," is a fine discussion of the whole problem of leadership and social action in the Negro and Puerto Rican groups.

69. *Ibid.*, p. 114.

70. "A Challenge to Negro Leadership," an address by John H. Johnson, to the National Urban League, New York, September 7, 1960.

71. "Are Negroes Ready for Equality?" *Saturday Evening Post*, October 22, 1960.

THE PUERTO RICANS

1. See the interesting paper by Cesar Garcia, "Spirits, Mediums, and Social Workers," student project #4570, 1956, New York School of Social Work.

2. Joseph R. Fitzpatrick, "Mexican and Puerto Ricans Build a Bridge," *America*, December 31, 1955, p. 374.

3. The material on the Puerto Rican family is very extensive. See: Paul K. Hatt, *Backgrounds of Human Fertility in Puerto Rico*, Princeton, N.J.: Princeton University Press, 1952; Julian M. Steward, *et al.*, *The People of Puerto Rico*, Champaign, Ill.: University of Illinois Press, 1956; Reuben Hill, Mayone Stycos, and Kurt W. Back, *The Family and Population Control*, Chapel Hill, N.C.: University of North Carolina Press, 1959; Sidney W. Mintz, *Worker in the Cane*, New Haven: Yale University Press, 1960; Dorothy Dohen, "The Background of Consensual Union in Puerto Rico," unpublished Master's thesis, Fordham University, 1959.

4. Hatt, *op. cit.*, p. 129.

5. In Clarence Senior, "Puerto Rican Emigration," Social Science Research Center, University of Puerto Rico, Rio Piedras, Puerto Rico, 1947 (mimeographed), p. 13.

6. Lawrence R. Chenault, *The Puerto Rican Migrant in New York*, New York: Columbia University Press, 1938, pp. 82–84.

7. Earl Parker Hanson, *Puerto Rico: Land of Wonders*, New York: Knopf, 1960; Ralph Hancock, *Puerto Rico: Success Story*, Princeton, N.J.: Van Nostrand, 1960.

8. For this description of the early Puerto Rican community in New York, we draw principally on Chenault, *op. cit.*

9. *Ibid.*, p. 99.

10. Clarence Senior, "The Puerto Ricans of New York City," Bureau of Applied Social Research, Columbia University, no date (mimeographed), p. 62.

11. Chenault, *op. cit.*, pp. 82, 150–151.

12. On the relations of Puerto Rican and Italian youths, see Agustin Gonzalez, "Problems of Adjustment of Puerto Rican Boys. . . . ," student project #4593, 1956, pp. 6–7; and Janet N. Reville and Alfonso Rivera, "The Psychosocial Adjustment of Puerto Rican Boys. . . . ," student project #4623, 1956, p. 65—both New York School of Social Work; and "The Leisure-Time Problems of Puerto

Rican Youth in New York City," Catholic Youth Organization, Arch-diocese of New York, 1953, pp. 39–40.

13. One explanation must be that many more Puerto Ricans coming to New York were leaving for other cities. But it is also not unlikely that there was considerable underenumeration among Puerto Ricans.

14. Morris Eagle, "The Puerto Ricans in New York," in Nathan Glazer and Davis McEntire, Eds., *Studies in Housing and Minority Groups,* Berkeley, Calif.: University of California Press, 1960, p. 145; and press release, Migration Division, Department of Labor, Commonwealth of Puerto Rico, August 11, 1961.

15. For the spread of Puerto Ricans through the city, see Eagle, *op. cit.,* pp. 144–177.

16. Hancock, *op. cit.,* p. 164. The boom in Puerto Rico's industrial production was steady through the early 1960's. The president of the Planning Board announced in San Juan on August 26, 1961, that by 1962 there would be 750 plants and 94,000 jobs as a result of the industrialization drive (*New York Times,* August 27, 1961). A *New York Times* report of September 2, 1962, raised this to 900 plants.

17. For a comparison of migrants and the general Puerto Rican population, see "A Summary in Facts and Figures," January 1, 1959, Migration Division, Department of Labor, Common-wealth of Puerto Rico, New York, p. 19.

18. *Ibid.,* p. 12.

19. *Ibid.,* p. 8.

20. *Ibid.,* p. 3.

21. Hill, Stycos, and Back, *op. cit.,* pp. 14–15.

22. Beatrice Bishop Berle, *Eighty Puerto Rican Families in Sickness and in Health,* New York: Columbia University Press, 1958, pp. 138–139.

23. Hill, Stycos, and Back, *op. cit.,* pp. 129–130.

24. There is a large literature on this subject, best summarized in Hill, Stycos, and Back, *op. cit.;* and in Evelyn Katz Furman, "Factors Influencing Choice of Population Control Methods in Puerto Rico," student project #4923, 1959, New York School of Social Work.

25. "West Side Notes Big Pupil Shift," June 1, 1960, *New York Times.*

26. "City Spanish Vote at Record High," *New York Times,* November 2, 1960; "Puerto Rican Fights State Literacy Law," *ibid.,* August 7, 1960; "Wagner Primary Cost Half Million," *ibid.,* September 21, 1961.

27. Roy B. Helfgott, "Puerto Rican Integration in the Skirt Industry in New York City," in *Discrimination and Low Incomes, op. cit.* (Note 6, "The Negroes," this volume), p. 268.

28. See letter by Monsignor James J. Wilson, in *New York Herald Tribune,* May 20, 1960.

29. Hatt, *op cit.,* p. 38.

30. C. Wright Mills, Clarence Senior, and Rose Kohn Goldsen, *Puerto Rican Journey,* New York: Harper, 1950, p. 110.

31. "A Report on the Protestant Spanish Community in New York City," Department of Church Planning, Protestant Council of the City of New York, 1960, pp. 47–50.

32. "The Puerto Rican Opportunity," an address by

Meryl Ruoss to the Division of Home Missions, National Council of Churches of Christ in the U.S.A., December 14, 1953, gives a picture of this Puerto Rican religious energy.

33. "A Report on the Protestant Spanish Community. . . . ," *op. cit.*, p. 35.

34. Renato Poblete and Thomas F. O'Dea, "Anomie and the 'Quest for Community' among the Puerto Ricans of New York," *American Catholic Sociological Review*, Vol. 21, No. 1, Spring, 1960, pp. 18–36.

35. The best account of Spiritualism among New York Puerto Ricans and its relation to the major religious tendencies is Dan Wakefield, *Island in the City*, Boston: Houghton Mifflin, 1959, pp. 49–84.

36. Mills, Senior and Goldsen, *op. cit.*, p. 105.

37. Clarence Senior, "The Puerto Rican Migrant in St. Croix," Social Science Research Center, University of Puerto Rico, Rio Piedras, P.R., 1947 (mimeographed), p. 18.

38. Mills, Senior, Goldsen, *op. cit.*, p. 220.

39. Another example of the closeness of the two labor markets: "Many of the bootstrap industries have opened employment offices in New York and Chicago, in an attempt to lure back to the island those Puerto Ricans who have acquired English and some skill." Hancock, *op. cit.*, p. 154.

40. "Complaints Alleging Discrimination Because of Puerto Rican National Origin, July 1, 1945–Sept. 1, 1958," New York State Commission Against Discrimination.

41. A. J. Jaffe, Ed., "The Puerto Rican Population of New York," Bureau of Applied Social Research, Columbia University, January 1954, p. 61.

42. *Discrimination and Low Incomes, op. cit.*, pp. 338–339, 351–353.

43. Bulletin, New York City Department of City Planning, November 22, 1954.

44. *Ibid.*

45. Jaffe, *op. cit.*, pp. 11, 34.

46. Rita Ortiz, "A Study of Well-Adjusted Puerto Rican Families in New York City. . . . ," student project #3173, 1947; and Wilson Gonzalez, "A Study of Ten Self-Sufficient Puerto Rican Families in New York City," student project #4595, 1956; both New York School of Social Work.

47. "Public Assistance Recipients in New York State, January–February 1957. . . . ," by Eleanor M. Snyder, State of New York, Interdepartmental Committee on Low Incomes, 1958, pp. 9, 35, 97; James R. Dumpson, Commissioner of Welfare, City of New York, address on June 6, 1960; speech by City Administrator, "Crime Data Cited on Puerto Ricans," *New York Times*, October 11, 1960.

48. Berle, *op. cit.*, pp. 202–203, 205–208.

49. Paul J. Reiss, "Backgrounds of Puerto Rican Delinquency in New York City," unpublished Master's thesis, Fordham University, 1954, p. 95; Ruth Narita, "The Puerto Rican Delinquent Girl in New York City," unpublished Master's thesis, Fordham University, 1954, p. 43. In the speech cited in Note 45, Preusse said: "The delinquency rate among Puerto Rican children is not the highest in the city, but it is high. Even more disturbing than the rate is the savagery of some recent incidents."

50. Benjamin Malzberg, "Mental Disease Among Puerto Ricans in New York City," *Journal of Nervous and Mental Disease,* Vol. 123, March, 1956, pp. 263–269.

51. Leo Srole *et al., Mental Health in the Metropolis,* New York: McGraw-Hill, 1962, pp. 291–293.

52. Manuel Alers-Montalvo, "The Puerto Rican Migrants of New York City, A Study of Anomie," unpublished Master's thesis, Columbia University, 1951, pp. 107–108.

53. This discussion of the Puerto Rican family in New York City is drawn principally from Berle, *op. cit.,* and Elena Padilla, *Up From Puerto Rico,* New York: Columbia University Press, 1958.

54. There is a good discussion of this problem in Vera M. Green, "Courtship Patterns in Eastville," unpublished Master's thesis, Columbia University, 1955.

55. See Elsie Cespedas, "A Study of Concerns and Interests Revealed by a Puerto Rican group in a New York Settlement," student project #4190, New York School of Social Work, 1953; and Padilla, *op. cit.,* p. 182, and elsewhere.

56. See Dorothy P. Wolf, "The Mother-Son Relationship in 12 Puerto Rican Families. . . . ," Student project #3747, 1950, New York School of Social Work.

57. Leona Thompson, "Problems of Puerto Rican Adolescent Girls. . . . ," student project #4880, 1950, New York School of Social Work, p. 49.

58. Joan Mencher, "Child Rearing and Family Organization Among Puerto Ricans in Eastville," unpublished doctoral dissertation, Columbia University, 1958.

59. *Toward Greater Opportunity,* Board of Education of the City of New York, 1960, p. 16.

60. "West Side Notes Big Pupil Shifts," *New York Times,* June 1, 1960.

61. There are as yet only handfuls of Puerto Rican graduates from the free city colleges. Maria Morales, a teacher, asserted at the Third Annual Puerto Rican Youth Conference that of 2,500 Regents' Scholarships offered in New York City, only 10 were held by Puerto Ricans; of 12,755 students in the four specialized academic high schools, only 83 were Puerto Ricans ("Counselling Hit by Puerto Rican," *New York Times,* April 30, 1961).

62. Renzo Sereno. "Crypto-Melanism: A Study of Color Relations and Personal Insecurity in Puerto Rico," *Psychiatry,* Vol. 10, No. 3, 1947, pp. 261–269.

63. Frederick P. Thieme, *The Puerto Rican Population: A Study in Human Biology,* Anthropological Papers, Ann Arbor, Mich.: University of Michigan, 1954, pp. 47–48.

64. Joseph P. Fitzpatrick, "Attitudes of Puerto Ricans Toward Color," *American Catholic Sociological Review,* Vol. 20, No. 3, Fall, 1959, pp. 219–233.

65. Mills, Senior, Goldsen, *op. cit.,* pp. 133–134.

66. Berle, *op. cit.,* p. 49.

THE JEWS

1. The population figures in this chapter are from C. Morris Horowitz and Lawrence J. Kaplan, *The Jewish Population* *of the New York Area, 1900–1975,* Federation of Jewish Philanthropies of New York, 1959.

2. An analysis of three surveys in 1957 and 1958 contrasted synagogue attendance among New York City Jews and Jews in the rest of the country. Among the former, 19 per cent never went to a synagogue, 53 per cent only a few times a year; nationally, 12 per cent never went, 50 per cent only a few times a year. See Bernard Lazerwitz, "Jews In and Out of New York City," *The Jewish Journal of Sociology,* III:2, December, 1961, pp. 254–260. This study, as others, indicates that only a small proportion of Americans answer "no religion" when asked what their religion is. The proportions are roughly the same in the United States (1.7 per cent) and in New York City (2 per cent). The great majority of nonobserving Jews thus report their religion as Jewish.

3. The first part of this chapter reflects the conception of the Jewish group developed by Nathan Glazer in *American Judaism,* Chicago: University of Chicago Press, 1957. Economic and social materials are drawn in part from his "Social Characteristics of American Jews," in *The Jews,* Louis Finkelstein, Ed., 3rd ed., New York: Harper, 1960, pp. 1694–1735.

4. Lazerwitz (*op. cit.*) reports on income figures in his study. His Jewish samples, as is true of all national samples for public opinion surveys, are tiny and include only 82 New York City Jews, and 105 non-New York City Jews, and his figures on income must be treated with caution, but they nonetheless are suggestive:

	Under $2,999	$3,000–4,999	$5,000–7,499	$7,500–$14,999	$15,000 or more
U.S. Protestants	28	27	27	15	3
U.S. Catholics	19	29	34	16	2
New York City Catholics	26	35	28	10	1
New York City Jews	13	20	30	25	12
Non-New York City Jews	7	9	30	37	17

5. The employment figures in this chapter are from a special tabulation made from the 1952 Health Insurance Plan Survey by *Fortune* magazine, as part of the background research for the article by Sam Welles, "The Jewish Elan," February, 1960. We are indebted to *Fortune* and to Eleanor Carruth, researcher for this article, for permission to consult this material.

Lazerwitz, *op cit.,* has later information on occupational breakdown. Once again, while his samples are small, the same pattern emerges as in the 1952 study. Here are comparisons for New York City Jews and Catholics, and non-New York City Jews:

	Professions	Owners, Managers, Officials	Clerical and Sales
New York City Catholics	3	6	10
New York City Jews	17	23	18
Non-New York City Jews	21	38	15

Skilled	Semi-skilled	Unskilled	Without an Occupation
21	19	23	18
12	15	2	13
7	4	0	15

6. Roy B. Helfgott (see Note 27, "The Puerto Ricans," this volume).

7. Interview in *New York Post*, February 11, 1960.

8. Katherine Hamill, "Junior Executive in Manhattan," *Fortune*, February, 1960, pp. 77 ff.

9. "Jews Charge Bias in Executive Jobs," *New York Times*, April 22, 1960; "Manpower Waste Charged to Bias," *New York Times*, October 25, 1960.

10. *Rights* (published by the Anti-Defamation League of B'nai B'rith), Vol. 2, No. 8, November–December, 1959.

11. "Equal Employment Opportunity Hearings, "Special Subcommittee on Labor of the Committee on Education and Labor, House of Representatives, 87:1, Part I, pp. 582–583.

12. I am indebted to Lawrence Bloomgarden of the American Jewish Committee for an unpublished tabulation by religion of a study of values of college students conducted by Rose K. Goldsen, Morris Rosenberg, Robin M. Williams, and Edward Suchman.

13. Lawrence Bloomgarden, "Harvard Looks at the Executive Suite," American Jewish *Committee Reporter*, Vol. 17, No. 4, October, 1960, p. 29.

14. "The Unequal Treatment of Equals," an address by John Slawson, 1959, New York, American Jewish Committee: ". . . Among the twenty-eight University Clubs throughout the country [not to be confused with the alumni clubs of individual colleges and universities] only two have any Jewish members. In New York City, out of the top ten social clubs, only one has Jewish members." See also his "Social Discrimination, The Last Frontier," 1955.

15. Judith R. Kramer and Seymour Leventman, *Children of the Gilded Ghetto*, New Haven: Yale University Press, 1961.

16. On Zeckendorf, see "Man in a $100-Million Jam," *Fortune*, July, 1960, pp. 104 ff.; on his earlier career, see *Fortune*, March, 1954. On the office-building boom, see John McDonald, "The $2-Billion Building Boom," *Fortune*, February, 1960, pp. 119 ff.; Daniel M. Friendenberg, "Real Estate Confidential," *Dissent*, Vol. 8, No. 3, Summer, 1960, pp. 260–276. The career of the Tisch brothers, who began with a small loan from their garment-manufacturing father after the Second World War and have built up a fortune estimated at $65,000,000 in the renting, management, and most recently, building of hotels, neatly sums up the relations, in size and source, of two Jewish generations to wealth and business; see "The Tisches Eye Their Next 65 Million," *Fortune*, January, 1960, pp. 132 ff.

17. "The Company That Started with a Gold Whisker," *Fortune*, August, 1959, pp. 98 ff.; "The Egghead Millionaires," *Fortune*, September, 1960, pp. 172 ff.

18. John Higham, "Social Discrimination Against Jews in America, 1830–1930," *Publications of the American Jewish Historical Society*, Vol. 18, No. 1, September, 1957, p. 16.

19. Robert J. Shosteck, *The Jewish College Student*, Washington: B'nai B'rith Vocational Service, 1957.

20. Lawrence Bloomgarden, "Medical School Quotas and National Health," *Commentary*, Vol. 15, No. 1, January, 1953; and "Who Shall Be Our Doctors?," *Commentary*, Vol. 23, No. 1, January, 1957, pp. 506–515.

21. *Rights*, Vol. 4, No. 2, February, 1961. Will Maslow of the American Jewish Congress has made available to us useful material of his organization on this question.

22. Again, we are indebted to Will Maslow for an unpublished survey of the experience of a cross section of New York State high school graduates of 1958 in gaining admission to colleges.

23. Lawrence Bloomgarden, "Our Changing Elite Colleges," *Commentary*, Vol. 29, No. 2, February, 1960, pp. 150–154.

24. "Policy to Change at Bard College," *New York Times*, October 15, 1960.

25. Higham, *op. cit.*; John Higham, "Anti-Semitism in the Gilded Age: A Reinterpretation," *Mississippi Valley Historical Review*, March, 1957. We have also benefited from *The Protestant Establishment*, by Digby Baltzell, New York: Random House, 1964.

26. "East Side Coops Still Show Bias," *New York Times*, June 19, 1961. A hearing before the Connecticut Commission on Civil Rights gives evidence on the existing suburban discrimination: "Realty Broker Conceded Writing Anti-Jewish Note in Greenwich," *New York Times*, September 15, 1961.

27. Bureau of the Census, "Religion Reported by the Civilian Population of the United States," *Current Population Reports: Population Characteristics*, Series P-20, No. 79, February 2, 1958.

28. Ruby Jo Reeves Kennedy, "Single or Triple Melting Pot: Intermarriage in New Haven," *American Journal of Sociology*, Vol. 58, No. 1, July, 1952, pp. 56–66.

29. On the dynamics of this process, see Alan Wood, "I Sell My House," *Commentary*, Vol. 26, No. 5, November, 1958, pp. 383–390.

30. John Slawson, "Integration and Identity," New York, American Jewish Committee, 1959, pp. 11–12; see also "The Riverton Study," by Marshall Sklare and Marc Vosk, New York, American Jewish Committee, 1957, pp. 32–42.

31. A good sample in the East Midtown area of Manhattan (the same sample that served as the basis for *Mental Health in the Metropolis*, by Leo Srole and others, New York: McGraw-Hill, 1962) showed a rather high rate (for Jews) of intermarriage—10 per cent of all Jews who were married were married to non-Jews. See "Premarital Characteristics of the Religiously Intermarried in an Urban Area," by Jerold S. Heiss, *American Sociological Review*, Vol. 25, No. 1, February, 1960, pp. 9–21.

32. Jewish Education Committee *Bulletin*, January, 1960, pp. 1–12.

33. Alexander M. Dushkin and Uriah Z. Engleman, "Jewish Education in the United States," *Jewish Education*, Vol. 30, No. 1, Fall, 1959, p. 7.

34. Erich Rosenthal, "Acculturation Without Assimilation," *American Journal of Sociology*, Vol. 66, No. 3, November, 1960, pp. 285, 287.

35. See, for example, Thomas P. Monahan and William M. Kephart, "Divorce and Desertion by Religious and Mixed Religious

Groups," *American Journal of Sociology*, Vol. 59, No. 5, March, 1954, pp. 454-465.

36. This was the conclusion of August B. Hollingshead and Frederic C. Redlich, in their careful study of prevalence of treatment for mental illness in New Haven, *Social Class and Mental Illness*, New York: Wiley, 1958. Srole *et al.* in *Mental Health in the Metropolis* (*op. cit.*) came to the same conclusion. In their East Midtown area somewhat less Jews than Catholics or Protestants were well, but also somewhat less were impaired. A higher proportion showed mild or moderate symptom formation. Srole suggested as one possible hypothesis:

Midtown respondents of Jewish parentage tend to reflect some kind of impairment-limiting mechanism that operates to counteract, or in some degree contain, the more extreme pathogenic life stresses during childhood. This hypothesis appears to be consistent with the repeatedly confirmed relative immunity of Jews to such self-impairing types of reactions as alcoholism and suicide. . . . One factor often hypothesized by psychiatrists as potentially pathogenic is the strong Jewish family structure. However, this factor may conceivably be eugenic on balance, in the specific sense that powerful homeostatic supports are brought into play at danger points of crisis and stress that in other groups may be unbalancing for the family and impairing for the individual. (P. 306.)

37. Charles P. Snyder, *Alcohol and the Jews*, Glencoe, Ill.: The Free Press and Yale Center for Alcohol Studies, 1958.

38. Library of Jewish Information, American Jewish Committee, "The Ethnic Religious Factor in the 1956 Elections," by Moses Rischin, September, 1957. All the Yiddish newspapers supported Mayor Wagner (Catholic) against Javits (p. 26).

39. Lawrence H. Fuchs, *Political Behavior of American Jews*, Glencoe, Ill.: The Free Press, 1956, p. 71.

40. William Spinrad, "New Yorkers Cast Their Ballots," unpublished doctoral dissertation, Columbia University, 1955, pp. 109 ff., on Jewish voting in the O'Dwyer elections, and on its ideological and nonparty character.

41. From an unpublished paper, "Political Behavior of Ethnic Groups," delivered at the Conference on Group Life in America conducted under the auspices of the American Jewish Committee at Arden House, November 9-12, 1956.

42. For most of the preceding history, see Fuchs, *op. cit., passim.*

43. Kurt List, "Jerome Kern and American Operetta," *Commentary*, Vol. 3, No. 5, May, 1947, pp. 433-441.

44. *Mental Health in the Metropolis, op. cit.,* asked the question: "Let's suppose some friends of yours have a serious problem with their child. I mean a problem with the child's behavior. . . . The parents ask your advice. . . . What would you probably tell them to do . . . ?" One-half of the Jewish respondents suggested a psychotherapist; 31 per cent of the Protestants; only 24 per cent of the Catholics. The responses were standardized for socioeconomic status (p. 317). A study based on the Midtown material concludes: ". . . Jews as a whole were more likely than Catholics to be familiar with some type of child guidance resources; and both Jews and Protestants manifested greater knowledge of community resources available for help with marriage problems." (Margaret Burton Bailey, "Community

Orientations Toward Social Casework and Other Professional Resources," unpublished doctoral dissertation, New York School of Social Work, 1958, p. 86.)

45. See Paul Jacobs, "David Dubinsky: Why His Throne Is Wobbling," *Harper's Magazine*, December, 1962, pp. 75–84; Daniel Bell, "Reflections on the Negro and Labor," *The New Leader*, January 21, 1963, pp. 18–20, "Testimony of Herbert Hill on Racial Practices of ILGWU," *Congressional Record—House*, January 31, 1963, pp. 1496–1499; Herbert Hill, "The ILGWU—Fact and Fiction," *New Politics*, Winter, 1963, pp. 3–23.

46. "Jewishness and the Younger Jewish Intellectuals: A Symposium," *Commentary*, Vol. 31, No. 4, April, 1961, pp. 306–359.

THE ITALIANS

1. The great work on Italian emigration to all countries is Robert F. Foerster, *The Italian Emigration of our Times*, Cambridge, Mass.: Harvard University Press, 1919. For Italians in early New York, see Lawrence Frank Pisani, *The Italian in America*, New York: Exposition Press, 1957; Federal Writers Project, *The Italians of New York*, New York: Random House, 1938; Robert Ernst, *Immigrant Life in New York City*, New York: King's Crown Press, 1949.

2. Foerster, *op. cit.*, pp. 223–310; *The Immigration and Naturalization Systems of the United States*, U.S. Senate, Committee on the Judiciary, 1950, 81st Congress, 2nd Session, Report No. 1515, p. 813.

3. Leonard Covello, *The Social Background of the Italo-American School Child*, doctoral dissertation, New York University, 1944, p. 42. Italian scholars used "scientific" arguments, based on presumed racial differences, to explain the inferiority of South Italians, pp. 35–36. This dissertation is now published: Leiden, The Netherlands: E. J. Brill, 1967.

5. Abstracts of the Reports of the Immigration Commission, U.S. Senate, 64th Congress, 3rd Session, Document No. 747, 1911, Vol. I, p. 97.

6. *Ibid.*, pp. 101, 103, 175.

7. *Ibid.*, p. 97. For 1899–1910, 21 per cent of the Italian immigrants were women, compared with 41 per cent of the German, 43 per cent of the Hebrew, 52 per cent of the Irish, 30 per cent of the Polish, 29 per cent of the Lithuanian. On the other hand, some new immigrant groups—Greek, South Slavs, Bulgarian, Russian—had even smaller proportions of women.

8. Census figures, and Immigration and Naturalization Bureau reports.

9. John H. Mariano, *The Second Generation of Italians in New York City*, Boston: Christopher, 1921, pp. 12–13, 24. On the high Italian birth rate, see William B. Shedd, "Italian Population in New York," Casa Italiana Educational Bureau, Columbia University, New York; also in *Atlantica*, September, 1934.

10. In 1950 Italian immigrants and their children made up 13 per cent of the population of the city; with the third generation included, a sixth seems a modest estimate. *United States Census of Population, 1950, Nativity and Parentage*, 3A-80.

11. Herbert Gans, Glencoe, Ill.: The Free Press, 1962.

12. Robert E. Park, and Herbert A. Miller, *Old World Traits Transplanted*, New York: 1921, pp. 146–151; Mariano, *op. cit.*, pp. 19–22. For a somewhat romanticized picture of such a village community in a New Jersey town, see Pietro Di Donato, *Three Circles of Light*, New York: Messner, 1960.

13. For a statistical demonstration of this slow movement of Italians out of original areas of settlement, see Leo Grebler, *Housing Market Behavior in a Declining Area*, New York: Columbia University Press, 1952, Chap. X.

14. For example, the economic level of the remaining Italian community in East Harlem is much higher than one might expect from the age of the housing. See Irving Abraham Spergel, *Types of Delinquent Groups*, unpublished doctoral dissertation, New York School of Social Work, 1960, p. 76.

15. Nat J. Ferber, *A New American*, New York: Farrar and Rinehart, 1938, p. 31.

16. W. F. Whyte, *Street Corner Society*, Chicago: University of Chicago Press, 1943.

17. We lean on Gans' brilliant description of this "peer-group" society, *op. cit.*

18. See, for example, for East Harlem, Leonard Covello, *The Heart is the Teacher*, New York: McGraw-Hill, 1958, p. 223. For a report of tension between an Italian-American neighborhood in Jersey City and the Negro residents of a housing project, see the *New York Post*, June 22, 1961, p. 3.

19. Edwin Fenton, *Immigrants and Unions, A Case Study: Italians and American Labor, 1870–1920*, unpublished doctoral dissertation, Harvard University, 1957, pp. 378, 209, 92.

20. As Fenton (*op. cit.*) sums it up in his excellent study: "They were village-minded, fatalistic, and self-reliant, three qualities which made them poor labor union members." P. 30.

21. *Ibid.*, pp. 406–407.

22. *Ibid.*, pp. 221–238.

23. *Ibid.*, pp. 491 ff.

24. *Ibid.*, pp. 60, 484.

25. *Ibid.*, p. 106. Fifty years after the event, Luigi Criscuolo, in his interesting personal newsletter of Italian-American life, *The Rubicon*, recalled bitterly Barsotti's skill in extracting "the pennies and dollars of the Italian working people," while necessary civic activities were starved. *The Rubicon*, Vol. 2, No. 2, 1942, and Vol. 5, No. 5, 1956.

26. John H. Mariano, *The Italian Immigrant in Our Courts*, Boston: Christopher, 1925, p. 22.

27. Foerster, *op. cit.*, p. 435.

28. Fenton, *op. cit.*, p. 50.

29. Edward Banfield, *The Moral Basis of a Backward Society*, Glencoe, Ill.: The Free Press, 1958.

30. Covello, *The Social Background of the Italo-American School Child, op. cit.*, p. 276.

31. *Ibid.*, p. 263.

32. See Norman Thomas Di Giovanni, "Tenements and Cadillacs," *The Nation*, 187: 443–445, December 13, 1958.

33. *New York Post*, March 10, 1960, p. 23.

34. On the Italian family, see Covello, *The Social Back-*

ground of the Italo-American School Child, op. cit.; Fred L. Strodtbeck, "Family Interaction, Values, and Achievement," pp. 135–194, in *Talent and Society*, by David C. McClelland *et al.*, New York: Van Nostrand, 1958; Paul Barrabee and Otto Van Mering, "Ethnic Variations in Mental Stress in Families with Psychotic Children," *Social Problems*, Vol. 1, No. 1, October, 1953, pp. 48–53; Ezra Vogel, "The Marital Relationship of Parents and the Emotionally Disturbed Child," unpublished doctoral dissertation, Harvard University, 1958.

35. On Italians and education, we draw on Covello, *op. cit.*

36. Federal Writers Project, *op. cit.*, p. 18.

37. Henry J. Browne, "The 'Italian Problem' in the Catholic Church of the United States," Catholic Historical Society, *Historical Studies and Records*, Vol. 35, 1946, pp. 46–72.

38. Pisani, *op. cit.*, p. 169. On Protestant work see also Antonio Mangano, *Sons of Italy*, New York Missionary Education Movement of the United States and Canada, 1917; William Payne Striver, *Adventure in Missions*, Board of National Missions of the Presbyterian Church in the United States of America, New York, 1946.

39. Newbold Morris writes of the selection of Impellitteri in 1945 (though the story must be highly colored):

O'Dwyer . . . had difficulties putting together a ticket. When Lazarus Joseph, a Jewish candidate from the Bronx, was selected for comptroller, it became desirable according to tradition [here Morris is wrong —this became a "tradition" only in this election] to place on the ticket a candidate of Italian extraction from Manhattan. . . . The hard pressed politicians picked up . . . the Official Directory of the City of New York . . . and thumbed through the listing of city officers and employees until they stopped at the name of Vincent Impellitteri, secretary to Supreme Court Justice Gavagan. He was drafted as President of the City Council. (*Let the Chips Fall*, New York: Appleton-Century-Crofts, 1955, pp. 208–209.)

40. Daniel Bell, *The End of Ideology*, Glencoe, Ill.: The Free Press, 1960, pp. 115–136.

41. Ed Reid, *The Shame of New York*, New York: Random House, 1953, pp. 111–112.

42. Theodore J. Lowi, "At the Pleasure of the Mayor," unpublished doctoral dissertation, Yale University, 1960, p. 54.

43. Arthur Mann, *La Guardia:* Philadelphia and New York, J. B. Lippincott, 1959, pp. 317–319.

44. William Spinrad, *New Yorkers Cast Their Ballots*, unpublished doctoral dissertation, Columbia University, 1955, pp. 56–130.

45. *Ibid.*

46. Luigi Criscuolo, in *The Rubicon*, the newsletter he published during the forties, took cruel delight in showing that *every* Italian American political leader, regardless of his outlook, had at some point or another said something favorable about Mussolini, or accepted a medal, or appeared at some function conducted by the Fascist Italian government.

47. See V. R. Tortosa, "Italian-Americans, Their Swing to the G.O.P.," *The Nation*, 177: 330–332, October 24, 1953.

THE IRISH

1. *Dictionary of American Biography*, New York: Charles Scribner's Sons, 1934, Vol. XIII, p. 621.

2. Allan Nevins and Milton Halsey Thomas, Eds., *The Diary of George Templeton Strong*, Vol. IV, New York: Macmillan, 1952, p. 236.

3. *Ibid.*, p. 342.

4. *Ibid.*, p. 368.

5. Florence E. Gibson, *The Attitudes of the New York Irish Toward State and National Affairs, 1848–1892*, Studies in History, Economics, and Public Law, No. 563, New York: Columbia University, 1951, pp. 17–18.

6. Eleventh Census: 1890, Part I, pp. cixii, cixix. New York City did not then include Kings, Queens, or Richmond Counties. However, the proportion generally carried over. In 1890 three-quarters of the Brooklyn Assemblymen were Irish, as against slightly less than half those from Manhattan.

7. E. Wilder Spaulding, *The State Government Under the First Constitution*, Vol. IV, *History of the State of New York*, Alexander C. Flick, Ed., New York: Columbia University Press, 1933, p. 158.

8. Frederick J. Zwierlein, *The Catholic Church in New York State*, Vol. IX, *ibid.*, p. 167.

9. John Tracy Ellis, *Documents of American Catholic History*, Milwaukee: Bruce, 1956, pp. 238–242.

10. *Dictionary of American Biography*.

11. Dixon Ryan Fox, *New York Becomes a Democracy*, Vol. VI, *History of the State of New York*, Alexander C. Flick, Ed., New York: Columbia University Press, 1934, p. 28.

12. Quoted in George W. Potter, *To the Golden Door, The Story of the Irish in Ireland and America*, Boston: Little, Brown and Co., 1960, p. 229.

13. Gibson, *op. cit.*, p. 390.

14. Thomas N. Brown, *Social Discrimination Against the Irish in the United States*, The American Jewish Committee, November, 1958 (mimeographed), p. 30.

15. Charles Frankel, *The Democratic Prospect*, New York: Harper & Row, 1962, p. 11.

16. In his autobiography, George B. McClellan, Jr., states that Cleveland told him the story was apocryphal. George B. McClellan, Jr., *The Gentleman and the Tiger*, Harold C. Syrett, Ed., Philadelphia: J. B. Lippincott Co., 1956, p. 311.

17. Potter, *op. cit.*, pp. 67–68.

18. Conrad M. Arensberg, *The Irish Countryman*, London: The Macmillan Company, 1937: p. 178.

19. Cecil Woodham-Smith, *The Great Hunger*, New York: Harper & Row, 1962, pp. 27 ff.

20. Potter, *op. cit.*, p. 105.

21. Peel describes this as a predominant role, but he would appear to be at least two generations early in this respect. Roy V. Peel, *The Political Clubs of New York City*, New York: G. P. Putnam's Sons, 1935, p. 32.

22. Arensberg, *op. cit.*, p. 93.

23. Lincoln Steffens, *Autobiography*, New York: Harcourt, Brace and Co., 1931, p. 236.

24. Arensberg, *op. cit.*, p. 107.

25. *Ibid.*, p. 179.

26. Peel, *op. cit.*, p. 38.

27. William L. Riordon, *Plunkitt of Tammany Hall*, New York: Knopf, 1948, pp. 107–108.

28. Thomas Beer, *The Mauve Decade*, New York: Knopf, 1926, p. 143.

29. Thomas F. O'Dea, *American Catholic Dilemma*, New York: Sheed and Ward, 1958, p. 152.

30. *Ibid.*, pp. 35–36.

31. Quoted in John Tracy Ellis, "American Catholics and the Intellectual Life," *Thought*, Vol. XXX, No. 118, Autumn, 1955.

32. Kevin Sullivan, *Joyce Among the Jesuits*, New York: Columbia University Press, 1958, p. 3.

33. C. J. McNaspy, S.J., "Patriarch of Parishes," *America*, Nov. 12, 1960.

34. John R. G. Hassard, Life of *The Most Reverend John Hughes, D.D.*, New York: D. Appleton and Co., 1866, p. 276.

35. John Tracy Ellis, *Documents of American Catholic History*, pp. 337–343.

36. *Diary of George Templeton Strong*, Vol. III, pp. 334–342.

37. Robert D. Cross, *The Emergence of Liberal Catholicism in America*, Cambridge: Harvard University Press, 1958, pp. 119–124.

38. William Oland Bourne, A.M., *History of the Public School Society of the City of New York*, New York: 1870, p. 5.

39. *Ibid.*, p. 7.

40. Quoted in "Report of the Secretary of State upon memorials from the city of New York, respecting the distribution of the common school monies in that city, . . ." *Documents of the Senate of the State of New York*, 64th Session, 1841, Document No. 86, Vol. III.

41. *New York Register*, 1840, pp. 337–338.

42. *New York Register*, 1840, p. 336.

43. *Documents of the Assembly of the State of New York*, 63rd Session, 1840, Document No. 2, pp. 5–6.

44. See Richard J. Purcell and Rev. John F. Poole, "Political Nativism in Brooklyn," *Journal of the American Historical Society*, Vol. XXXII, 1941.

45. "Report of the Secretary of State," 1841, *op. cit.*, p. 6.

46. *Ibid.*, p. 12.

47. Edwin R. Van Kleek, "The Development of Free Common Schools in New York State—The Campaigns to Eliminate the Rate Bill and to Divert Public Funds from Sectarian Schools," unpublished doctoral dissertation, Yale University, 1937, p. 162. Quoted in William Kailer Dunn, *What Happened to Religious Education? The Decline of Religious Teaching in the Public Elementary School, 1776–1861*, Baltimore: Johns Hopkins Press, 1958, p. 255.

48. Quoted in Robert D. Cross, *op. cit.*, p. 137.

49. Quoted in John Tracy Ellis, "American Catholics and the Intellectual Life," *Thought*, Vol. XXX, No. 118, Autumn, 1955, p. 368.

50. Thomas B. Macaulay, *The History of England*, New York: 1866 Vol. I, p. 72.

51. *Irish Quarterly Review*, September, 1938.

52. Thomas N. Brown, "The Origins and Character of Irish-American Nationalism," *The Review of Politics*, Vol. XVIII, No. 3, July, 1956, p. 331.

53. Thomas N. Brown, *Social Discrimination Against the Irish in the United States, op. cit.*, p. 23.

54. Elizabeth Gurley Flynn, *I Speak My Own Piece*, New York: Masses & Mainstream, 1955, p. 13.

55. Strong, *op. cit.*, Vol. 2, p. 276.

56. *Ibid.*, Vol. 2, p. 453.

57. From the litany of St. Lawrence O'Toole. Philip H. Bagenal, *The American Irish and the Influence on Irish Politics*, Boston: Roberts Brothers, 1882, p. 137.

58. George Templeton Strong, *op. cit.*, Vol. IV, pp. 90–91.

59. Carl Wittke, *The Irish in America*, Baton Rouge: Louisiana State University Press, 1956, p. 277.

60. Charles Callan Tansill, *America and the Fight for Irish Freedom, 1866–1922*, New York: Devin-Adair Co., 1957, pp. 134–135. Italics added.

61. *Ibid.*, pp. 302–303.

62. *You're a Grand Old Flag*, Copyright Richmond-Robbins, Inc.

63. Thomas Beer, *The Mauve Decade*, p. 153.

64. Morris R. Werner, *Tammany Hall*, New York: Doubleday, Doran, 1928, p. 290.

65. Thomas Beer, *op. cit.*, p. 152.

66. *Ibid.*, p. 152.

67. Quoted in Tansill, *op. cit.*, pp. 126–127.

68. Eugene O'Neill, *Long Day's Journey Into Night*, New Haven: Yale University Press, 1956, p. 127.

69. Eugene O'Neill, *A Touch of the Poet*, New Haven: Yale University Press, 1957, p. 168.

70. A. N. Whitehead, *Adventures of Ideas*, New York: Macmillan, 1935, p. 205.

71. *The Tablet*, December 10, 1960.

72. Eugene F. Moran and Louis Reid, *Tugboat, the Moran Story*, New York: Charles Scribner's Sons, 1956.

73. Oscar Handlin, *The Newcomers: Negroes and Puerto Ricans in a Changing Metropolis*, Cambridge: Harvard University Press, 1959, p. 26.

74. *Life*, February 17, 1947.

75. Charles R. Snyder, "Culture and Sobriety: Signs of Alcoholism," *Quarterly Journal of Studies on Alcohol*, Vol. XVII, No. 1, March, 1956, p. 128.

76. Robert Freed Bales, "Cultural Differences in Rates of Alcoholism," *Quarterly Journal of Studies on Alcohol*, Vol. VI, No. 1, March, 1946, p. 485.

77. Roger J. Williams, "The Etiology of Alcoholism: A Working Hypothesis Involving the Interplay of Hereditary and

Environmental Factors," *Quarterly Journal of Studies on Alcohol,* Vol. VII, No. 4, March, 1947, p. 583.

78. Robert Straus and Raymond G. McCarthy, "Non-addictive Pathological Drinking Patterns of Homeless Men," *Quarterly Journal of Studies on Alcohol,* Vol. XII, No. 4, December, 1951.

79. A. Meyer, "Alcohol as a Psychiatric Problem," in *Alcohol and Man,* H. Emerson, Ed., New York: Macmillan Co., 1932, Chap. 11.

80. Donald Davison Glad, "Attitudes and Experience of American-Jewish and American-Irish Male Youth as related to Differences in Adult Rates of Inebriety," *Quarterly Journal of Studies on Alcohol,* Vol. VIII, No. 3, December, 1947, p. 408.

81. John J. Kane, "The Social Structure of American Catholics," *The American Catholic Sociological Review,* Vol. XVI, No. 1, March, 1955, p. 30.

82. Gerhard Lenski, *The Religious Factor,* Garden City: Doubleday & Co., 1961, pp. 85–87, 247–248.

83. Bosco D. Cestello, "Catholics in American Commerce and Industry, 1925–45," *American Catholic Sociological Review,* Vol. XVII, No. 3, October, 1956.

84. See Table 1.

85. *New York Times,* August 31, 1919.

86. *Syracuse Herald,* October 23, 1936. See also the brilliant essay by Richard Hofstadter, "The Pseudo-Conservative Revolt," *The American Scholar,* Vol. XXIV, No. 1, Winter, 1954–1955.

87. James A. Farley, *Jim Farley's Story, The Roosevelt Years,* New York: Whittlesey House, 1948, p. 63.

88. James A. Farley, "What I Believe," *The Atlantic Monthly,* June, 1959.

89. Svetozar Tonjoroff, "Jews in World Reconstruction," *The American Hebrew,* Vol. 107, No. 17, September 10, 1920, pp. 434, 507.

90. Friendly Sons of St. Patrick, 1941.

91. Irving Kristol, "The Web of Realism," *Commentary,* Vol. 17, June, 1954, p. 610.

92. *The New York Times,* April 26, 1954.

93. Address to the Rotary Club of Los Angeles, July 8, 1960.

94. Emily Smith Warner with Hawthorne Daniel, *The Happy Warrior,* Garden City: Doubleday, 1956, p. 183.

95. Reinhold Niebuhr, "Catholics and the State," *The New Republic,* October 17, 1960, p. 15.

96. John D. Donovan, "The American Catholic Hierarchy: A Social Profile," *The American Catholic Sociological Review,* Vol. XIV, No. 2, June, 1958.

97. I.e., the names are Irish. Some could also be English, however. It should also be noted that Pope John has appointed a number of German-American cardinals.

98. Sister Joan Bland, Letter to the Editor, *The New Republic,* October 10, 1960.

99. Gustave Weigel, S.J., Introduction, Thomas F. O'Dea, *American Catholic Dilemma,* p. xi.

100. *Thought,* Vol. XXX, No. 118, Autumn, 1955, p. 353.

101. Denis W. Brogan, *U.S.A., An Outline of the Country, Its People and Institutions*, London: Oxford University Press, 1941, p. 66.

102. Joseph P. Fitzpatrick, S. J., "Catholics and Scientific Knowledge of Society," *The American Catholic Sociological Review*, Vol. XV, No. 1, March, 1954, p. 6.

103. Gustave Weigel, S.J., "American Catholic Intellectualism—A Theologian's Reflections," *The Review of Politics*, Vol. XIX, No. 3, July, 1957, p. 305.

104. O'Dea, *op. cit.*, pp. 112–113.

105. "A Survey of the Experience of 1235 New York State High School Graduates in Seeking Admission to College." American Jewish Congress, September, 1958 (mimeographed).

106. Leland Gartrell, "Religious Affiliation, New York City and Metropolitan Region," Department of Church Planning and Research, Protestant Council of the City of New York, November 1, 1958, (mimeographed).

107. *New York Times*, September 2, 1960.

108. *The Catholic News*, January 21, 1961.

109. *The Tablet*, February 17, 1962.

110. *New York Times*, October 18, 1962.

111. *New York Times*, May 11, 1959.

112. James B. Kelley, "Correspondence," *America* October 1, 1960.

113. John R. Strack, "Between the Lines," *The Fordham Ram*, November 17, 1960.

114. Right Reverend Monsignor John Tracy Ellis, "The American Catholic Laity—1962," Commencement address, Saint Mary's College of California, June 9, 1962 (mimeographed).

115. Joseph B. Schuyler, S.J., *Northern Parish*, Chicago: Loyola University Press, 1960, pp. 174–177.

116. John J. O'Brien, "Catholic Schools and American Society," *Social Order*, Vol. 12, No. 2, February, 1962.

BEYOND THE MELTING POT

1. J. Hector St. John Crèvecoeur (Michel-Guillaume Jean de Crèvecoeur), *Letters from an American Farmer*, New York: Fox, Duffield & Co., 1904, pp. 54–55.

2. Israel Zangwill, *The Melting Pot*, New York: Macmillan, 1909, pp. 37–38.

3. Joseph Leftwich, *Israel Zangwill*, New York: Thomas Yoseloff, 1957, p. 255.

4. Lee Benson, *The Concept of Jacksonian Democracy*, Princeton, N.J.: Princeton University Press, 1961, p. 165.

5. See Nathan Glazer, *The Social Basis of American Communism*, New York: Harcourt, Brace & World, 1961, Chap. IV.

6. For the complex interplay of religious, ideological, and socioeconomic factors within the American Jewish community, see *American Judaism* by Nathan Glazer, Chicago: University of Chicago Press, 1957.

7. Quoted in the *New York Herald Tribune*, July 2, 1962.

8. *The Tablet,* February 17, 1962. In an address given in Washington on April 30, 1962, Very Reverend William F. Kelley, S.J., President of Marquette University, implicitly proposed a secondary role for Catholic education. As reported in *The Washington Post,* Father Kelley suggested that Catholic schools leave "research and the exploration for new knowledge" to "research institutes" like Hopkins, Harvard, and M.I.T., it being "perfectly respectable and professionally honorable" to concentrate on the transmission of the knowledge of the past:

It is an entirely sound plan to be trailing along at a respectable distance with a trained and educated citizenry competent to appreciate and consume the discovery of the successful investigator. Let us remember that if there are no followers, there can be no leader.

9. See *A Tale of Ten Cities,* Albert Vorspan and Eugene Lipman, New York: *Union of American Hebrew Congregations,* 1962, pp. 175 ff.

10. Gerhard Lenski, *The Religious Factor,* New York: Doubleday, 1961, gives a great deal of evidence to the effect that value differences between Catholics and white Protestants and Jews (the latter two often linked, but not always) in Detroit have increased as the groups move from working-class and immigrant generation to middle-class and later generations. Parochial schooling plays some part in these differences. For an interesting evocation of the milieu in which Jewish-Catholic political cooperation flourished, see *Al Smith,* by Oscar Handlin, Boston: Little, Brown, 1958.

11. U. S. Bureau of Labor Statistics data for October, 1962.

12. James Q. Wilson, *The Amateur Democrat,* Chicago: University of Chicago Press, 1962, p. 304.

13. de Crèvecoeur, *op. cit.,* pp. 65–66.

14. Ruby Jo Reeves Kennedy, "Single or Triple Melting Pot: Intermarriage in New Haven," *American Journal of Sociology,* Vol. 58, No. 1, July, 1952, pp. 55–66.

Index

Abbey Theatre, 248
Acheson, Dean Gooderham, 270
Acculturation, xxiv
Adams, John Quincy, 222
AFL-CIO, 271
Africans, 1
  new African states 68, 78
Afro-American studies, xx*n*
Alcoholism, 165, 197, 257, 258
Algeria and Algerians, 10, 182
Alien and Sedition Acts of 1798, 222
Amalgamated Clothing Workers of America, 152
America, 296
American Catholic Sociological Society, 277
American Communist Party, xxiii, lix
American Federation of State, County and Municipal Employees, xlvi, li
The American Hebrew, 268
American Indians, xiv, lxxix, lxxxii
American Irish Historical Society, 252, 253

American Jewish Committee, 140, 143, 148, 149, 161, 194, 296
American Jewish Congress, ix, xc, 143, 194, 296
American Journal of Sociology, 164
American Labor Party, xxviii, 166, 170
American Mercury, 253
American Negro Labor Council, 78
Amsterdam News, 73, 74, 79, 85
Ancient Order of Hibernians, 240, 248, 251
Anglo-Saxons, 7, 13, 20
  See also White Anglo-Saxon Protestants
Anticlericalism, 282–285
"Anti-Defamation League," Italian-American, lxviii
Anti-Defamation League of B'nai B'rith, lxviii, 143, 148, 194, 296
Antidelinquency programs, xv
Antidiscrimination laws, *See* Discrimination
Anti-Negro attitude, 18, 19, 70, 71, 75, 132, 134
Antioch College, 158

Antipoverty programs, li
Anti-Semitism, 14, 71–73, 77, 139, 141, 151, 158, 172, 176, 270
Antonini, Luigi, 192
Apalachin, N. Y., 196
Apprenticeship programs, xlviii, xlix*n*
Archdiocesan Teachers Institute, 281
Arensberg, Conrad M., 224, 227, 228
Argentina, 141, 143, 172, 176, 182, 183
Armenians, xxxii, 37, 263
Aspira, 128
Assimilation, xxii–xxiv, lxxix, 13, 14, 20, 22, 100, 141, 163, 164, 256
Assimilation in American Life (Gordon), lxxix
Association of Black Social Workers, lxxv
Association of Catholic Trade Unionists, 261
Assuan Dam (first), 182
Atlanta, Ga., xxiv
Atlantic Monthly, 275
Atomic Energy Commission, 271
Aurelio, Thomas A., 212
Austria, 7, 139, 160
Austria-Hungary, 139

Badillo, Herman, xxvii, lxix
Bakalar brothers, 155
Baldwin, James, 71, 78, 81
Banfield, Edward C., 195
Banks, 5, 30, 42, 147, 148, 154, 255
Baptists, 61, 80, 81, 139
Barbados and Barbadians, 35, 36
Bard College, 158, 159
Barrett, Ronald A., 279
"El Barrio," 93, 94
Baruch, Bernard, 169
Batista, F., 9
Bayside–Oakland Gardens area, 162
Beame, Abraham D., xxviii, lxxi, 305
Bedford–Stuyvesant area, 38, 48, 57, 94
Beer, Thomas, 245, 247
Behan, Brendan, 254
Bell, Daniel, 210
Bellanca, August, 192
Benjamin Franklin High School, 201, 203
Bennett, James G., 237
Bennington College, 158
Benson, Lee, 291
Bensonhurst, 161
Bentley, Elizabeth, 269

Berle, Beatrice Bishop, 119, 120, 128, 130
Bigotry, interclass, lxxii–lxxvi, lxxxvii
Black Americans (Pinkney), lxxix
Black Chicago: The Making of a Negro Ghetto, 1890–1920 (Spear), lxxxi
Black Metropolis (Drake and Cayton), lxxvii
Black militancy, xxvi, xxxvi, xliii–xlvi, lii–lv, lxxv
Black Muslims, *See* Nation of Islam
Black Panthers, xvii, xviii
Black Power, xvi
Black Studies, xx*n*, lxxxii
"Blackness," as a cultural style, xxxix
Blacks, *See* Negroes
Blaine, James G., 222
Bloom, Sol, 169
Blue-collar workers, xxvi, xxvii
B'nai B'rith, 143, 194, 296
Board of Estimate, lviii, lxii, 70
Board of Home Missions of the Congregational Christian Church, 82
Bohemia (country), 139
Bohemia, 129
Booth, Charles, 116
Borough Park, 161
Borsatti, Carlo, 192
Brady, J. B. ("Diamond Jim"), 246
Brandeis, Louis D., 140, 169
Brazil, 88, 138, 183
Brighton Beach, 161
British West Indies, 34, 35, 36
Brogan, Denis, 276
Bronfman, Samuel, 151
Bronx, the, 28, 59, 66, 71, 93, 94, 111, 121, 145, 161, 173, 187, 215, 226, 251, 263, 271, 273, 285, 310
Brooklyn, xix, xxvii, lxxxii, lxxxiv, 8, 17, 24, 28, 35, 48, 59, 66, 71, 81, 93, 94, 121, 145, 152, 161, 169, 173, 190, 204, 220, 226, 262, 263, 272, 273, 279
Brooklyn College, 201
Brooklyn Museum, 24
Brooklyn Navy Yard, 24, 91
Brooklyn Technical High School, 25
Broun, Heywood, 282
Brown, Rap, lxxiv
Brown, Thomas N., lxxxi, 241
Brownsville, 161
Bruce, Herbert R., 35
Bryan, William Jennings, 168
Buenos Aires, 172, 182

Buffalo, N. Y., 263
Building trades, 192, 210
    See also Construction business
Buitoni Foods, 33
Bullock, Henry A., lxxxi
Bunche, Ralph J., xxii, 306, 308
Burchard, Samuel D., 222
Burke, Adrian P., 305, 308
Bushwick, 190
Businessmen, small, 31–33, 35, 36, 40, 91, 112, 113, 147, 149, 206, 207
    absence among Negroes, 30–34, 36–39

Cagney, James, 247
Cahan, Ab, 186
California, 43, 153, 183
Campagna, Anthony, 193
Campbell, Timothy J., 224
Canada, 7, 8, 11, 141, 172
Carey, Hugh, xxvii
Carroll, John F., 228, 229
Carroll Hall, 237
Casa Italiana, 193
Casals, Pablo, 129
Casement, Sir Roger, 244
Castro, Fidel, 9, 177
Catholic Association, 225
Catholic Big Brothers, 193
Catholic Charities, 107
Catholic Commission on Intellectual and Cultural Affairs, 277
Catholic Emancipation movement, 225, 238
Catholic-Jewish controversy, 295–299
Catholic World, 268
Catholicism, 103, 106, 107, 201, 202, 203, 204
    American Catholicism, 202, 203
    See also chapter "The Irish," 217–287
Catholics, viii, ix, xxvi, xxxiii, xxxvi, xxxviii, lvi, 14, 19, 60, 149, 157, 158, 166, 212, 213, 218
    decline of power of, lvii–lix, lxvi, lxix, lxxi
    and the Jews, lvii–lxx
    revolution in Church, xxxvii
    See also Irish Catholics, German Catholics
Cavan, Ireland, 224
Cayton, Horace, lxxvii
Celler, Emanuel, 169
Central Queens area, 162
Cestello, Bosco D., 259
Chalk, O. Ray, 103
Chambers, Whittaker, 269

Chaplin, Charles ("Charlie"), 247
Chelsea, 94, 112
Chenault, Lawrence R., 90, 92
Chicago, xvii, xviii, xxix, xxx, 3, 4, 81, 164, 172, 173
    Negroes in, 25, 27, 29, 70, 131
Chile, 106
Chinese, xiv, xxii, xxxii, lxxx, 7, 31, 37, 181, 276
Christ Stopped at Eboli, 195
Christian Frontiers, 168
Christianity and Crisis, 285
Churches, influence of, 33, 80–83, 103–107
    See also Religious groups and factors, separate denominations
City College of New York, xxviii, liv, lv, lxi, xc, 46, 155, 158, 172, 201, 202
City Commission on Human Rights, xliv, xlix*n*, xlix, lxxxix, 55, 68, 71
Ciudad Trujillo, 103
Civil rights movement, ix, x, xv
Civil service, 18, 42, 146, 207, 260
Civilian Police Review Board, ix, xxvi, lxxxiv
Clan-na-Gael, 243, 244
Clark, Kenneth B., lxxvii, 46, 71
Class groups, xxvi, xxvii, xxxv, xlix, l, li, lvii, lxv, lxxv, lxxvi
Cleveland, Grover, 224, 264
Cleveland, Negroes in, 25, 29
Client participation, advocated, xv
Coale, Ansley J., xi
Cohalan, Daniel, 243, 244, 248, 264
Cohan, George M., 244
Coleman, James, lxxix, lxxx
Columbia University, 3, 200, 213
Comerford, James A., 253
Coming Up Black (Schulz), lxxviii
Commentary, 71, 180
Commercial and trading classes, 5, 10, 14, 255
Commission on Intergroup Relations (COIR), *See* City Commission on Human Rights
Commissioner of Social Welfare, 73
Committee for Democratic Voters, 304
Committee on Civil Rights in Manhattan, 68
Committee on Racial Equality (CORE), 55, 78, 80, 176
The Commonweal, 285
Communists and Communism, 35, 173, 268–271, 282, 283, 292, 293
Conant, James Bryant, 38
Coney Island, 161

Congregationalists, 61
Conner, Robert T., lviii
Connoly, Richard B. ("Slippery Dick"), 219
Conservative Party, xxviii
Construction business, xlviii, 39, 210
Contracting business, 18, 39, 206, 210, 255
Cornell University Medical School, 156, 158
Corporations, big, 5, 30, 147–149, 207, 208
Corrigan, Bishop, 234
Corsi, Edward, 208, 209
Cosa Nostra, see Mafia
Costello, Frank, 209–212, 274
Cotillo, Salvatore, 188, 200
Coughlin, Father, 266
Covello, Leonard, lxxix, 184, 195, 200–203
Criminal elements, ix, x, xxiii, xxiv, xxix, lxvii, lxxi, 196, 197, 209–212, 258
Crisis in Black and White (Silberman), lxxvii
Croker, Richard (Boss), 219, 226–229
Crown Heights, 163
Cuba and Cubans, xxxii, lxx, 9, 74, 88, 102
A Cup of the Sun, 198
Cushing, Richard J., Cardinal, 238, 275
Czechoslovakia and Czechs, xxxii, 7, 8

Daddy Grace, 33
D'Allessandro, Dominic, 191
da Ponte, Lorenzo, 182
Dark Ghetto (Clark), lxxvii
Dartmouth College, 158
Davis, John W., 168
Davitt, Michael, 242
DeCapite, Michael, 195
de Crèvecoeur, M-G. Jean, 288, 313
Delaney, James J., 280
Democratic Financial Committee, 169
Democratic party and Democrats, viii, xxvi, xxxiv, xxxvii, lv, lxiii, lxvii, lxxi, lxxiv, 5, 12, 35, 69, 136, 166–170, 208–210, 215, 219, 221–229, 262, 263, 292
See also Political leadership
Demonstration Guidance project, 47
Derryck, Dennis A., xlixn
DeSapio, Carmine G., lxiii, lxviiin,

210, 212, 215, 260, 263, 266, 272–274, 303
Desegregation (of schools), 81
Detroit, xxix, xxx, 6, 173, 259
Negroes in, 25–30, 131
de Valera, Eamon, 243
Devoy, John, 243, 248
Dewey, Thomas E., 167, 263
DeWitt Clinton High School, 200
Diaspora, 177
Dickstein, Nathaniel, 169
Di Fede, Joseph, 305
Dillon, Read & Co., 256
DiMaggio, Joe, 218
Discrimination, xxxviii–xlii, xlviii, lii, lxv, lxxvi, 32, 35, 39–43, 49, 52–54, 68, 74, 112–114, 134, 147–149, 153, 156–159, 178, 207, 282
See also Housing
Domestic workers, 26, 27, 30, 37, 72, 73, 91
Dominica, 103
Dongan, Thomas, 220
Donovan, James B., 263
Donovan, "Wild Bill," 244
Douglaston–Little Neck–Bellerose area, 162
"Dozens, The," xvii
Drake, St. Clair, lxxvii
Dreiser, Theodore, 241
Dressmakers' Local 22, 144
Drug and Hospital Workers Union, xlvii
Dubinsky, David, 261, 304
Du Bois, W. E. B., 32
Dudley, Edward R., xxi, xxii
Dumpson, James, 73
Dunn, Thomas J., 228
Dutch, 1, 7, 8, 20, 256

East Bronx, 92
Hunts Point area of, xxv
East Harlem, 28, 91–94, 99, 136, 187, 188, 190, 200–203, 208, 213, 302
East Midtown area, 122
East New York, 161
East Side, 68, 152, 169, 179, 292
Easter Rebellion, 244
Eastern Parkway, 163
Eastman, Max, 172
Ebony, 84
Education, attitudes toward, xv, lxxix, 35, 39–52, 127–129, 155–159, 199, 201, 202, 276–281, 285, 286, 297, 298
See also Schools
Educational Alliance, 192
Eichler, Edward, 153

Einstein, Albert, 156
Eire, Republic of, 12, 252, 253
El Diario, 103
Elite, the, lx, lxvii, lxx, lxxiii, lxxvi, 10, 11, 25
Elite institutions, 42
Ellis, John Tracy, Msgr., 238, 276, 277, 284
Emerald Society, 261
Emigrant Industrial Savings Bank, 256
Emmet, Robert, 242
Emmet, Thomas Addis, 221
England and Englishmen, 2, 8, 141, 143, 256, 262
Entertainment business, 151, 154, 174
Episcopalians, 60, 275
Equality of Educational Opportunity (Coleman), lxxix
Ethical Culture Society, 295
Ethnic Patterns in American Cities (Lieberson), lxxix
Ethnicity, xxi, xxiv, xxvi, xxvii, lxix, lxx
  groups, vii, xiii, xiv, xxiii, xxv, xxxiii
  importance of, vii, ix, xxii, xxvii, xxix
  persistence of, xxxii–xxxix
  policy of, lxxxiii–xc
  resurgence of, xxxi–xlii
  studies in, lxxvi–lxxxii
Ettor, Joseph J., 192

Fair employment practices, 74
  See also Discrimination
Family structure, viii, 14, 19, 33, 43, 49–53, 89–91, 122–127, 154, 164, 186, 194–202
Far West, 5, 10
Farley, James A., 266, 267, 271, 308
Father Divine, 33, 82
FBI, 271
Federation of Jewish Charities, 140
Federation of Jewish Philanthropies, 153, 176
Fenians, 242, 243, 248
Ferré, Luis, 100
Finland and Finns, 1, 7
Finn family ("Battery Dan," "Sheriff Dan," "Bashful Dan"), 260
Fino, Paul, 187, 305
Fishman, Joshua, lxxix
Fitzpatrick, Joseph P., S.J., of Fordham, lxxix, 133, 135, 277
Flatlands, 161
Flynn, Edward J., 226, 263

Flynn, Elizabeth Gurley, 241, 242, 268
Foerster, Robert F., 193
Fordham, 161
Fordham Ram, 282
Fordham University, 202, 231, 239, 254, 271, 272, 276–278
Foreign Conspiracy Against the Liberties of the United States, 240
Foreign-language press, *See* Press
Forest Hills–Rego Park area, 162
Forrestal, James V., 256
Fort Amsterdam, 1
Fort Greene Houses, 24, 25
Fortune, 147, 150, 151, 155
Foster, William Z., 267, 268
France and Frenchmen, 2, 8, 141, 182
Frankel, Charles, 223
Frazier, E. Franklin, lxxvii, 34, 52
Free School Society, 234
French Revolution, 232
Freud, Sigmund, 175
Friendly Sons of St. Patrick, 239, 254, 269, 287
Friends of Irish Freedom, 264
  See also Irish nationalism
From the Terrace, 150
Frost, Robert, 250

The Gaelic-American, 243
Galamison, Milton, 48, 80
"Galveston Project," 109
Gamso, Raphael, 73
Garibaldi, Giuseppe, 182
Garment industry, 18, 39, 43, 72, 131, 140, 144, 145, 151, 154, 155, 192, 210
Garry, Charles, xviii
Gartrell, Leland, 279
Garvey, Marcus, 35, 78, 82
Genoa, 182
Genocide, fear of, xviii, lxxvi
George, Henry, 233, 234
German American Bund, 312
German Catholics, 202, 286
Germany and Germans, vii, xxxii, xxxiii, 1, 7–10, 12, 13, 15, 16, 18–20, 138, 139, 147, 160, 182, 201, 243, 244, 256, 277, 291, 311–313
Gerosa, Lawrence E., ix, 214, 304
Gilhooley, John J., 305
Giovanitti, Arturo, 192
Glad, Donald D., 257
Glazer, Joe, xci
Go Tell It on the Mountain, 81
Goff, John W., 219
Godfather, The (Puzo), lxviii

Goldscheider, Calvin, lxxix
Goldsen, Rose Kohn, lxxviii, 105, 112
Goldstein, Jonah, 213
Goldstein, Sidney, lxxix
Gompers, Samuel, 261
Goodman, matzoh makers, 33
Gordon, Milton, lxxix
Government, responds to recognized need, xvi
Grace, William R., 218, 221
Graham, Billy, 107
Great Britain, 7, 15
    See also England
Great Neck, 59, 66, 67
Greece and Greeks, xxxii, 7, 10, 37, 140
Greeley, Andrew, lxxvii, lxxxii
Greenblum, Joseph, lxxviii
Greene Country, 251
Greenpoint, 2, 169
Greenwich, Conn., 272
Greenwich Village, 20, 66, 172, 173, 187, 254, 260, 274
Groppi, Father, xxxvii
Group relations, Northern model of, xxiii, xxiv
    Southern model of, xxiii–xxv
Gusweller, James, Father, 105

Haiti, 88
Hamilton, Alexander, 222
Handlin, Oscar, lxxvi, 18, 22, 79, 80, 256
Hansberry, Lorraine, 78
Hansen, Marcus, lxxvi, 22
Hargraves, J. Archie, 92
Harlem, 27, 28, 32, 34, 38, 49, 57–59, 65, 67, 74, 78, 92, 300
Harlem: The Making of a Ghetto (Osofosky), lxxxi
Harlem Hospital, 73, 74
Harriman, William Averell, 263, 305, 309
Harrington, Michael, xi
Harvard Business School, 148
Harvard University, 158, 270, 271, 274
Haskin, John B., 245
Hawaii, 90
The Heart is the Teacher, 200
Hebrew Immigrant Aid Society, 192
Herberg, Will, xxxvi, xxxviii
Herbert, Victor, 246, 254
Higham, John, 159
Higher Horizon project, 47, 74
Hill, Herbert, 178
Hispanic-America, See Spain and Spanish culture

Hiss, Alger, 269
History of Negro Education in the South, A: From 1619 to the Present (Bullock), lxxxi
Hod Carriers, 191
Holden, Matthew, Jr., critique by, xliv
Holland, 7, 138, 160
Homeowning, ix, xxvi, xxxiv, 17, 18, 35, 70, 161, 201
Hopkins, Ernest M., 158
Horwitz, Julius, 120
Hotel industry, 42, 43, 131
The House by the Medlar Tree, 195
Housing, 17, 18, 49, 51, 53–67, 69, 92, 94, 95, 107, 152, 159
    co-op, See Housing projects
Housing projects, See Public housing projects, Morningside Gardens, Park West Village
Houston, Tex., 3
Hughes, Everett C., lxxvi
Hughes, John Bishop, 232, 233, 235, 240, 255, 280
Human Resources Administration, li
Humphrey, Hubert H., lxxii
Hungary and Hungarians, xxxii, 7, 8, 139, 160
Hunter College, 201
Hunts Point, 161
Huron Club, 260
Hylan, John F., ("Red Mike"), 219

Illegitimacy, 50–52, 89
Illinois, 10
Il Progresso Italo-Americano, 192
Immigrant societies, 12, 18
Immigration laws, 9, 36
Impellitteri, Vincent R., 208, 209, 212
Indian Americans (Wax), lxxix
Indianapolis, 10
Indians, American, 16
Indians, Puerto Rican, 88
Indians, West, See West Indians
Indonesians, 12
The Inhabitants, 120
Insurance companies, 5, 30, 147, 148, 154
Integration, 47, 57, 61, 62, 65, 67, 105, 159–166, 171
    See also Segregation
Intelligentsia, xvi–xviii, xxxiv, xxxv, lxxxvi
Interest groups, 17–19
Intergroup relations, 42, 43, 70–80, 82, 91–93, 126, 128, 147, 190, 203, 204

Intermarriage, 13, 132, 133, 135, 160, 162, 164, 204, 313
International Ladies' Garment Workers' Union (ILGWU), xlvii, 102, 144, 145, 152, 178, 191 218, 302
Iowa, 10
Ireland, 7, 103, 206
Irish, character of, 238–250
  decline of, in NYC, 250–262
  decline of political influence, 262–274
  numbers of, 219–222
  in politics, 220
Irish-American Nationalism 1870–1890 (Brown), lxxxi
Irishmen in NYC, vii, xiv, xxii, xxxi, xxxii, xxxvi, xxxvii, xlviii*n*, lv–lviii, lxiii, lxiv, lxxii, 1–19 *passim*, 70, 71, 138, 147, 166, 169, 170, 178, 185, 190, 197, 204–206, 210, 217–287, 291
Irish Catholics, 5, 168, 201, 202, 204, 294–299, 301
Irish Emmigrant Society, 255, 256
Irish Free State, 253
Irish nationalism, 240, 241, 244, 245, 253
  See also Friends of Irish Freedom
Irish Republican Brotherhood (I.R.B.), 244
Irish World, 243
Israel and Israeli, lix, 9, 12, 79, 141, 167, 176, 180, 293
Italian Child Welfare Committee, 193
Italian Home, 192
Italy and Italians, vii, ix, xiv, xix, xxii, xxvii, xxx–xxxiii, xxxvii, lv–lvi, lxiii–lxix *passim*, lxxii, lxxix, lxxxiv, 1, 6–19 *passim*, 70, 71, 106, 166, 169, 170, 178, 181–216, 252, 258, 259, 261, 263, 272, 276, 291
  community in NYC, 186–194
  family influence, 194–202
  numbers of, 184–186
  occupations, 205–208
  politics, 208–216
  religion among, 202–205
Ivy League schools, 157, 279
IWW, 192, 268

Jack, Hulan E., 76, 77, 81, 153
Jackson, Andrew, 222, 246, 250
Jackson, J. H., 81
Jamaica, B.W.I., 34–36, 132, 133
Jamaica race track, 152
James, Henry, 251

Japan and Japanese, xiv, xxii, 7, 14, 43, 44
Japanese Americans (Kitano), lxxix
"Jardin Botanicas," 106
  See also Spiritualism
Javits, Jacob K., 167, 263, 306, 307
Jay, John, 220, 222
Jefferson, Thomas, 222
Jesuits, 1, 181
Jet, 84
Jewish Americans (Goldstein and Goldscheider), lxxix
Jewish Daily Forward, 129, 186, 192, 292
Jewish Identity on the Suburban Frontier (Sklare and Greenblum), lxxviii
Jewish Old Age Homes, 176
Jews, vii–ix, xiv, xxii, xxvii, xxxi, xxxii, xxxvi, lv, lvi, lxxii, lxxviii, lxxxiii, lxxxix, 1–20 *passim*, 34, 43, 52, 57, 59, 60, 71, 109, 137–181, 197, 207, 208, 210, 213, 218, 246, 251–281 *passim*, 301, 303
  in America, xxxviii, lxxx
  "Brazilian," 138
  and the Catholics, lvii–lxx
  community, neighborhood, integration, 159–166
  Conservative, 142, 165, 203
  cultural factors, 171–180
  "Dutch," 138
  East European, 16, 17, 102, 139, 140, 143, 145, 154, 155, 168, 169, 172, 175, 291
  economic base of, 143–155
  education, 155–159, 164
  German, 6, 16, 17, 102, 139, 140, 151, 168, 169, 172, 174, 175
  Hasidic, 163
  and the Negroes, lxv, lxxxviii, lxxxix
  Orthodox, 139, 141, 142, 163, 165, 203, 296
  politics, 166–171
  recent studies on, lxxviii
  Reform, 139, 142, 165, 203
  Russian, 292
  "Sephardic," 138, 140, 141, 145
  shaping of their community, 292–294
  Socialist, 139
Jogues, Isaac, 1
John XXIII, Pope, 285
John Birch Society, 282
Johnson, James Weldon, 27, 35
Johnson, John H., 84
Johnson, Philip, 151
Jones, J. Raymond, 300

Jordan, Winthrop D., lxxxi
Joyce, James, 253
Judges and judicial officers, 263
Juvenile delinquents, 26, 52, 90

Kane, John J., 258, 259
Kantrowitz, Nathan, xii, xli, xlii, lxxix
Kaplan, Mordecai, 179
Kansas City, 10
Kazan, Abraham, 152
Kefauver investigations, 211
Keil, Charles, lxxvii
Kelly, Colin, 267
Kelly, John ("Honest John"), 218, 221, 226
Kennedy, John F., 167, 168, 272, 280
Kennedy, Robert F., lxvii
Kennedy, Ruby Jo, 314
Kerner Commission, xiv, xvi
Khrushchev, 177, 272
Kieft, William, 1
King, Martin Luther, xxxvii, 81
Kitano, Harry, lxxix
Klebanoff, Arthur, xiv
Knopf, Alfred A., 174
Know-Nothing party, 240
Koenig, Samuel, 169
Kossuth, Lajos, 233, 238
Kramer, Judith, 150, 151
Kristol, Irving, 269

Labor leaders, 35, 78, 144, 145
See also Unions
Laborers, 30, 37
La Guardia, Fiorello H., lix, 168, 170, 187, 192, 202, 209–218 passim, 273, 274, 303
Lakeview, Long Island, 58
Language Loyalty in the United States (Fishman), lxxix
Languages, different, 11, 13, 17, 18, 19, 22, 34, 87, 200
Italian, 101
Portuguese, 138
Spanish, 92, 101, 102, 104, 105, 129, 141
Yiddish, 101, 139, 141, 146, 162
Lanigan, James S., 274
Lanzetta, James J., 213
La Prensa, 102, 103
La Rosa, V., and Sons, 33
Latin American and Latin Americans, 11, 17, 74, 102, 103, 107, 114, 183, 283
Laundry industry, 72, 131
Laurelton, 58
La Vida (Lewis), lxxviii
Law firms, 147, 148, 255

Lawrence (Mass.) strike, 192
League of Nations, 265
"Learning Patterns in the Disadvantaged" (Stodolsky and Lesser), lxxx
Lefkowitz, Louis J., 305
Lehman, Herbert, 167, 168
Lehman family, 151
Lenox Terrace, 49
Lenski, Gerhard, 259
Lerner, Michael, on interclass bigotry, lxii–lxxvi
Lesser, Gerald, lxxx
Leventman, Seymour, 150, 151
Levi, Carlo, 195
Levinson, Frances, 66
Levitt, Arthur, lxxi
Levitt, William J., 305
Levitt family, 152, 153
Levittowns, 152
Lewis, Oscar, lxxviii
Lexow Committee, 219
Liberal Party, xxviii, 81, 170, 304
Liberalism, lxiii, 77, 165, 166, 167, 168, 176, 177, 315
Lieberson, Stanley, lxxix
Liebow, Elliot, lxxvii
Life, 130, 256
Limerick, Earl of, See Dongan, Thomas
Lindsay, John, ix, xiv, xxvi–xxix, lxvi, lxviii, lxxi, lxxii, lxxiv
Lippmann, Walter, 281
Lipset, Seymour Martin, xci
List, Kurt, 174
Lithuanians, xxxvii
Litwack, Leon F., lxxxi
Long Day's Journey Into Night, 248, 249
Long Island, 66, 161, 203
Los Angeles, xviii, xxix
Low, Seth, 303
Lowell, Abbott Lawrence, 158
Lower East Side, 66, 94, 145, 160, 180, 246, 271
Lowi, Theodore, 303
Lubell, Samuel, 168
Luchow's, 260
Luz, See Sexology

Macaulay, Thomas B., 238
McCarran-Walter immigration law, 36
McCarthy, Eugene, lxin, lxxii
McCarthy, Joseph, 269, 270, 271, 272
McCarthy, Mary, 254
McCarthy, Raymond G., 257
McCoocy, John H., 226, 272
MacCool, Finn, 221

MacDonald, George, 287
McEntegart, Bishop of Brooklyn, 297
McGlynn, Edward, Father, 233
McGoldrick, Joseph D., 209
McGuire, Peter J., 219, 261
Mackay, Claude, 28, 35
Mackell, Thomas J., 305
McKim, Mead & White, 24
McLaughlin, Hugh, 226
McManus, Thomas J. ("The"), 225, 274
McNaspy, C. J., Father, 232
MacNeven, William J., 221
Mafia, lxvi–lxviii
Malcolm X, xvii
Mancuso, Francis X., 211
Manhattan, 28, 39, 48, 54, 56, 57, 58, 60, 65, 70, 71, 91, 152, 153, 160, 162, 165, 169, 179, 188, 263
"Manhattan arrangement," xxvi, lxxii
Manhattan Beach, 161
Manhattan College, 269
Manhattantown, 152
Manischewitz, M., and Company, 33
Manpower training programs, xv
Marcantonio, Vito, 187, 302
Marchi, John J., xxvi, lxxiv
Maria, 195
Mariano, John H., 193
Marshall, George Catlett, 270
Marshall, Louis, 140
Marshall, Paule, 35
Mass media, ignores affluent Negroes, xlii, xliii, li
  role of, xvi, xviii, xxvi, xxxv, lxvii
The Masses, 172
Mater et Magistra, 285
Maynard, Aubrey, 73, 74
Mead, James M., 263
Meagher, Peter P., 274
Meagher, Thomas F., 242
Meany, George, 261, 271
Medalie, George Z., 167
Medical Fellowships, Inc., 45
Meier, August, lxxxi
Melbourne, Viscount (William Lamb), 23
Mellon family, 4
Melrose area, 94
The Melting Pot, 289, 290, 292
Mendelsund, Henoch, 145
Merchandising, 151, 210
Merchants, See Commercial and trading classes
Methodists, 60
Mexican-Americans, xiv, lxxxii

Mexico and Mexicans, 7, 16, 52, 74, 88, 102, 208
Meyer, A., 257
Midtown study, 122
Midwest, 30, 173
Mies van der Rohe, L., 151
Migration Division of the Department of Labor of the Commonwealth of Puerto Rico, 109, 201
Milgram, Morris, 153
Militancy, See Black militancy
Miller, Herman P., xi
Mills, C. Wright, lxxviii, 105, 112, 134
Mitchel, John Purroy, 213, 219, 303
Mobility, xii, lii
Model cities programs, xv, xxv
Modern Community Developers, 153
Monserrat, Joseph, 109
Montreal, 172
Mooney, William, 229
Moran, Michael, 255
Morgenthau, Henry, Sr., 169
Morgenthau, Robert M., viii, xxi, 305, 309
Morningside Gardens co-ops, 65, 66
Morris, Newbold, 209, 213
Morrisania, 2, 94, 161
Morrissey, John, 245
Morse, Samuel F. B., 240
Moses, Robert, 3, 4, 24
Mt. Sinai Hospital, 73, 74
Mount Vernon, N. Y., 67
Muhammed, Elijah, 34, 82, 83
  See also Nation of Islam
Muñoz Marin, Luis, 91, 95, 98
Murphy, Charles F., lxiii, 226, 228, 229, 264
Murray, Thomas B., 271
Muslims, Negro or Black, See Nation of Islam
Mussolini, Benito, 214
Mutual Aid Societies, 194

NAACP (National Association for the Advancement of Colored People), lxxxix, 39, 41, 78, 79, 80, 109, 110, 176, 178, 194
Nassau and Suffolk Lighting Company, 287
Nassau County, 59, 157, 263
Nation of Islam, xvii, xxiii, 33, 78, 82, 83
  See also Muhammed, Elijah
National Advisory Commission on Civil Disorders, See Kerner Commission

National Association of Social Workers, lxxv

National Baptist Convention, 81

National Conference of Catholic Charities, 91

National Defense Education Act of 1958, 282

National Order of the Sons of Italy, 194

National Review, 285

National Scholarship Service and Fund for Negro Students (NSSFNS), 45

National Urban League (NUL), lxxv, lxxxix, 29, 40, 78, 80, 84, 109, 110

Native American Ticket, 240

The Native Moment, 248

Nazarene Congregational Church (Brooklyn), 82

Negro Protestants, 25, 60, 259, 315

Negroes, vii, x–xxv, xxix, xxxv, xxxvi, xxxvii, xxxix, xli, xlii, lviii, lxii, lxiii, lxiv, lxv, lxix, lxxii, lxxx, lxxxiv–xc, *passim*, 4–11, 14, 17–20, 24–85, 147, 159, 163, 166, 177–179, 187, 196, 201, 207, 211, 261, 273, 302, 303

affluent, and poor whites, xliii–lvii

African origins of, xx*n*

creation of stable working class, xlvi–xlix

jobs, 29–44, 51, 68, 69, 299, 300

numbers of, xxxi, xxxii, xxxiii, 25–29, 112

political leadership, 67–70, 84, 85

recent studies on, lxxviii, lxxix, lxxxii

Southern, xv, 12, 27, 291

West Indian, 17, 27, 34, 35, 36

Negro Family in the United States, The (Frazier), lxxvii

Negro Thought in America, 1880–1915: Racial Ideologies in the Age of Booker T. Washington (Meier), lxxxi

Negroes in Cities (Taeuber), lxxix

Neighborhood-oriented programs, li

Netherlands, *See* Holland

The New American, 208

New England, 2, 6, 7

New Haven, Conn., 160, 314

New Hyde Park, 295

New Jersey, 66, 94, 203

The New Masses, 172

New Netherland, 1

New Rochelle, N. Y., 67

New York City, ethnic mix of, xxviii 1969 election, viii, xxv, xxviii uniqueness of, xiii, xxix

New York City Board of Education, 46–49, 68, 80, 109, 127, 146, 200, 237

New York City Department of Welfare, 118

New York City Housing Authority, 61, 63, 65

New York Constitutional Convention of 1777, 220

New York County Democratic Committee, 218

New York Post, 76, 196

New York State Committee Against Discrimination in Housing (NYSCDH), 67, 75

New York State Crime Commission, 211

New York State Federation of Citizens for Educational Freedom, 281

New York State Medical School, 156

New York Times, 76, 260, 281

New York University School of Education, 201

The New Yorker, 263

Newark, N. J., 26, 59, 94

Newspapers, *See* Press

Niebuhr, Reinhold, 275, 285

Ninfo, Salvatore, 192

Nixon, Richard M., 272

Nondiscrimination agencies, l

North Africa, 182, 183

North Bronx, 17, 187

North of Slavery (Litwack), lxxxi

Northwestern Europe, settlers from, 8

Norwegians, xxxii

Notre Dame (University), 258

Nuñez, Emilio, 102

N.Y.U. Hall of Fame, 24

Oakland, Calif., xviii, 16

O'Brien, John J., 286

O'Brien, Pat, 246

The Observer, 240

Occupational identities, role of, xxxiv–xxxvii

O'Casey, Sean, 253

O'Connell, Daniel, 225, 243

O'Conor, Charles, 217, 221

O'Dea, Thomas F., 231, 278

O'Dwyer, William, 168, 208, 209, 213

O'Faolain, Sean, 239, 255

Office of the Commonwealth of Puerto Rico, 109

Office of Economic Opportunity, xxv

O'Hara, John, 254
Oklahoma, 10
"Old stock," *See* White Anglo-Saxon Protestants (WASP)
O'Neill, Eugene, 248, 249, 255
Oppenheimer, Robert, lx
Order of the Garter, 23
The Organization Man, 150
Oriental Americans, lxxix
Osofsky, Gilbert, lxxxi
O'Sullivan, John, 247

Pacem in Terris, 285
Park, Robert E., lxxvi
Park West Village, 65, 152
Parker, Alton, 168
Parnell, Charles, 242
Partisan Review, 172
Paterno brothers, 193
Pecora, Ferdinand, 202, 208, 209
Pelham Parkway, 161
Pennsylvania Station, 24
Pentecostalists, 105, 106
Perlman, Selig, lxii
Pernicone, Joseph M., 204
Peru, 88
Philadelphia, 2, 25, 131, 153, 232
Pinkney, Alphonso, lxxix
Pittsburgh, 3, 4
Plant, Richard, 45
Platero and I, 129
Playboy of the Western World, 248
Plunkitt, George Washington, 228, 229
Poland and Poles, xxxii, xxxvii, lxxix, 7, 103, 259, 261
Poletti, Charles, 202, 216
Police Department Holy Name Society of the New York Diocese, 270
Political leadership, ix, 27, 35, 42, 67–70, 136, 262–274
   attitudes toward Negroes, xxi, xxii, xxvii, xxviii
Politics, x, lxii, lxiii, lxxi–lxxvi, 4, 5, 18, 19, 20, 60, 166–171, 208–216, 226, 259, 301–310
   See also 217–287
Poll, opinion, in 1962 results, 305–310
Pope, Fortune, 103
Pope, Generoso, 192, 210, 212
Portnoy's Complaint (Roth), lxviii
Portugal, 7, 138
Poston, Ted, 196
Potter, George, 224, 225
Poverty, problems and programs, xii, xv
Powell, Adam Clayton, 69, 76, 79, 80, 196

Power, Father, 232
Prendergast, Michael H., 303, 304
Presbyterian Church of the Master, 81
Presbyterians, 81, 239
Press, 12, 17, 62, 67, 75, 80, 81, 84, 102, 103, 129, 130, 146, 172, 186, 192, 243, 244
   See also Languages
Princeton, N. J., 153
Procaccino, Mario, ix, xxvi, xxvii, xxxv, liv, lxxii, lxxiii
Professional employment, lvi, lvii
Progress and Poverty, 234
Proskauer, Joseph M., 275
Protestant Council of New York, 82, 105
Protestant Episcopal Church, 105, 158, 208
Protestantism, lxix, 82, 104, 105, 107, 234, 237, 253, 283, 296, 297
Protestants, 1, 8, 16, 19, 25, 61, 88, 104, 105, 166, 200, 202, 212, 213, 217, 221, 240, 243, 254, 268, 269, 272, 274, 279, 281
   See also Negro Protestants, White Protestants
Psychoanalysis and the Jews, 175, 298
Public Education Association, 46
Public Housing projects, 24, 25, 54, 61, 94, 107, 152
Public School Society, 234, 236, 237
Public utility companies 5, 147, 148, 210
Publishing houses, 174
Puerto Rican Americans (Fitzpatrick), lxxix
Puerto Rican Educational Alliance, 129
Puerto Rican Journey, The (Mills, Senior, and Goldsen), lxxviii
Puerto Ricans, vii, viii, xviii–xx, xlii, xliii, xlvi, lvi, lxiii, lxviii, lxx, lxxx, lxxxiv, lxxxvi, lxxxvii, 5, 7, 9, 10, 11, 17, 19, 24, 26, 86–136, 147, 163, 166, 178, 179, 187, 196, 201, 207, 211, 213, 259, 261, 291, 315
   attitude toward education, 127–129
   color problem, xii, xiv, xxv, xxvi, 132–136
   creation of stable working class, xlvi–xlix
   culture and contributions, 129–136
   family structure, 122–127
   low incomes, 116–122, 299, 300
   migration, 91–99, 100

Puerto Ricans (*continued*)
  mobile element, 110–116
  number of, xxxii
  recent studies on, lxxviii
Puerto Rico, Commonwealth of, 109, 110, 124
Puerto Rico: Land of Wonders, 91
Puerto Rico: Success Story, 91
Puzo, Mario, lxviii

Quadragesimo Anno, 285
Queens College, 201, 282, 283
Queens County, 17, 28, 58, 59, 66, 71, 94, 111, 152, 161, 187, 273, 280
Quinn, John, 248

Race relations, etiquette of, lxxiv–lxxvi
  faulty policies of, lii–lv
  Northern and Southern, x, xxiv, lxxv
Racism, viii–x, xiii, xiv, xxii, xxvi, xxxix, xl, xli, lxii
  and the intelligentsia, xvi, xvii
  as issue in politics, xxiv–xxxi, lxiv
  resurgence of, ii, xxxvii
Radicalism, among Irish, 267
  among Italians, 192
  among Jews, 172, 180, 292, 293, 314
  among Negroes, 35
Rainwater, Lee, lxxviii
Raisin in the Sun, 78
Randolph, A. Philip, 78
Randolph, A. Philip, Educational Fund, xlviii, xlix*n*
Random House, 174
Reader's Digest, 130
Real estate business, 32, 151, 152, 153, 154, 155, 255
Reform Democrats, xxviii, 55, 167, 170, 171, 176
Reform movements, 213, 219, 223, 227, 274, 303
Regents' Scholarships, 157
Reilly and the 400, 248
Religions, variety of, 14, 18, 19, 22, 35
Religious groups and factors, viii, ix, xxxvi–xxxix, 8, 11, 25, 56, 59, 60, 62, 88, 140, 141, 161, 172, 202–205, 279, 280, 313, 314
  See also Catholics, Jews, White Anglo-Saxon Protestants
Remington, William, 269
"The Remnant of Israel," *See* Shearith Israel
Republican party and Republicans, lxxi, 12, 166, 169, 208, 215, 222,

Republican party (*continued*)
  223, 240, 262, 263, 266, 271, 272, 281, 292, 297
Rerum Novarum, 284
Richmond County, 273
Riders to the Sea, 248
Riesman, David, xci
Riverton, 49
Robinson, James H., 81
Rockefeller, Nelson A., lxxi, 305
Rockefeller family, 4
Rockwell, George, 176
Roman Catholic Church, 88, 98, 104, 140, 204, 205, 208, 230–238, 274, 287
Roman Catholic Free Schools, 234
Roman Catholicism, *See* Catholicism
Roosevelt, Eleanor, 267
Roosevelt, Franklin D., 167, 168, 214, 218, 264, 265, 266, 270, 305
Roosevelt, Franklin D., Jr., 167
Roosevelt, Theodore, 313, 314
Rose, Alex, 304
Rosedale, 58
Rosenberg, Ethel and Julius, 269
Rosenthal, Erich, 164
Rosh Hashana, 146
Rossa, O'Donovan, 242
Roth, Emery, 151
Rothstein, Arnold, 210
Rowan, Carl T., 85
Rudin Management Company, 151
Rumania, 7, 139, 256
Russia and Russians, xxxii, 10, 12, 14, 139
  See also U.S.S.R.
Ryan, Thomas Fortune, 219
Ryan, William Fitts, 167

St. Croix, Island of, Puerto Ricans on, 110, 111, 112, 117
St. Patrick's Cathedral, 274
St. Peter's Church, 232, 238
San Francisco, 3, 4
Santangelo, Alfred E., 187
Saturday Evening Post, 85
Scandinavians, 8
Scanlan, Patrick, 304
Scarsdale, N. Y., 67
Schapiro's Wine Company, 33
Scheuer, James H., 153
Schiff, Jacob, 140
Schiff, family, 151
Schools, parochial, lxii, 26, 48, 56, 104, 163, 202, 204, 234, 235, 237, 238, 269, 279, 280, 281
  private, 26, 48, 56, 234, 237
  public, 26, 48, 56, 100, 104, 200, 203, 235, 236, 237, 280, 281

Schools (*continued*)
teachers' strike in, xxvi, xxviii
threatened by black militants, lxv
Schreiber, Daniel, 74
Schulz, David A., lxxviii
Scotch-Irish, 20
Scots, 7, 8, 262
Screvane, Paul R., 215, 305
Seagram's Building, 151, 152
Segregation, xli, xlii, liii, lxii, 26,
27, 46, 49, 56, 300
See also Housing
Senior, Clarence, lxxviii, 105, 109,
110, 112
Separatism, issue of, ix, xvii, xxi–
xxiv *passim*, xli, lxxv
"Seven Sisters" colleges, 157
Seward, William H., 235
Sexology, 130
Sharkey, Joseph T., 315
Shaw, George Bernard, 253
Shearith Israel, 138
Sheen, Fulton J., Msgr., 269
Shopkeeper, 17, 30, 31, 71, 112, 113
See also Businessman, small
Sicily, 183, 184
Silberman, Charles, lxxvii
Siloam Presbyterian Church, 48
Sinatra, Frank, 194, 218
Sinn Fein, 243
Skirtmakers' Union, 102, 145
Sklare, Marshall, lxxviii
Slavs, lxxix
Slawson, John, 148, 161
Sloan, John, 248
Slums, *See* Negroes, Housing
Smith, Alfred E., 167, 168, 169, 218,
229, 230, 246, 263, 265, 266, 275
Smith, Alfred E., Jr., 272
Smith, Timothy L., lxxxi
Snyder, Charles R., 257
*Social Background of the Italo-
American School Child, The*
(Covello), lxxix, 195
*Social Order of the Slum, The:
Ethnicity and Territory in the
Inner City* (Suttles), lxxviii
Socialism and Socialists, lix, 141, 169,
172, 173, 192, 202, 241, 261, 293
Society of the Friendly Sons of Saint
Patrick, *See* Friendly Sons of St.
Patrick
Sons of St. Patrick, *See* Friendly
Sons of St. Patrick
Sons of St. Tammany, 221
See also Tammany Hall
South Africa, 141, 143
South American and South Amer-
ica, 102, 183
South Brooklyn, 91

South Village, 187
Southerners and the South, 2, 9, 68,
78
Southwest, 5, 52
Southwest Washington, 153
Spain and Spanish culture, 17, 88,
102, 129, 138, 283
Spanish Catholic Church, 283
Spanish-speaking migrants, lxx
Spear, Allan H., lxxxi
Spellman, Francis J., Cardinal, lvii,
274, 280, 281, 295, 296
Spencer, John C., 235–237
Spiritualism and Spiritualists, 88,
105, 106
Springfield Gardens, 58
State Board of Regents, 263
State Commission for Human
Rights, 68, 303
State Committee Against Discrimi-
nation (SCAD), 39–42, 62, 71,
115
Staten Island, 17, 187, 263
Steffens, Lincoln, lxiii, 227, 229
Steinbrink, Meier, 169
Stevenson, Adlai, 168, 271, 272, 315
Stodolsky, Susan S., lxxx
Story, Joseph, Justice, 221
Straus, Oscar, 140
Straus, Robert, 257
Strauss, Lewis, lx
Street Corner Society, 189
The Stricken Land, 86
Strong, George Templeton, 218, 242,
243, 311
Stuyvesant Town, 75
Suburbia, 5, 28, 57, 60, 64, 66, 67,
157, 160–166 *passim*, 187, 203
Suffolk County, 59, 157, 263
Sullivan, Timothy, 228, 229
Sullivan County, 251
Sulzer, William, 228
"Superettes," 113
Suttles, Gerald D., lxxviii
Sweden and Swedes, xxxii, 1, 10
Sweeney, "Brains," 219
Switzerland, 7, 182
Swope, Herbert Bayard, 230
Sydenham Hospital, 80
Synagogues, influence of, 59, 60
See also Religious groups

Tablet, 253, 282, 283, 296, 304
Taeuber, Alma F., lxxix
Taeuber, Karl E., lxxix
Tally's Corner (Liebow) lxxvii
Tammany Hall, 213, 218–228 *pas-
sim*, 243, 245, 260, 264, 266, 272,
273, 282, 292
Taylor, Gardner, 80–82

Teaneck, N. J., 58
Teller, Edward, lx
Teller, Ludwig, 167
Temples of Islam, *See* Nation of Islam
Thomas, Norman, 202
Thomas, W. I., lxxvi
Thought, 276
Time, 231
Tishman Realty and Construction, 151
Tocqueville, Alexis de, 220, 232, 235
Tokyo, 10, 11
Tone, Wolfe, 242
A Touch of the Poet, 249
Trade Unions, *See* Unions
Transitron Company, 155
Transport Workers Union, xlvi, xlvii*n,* xlviii*n*
Tresca, Carlo, 192
Tri-Community Council, 58
Trucking business, 18, 206, 210
Truman, Harry S, 167, 168
Tugwell, Rexford, 86, 95
Tunis, 182
Turkey, 140
Tweed, William March (Boss), 217, 218, 219, 245
Tyrone family, 248, 256, 257
    See O'Neill, Eugene

"Ulster Irish," 240, 253
Unger, Sidney, 77, 153
Unions, xlvi, xlvii, lxii, lxv, lxxxviii, 6, 40, 68, 72, 140, 144, 178, 191, 192, 204, 261, 264, 302, 303
    See also Labor leaders
Unitarians, 139, 295
United Jewish Appeal, 140, 153, 176
United Nations, 152
United Parents Association, 48
University Club, 24
University of Chicago, 3, 277
University of Puerto Rico, 134
University of San Juan, 114
Upper East Side, 160
Upper West Side, 152
Urban Blues (Keil), lxxvii
Urban renewal, 179
    See also Public housing projects
The Urban Villagers, 186
Uris Brothers, 151
Uruguay, 183
U.S.S.R., 7, 206, 268

Valente, Louis, 212
Vegetable business, 18
Venice, 182
Verga, Giovanni, 195

Viereck, Peter, 231
Virgin Islands, 110

Wagner, Robert F., Sr., 167
Wagner, Robert F., vii, 4, 5, 101, 167, 214, 215, 262, 273, 274, 300, 303, 304, 305, 312
Waldo, Octavia, 198
Walker, James J. (Jimmy), 210, 217, 218, 246, 265
Wallace, Henry, 167, 168
Wallace movement, xxxv
Warburg family, 151
Washington, Booker T., 32
Washington, George, 241
Washington, D. C., 68
Washington Heights, 94, 111, 160, 162
Wax, Murray, lxxix
Webb and Knapp, 151, 152
    See also Zeckendorf, William
Wechsler, James A., 304
Weigel, Gustav, S.J., 276, 277
Welfare population, ix, xlvi, lxxxv
Werner, Morris R., 245
West, Anthony, 248
West Bronx, 161
West Indians, 92
    See also Negroes, West Indian
West Side, 2, 65, 94, 108, 112, 113, 121, 127, 179, 274
West Side Church of St. Matthew and St. Timothy, 105
West Side Urban Renewal Project, 108
Westchester County, 59, 66, 157, 263, 310
White Anglo-Saxon Protestants (WASPS), xxvi, xxxi–xxxii, xxxvi, lvi, lx, lxiii, lxxii, 6, 8, 10, 15, 16, 19, 20, 105, 139, 147, 149, 154, 157–159, 166, 170, 173, 194, 213, 220, 238, 259 261, 270, 301, 305, 311, 314, 315
White Over Black (Jordan), lxxxi
White Protestants, 5, 8, 9, 19, 60, 81, 82
    See also White Anglo-Saxon Protestants
Whitehead, Alfred North, 247, 253
Whites, poor, and affluent Negroes, xii, xliii–lvii (esp. lvi, lviv)
    upper-class and Negroes, xxvi
Whyte, William F., 189
Whyte, William H., 147
Wickham, William H., 245
Wilde, Oscar, 253
Williams, Roger J., 257
Williamsburg area, 161, 163
Wilson, James Q., 70, 75, 303

Wilson, Malcolm, lviii
Wilson, Woodrow, 168, 169, 241, 244, 264
Wirth, Louis, lxxvi
Wise, Stephen S., 179
Wittke, Carl, 244
Wolfson, Erwin, 151
Woodham-Smith, Cecil, 225
Workers' Defense League, xlviii, xlix*n*
The Workmen's Circle, 146, 292
Wright, Frank Lloyd, 174

Yale University, 274

Yankees, 2
Yeats, William B., 253
Yeshiva University Medical School, 156
Yeshivas, 163
Yom Kippur, 146, 177
Young, Whitney M., Jr., lxxv, lxxvi
Yugoslavia, 7

Zangwill, Israel, 289, 290, 293
Zeckendorf, William, 151, 152
    See also Webb and Knapp
Zionism, 79, 140, 141, 290, 292
Zuber, Paul, 48

Publications

OF THE JOINT CENTER FOR URBAN STUDIES

The Joint Center for Urban Studies, a cooperative venture of the Massachusetts Institute of Technology and Harvard University, was founded in 1959 to organize and encourage research on urban and regional problems. Participants have included scholars from the fields of anthropology, architecture, business, city planning, economics, education, engineering, history, law, philosophy, political science, and sociology.

The findings and conclusions of this book are, as with all Joint Center publications, solely the responsibility of the author.

The Joint Center also publishes monographs and reports.

PUBLISHED BY HARVARD UNIVERSITY PRESS

The Intellectual versus the City: From Thomas Jefferson to Frank Lloyd Wright, by Morton and Lucia White, 1962

Streetcar Suburbs: The Process of Growth in Boston, 1870–1900, by Sam B. Warner, Jr., 1962

City Politics, by Edward C. Banfield and James Q. Wilson, 1963

Law and Land: Anglo-American Planning Practice, edited by Charles M. Haar, 1964

Location and Land Use: Toward a General Theory of Land Rent, by William Alonso, 1964

Poverty and Progress: Social Mobility in a Nineteenth Century City, by Stephan Thernstrom, 1964

Boston: The Job Ahead, by Martin Meyerson and Edward C. Banfield, 1966

The Myth and Reality of Our Urban Problems, by Raymond Vernon, 1966

Muslim Cities in the Later Middle Ages, by Ira Marvin Lapidus, 1967

The Fragmented Metropolis: Los Angeles, 1850–1930, by Robert M. Fogelson, 1967

Law and Equal Opportunity: A Study of the Massachusetts Commission Against Discrimination, by Leon H. Mayhew, 1968

Varieties of Police Behavior: The Management of Law and Order in Eight Communities, by James Q. Wilson, 1968

The Metropolitan Enigma: Inquiries into the Nature and Dimensions of America's "Urban Crisis," edited by James Q. Wilson, revised edition, 1968

Traffic and the Police: Variations in Law-Enforcement Policy, by John A. Gardiner, 1969

The Influence of Federal Grants: Public Assistance in Massachusetts, by Martha Derthick, 1970

The Arts in Boston, by Bernard Taper, 1970

Families Against the City: Middle Class Homes of Industrial Chicago, 1872–1890, by Richard Sennett, 1970

PUBLISHED BY THE M.I.T. PRESS

The Image of the City, by Kevin Lynch, 1960

Housing and Economic Progress: A Study of the Housing Experiences of Boston's Middle-Income Families, by Lloyd Rodwin, 1961

Beyond the Melting Pot: The Negroes, Puerto Ricans, Jews, Italians, and Irish of New York City, by Nathan Glazer and Daniel Patrick Moynihan, 1963

The Historian and the City, edited by Oscar Handlin and John Burchard, 1963

The Federal Bulldozer: A Critical Analysis of Urban Renewal, 1949–1962, by Martin Anderson, 1964

The Future of Old Neighborhoods: Rebuilding for a Changing Population, by Bernard J. Frieden, 1964

Man's Struggle for Shelter in an Urbanizing World, by Charles Abrams, 1964

The View from the Road, by Donald Appleyard, Kevin Lynch, and John R. Myer, 1964

The Public Library and the City, edited by Ralph W. Conant, 1965

Regional Development Policy: A Case Study of Venezuela, by John Friedmann, 1966

Urban Renewal: The Record and the Controversy, edited by James Q. Wilson, 1966

Transport Technology for Developing Regions, by Richard M. Soberman, 1966

Computer Methods in the Analysis of Large-Scale Social Systems, edited by James M. Beshers, 1968

Planning Urban Growth and Regional Development: The Experience of the Guayana Program of Venezuela, by Lloyd Rodwin and Associates, 1969

Build a Mill, Build a City, Build a School: Industrialization, Urbanization, and Education in Ciudad Guayana, by Noel F. McGinn and Russell G. Davis, 1969

Land-Use Controls in the United States, by John Delafons, second edition, 1969

Beyond the Melting Pot: The Negroes, Puerto Ricans, Jews, Italians, and Irish of New York City, by Nathan Glazer and Daniel Patrick Moynihan, second edition, 1970